AF478269

PREFACE

This volume celebrates the fact that Milton Fox was an outstanding editor. It's tempting for me to recall his intellectual curiosity and versatility, his tirelessness in pursuit of the finest possible product, but the evidence for his great talent is in the books produced under his supervision and nothing I might say could add luster to his remarkable achievements.

As well as being a great editor, Milton was a wonderful friend and a valued associate. From the time I founded this publishing house, twenty-five years ago, until his untimely death in 1971, Milton was vitally involved with every aspect of the company's growth. It's easy to remember the excitement with which we embarked on the first Abrams publications. Working out of a single room, we produced the trio of books which launched our series "The Library of Great Painters"—*Renoir* by Walter Pach, *Van Gogh* by Meyer Schapiro, and *El Greco* by Leo Bronstein. Milton and I were the entire editorial and production staff—with the help of our first employee, Dore Ashton, fresh out of school on her first job—but we somehow had these three titles ready for production within just a few months of commissioning the texts, a feat that would be impossible to duplicate today. To do so, we worked around the clock—if we were not at the office we were generally to be found working in my apartment—and without Milton's enthusiasm, good humor, and hard work we could never have done it. It was his great wit and enthusiasm, too, that pulled us through many of the difficult periods that were common enough in those early days.

It goes without saying that all of us who worked with Milton miss him so very much, and equally we miss the inimitable way in which he exercised his gifts. Like many creative people, he did not appear to be the most organized of men. In part this was because he gave so freely of his energies—he was apt to be involved in a dozen things at any given time—but mostly it was because he was by nature flexible rather than rigid, open rather than closed. He was not the kind of person to shut himself away in an ivory tower. He loved nothing better than to be with his peers, exchanging ideas and hammering out new projects.

If Milton had one gift that was more significant than the rest, it was his generous ability to recognize talent in others. In this volume, his friends return the tribute.

HARRY N. ABRAMS

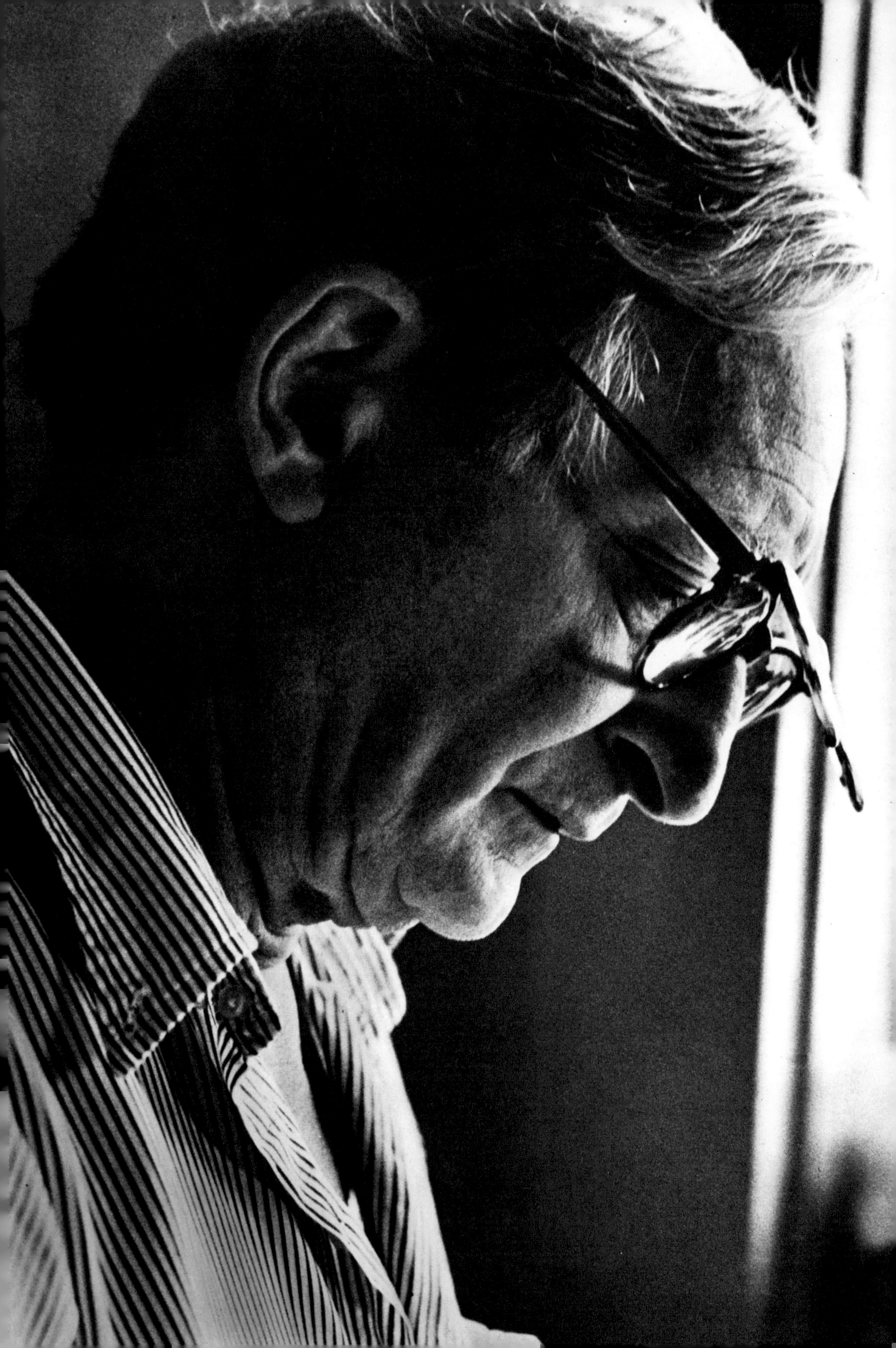

ART STUDIES
FOR AN EDITOR:

25 ESSAYS IN MEMORY OF
MILTON S. FOX

HARRY N. ABRAMS, INC., PUBLISHERS, NEW YORK

Photograph of Milton S. Fox by Timothy Barnhart, 1969
Photograph of *Ruby,* on page 12, by George Roos

Nai Y. Chang, Vice-President, Design and Production
John L. Hochmann, Executive Editor
Margaret L. Kaplan, Managing Editor
Barbara Lyons, Director, Photo Department, Rights and Reproductions
Patricia Egan, Editor
Lisa Pontell, Picture Editor
Robin Fox, Designer

Library of Congress Cataloging in Publication Data
Main entry under title:

Art studies for an editor.

1. Art—Addresses, essays, lectures.
2. Fox, Milton S., 1904–1971. I. Fox, Milton S., 1904–1971.
II. Hartt, Frederick, ed. III. Egan, Patricia, ed.
N7442.2.F692   709   74–30303
ISBN 0–8109–0279–6

Library of Congress Catalogue Card Number: 74–30303
Published by Harry N. Abrams, Incorporated, New York, 1975
All rights reserved. No part of the contents of this book may be
reproduced without the written permission of the publishers
Printed and bound in Japan

It is unusual for a volume of essays to be offered to the memory of an editor. But Milton Fox was an unusual editor—in the experience of the contributors to this book, unique. It is indicative of his special qualities that the idea of such a collection occurred to several of us independently. Yet we felt this was not the occasion for a conventional series of scholarly papers. A miscellany of essays reflecting at times highly personal notions of the authors on a wide variety of artistic topics, and written in styles representative of the authors' personal approaches to art, seemed to us a more suitable tribute to a man whose imagination was anything but conventional, and whose relation to each of us was personal and unforgettable.

All authors of books initiated by Abrams and edited by Milton Fox were approached. All gave the project their blessing, but some either had at the moment nothing appropriate to submit or had already dedicated an article or a book to Milton's memory. I am deeply grateful to them for their goodwill, to all those who were able to contribute for their essays, and to Milton's close associates over many years, Harry Abrams and Fritz Landshoff.

Milton S. Fox was born March 29, 1904, in New York City. He was first trained as a painter at the Cleveland School of Art, and subsequently in Paris, at the Académie Julian; in a concours in 1926 he was invited to become "élève Ecole des Beaux-Arts." In 1928 he and Ruby Canfield were married, and they had two children,

Robin and Michael. In Cleveland he had considerable success as a portraitist, and painted two murals for the Cleveland Public Auditorium. During this period he also taught at the Cleveland School of Art, Cleveland College, the Cleveland School of Architecture, and Western Reserve University. He was a member of the Education Department of the Cleveland Museum of Art, and from 1942 to 1944 was a trained specialist and instructor in camouflage for Civil Defense.

He began the literary phase of his career as art critic for the Cleveland *News,* for which he wrote more than 150 articles. From 1944 to 1950 he wrote film scripts in Hollywood, and was Chairman of the Education Committee of the Beverly Hills Institute of Modern Art.

In 1950, the year the company was organized, Milton Fox joined the Harry N. Abrams publishing house, of which he was Vice-President and Editor-in-Chief. For the next twenty-one years he edited hundreds of books on art, including many first published abroad. As the company—at that time an unprecedented venture in the field of art publishing in America—grew from modest beginnings he helped Harry Abrams shape its policy and direction. At the inception of the company he and Mr. Abrams did in person most of the work toward the creation and publication of the books. Milton Fox was thus intimately familiar with all details of the selection and editing of manuscripts, and color photography and color printing.

He helped develop the highly successful series, the *Library of Great Painters,* initiated by Harry Abrams, and many of the best-known Abrams publications. In the course of his editorial work he came to know, and to attract to the company, many of the leading art historians and critics in the United States and in Europe. Through these contacts, which often ripened into lifelong friendships, and through the publications he edited, his influence on the teaching and understanding of art was incalculable. In the 1960s his interests expanded to include telecasting, and he was involved in instrumenting two memorable television programs, "Museum without Walls" and "The Louvre, Golden Prison," for the National Broadcasting Company.

A morning or afternoon spent in Milton Fox's office could be a startling experience. In an atmosphere of benign confusion he received a steady procession of colleagues and assistants, authors, artists, critics, and museum directors (with or without appointments), dealing sometimes with two or three problems at once, in person, by correspondence, or over the constantly ringing telephone. To each problem and to each visitor he brought his own special blend of sensitivity, personal understanding, and gently disparaging humor. And out of the innumerable problems the beautiful books emerged.

His knowledge of art grew steadily in range and depth, and so did the collection which filled his apartment to bursting with unusual works from many periods but especially from the twentieth century. In later years he was able to indulge his love of Japanese art and culture by frequent trips to the Far East. He made strenuous efforts to learn the Japanese language, and splendid works of Japanese painting, sculpture, calligraphy, and minor arts joined their Western counterparts in his home.

In recent years Milton's life was often shadowed by serious illness, and the danger of death was always near. Nevertheless he could see no reason to conserve his strength for a life of inactivity which would have bored him. After each recovery he returned to work with characteristic energy and imagination. When the end came, quite suddenly, at home with his family early in the morning of October 25, 1971, the Abrams company and its authors suffered a great loss. Milton Fox was well aware of his limitations and would have been the last to want a eulogy. Nonetheless his associates and friends feel a deep personal obligation to record something of the extraordinary quality of his personality and range of his achievements.

Frederick Hartt

CONTENTS

MILTON S. FOX. *Ruby*. 1933
(1st prize, May Show, Cleveland Museum of Art).
Oil on canvas, 53 3/4 × 39″.
Collection Mrs. Milton S. Fox

ART STUDIES
FOR AN EDITOR

1

GERMAIN BAZIN

Aperçus nouveaux sur l'art du XVIIIe siècle français

France in the Eighteenth Century, la grande manifestation organisée en 1968 par la Royal Academy, illustre bien la crise que connaissent actuellement les expositions. Celle-ci fut une des plus importantes qui aient été consacrées au sujet avec 1034 numéros, contre 1084 à l'exposition l'*Art français au XVIIIe siècle* qui eut lieu à Copenhague en 1935, et 653 à l'*Ausstellung Kunst und Geist Frankreichs im 18. Jahrhundert* dont Hélène Adhémar fut le commissaire général à Vienne en 1966. Cependant l'exposition de Londres fut, en général, peu favorablement accueillie par la presse en Angleterre comme à l'étranger, les critiques, plus ou moins spécialisés, s'étant perdus dans cet ensemble touffus. Et tous d'entonner pour finir, l'hymne à la collection Wallace, promue à la hauteur d'un mythe. Encore qu'on ne voit pas très bien quel intérêt il y aurait eu à répéter la collection Wallace dans la ville qui la possède—sinon d'amener à voir des tableaux du XVIIIe siècle un public qui ne fréquente plus les musées, mais se précipite vers les expositions—il aurait suffit de choisir dans la masse des tableaux présentés à la Royal Academy cent cinquante toiles et de les présenter différemment pour assurer à cette exposition un succès plus évident. Et c'est là qu'apparaît bien le malentendu qui risque désormais de fausser le sens des expositions. Guidé par des critiques, à qui il importe de juger un fait artistique, non au fond, mais comme un "évènement," le public a tendance à chercher dans une exposition un spectacle, plus qu'un enseignement, à proprement parlé une "représentation," un *show;* la séquence des oeuvres qui lui seront proposées l'interessera plus que celles-ci et un habile étalagiste, qui saura flatter ce goût de la mise en scène, obtiendra de meilleurs résultats qu'un conservateur consciencieux, mais peu soucieux de ses effets. La présentation d'une exposition est-elle confuse, la matière trop abondante, les chefs d'oeuvre sont-il accompagnés par le cortège des "petits maîtres," que toute école traîne après soi, la voici condamnée par la critique, quelque soit sa valeur. Il fallait être dépourvu de toute sensibilité artistique pour n'avoir pas été bouleversé à Londres par la seule réunion des cinquante-trois dessins de Watteau, car la main de l'artiste, maniant la pierre noire ou la sanguine, confie au papier les sentiments de son âme émue par tout ce qui vit. Que le critique d'un hebdomadaire politique français soit indifférent à ces choses, car, dit-il, "la fatigue de l'ennui imposée au visiteur l'empêche de saisir ces découvertes," on peut le concevoir. On s'étonne plus qu'une grande revue d'art anglaise, qui se donne pour mission de servir l'érudition, aît pû juger avec la même légèreté une exposition qui apportait au connaisseur et à l'amateur un matériel considerable d'étude. Doit-on admettre comme acquis que plus on organisera d'expositions et plus les foules s'y porteront, moins il sera possible d'en faire qui soient propres à seconder les recherches des historiens d'art? Seules échapperont peut-être à ce verdict de la critique—qui n'est pas toujours celui du public—les expositions d'archéologie, protégées de l'incompréhension par une incompétence qu'on avoue pas pour la peinture, où tout le monde se croit apte à porter un jugement.

Il faut avouer que ceux qui avaient accroché et disposé les oeuvres à la Royal Academy n'avaient pas facilité la visite ni du public ni des érudits. Un grand nombre de tableaux ayant pû être réunis pour les peintres majeurs, sans doute par crainte de la monotonie, au lieu de concentrer chaque groupe, on l'avait dispersé dans plusieurs salles, ce qui réduisaît le profit de ces rassemblements et produisait une impression labyrinthique. Il fallait chercher les Jean-François de Troy dans quatre salles, et que dire de la présentation des plus beaux Subleyras dans une salle encombrée de vitrines et de surcroît en compagnie de Prud'hon et de David!

Enfin, il faut noter les difficultés croissantes pour l'examen des oeuvres, qui résultent des modes de restauration de plus en plus divergents, employés dans les diverses régions du monde. Les états de certains tableaux du même maître sont si différents que ceux-ci ne sont même plus comparables. L'emploi de certains vernis synthétiques, dont l'indice de réfraction est très éloigné de celui des vernis naturels, produit notamment des effets d'optique opposés à ceux que procurent ces derniers et l'on a trop tendance, dans certains ateliers de restauration, a négliger ce fait que le vernis est un facteur artistique d'un tableau, aussi bien que la couche picturale.

On s'était efforcé, dans cette exposition, d'une part de montrer le plus grand nombre de petits maîtres, et d'autre part de réunir des ensembles importants des plus grands. Deux peintres sortirent grandis de cette confrontation, deux peintres que tout oppose: Jean-François de Troy et Subleyras.

La méconnaissance de l'art de Jean-François de Troy a masqué jusqu'ici une tendance profonde de la peinture française qui découle ce l'art du XVIIe siècle et qui montre l'assimilation du lyrisme baroque, tandis que ce qu'on appelle généralement "la Régence," issu de l'art intimiste de Watteau, et qui, mis en imagerie par Pater et Lancret s'est transmué en galanterie, voire en gaillardise par Boucher, est une expression du style rococo. Comme le montrent les trois compositions peintes pour Monsieur de St-Aiguan sur des sujets tirés de l'histoire romaine (nos. 672, 673, 674, Musée de Neufchâtel), tout-à-fait comparables au *Repas chez Simon* de la collection Walter P. Chrysler, Jean-François de Troy a le sens de la composition large, très étoffée, dont il a emprunté la rhétorique à Solimène et à Luca Giordano. La curieuse exposition qu'avait faite Hazlitt Gallery de Londres en Mai 1961, où l'on voyait deux esquisses de Jean-François de Troy pour les tapisseries de Jason (exposées à la Royal Academy sous les numéros 680 et 681) rapprochées d'oeuvres des deux napolitains et de quelques autres italiens baroques, attestait cette filiation. Cependant pour le coloris clair, de Troy s'orientait plutôt vers Rubens. Son métier est très varié; dans ses esquisses, qui révèlent l'impétuosité de son tempérament, il procède par franches coulées de pâtes à l'italienne. Aux pâtes généreusement étalées de ses tableaux d'histoire, de Troy mêle, au moins dans les chairs, des glacis. Pour ses tableaux de genre, d'une manière plus fine, il fait un usage subtil de ces transparences qui donnent un charme fruité à ces petites oeuvres, évoquant Renoir, du moins quand elles sont intactes comme la *Lecture de Molière* du marquis Cholmondeley, qui est dans un état de conservation miraculeux.

La véritable ascendance de Jean-François de Troy dans l'école française, doit être recherchée dans le style de Vouet, qui n'avait pas eu de lendemain, cette veine ayant été tarie par l'académisme de Le Brun. De Vouet, Jean-François retrouve la sensualité saine, la franchise des coloris clairs, cette générosité de tempérament qui a toujours peine à s'épanouir dans l'école, où elle se trouve paralysée par le dogmatisme au XVIIe siècle, apauvrie par les futilités de l'art de société au XVIIIe siècle.

Toutes les manières de ce peintre, si doué, et qui semble avoir fait preuve d'une remarquable égalité de talent, étaient bien représentées à la Royal Academy où se trouvaient réunies seize de ses toiles; toutes sauf l'aisance qu'il était capable de déployer dans les très grandes compositions, comme les cartons des tapisseries de l'*Histoire d'Esther* ou l'admirable *Ex-Voto à Sainte Geneviève* de Saint-Etienne du Mont, une des oeuvres les plus monumentales de l'école française. Pour prouver que le XVIIIe siècle n'a pas excellé que dans le petit, j'évoquerai ici un exemple peu connu de ce sens baroque de la grande composition, le *Saint Vincent de Paul administrant Louis XIII mourant* (3m.25 × 2m.85), curieux tableau historique qu'on dirait quelque peu romantique. C'est le tableau faisant partie de la série de la vie de Saint Vincent de Paul, peinte vers 1730 pour la maison de Saint Lazare, qui gravé par Herisset, fut catalogué par Brière en 1930 parmi les manquants[1] sous le numéro 21, je l'ai retrouvé au château de Kronborg en Suède.

J'ai revu avec plaisir (no. 675) une petite toile que j'avais remarquée dans ma jeunesse à l'exposition du *Paysage français de Poussin à Corot* au Petit Palais en 1925, retrouvée à l'exposition *Landscape of French Art* à Londres en 1949. Appartenant maintenant au Fitzwilliam Museum de Cambridge, c'est un "Paysage avec un homme chassant un canard" (fig. 1). Cette oeuvre qui a toute la fraîcheur et la profondeur d'un sous-bois de Rubens, fait regretter que ce peintre d'histoire et d'historiettes ne se soit pas plus souvent échappé vers la nature.

Ce courant baroque qui s'épanouit dans l'école française, comme à retardement, dans la première moitié du XVIIIe siècle, parallèlement à l'éclosion du style rococo risque de passer inaperçu depuis que les musées ont enfoui dans leurs réserves les grandes compositions qu'il a produites. Lemoine, La Fosse, Jouvenet, Antoine

Coypel, Carle Van Loo (qui au demeurant est un peintre assez médiocre) n'apparaissaient guère au Burlington House que sous la forme de leurs esquisses qui ne peuvent rendre compte de leurs tentatives vers le style noble. Peut-être, malgré les difficultés de transport, eut-il été utile d'accrocher quelques-unes de ces grandes toiles qui, d'ailleurs, eussent mieux rythmé l'exposition en ponctuant de temps forts les grands murs tristes de la Royal Academy. On pouvait s'en rendre compte en admirant l'effet de l'éffigie équestre du *Comte Potocki* de David (no. 176), prêtée par le musée de Varsovie, sans comprendre toutefois la raison de son voisinage avec Largillière, François Hubert Drouais et Boucher, et son apparition avant Oudry et Desportes.

Malgré la présence du radieux *Canard blanc* d'Oudry (no. 511) et de deux exquis paysages de Desportes, ces deux peintres de "l'art royal" étaient peut-être les moins bien servis à l'exposition.

Unique est la position dans l'école française du XVIIIe siècle de Subleyras, contemporain plus jeune de Jean-François de Troy et dont la carrière s'achève comme celle de celui-ci au mitan du siècle. Ce fut l'un des apports de l'exposition du Burlington House que la mise en valeur de cet admirable peintre, malgré la dispersion de ses toiles (au nombre de onze) qui eussent gagné d'autant plus à être regroupées qu'elles ne s'apparentent à aucune autre. Comme Poussin avait fui deux fois l'ambiance de la cour de France, pour approfondir en soi au contact de Rome son âme française, c'est à Rome, où il s'établit, que Subleyras, loin du rococo du boudoir ou du baroque décoratif du temps de Louis XV, fait rejaillir une source profonde de notre génie national. Ce sont les nobles cadences de Philippe de Champaigne qui revivent dans ces tableaux, où la matière picturale est étendue d'une main calme et sûre par larges aplats de couleur, nuancés cependant d'une cendre légère et comme pastellisée. Des blancs, généreusement prodigués, apportent la chanterelle à ces harmonies sourdes. Dans le *Bienheureux Jean d'Avila* (fig. 2) du musée de Birmingham (no. 653) l'immense surplis blanc envahit toute la toile. Comment cette énorme tache de blancheur, au lieu de trouer la toile, l'emplit-elle d'une résonnance discrète? C'est le secret de Subleyras que celui-ci partage avec Zurbaran. N'est-il pas le Zurbaran du XVIIIe siècle, ce peintre de saints et de moines dont les oeuvres, comme celle de Sévillan, sont toutes enveloppées de silence? C'est sans doute le seul peintre religieux de ce siècle profane. Il y a dû Fra Angelico dans la grâce du *Mariage mystique de Sainte Catherine de Ricci*, et dans le *Saint Camille de Lellis sauvant les malades* de l'hôpital du Saint Esprit, envoyé par le musée de Rome (no. 650), le peintre se hausse là aux accents les plus sublimes. Quand au sens de la composition de ce grand classique, composition traitée en bas-relief à la française, elle découle d'une ascendance de sculpteurs. On pourra à nouveau l'apprécier quand on pourra revoir au Louvre l'admirable *Repas chez Simon* peint en 1737.

On a souvent insisté sur l'apport nordique dans la peinture du XVIIIe siècle (Watteau, Pater), ou parisien (Boucher, Chardin). Les languedociens de Troy et Subleyras s'ajoutent à Fragonard, le provençal, pour attester que toute la France a collaboré à l'art du XVIIIe siècle.

L'art d'imagerie facile, à quoi ce siècle s'est complu, qui déferlait sur les murs du Burlington House, a sans doute quelque peu empêché de saisir la persistance des courants profonds de l'âme française au cours du XVIIIe siècle. Et, pourtant, il y avait ici une admirable suite de ces dessins de Watteau, où l'ingénuité du coeur est servie par la plus haute science de la main. Chardin poursuit la tendance française de la sympathie pour tout ce qui est humble, choses et êtres, tradition qui fut celle des Le Nain et avant ceux-ci des imagiers du moyen âge. On pouvait voir de lui à Londres quelques fort belles toiles.[2] Les cinq dessins qui étaient présentés sous son nom formaient un ensemble cohérent. Est-il bien de Chardin? Et Chardin a-t-il jamais dessiné? Mariette dit qu'il ne s'aidait d'aucun croquis pour ses tableaux. Le travail de son pinceau, qui fait naître la forme de la lente trituration des pâtes (travail spécifiquement français), ne permet guère de penser qu'il dessinait. Sans doute n'y a-t-il pas plus de dessins de cet artisan peintre qu'il n'y en a des Le Nain.

Une autre issue de l'âme française traditionnelle au XVIIIe siècle est le paysage. Là encore Rome a joué un rôle primordial, Rome, où le peintre français s'évade pour fuir les pompes de la Cour et les futilités de la Ville, afin de se retrouver lui-même. J'ai montré jadis[3] que l'étude dessinée d'après nature dans les sites du Latium étaient un des exercices obligés de l'Académie de France à Rome et que Pierre de Nolhac s'était trompé en nous décrivant le vieux Natoire, directeur de l'Académie, "débauché" par Fragonard et Hubert Robert qui en firent un "tardif paysagiste." C'est Natoire au contraire qui emmenait les élèves sur le motif et déjà en 1724 Wleughels, quand il était arrivé à Rome, avant même d'occuper en titre le poste de directeur de l'Académie, avait pris l'habitude de conduire à travers la campagne de Frascati et de Tivoli les pensionnaires, dans l'intention de faire renaître le genre de paysage historique et pour chercher dans la nature un dérivatif aux excès stérilisants de la copie d'après les maîtres. Lorsqu'en 1734 arrive à Rome Joseph Vernet, l'intelligent Wleughels, appréciant les talents de peintre de marine de "l'Avignonnois," l'encourage à suivre son penchant. Passé le milieu du siècle, l'étude d'après nature va provoquer une véritable frénésie du dessin chez Fragonard et Hubert Robert que suivront bientôt tant d'autres, et parmi eux les artistes illustrateurs des *Voyages pittoresques*, tels Desprez et Houel. Ce dernier, passant du dessin à la gouache, opère la transition vers l'étude peinte, étape que franchira Valenciennes, mais après Desportes.

Cependant, parallèlement à cette école latine du paysage français, se développe le courant nordique, dont l'origine remonte aux dessins d'Oudry et aux admirables études peintes d'après nature en Ile de France par Desportes, ce précurseur. Cette intimité recherchée avec la nature aboutit à la fin du siècle aux gouaches frémissantes de Moreau le Jeune qui sort des frondaisons ombreuses des parcs, pour s'ébrouer dans les étendues aérées des plaines.

La tradition du paysage poétique de Claude Lorrain, où les formes sont noyées dans la lumière irradiée par le soleil, ou diffusée par la brume, fut transmise par Manglard à Joseph Vernet. Revenu en France après dix-huit ans d'Italie, celui-ci inspira Delacroix de Marseille. Il faudra réviser l'opinion qu'on se fait d'ordinaire sur cet artiste dont il fut montré au Burlington House deux tableaux (nos. 358 et 359) d'une qualité presque égale à celle des oeuvres de son maître. Au hazard des cimaises on pouvait glaner encore dans ce genre une étonnante marine de Pillement, une *Vue du Tage* datée de 1785 (no. 365); d'après ses morceaux de pratique, on n'aurait pas cru cet artiste si sensible à une impression naturelle.

Nombreux étaient à Londres les témoins de cette veine paysagiste du XVIIIe siècle, mais sans doute fut-elle peu sensible aux visiteurs, parce que les exemples en avaient été dispersés aux quatre coins des galeries.

Heureusement sélectionné, l'ensemble des tableaux de Fragonard soutenait bien la réputation d'un des plus grands virtuoses de la peinture; on pouvait y apprécier tous les aspects de son art, aussi bien dans la figure que dans le paysage, sauf peut-être son talent d'animalier. Quant à Greuze, le drame de sa carrière était illustré par le conflit de ses divers genres et manières.

S'il y avait eu à Londres de ces têtes d'étude, où Greuze inaugure avec succès cette technique des frottis, qui sera celle de David et de Géricault, ç'aurait été lui qui nous aurait introduit au néo-classicisme.

La réaction qui mit fin à l'art du XVIIIe siècle n'était indiquée à Londres que par quelques tableaux, trop peu nombreux pour exprimer la vigueur du mouvement. Les deux tableaux de Vien (1705 et 1706) préfacent Ingres. Quant au *Marat assassiné*, cette sublime toile de David—déjà romantique—la force en était atténuée par son voisinage avec un tableau de piété de Subleyras et une femme dénudée de Vestier. Quelques beaux tableaux de Madame Vigée-Lebrun, eux aussi dispersés, définissaient mieux peut-être le néo-classicisme; parmi eux, il y avait le *Portrait d'Elisabeth Stroganoff* dont une réplique fut l'objet d'une amusante bévue lors de l'exposition des *Chefs-d'oeuvres des musées russes* à Paris en 1965. Désappointée par cette exposition, chiche en vrais tableaux de maîtres, la critique parisienne se rabattit avec enthousiasme sur ce "chef d'oeuvre d'un maître inconnu," Jean-Louis Voille, sous le nom duquel cette réplique était présentée, au grand étonnement du prince Paul de Yougoslavie qui possède l'original dû au pinceau de Madame Vigée-Lebrun.

En marge du néo-classicisme à la romaine, dont les *Horaces* de David furent le manifeste, il y eut auparavant une fort interressante tentative de retour aux sources, c'est-à-dire à Poussin. Un curieux tableau de Lagrenée, le *Vieux Télémaque et Thermosiris* (no. 368) exposé dans la dernière salle, marquait bien cette tendance; il ressemblait comme un frère à un Louis de Boullogne figurant dans la salle I: la *Conversion de Saint Augustin* (no. 107).

Ces quelques réflexions suffiront, je l'espère, à indiquer quelques-unes des ressources qu'offrait au visiteur de bonne volonté cette exposition de la Royal Academy, rendue difficile par son abondance même et sa présentation confuse. Les critiques, distraits ou prévenus, qui refusèrent de faire l'effort exigé par cet important ensemble, me font penser à des sylviculteurs qui se mettraient la tête à ras terre, afin que les buissons leur masquent mieux les arbres de le forêt.

NOTES

1   Brière dans Dimier, *Les peintres français du XVIIIe siècle,* tome II, p. 43.

2   Le rédacteur de l'éditorial du *Burlington Magazine* (February 1959) dit que la *Table à la nappe blanche* (fig. 3; de l'Art Institute de Chicago; no. 139) non seulement n'est pas de Chardin, mais n'est certainement pas du XVIIIe siècle. Il suffit d'être familier des toiles de Chardin pour reconnaître dans celle-ci les craquelures caractéristiques des pâtes de cet artiste ou de ses imitateurs. Je crois d'ailleurs fort possible que Chardin —qui est un peintre lent—ait brossé à la hâte cette nature morte de format inhabituel, pour faire un devant de cheminée qui lui était commandé. Par contre, comme le rédacteur du *Burlington Magazine,* je ne me sens point de goût pour le numéro 131.

3   Catalogue de l'exposition *L'Italia vista dai pittori francesi del XVIII e XIX secolo,* Rome et Turin, 1961.

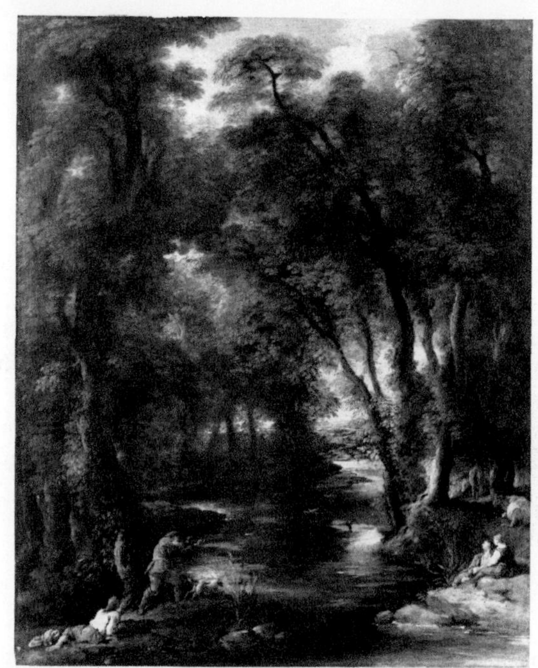

1

2

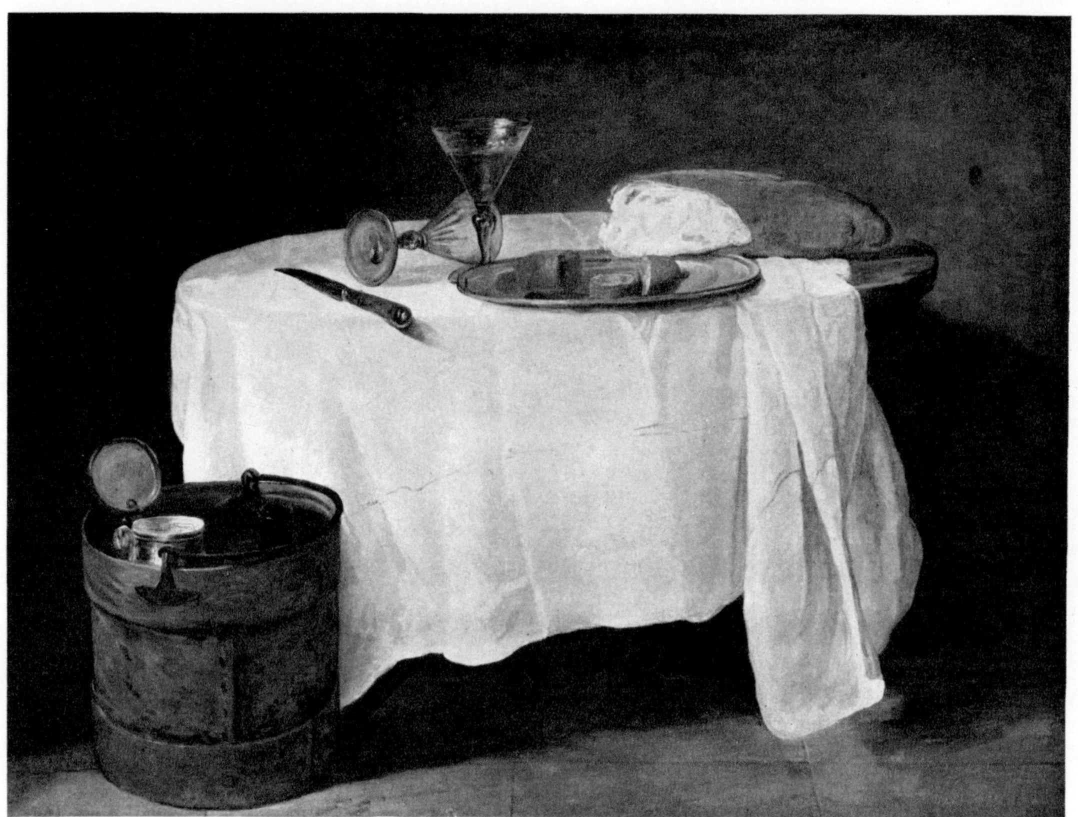

1. JEAN-FRANCOIS DE TROY. *Paysage avec un homme chassant un canard (Duck-Shooting in a Wood)*. 1730.
Fitzwilliam Museum, Cambridge, England

2. PIERRE SUBLEYRAS. *Bienheureux Jean d'Avila (The Blessed John of Avila)*.
Birmingham Museum and Art Gallery, England

3. JEAN-BAPTISTE CHARDIN. *Table à la nappe blanche (The White Tablecloth)*. c. 1737.
The Art Institute of Chicago.
Mr. and Mrs. Lewis L. Coburn Memorial Collection

2

BLANCHE R. BROWN

Questions about
the Late Hellenistic Period

Periodization is inevitably in error, since it imposes a simple grid on a very complicated situation. But it is convenient, and we continue to write art history along such lines, following the conventions of our ancestors as long as we possibly can, and asking of our system of periodization, I believe, only that it should not confuse more than it clarifies. The last proposition brings me to my first question about the Late Hellenistic period: Why is it so confusing to us? Why have we found in it more stylistic trends than anyone has learned to cope with? Why are we still arguing the most rudimentary problems of configuration and chronology?

Inevitably also, when we write survey histories of art, we move from crest to crest, following the centers of creativity. The tone tends to be one of glad discovery, as we view the unfolding variations in the expressive use of art which accompany the historic reshaping of society and people. This proposition brings me to my second question about the Late Hellenistic period: Why does it make us so sad? Hardly any of the stipulated stylistic trends is found pleasing. We lament the loss of earlier energy, so that barely enough was left, we say, for the feebler continuation of earlier styles or the playful preoccupation with rococo diversions or the nostalgic recapitulation of past glories. "Declines" of course are dealt with in our surveys. Next question: Is "decline" the most relevant word for what was happening during the Late Hellenistic period?

Facts are available, and are generally known. In relation to the arts, in the

Hellenistic areas during the Late period, production seems to have been limited in dimension and ambition. Relatively little building was going on and there were few if any great and noble projects. Much of the smaller art was made not to enrich local lives, but to be exported, specifically to Rome. Many artists, including some of the best, themselves left home and went to Rome. In the verbal arts also, the syndrome was the same. The words that were spoken and written ran heavily to didactic prose, and they do not reverberate down the centuries as the older ones do. Among the best writers were Polybios, historian of the second century B.C., and Posidonios, philosopher and scientist of the first half of the first century B.C., who was more respected in his own day than he is today, and they also had important connections outside the Hellenistic region, with Rome.

In relation to political and military matters, the facts are written large in every book on classical history, whether ancient or modern. During the Late Hellenistic period, Rome was the predominant power in all of the Mediterranean world. Even earlier, still in the full Early Hellenistic flush, by 272 B.C. Rome had conquered and subdued the Greeks of South Italy, and after the First Punic War, 264–241 B.C., Sicily was made Rome's first province, its Greeks of course included. During the Second Punic War, 218–201 B.C., South Italy was ravaged, save only Campania, and after the war both it and Sicily were rapidly Romanized, in the devastating terms of the *latifundia,* which were then new to the Romans themselves. In 89 B.C., all Italians were given Roman citizenship. In the eastern Mediterranean, Rome entered in 229 B.C., and was the strongest power by 197 B.C., after the Second Macedonian War. From 189, when she stopped Antiochos III at Magnesia, she controlled Asia Minor, circumscribed Syria, and assumed a dominating role throughout the region. In 168, after the Third Macedonian War, she subdivided Macedonia and stopped Antiochos in his tracks in Egypt. An overt stage of domination was introduced in 148 and 146, when Macedonia and Greece became provinces of Rome, and it climaxed in 133, when Pergamon was willed to her. A last anti-Roman convulsion was instigated by Mithridates of Pontus, from 88 to 69 B.C. One by one, the rest of the eastern Mediterranean communities were made into provinces, with Egypt the last, of the epoch as now calculated, in 30 B.C.

As conquerors, during this time, the Romans were sometimes devious, often ruthless and greedy, usually disorganized in governance. The Greek and Macedonian states were (with variations) subordinated completely, manipulated rudely, ruled severely, sacked and looted repeatedly, taxed immoderately, and bled white in terms of art and artists, property and people. Money was drained out by Roman *publicani* with only occasional restraint. People were enslaved in large numbers, and taken as hostages. From the beginning of the second century, conquering generals carried artistic loot back to Rome in vast quantities.[1] After 187 B.C., they took artists as well as art.[2] On their own, many more artists must have gone to Rome to look for rich customers than ever went before, since there were so many more rich customers to be found there. Art workshops were set up in the east to sell their wares to Rome, as well.

In sum, the operative word seems to be not so much "decline" as "defeat." The independent Greek and Macedonian states which had been characteristic of the earlier Hellenistic period had first undergone an historic change of status and *seriatim* had ceased to exist as such. They were no longer centers of power. They were not self-generating entities, but dependent and/or provincial. An exterior, stronger force influenced and limited their acts and siphoned away their people, their money, and their products. The generative power lay in Rome now, and the Hellenistic states were a backwater. The "Roman Empire" was already in broad, if inefficient, operation.[3]

Was there, then, an ebb in artistic creativity in all of the classical world during the "Late Hellenistic"—or "Early Roman Imperial"—years? Or, since both power and pelf were now in Rome, was artistic creativity there too? Let us take a look, and make a list.

Physically, of course, Rome was expanding at a breathtaking pace. We have seen that her area of domination and the number of her provinces were growing, and we know that they were exploited ruthlessly for the enrichment of Rome, Latium, and eventually Italy, for individuals as well as the state. The result was physical growth and elaboration of the environment, both public and private. Since colonies had to be planted in Italy, whole cities were planned and raised. Complex sanctuaries were built or rebuilt. The city of Rome itself grew apace. Homes were built and expanded, and gardened villas rose in the countryside. This, of course, means the expansive application of urban and suburban planning, horticulture, engineering, and architecture. Building went on, energetically. There were many great and noble projects. Dimensions were large and ambitions were high.

In the past, Rome, as a lesser member of the Mediterranean community, had found her own forms within the formal language that was shaped predominantly by the Etruscans, Greeks, and Macedonians who were then in power. Now, responding to contemporary Hellenism from a position of strength, she continued to make her own way, but rather more aggressively, seizing and procuring, taking and rejecting, resisting and adoring, adapting and transforming, with many fits and starts finding a level of sophistication and monumentality and splendor which was commensurate with her increasing importance.

Romans continued to develop the building forms that they had previously established. Also, they took new ideas from Hellenism—from theaters, temples, houses, and fortifications—and adjusted them to their own needs. In addition, they developed a large repertoire of more original building formats: arched bridges and aqueducts, paved roads and porticoed streets; giant terraces honeycombed with vaulted chambers; basilicas, baths, amphitheaters, villas, tombs, triumphal arches, civic buildings, and commercial buildings. Out of the earth of Italy they made concrete, a material new to monumental architecture, and they cast it in a new set of basic shapes, which were vital both structurally and aesthetically. Aesthetically also, they translated the Greek orders into an ornamental, articulating system applied to the concrete surface, at the same time serving to enrich and monumentalize it. Compositionally, they used a very rational, coherent, compartmentalized, axial system, as simple or as complex as suited need or fancy; they often contained this system strictly within a basic block of space, and they applied it on a scale that went from small to phenomenally large. Among many individual monuments that are memorable, whether extant or not, let me choose the large basilicas of the Forum Romanum; the Sullan Tabularium and Temple of Jupiter; the

Portico of Metellus and the Forum of Julius Caesar; the utilitarian vaults of bridges, aqueducts, and the Porticus Aemilia; any number of bourgeois houses and even more the studied pleasures of the villa-with-view; the Amphitheater in Pompeii and the Theater-complex of Pompey in Rome; the sanctuaries of Jupiter in Terracina and of Hercules in Tivoli; and the vast Sanctuary of Fortuna Primigenia in Palestrina, the super-spectacular that illustrates all points.

Painting seems to have continued to play an important role in Roman life, in ways that were traditional, and were in part peculiar to it. Military subjects—scenes of battle or incidents of campaigns—were still dear to Roman hearts, and they were used in preestablished ways—put into temples, or displayed publicly in the Forum or Capitoline, or carried in triumphal processions. More tombs than the several we know must have had painted walls. On domestic and public walls, the Romans first took over the structural style previously developed in Hellenistic areas, and then, from the beginning of the first century, transformed it into a mural-and-ceiling system by which the total room is united in a pseudoarchitectural scheme of increasing pomp and splendor. Simulated structures of palatial richness and grandeur occupy a complex simulated space. Architectural forms and spatial areas both are large and vigorous, with a great energy of projection and recession. They are painted in robust colors, with much painterly élan. The composition is multiform, intricate, and grandiose, but held within a highly controlled, rational, coherent, compartmentalized, usually axial, order. Into this architectural system, in the course of the decades, there were assimilated, first, a correspondingly heroic, megalographic kind of figurative composition and, then, a remarkably numerous and diverse repertoire of smaller pictures of many shapes, types, and subjects. One of the subjects is landscape, which may have been invented then. Other subjects seem to be connected with earlier traditions. Within the pictures, diverse styles as well as subjects are introduced, but all are made to coexist plausibly enough within the persistently coherent, often very imaginative, scheme. This style spread broadly through the Roman environment, bringing a sumptuous painterly setting into even those comfortable middle-class houses mentioned above and achieving a degree of cultural dispersion which is not easily found again in civilized society.

Terracotta and bronze were Rome's traditional sculptural materials, and they apparently continued in use. The *Arringatore* and maybe the *Brutus* indicate what was possible, regionally and locally, at this time, in bronze. Many individual terracottas persist, although not many are on a high level. Traditional Roman temples had long burgeoned with figurative sculptures and elaborate ornament in terracotta, even during the time when Greek temples were sculptureless. Examples in terracotta survive through the first century B.C., and we learn from representations on coins and reliefs that the practice was transferred to the new stone temples as well.[4] Marble sculpture was a new idea for Rome, introduced there in the second century B.C. from Hellenistic areas. Marble obviously seemed a very stylish material to Romans, and it was the vehicle for some of the more sophisticated, Hellenizing ideas. However, in the first century B.C. even marble was adapted, in statuary, to the Roman taste for verism in portraiture, the style which is now understood as a "special variant on Hellenistic realism."[5] In architectural decoration, it was used for a sophisticated Roman mode of surface-covering ornament, which can also be understood as a "special variant." Related to this last, as well as to painting, is the Roman use of stucco to cover whole architectural areas, usually interior, and particularly vaulted ceilings.[6] It has been found on tombs, in houses, and in thermae. A. M. G. Little described the development of the painted-prospect wall, combined with the newly vaulted ceiling, as "the transformation of a Hellenistic into a genuine Roman interior."[7] Add to this image stucco relief as an alternative to painting, on the vault.

For literature, it is a well-established fact that the great writers of the period were Roman. This verbal shift had begun earlier. Following the Athenian Menander, the best-known playwrights of the classical world are Plautus, already in the late third century B.C., and Terence, before the mid-second century. Following Apollodoros Rhodios, the best-known epics were written by Livius Andronicus, who was only about eleven years younger than Apollodoros, by Naevius, about twenty-five years younger, and, in the second century, by Ennius. During the Late Hellenistic years which are under discussion, a variety of verbal arts crescendoed in Rome. Among historians there were Sallust and Julius Caesar. Among didactic writers there was Varro. Didactic poetry of a high artistic order was written by Lucretius. Rhetoric reached its greatest heights with Cicero. Poetry soared with Catullus, Horace, and Virgil. In categories that were more specifically Latin, poetic satires were written by Lucilius, and the first systematic treatise on civil law was published by Scaevola. Among these men there are easily recognizable giants of the whole extended human vista; and this last period, the first century B.C. at least, has long since been designated as the beginning of a "golden age."

This list of what was going on in Rome in the arts is long and resounding. That energy and activity were exploding there during this period can hardly be doubted and it seems to me that "creativity" is the word for it too. If I hesitate a little, before saying so, it is because we are still struggling with the bad press that the Romans have had in the past on the subject of creativity. By now, it is true, the ultimate originality of Roman art has been firmly established by many fine scholars, along lines that have been summarized and reconfirmed very cogently, recently, by T. Kraus.[8] But Kraus himself sees no Roman originality in art until the Augustan age, and such noble Romanists as Ward-Perkins and Bianchi Bandinelli acknowledge it for architecture only as late as the reign of Nero, and, for sculpture, in the reign of Trajan.[9]

The anti-Roman argument inevitably begins out of the mouths of the Romans themselves. Repeatedly it is pointed out that Virgil said, "Others, I doubt not, shall beat out the breathing bronze with softer lines, shall from marble draw forth the features of life; shall plead their causes better; with the rod shall trace the paths of heaven and tell the rising of the stars: remember thou, O Roman, to rule the nations with thy sway—these shall be thine arts—to crown Peace with Law, to spare the humbled, and to tame in war the proud."[10] These lines of course must be weighed in the scale of Augustus' policy and propaganda, and in the specific context of Anchises' ghostly exhortation of Aeneas to the Roman destiny of conquest. But shouldn't they also be considered in terms of the historicity of taste? This factor has been adduced by scholars previously to explain Pliny's rejection of earlier Hellenistic art (from the 121st to the 156th Olympiad, 296/2–156/2 B.C.).[11] Now let us remember that Virgil spoke from the august and Augustan viewpoint of official imperial Neoclassicism, stately, educated, and grand. For him Greek classicism could be a lodestar, white marble a preferred material, and subtle, elegant decorum the proper stance. It seems relevant that he selects marble and bronze as his criteria, and that of bronze he uses not an absolute but a comparative adjective: "mollius," "softer." Does the latter perhaps mean only that he prefers the softer lines of, let us say, an Augustan imperial portrait to the harder lines of a portrait in the tradition of the *Brutus*? If this is so, would we agree with him? Do we find softer art better? Do we find less classicizing art less good? Do we doubt that it is art? He does not mention terracotta, wood, tufa, or paint, which, together with bronze, were Rome's traditional materials. Does that mean that he does not consider them worth mentioning? Or that he does not cede superiority in those arts? Whatever it implies for Virgil, his contemporary, Horace, said in *Epistles* II, 1, "We have come to fortune's summit; we paint, we play and sing, we wrestle with more skill than the well-oiled Greeks,"[12] and Pliny later, in Flavian times, appreciated the merits of traditional Roman terracottas. "Effigies of clay still exist in many places," he says, "they survive, in fact, even on rooves of temples in Rome as well as in provincial towns—images which are to be marveled at for their surface detail and artistry and for their strength, more revered than gold, and certainly more innocent."[13] As for Virgil, also, some question must be raised about the aesthetic (though not the political) judgment of a man who is willing to give away the orator's palm (note, above, "shall plead their causes better; . . .") less than a generation after the death of Cicero.

Finally, it has often been pointed out in connection with Virgil's statement that he also implies that artists of Greek nationality, rather than Roman, were making those softer bronzes and lifelike marbles. That this was so seems, on our present evidence, to be overwhelmingly true, although there apparently were more Roman artists working in other materials and other arts.[14] Of course the nationality of artists is an interesting and significant factor in the history of art. But many scholars have already made it clear how basically significant are the positive force of patronage and the molding effect of the environment in which art is made.[15]

It is still often said that the Romans were not traditionally artistic. But did they in fact neglect the arts? Certainly they were relatively obscure during earlier years, relatively provincial, at times relatively poor—and so, presumably, was their art. How could it be otherwise? But literary and archaeological sources, partial as they are, give evidence of a community which, at least from its urban beginnings, was as well stocked with architecture, sculpture, and painting as any comparable one.[16] Many temples were built in Rome, and they were richly ornamented, we have every reason to believe, with terracotta revetments, as well as with figurative sculpture on rooftops and in pediments. Their doorways received bronze frames, and their walls received mural paintings. At first, we are told, they did not have cult images, but soon they had many of them, made of wood, terracotta, and bronze, and many votives were offered to the gods as well. The Temple of Jupiter, already in the sixth century B.C., was the largest temple of the region, and it had a superlative cult image and roof-quadriga of terracotta. Bronze seems to have been the favorite material for honorary statues, mostly portraits, that were set up from early times in public places, particularly in the Forum and Comitium, on the Capitoline, in various temples, and in public buildings like the Curia. The Capitoline Wolf and the portrait called "Brutus" indicate the quality that existed among these works. So numerous were the portraits that they were thinned out from time to time, in 179 B.C. on the Capitoline,[17] in order to clear the view to the Temple of Jupiter, and in 158 B.C. in the Forum.[18] The Romans made particular use of paintings of military subjects, in a variety of ways. (The fact that they were a militaristic people seems to have turned them not away from art, but toward specific kinds of art.) They also made particular use of portraiture in their homes, in connection with ancestral cult and family custom. Tombs could be large, whether above ground or below, and enriched with mural paintings. Is all of this nonartistic? Only in the sense that art was directed primarily toward religions and civic and funerary ends. But this was quite normal in most periods of world history, and it certainly was also true of the Greeks at a similar level of historic development, except that the Greeks at that level did less in the secular-civic and individual categories. For a long time, Roman houses were simple and the code was against individual display, according to the austere ethic of the old Senatorial class. Exactly so was it among the Greeks, as long as they followed the similar ethic of their similar eupatrids.

That there were differences in the use of art between the Greeks and Romans is an idea that the Romans themselves held. One reason for that probably was that Rome was historically rather laggard, so that she was still at a simpler level of development when Greeks and Macedonians were at a more complex level, and she was still relatively provincial when they were central powers. When Rome rose in the world, in the later stages the process went fast. She progressed from isolated city to regional leader, to conqueror of other Italian cities and districts, to imperial center, and to imperial capital with a speed which often took her by surprise, and she had to make her way culturally from level to level sometimes quite precipitously. Repeatedly, she took over avalanches of booty and ideas, with which she helped herself learn, step by step, how to be a sophisticated world center. One of the differentials most noticeable to the Romans, apparently, was in the habit of individual luxury and the private use of art, practices which the Greeks themselves had developed only since the fourth century B.C. In this connection, the Romans were first shocked by what they saw, and then delighted, as their own personal fortunes swelled and as the old Senatorial class waned, together with its morality of austerity. The new Romans, in fact, were remarkably apt pupils in self-indulgence and self-expression[19] once they started, absorbing lessons as they wished and augmenting them with many ideas of their own, as we have already seen in part. During the last century or more of the Republic they were already making their own pattern of private environment, including house type and villa type, garden and pleasure dome, painted decorations and household appurtenances, retrospective interests as well as contemporary ones, and rabid art collecting, all of it done intensely, by numbers of people and to a degree that was new in the world.

In discussing the artistic capacities of the Romans, perhaps what is needed now is a closer definition of just how much originality one has in mind. Obviously, we are not speaking here of the degree of originality that means reinventing art from the ground up. Nor was a drastic new direction taken in art any more than it was in life. Rome had been backward for a long time, but was now catching up with the Hellenistic world, at least enough to exploit it and assimilate to it. Under her control, the classical imperial system was enlarged and unified to include the whole Mediterranean community, and it was modified by some practices and systems that were particular to the Romans. The basic economic structure continued, but the burgeoning demands of the lower classes to share its benefits were suppressed, ultimately with severe controls, and instead there was a decrease in the percentage of people who received its benefits during the late second and first century B.C., while individual fortunes became larger. All of this constituted a continuation of the classical imperial world, with differences, and that is true culturally as well. Rome now presided over a new period, although not a new epoch, in which the arts in Rome were modified enough to express the content of the Roman organization of empire and the Roman character.

Concerning the style of the art that was made during this time, first let me make a generalization: The fact that people collect art, and what they collect, is related to but distinct from what is produced in their own time, and the two should not be confused. What the Romans collected was, in fact, diverse. It included objects not only in many techniques but also in many styles, from Classical, if not earlier, to contemporary "Hellenistic." The copies of famous works which they collected were equally diverse, as Miss Richter has pointed out, not confined to Classical originals but also covering the same wide range.[20] Second, the wall paintings that we know in Rome and the region of Mt. Vesuvius show that a very stately and firmly-organized version of the style that is usually called "Baroque" persisted to the end of the Republic, beginning to solidify plastically and simplify spatially only in the last decade before the Principate. This would seem to indicate a widespread, continuing taste for such a style which, if basic art historical logic holds at all, must have applied to other arts as well. Therefore I cannot sympathize with Miss Richter's attempt to clear all but revivalist work from the first century B.C.[21] If we did not have "stately-Baroque" sculpture to ascribe to this period, we would have to invent it. Third, it is still necessary to winnow out what is Neoclassic in this period from the list of works that are called Neoclassic. It must be obvious to all that, in general, philhellenism does not equal Neoclassicism, neither does Neo-Atticism. One must still cast a careful eye over individual works, one by one. However, even now it seems plain that whatever Neoclassicism existed before the Principate was limited and concentrated within certain, particularly interested groups. Concerning the basic nature of Neoclassicism, is it necessary to note that it is a new style that refers in certain ways to an old one, not an old one repeated? This goes without saying to people who admire the late eighteenth and early nineteenth centuries A.D. among others, and who have listed among creative geniuses Jacques-Louis David, Jean-Auguste-Dominique Ingres, and William Blake; Percier and Fontaine, and John Nash; Jacques-Ange Gabriel and Robert Adam; Claude-Nicolas Ledoux, John Soane, and Thomas Jefferson.

That influence moved from Hellenistic centers to Rome, even during this period, when the Hellenistic countries were dominated and conquered by the Romans, is a circumstance that has been long known and much discussed. Less often discussed is the influence that went from the dominant and conquering Romans to the Hellenistic centers. After all, the former is stressed because it seems odd. The latter is what is expected.

In South Italy and Sicily, the flow of influence is only too clear. There the Romans took over and Romanized, in provincial Sicily in an especially brutal way. In the eastern Mediterranean, as we have seen, Roman greed and mismanagement during this period led to relative impoverishment. Rome's power dominated both friends and foes. She was able to degrade Rhodes and elevate Delos at will. Even in Egypt, the last state to fall into overt submission, all the contending Ptolemaic factions had long been Rome's "obedient servants."[22] From the beginning of the second century B.C., not only Roman soldiers but other Romans, also in tens of thousands, poured into the east to practice banking, industry, trade, and agriculture, to represent the Roman government, and to collect tribute and taxes.[23] In addition to settlers, there were many Roman students, visitors, and exiles. But in the eastern Mediterranean, Greek and Macedonian governmental organization persisted, as well as cultural and religious organization, and many members of the upper class collaborated in the management of affairs. They had found a measure of rapport with the Romans from the beginning, eager for their help in suppressing not only each other but also the demands of the restive classes below them, and many continued to serve in old capacities, under the new overlords. Following the general trend, they became both richer and fewer during the late second and first century B.C. Because of this continuity, Hellenistic language, customs, forms, and daily habits persisted to a considerable extent, and there was still some local money to spend on art. But obviously things were not the same as they had been before.

There is no sign that Roman artists invaded the east, except for Cossutius, who was hired by Antiochos IV in 174 B.C. to work on the Olympeion in Athens, and brothers named Stallius, who were hired by Ariobarzanes of Cappadocia in 60 B.C. to rebuild the Odeion of Pericles.[24] But there are abundant signs of Roman customers. Note those tens of thousands of Romans who streamed in, after the beginning of the second century B.C. Eventually they must have added up to hundreds of thousands, since in 88 B.C., when Mithridates called on the people of Asia Minor to rise up and massacre the Romans who lived among them, they killed 80,000 of them, according to ancient historians, and some 20,000 more Romans were killed on Delos and other Aegean islands in the course of the Mithridatic Wars.[25] As members of the conquering country, those resident Romans must have been in a privileged position, and many of them had wealth even if they did not have direct political power.[26] How much of it did they spend on art? How much did their demands and inclinations influence what the artists produced? How much, on the other hand, were they themselves influenced by their milieu?[27]

We know of some prominent Roman commissions, among them Aemilius Paullus' victory monument in Delphi in 168 B.C., the Agora of the Italians and much else on Delos, a number of portraits that are identified as representing Romans, and Appius Claudius Pulcher's propylon in Eleusis of the mid-first century B.C. How many more were there? It has been pointed out that the frieze of Aemilius Paullus' monument represents the specific battle of Pydna, which is rather the Roman than the Greek approach to the subject. The Agora of the Italians, the largest public building raised in the eastern Mediterranean during the last century of the Roman Republic, is a four-sided enclosure with what may be read as inclinations toward axiality.[28] The painted altars of Delos represent

Roman games, painted in the same calligraphic way as they were painted in Rome already in the third century B.C.[29] The eastern Romans are represented in their portraits in the same veristic style as western Romans. It can be asked, concerning the Eleusis propylon, how much the Neoclassicism of taste, the eclecticism of sources, and the originality of composition had to do with its Roman patron.

We know that a great deal of art was made in the east specifically for Roman markets in the west. Much of the "Neo-Attic" sculpture and the Rhodian sculpture, the sculptured copies of earlier works, and the gold and silver plate were destined for the Roman market,[30] and a Roman firm, the Cossutii, set up branches throughout Greece, employing Greek workmen, exactly for this purpose.[31] How much was that art shaped by the taste of its Roman customers?

Negatively, A. W. Lawrence has pointed out that there were "no temples of any consequence built during the first century B.C. in the East Mediterranean," and noted quietly and briefly that "The weight of Roman taxation must have discouraged building" in much of the area.[32]

We know that the prosperity of any given center in the east, from the beginning of the second century, depended heavily on its relationship with Rome, and that its art production often prospered at the same time. The high "Baroque" style, that most "typical" Hellenistic style, flourished in Pergamon and Rhodes, when they were Rome's principal allies and instruments. Was this a function only of their opportunity to prosper? Did the connection with Rome influence their style in any way? After 168 B.C., when Rome's favor moved to Athens and Delos, they in turn were responsible for a large production of art. Then the possibility of Roman influence becomes more explicit, since we know that much of the art that was made in Athens or Delos was bought by Romans, who resided either in those two cities or in Rome.[33] On the other hand, Rome dealt with Syria and Egypt by circumscribing and isolating them, cutting them off from possessions and markets overseas. Did that influence the Greeks and Macedonians in those countries to turn inward instead, assimilating with native peoples and native customs, in art as in other matters?

More generally, how far did Roman taste spread beyond the Romans themselves, in the east? We talk a great deal about philhellenism among the Romans. What of philromanism among the Greeks and Macedonians? That the latter existed as well as the former, we know. Among the intellectuals, it is spelled out quite explicitly in their surviving writings. Many admired the Romans for their energy, their organizational ability, their morality, their Republican government, and their success. A number of them went to Rome, for long or short stays, including the historian Polybios, who spent eighteen years there as a hostage, from 168 B.C.; the philosopher Panaitios, his contemporary, who like Polybios was a welcome member of the philhellenic circle of Scipio Africanus; the philosopher Posidonios of the first half of the first century B.C., who found similar Roman friends in his own generation; and ambassadorial agents like Krates, Pergamene librarian, who represented Eumenes II in 168 B.C., and the heads of the three major philosophic schools of Athens who were sent to Rome in 155 B.C.[34]

The admiration between Greeks and Romans apparently could be mutual, and such sojourns in Rome, says Stahl, "had much to do with turning the minds of Greek philosophers from the passive to the active virtues and with moulding eclectic philosophies which would have enough application and adaptability to appeal to practical men in this dynamic new world that was coming into being."[35] It was in this direction that the Stoa was developed by Panaitios and Posidonios, both greatly influenced by their Roman friends and both personally traveling between Rome and Athens or Rhodes. In this way they made Stoicism into the most useful, and characteristic, philosophical instrument of the period. They taught this philosophy both to local students and to the Romans who, from the later second century B.C., came to the eastern schools of philosophy and rhetoric for their higher education. Polybios returned to his native Achaia as Rome's enthusiastic admirer and friend, and devoted his history primarily to the story of her deserved rise to greatness, which was predestined by Tyche, conceiving his book in terms of universal history because Rome had made the world into an organic whole. When Posidonios wrote history, he followed the universalism of Polybios, and he pictured the new, unified world empire of the Romans as the fulfillment of the commonwealth of God. Political leaders, perhaps even more naturally, learned to admire Rome, and those included not only her friends but also her foes, such as the Seleucid Antiochos IV, who had lived in Rome for fourteen years. Also political rebels on both east and west sides of the Mediterranean shared a philosophic point of view, and in at least one instance shared a famous philosopher. The Stoic Blossios of Cumae was advisor first to Tiberius Gracchus and then, in 132 B.C., to Aristonikos, who led a massive social uprising in Pergamon.

The admiration of Rome was institutionalized officially very widely, and if it was often done in ways that were more ordained than spontaneous, it is hardly therefore to be discounted. The goddess Roma was worshiped as early as 195 B.C. in Smyrna, and in many additional cities afterward. Roman conquerors were worshiped together with Roma, beginning with Flaminius, the victor at Kynoskephalai in 197 B.C. By the first century B.C., Roman governors were "worshiped indiscriminately."[36] Festivals called *Romaia* were established in many sanctuaries, beginning in 189 B.C., in Delphi.

Given such an atmosphere, could Roman-influenced attitudes have found their way generally not only into historiography, philosophy, rhetoric, and civic and religious practices, but also into art? It seems logical enough that it should. But how? Is it recognizable? Where? Specifically in relation to gold jewelry, Pfeiler-Lippitz recently suggested that a decisive stylistic change which began in the mid-second century B.C. is to be connected with the taste of the dominant Romans.[37] A few other suggestions rear their heads, at least in the form of questions. Do all veristic portraits that exist in the east represent Romans, or did the taste spread to others as well? Did the revival of architectural sculpture in the Late Hellenistic period have to do with its continuing popularity among the Romans? Was the use of the trophy motif in the second-floor banister of the Athena Stoa in Pergamon and on the frieze of the propylon of the Bouleuterion in Miletos related to Roman usages?[38] Did Roman custom, if not Roman customers, influence such axial temples-on-podiums as the Temple of Dionysos at Pergamon or the two temples near the harbor in Kos?[39] What is the relationship to Roman aesthetic of the terraced symmetry of the later additions on the acropolis of Lindos and the Asklepieion of Kos, the block composition of the Bouleuterion of Miletos, or the alignment side by side of the same two temples in Kos, and their enclosure in a tight, symmetrical, four-sided colonnade? If our first copies of earlier statues have turned up in Pergamon and Delos, is that for Greek or Roman reasons? Can we take it as a clue to the significance of the classicizing movement that it found its culmination in the Rome of Augustus and the Julio-Claudians?

Most generally and most basically, how did the new conditions of this period, which included the adjustment that every Macedonian and Greek had to make to the fact of Roman domination, affect their lives, their character, and their mentality, and therefore the content of their art?

If the basic question proposed here is valid, systematic research will provide answers. It is hardly likely that those answers will be simple, since the situation was complex, involving a layered population; interplay between Romans and Greeks, and others as well; many regional variations; and not only different but also changing relationships among the regions, and with Rome.

And now for almost the last of these many questions: Is it possible at all to understand the eastern Mediterranean during this period without looking at it together with the west, any more than one can understand the west without the east? If the Romans, with the help of Tyche and the Stoic God, had already made the Mediterranean into an organic whole, does it not behoove us to learn to understand it in this way? How can we make sense of it if we do not keep in mind always which is the center of power and which is the periphery?

We have organized the chapters of our books on this coordinated basis only from the Principate of Augustus. Now we would have to begin earlier. But when? 220 B.C.? 197? 168? 146? 133? 88? Or what other decisive year? How many subdivisions would there be? Among historians, Rostovtzeff made the divisions as follows: After the periods of "Alexander and the Successors" (334–282 B.C.) and "The Balance of Power" (281–221), came "Disintegration of the Balance of Power and Roman Intervention" (220–168), "The Roman Protectorate and the First Stage of Roman Domination" (168–88), and "Roman Domination" (from 88).[40] Among cultural historians, C. Schneider postulated, after an "Early Hellenistic" period (323–c. 280 B.C.) and a "High Hellenistic" period (280–220), a time of "Inner Crises and Roman Invasion" (220–133), and then a "Late Hellenistic" period (133–30).[41] The Romans of course shared many of the Hellenistic crises, but they also lived through others, both internal and external. How would we reconcile Hellenistic and Roman history? How could we reconcile the periodization of art styles with the periodization of history? These are difficult problems. But if we deal more accurately with historic relationships, we should be better able to make a periodization which clarifies more than it confuses.

NOTES

*   I thank Moshe Barasch, Phyllis Bober, Elsbeth Dusenbery, and Milton W. Brown for reading the manuscript of this article and giving me good advice for its improvement.

1   J. J. Pollitt, *The Art of Rome, c. 753* B.C.*–337* A.D. (Sources and Documents), Englewood Cliffs, N. J., 1966, pp. 24–25, 32–33, 42–48, 63–74.

2   Livy, XXXIX, 22, 1–2.

3   From the beginning of the Principate, the government of the Roman empire was to be organized more efficiently and constructively, which led to a revival of prosperity and activity in the eastern, as in the other, provinces. During the late Republic, the government of empire was not yet well organized, so that it functioned in haphazard and unprincipled ways, which led to the impoverishment cited here. In both cases, the explanation lies in Rome.

4   The use of stone pedimental sculpture continued abundantly with the Principate, and most of the illustrated examples are of the later times, but even these testify to the Republican practice. For coins: D. F. Brown, *Temples of Rome as Coin Types,* New York, 1940 (Numismatic Notes and Monographs, XC). For reliefs, and other evidence: P. Hommel, *Studien zu den römischen Figurengiebeln der Kaiserzeit,* Berlin, 1954.

5   R. Bianchi Bandinelli, *Rome: The Center of Power, 500* B.C. *to* A.D. *200,* London, 1970 (Arts of Mankind, 79). O. Vessberg, *Studien zur Kunstgeschichte der römischen Republik,* Lund, Leipzig, 1941 (Swedish Institute in Rome, Skrifter, VIII), calls it "der sachliche Stil."

6   Stucco decoration has not been adequately published. For a brief but comprehensive treatment, with bibliography: S. De Marinis, "Stucco," *Enciclopedia dell'arte antica,* Rome, VII, 1966, pp. 524–33. The Roman architectural use of stucco relief apparently began in the early first century B.C., although remains of the Republican period are not extensive. To those mentioned by De Marinis, add the ceiling fragments from the late Republican House of the Cryptoporticus in Pompeii: H. G. Beyen, *Die pompejanische Wanddekoration vom zweiten bis zum vierten Stil,* The Hague, II, 1960, fig. 36, pp. 44–49.

7   A. M. G. Little, "The Formation of a Roman Style in Wall Painting," *American Journal of Archaeology,* XLIX, 1945, p. 134; K. Schefold, *Vergessenes Pompeii,* Berne, Munich, 1962, p. 40, said, "Der zweite Stil ist die erste reife Schöpfung der lateinisch-abendländischen Kunst."

8   T. Kraus, *Das römische Weltreich,* Berlin, 1967 (Propyläen Kunstgeschichte), n.s. II, pp. 11–16.

9   A. Boëthius and J. B. Ward-Perkins, *Etruscan and Roman Architecture* (Pelican History of Art), Harmondsworth, 1970, pp. 248 ff.; Bianchi Bandinelli, *op. cit.,* pp. 223 ff.

10   Virgil, *Aeneid,* VI, 847 ff. The *Aeneid* was begun 26 B.C. and left almost finished when Virgil died, 19 B.C.

11   Pliny, *Natural History,* XXXIV, 52.

12   *Epistles* II, 1, 33–34. Written after 17 B.C., and dedicated to Augustus. These lines are in the same *Epistle* in which Horace also said, lines 156–157, "Greece, the captive, made her savage victor captive, and brought the arts into rustic Latium," a statement which refers so specifically to the drama, *i.e.,* to the opposition between Fescennine license and the Saturnian measure on the one hand and Greek dramatic forms on the other, that it does not seem applicable to anything else.

13   Pliny, *Natural History,* XXXV, 157.

14   Lists of artists were made by H. Brunn, *Geschichte der griechischen Künstler,* Stuttgart, 1889; Vessberg, *op. cit.,* part I; G. Ricci, "Relazioni artistico-commerciali tra Roma (Italia) e la Grecia negli ultimi secoli della Repubblica e nel primo dell'Impero," *Antichità,* II, 1950, appendix. The subject is discussed at some length by J. Toynbee, *Some Notes on Artists in the Roman World,* Brussels, 1951 (Collection Latomus, VI). She strains every sinew and stretches every point to prove that all artists in Rome were Greeks, going so far as to say that all painters with Roman names were eccentrics and all others may have been renamed Greeks. This surely goes too far. K. Michalowski, "La fin de l'art grec," *Bulletin de la correspondance hellénique,* LXX, 1946, 385–392, points out that for painters there are more Roman than Greek names in the total lists of artists who worked during the Roman Republic and Empire, which are published by Brunn, *op. cit.,* and J. Overbeck, *Die antiken Schriftquellen zur Geschichte der bildenden Künste bei den Griechen,* Leipzig, 1868. It would be very desirable to have an up-to-date exhaustive list of such names, culled from all presently available sources, upon which to base further argument.

15   One of the clearest statements was made by Toynbee, *op. cit.,* p. 6. For a fuller, more recent statement of the position: Kraus, *op. cit.,* pp. 11–16.

16   Literary sources: Vessberg, *op. cit.*; Pollitt, *op. cit.* Archaeological sources and topography: T. Ashby, S. B. Platner, *A Topographical Dictionary of Ancient Rome,* Oxford, 1929; G. Lugli, *I monumenti antichi di Roma e suburbio,* Rome, 1931–40; I. S. Ryberg, *An Archaeological Record of Rome from the VIIth to the IInd Century* B.C., London, 1940 (Studies and Documents, XIII), 1, 2; G. Lugli, *Roma antica, il centro monumentale,* Rome, 1946; D. R. Dudley, *Urbs Roma: A Source Book of Classical Texts on the City and its Monuments,* Aberdeen, 1967; E. Nash, *Pictorial Dictionary of Ancient Rome,* rev. ed., London, 1968.

17   Livy, XL, 51, 3.

18   Pliny, *Natural History,* XXXIV, 30–31.

19   G. E. Rizzo, "I Romani e l'arte greca," *L'Urbe,* X, 1947, July-Aug., 3–13, Sept.-Oct., 3–9, Nov.-Dec., 3–15; H. Jucker, *Vom Verhältnis der Römer zur bildenden Kunst der Griechen,* Frankfurt-am-Main, 1950; G. Becatti, *Arte e gusto negli scrittori latini,* Florence, 1951; J. H. D'Arms, *Romans on the Bay of Naples; a social and cultural study of the villas and their owners from 150* B.C. *to* A.D. *400,* Cambridge, Mass., 1970 (Loeb Classical Monographs).

20   G. M. A. Richter, "Was Roman Art of the First Centuries B.C. and A.D. Classicizing?" *Journal of Roman Studies,* XLVIII, 1958, 10–19.

[21]   *Idem,* "Chronologie hellénistique, le second et le premier siècle av. J. C.," *Actes du Premier Congrès de la Fédération Internationa ledes associations d'études classiques, à Paris, 1950,* Paris, 1951, 185–191. This is true, she says, of art representing mythological or ideal subjects.

[22]   M. Rostovtzeff, *The Social and Economic History of the Hellenistic World,* corrected edition, Oxford, 1953, p. 69.

[23]   J. Hatzfeld, *Les Trafiquants italiens dans l'Orient hellénique,* Paris, 1919 (Bibliothèque des Ecoles françaises d'Athènes et de Rome, CXV), said that these men, who were called Ῥωμαῖοι by the local inhabitants, and often by themselves, in fact were rarely Romans or even Latins, and almost never came from Rome itself; he said that most were Italiotes or Greeks, from Campania or South Italy. They were divided among free, freed, and slave. A. J. N. Wilson, *Emigration from Italy in the Republican Age of Rome,* Manchester, New York, 1966, pp. 87–93, disputes this. He says that a larger portion of them than Hatzfeld indicates must have been Roman or Latin, including those from Campania and South Italy, since there were Roman colonies there. He emphasizes the degree of Romanization already achieved generally in those areas in the second and first centuries B.C., as well as the degree of "hybridization" between Oscans, other Italiotes, Italiote Greeks, Latins, and Romans. Cf. also A. Donati, "I Romani nell' Egeo. I documenti dell'età repubblicana," *Epigraphica,* XXVII, 1965, 1–37. E. Badian, *Roman Imperialism in the Late Republic,* new ed., Ithaca, N. Y., 1968, p. 17, note 4, says, "The whole matter needs renewed study in the light of what facts we possess." Hatzfeld, *op. cit.,* says that the first Italian *trafiquants* came to the east c. 240 B.C., but Wilson, *op. cit.,* disputes that also. He says, pp. 86–87, that they had begun to come earlier, and that "a new age in economic relationships" between Italy and the east came not c. 240 B.C., but in the first half of the second century, together with new political relationships.

[24]   Vitruvius, VII, praef. 15. W. Dittenberger (ed.), *Inscriptiones Atticae aetatis Romanae,* Berlin, 1878 (*Inscriptiones Graecae,* III, 1), p. 541.

[25]   Appian, *Mithridatica,* 22–23, 28; Valerius Maximus, IX, 2–3; Memnon of Heraclea Pontica, 31, 9 (F. Jacoby, *Die Fragmente der griechischen Historiker,* Berlin, III B, 352, 16–21). Plutarch, *Sulla,* 24, 7, puts the number of Romans killed at 150,000, but that number is generally dismissed as inflated. Wilson, *op. cit.,* p. 126, points out that Cicero, *De imperio Cn. Pompeii,* 11, does not give an exact figure. Rostovtzeff, *op. cit.,* p. 818, says, ". . . at the bidding of Mithridates 80,000 Romans were massacred all over Asia, and . . . many more escaped. The figures are trustworthy and are derived in one way or another from official sources, though these may for some reason have exaggerated the greatness of the catastrophe."

[26]   W. W. Tarn, *Hellenistic Civilisation,* 3rd ed., revised with G. T. Griffith, London, 1952, p. 263, ". . . they could, and often did, appeal from the city law to Roman law, and got the benefit of edicts or allowances from complacent Roman governors; the dice were, politically, weighted in their favor." Wilson, *op. cit.,* p. 128, "For Romans of any standing enjoyed, as such, a position of special advantage in the provincial system . . ."

[27]   Philhellenism among some Romans in the east is as well known as in the west: e.g., Cicero's friend Titus Pomponius Atticus. On a more basic level, says Tarn, *op. cit.,*

p. 262, in Greece and Asia at least, "The Roman trader . . . often became a citizen, married a Greek wife, owned land, took part in city life, perhaps held a magistracy, and sent his son to the gymnasium and through the ephebate." The community leaders among them are known to have followed the Hellenistic custom of public benefaction.

[28]   L. Crema, *L'Architettura romana,* Turin, 1959, *Enciclopedia classica,* III, xii, 164, sees no axiality, but notes its four-sidedness, and its distinctness in the east: ". . . essa a forma di recinto rettangolare circondato in maniera piuttosto irregolare da esedre e ambienti vari, a cui è riconosciuto un carattere differente da quegli altri edifici ellenistici." A. W. Lawrence, *Greek Architecture,* 2nd ed. (Pelican History of Art), Harmondsworth, 1967, p. 279, points out its size.

[29]   Naevius, *Tunicularia,* Festus v. penis (ed. Müller, 230). The grammarian Festus quotes an excerpt from Naevius in which he says that a certain Theodotus painted the *Lares ludentes* on altars for the Compitalia "with an ox's tail."

[30]   D. E. Strong, *Greek and Roman Gold and Silver Plate,* Ithaca, N. Y., 1966, p. 107, makes one of the clearest statements in this connection: ". . . 31 B.C. . . . has no special significance in the history of ancient plate. By that time the Romans had become ardent collectors and much of the plate that was produced was made for the Roman market, so that the 'Hellenistic' merges completely with the 'Roman' in the late Republic."

[31]   Hatzfeld, *op. cit.,* 227.

[32]   Lawrence, *op. cit.,* p. 221.

[33]   J. Hatzfeld, "Les Italiens résidant à Délos mentionnés dans les inscriptions de l'Ile," *Bulletin de la correspondance hellénique,* XXXVI, 1912, 5–218. Tarn, *op. cit.,* p. 265, summarizes that especially after c. 130 B.C., on Delos, "Far the strongest element now was the Romans; they were favored by the Athenian governors, Athens having consistently been Rome's friend, and became the real power in the island."

[34]   The three were Kritolaos the Peripatetic, Diogenes the Stoic, and Karneades, founder of the New Academy. They were sent when Athens found herself in disfavor with the Roman Senate.

[35]   W. H. Stahl, *Roman Science: Origins, Development, and Influence,* Madison, Wis., 1962, p. 45.

[36]   Tarn, *op. cit.,* p. 55.

[37]   B. Pfeiler-Lippitz, "Späthellenistische Goldschmiedearbeiten," *Antike Kunst,* XV, 2, 1972, 107–119. She bases her statement on jewelry found in datable contexts in Thessaly, Kurgan, Delos, Samothrace, Macedonia, Eretria, Syria, Piraeus, Damascus, and Olbia. Until the third century B.C., she says, Greek and Macedonian jewelry depended upon naturalistic animal motifs, made in monochrome gold, with color used only to accent naturalistic details. From about the mid-second century B.C., color became important, used in flat areas, often with multiple colors playing against one another as well as against the gold, and making independent, geometric, decorative effects. She says (p. 119), "Dies alles bedeutet, dass etwa in der Mitte des zweiten vorchristlichen Jahrhunderts ein grundsätzlicher Wandel in der Konzeption hellenistischer Schmuckarbeiten beginnt, der das Ende griechischer Goldschmiedetradition

einleitet und dessen logische Fortsetzung der frühkaiserzeitliche römische Schmuck ist. Es wird kein Zufall sein, dass dieser Wandel etwa gleichzeitig mit dem Eingreifen Roms im griechischen Osten beginnt und die weitere Entwicklung zeitlich parallel geht mit seiner immer stärkeren Einflussnahme in der hellenistischen Welt.

"Die Bedeutung der Zentren des griechischen Kunsthandwerks endete weitgehend mit dem Niedergang und der Auflösung der hellenistischen Königshöfe. Zahlreiche Kunsthandwerker gingen nach Rom, dem neuen Zentrum politischer und wirtschaftlicher Macht. Sie brachten ihr technisches Können mit, passten sich bald aber immer mehr der künstlerischen Auffassung ihrer neuen Auftraggeber an. Und diese wurde bestimmend im gesamten römischen Imperium. Dies erklärt die engen stilistischen Beziehung zwischen späthellenistischen und frühkaiserzeitlichen Schmuckarbeiten." (Elsbeth Dusenbery referred me to this article, for which I thank her.)

[38]   The Bouleuterion was at least partly subsidized by Antiochos IV (175–164 B.C.).

[39]   The foundations of the temple in Pergamon are Hellenistic; it was rebuilt during the reign of Caracalla: R. Bohn, *Die Theater-Terrasse,* Berlin, 1896 (*Altertümer von Pergamon,* IV). Kos: L. Laurenzi, "Coo," *Enciclopedia dell'Arte Antica,* II, Rome, 1959, p. 796, fig. 1043. Kos was part of the Roman province of Asia from 129 B.C.

[40]   Rostovtzeff, *op. cit.*

[41]   C. Schneider, *Kulturgeschichte des Hellenismus,* Munich, 1967, I, p. 2, says of the period from 323 to 30 B.C. that only the earliest century was "Hellenistic," since the other two were increasingly Roman. Cultural historians in other fields tend to remark more than art historians do on the presence of the Romans in the east Mediterranean during the Late Hellenistic period. Among historians of the major visual arts, the most explicit acceptance of Roman rule during this period has come as a result of looking backward, by some who have undertaken to describe what happened to the east, or a part of it, under the Roman Empire, and therefore were forced to look beyond 30 B.C., except in Egypt, for even the most overt and official Roman takeover: A. Giuliano, *La cultura artistica delle province della Grecia in età romana: Epirus, Macedonia. Achaia, 146 a.C.– 267 d.C.,* Rome, 1965 (Studia Archaeologica, VI); C. C. Vermeule, *Roman Imperial Art in Greece and Asia Minor,* Cambridge, Mass., 1968. Vermeule, p. vii, says, "I believe a new picture of Roman art in the Hellenic world can be formed by tracing its development from the impact of Rome on the Hellenistic states in the second century B.C. to the flowering of Eastern Rome in the sixth century A.D. . . ."

3

JOAN LEBOLD COHEN

The Domestication of the Fourth Dimension

What is to be learned about western civilization from a comparison between a knight's fortified castle and an astronaut's split-level, terraced house? Assuming the risk of Herculean generalities, I suggest that apart from what each building tells us about the differing degree of personal security enjoyed and the technology available to the individual in his community, these buildings reflect dramatically altered views of the universe. Man's creations, indeed his entire life style, inevitably reveal the contemporary understanding of his relationship to the environment.

In the twentieth century, this realization came to be popularized in words borrowed from the scientific terminology of Einstein's theory of relativity. Ignoring the complexities of the theory, nonscientists began to use the term "fourth dimension" to express consciousness of universal change, impermanence, the absence of absolutes, and the motion of objects in space and time. All things in the world were seen as relative to one another within a universal flux.

This image of the nature of things was translated into man-made form. Just as the formally arranged plan of Washington, D.C., with rectangular and diagonal avenues lined with dignified government buildings, reflects the eighteenth-century notion of an ordered environment, so, too, twentieth-century planners have sought a host of new solutions to urban problems in the context of a far more complex series of relationships symbolized by the term "fourth dimension."

The avant-garde artists of the first decades of the twentieth century heralded this new vision. For the four centuries preceding Cubist painting artists had drawn an object from a single viewpoint, reflecting the older notion that fixed bodies in a universe were measurable in three dimensions. The Cubists examined objects in space in a way that showed many points of view. Their aim was to express an image, such as a bottle, according to their new understanding of how it *really* exists. But trying to paint this four-dimensional idea of the object in space and time on a flat canvas posed serious representational problems. In order to show many views at once, the Cubists broke up the object into planes or facets.

The Cubist vision of revolution invaded the American art scene in 1913 at New York's "Armory Show" with Marcel Duchamp's *Nude Descending a Staircase* (Essay 4, fig. 3). Outraged critics looking for the nude described the composition as "an explosion in a shingle factory" and "a collection of saddle bags." Duchamp himself said: "It is an organization of kinetic elements, an expression of time and space through abstract presentation of motion." But the public understood neither his abstract vocabulary of form nor his expression of time/space. Referring to three-dimensional vision, he asked ". . . why must we worship principles which. . . no longer apply?" In considering form in space at a given time, he said he had to "enter the realm of geometry and mathematics." Theodore Roosevelt, however, voiced a majority opinion on this new artistic vision: "The Cubists are entitled to the serious attention of all who find enjoyment in the colored puzzle pictures of the Sunday newspapers."

Would this four-dimensional idea find specific form in our daily lives? Was the home going to reflect the universal pattern? Frank Lloyd Wright was the outstanding American architect to build with this new vision (fig. 1). During the first half of the twentieth century he designed structures that he said expressed a truly modern architecture. He believed that a house must relate to valley, hill, or flat, that exterior space must be conceived to relate to interior space. He wrote: "There is no outside independent of the inside—the two are one—organic—integral." Within the house itself, the notion of separate cubes of space for living and dining rooms is rethought to express the pattern of use of those rooms. Enclosing walls give way to interpenetrating space for the continuous activities of living. Wright's approach epitomizes "fourth-dimensional" thinking about the complexities of ever-changing, interrelating space.

Although the mid-twentieth-century contractor may be unaware of his participation in the ideological revolution, tract houses with split levels and combined living-dining areas with related patios are the evidence of a general acceptance of the notion of interpenetrating space as the key to house planning. Wright organized living space in a "truthful" way: his prophetic credo was "form follows function," and he indicted the bizarre borrowing of styles of the past. He said "Architecture . . . after five centuries of decline, culminated in the imitation of imitations . . . Mrs. Plasterbuilt, Mrs. Gablemore, and Miss Flattop . . ." He also said that the nature of materials must be respected. Why should a papier-mâché form pretend to be a stone vault, or a wooden house pretend to be a stone palazzo? Technology developed materials to make new kinds of structures possible and they too must be used truthfully—as themselves.

Art and technology has been the theme of at least a dozen exhibitions in recent years. Artists today concerned with art and the machine are indebted to the Bauhaus masters of Germany in the 1920s who sought to reform art and industrial design. The problem they faced was, how can the artist marry the machine to create a new language of forms? Many thoughtful Bauhaus artists came to America in the '30s after the Nazis closed down that school. These émigrés became prophets in a new land leading the revolution in ideas and images.

One of the most distinguished Bauhaus leaders was the architect Mies van der Rohe, whose philosophy of building was based on the notion that "less is more" (fig. 3). For a richer architecture you must simplify—exclude all but the essential, use the industrial materials beautifully, and the result is a kind of classic twentieth-century form. The structure, a steel skeleton sheathed in a glass skin, invites the visual continuity of the environment in quite a different way from Wright's forms. Seeing through the glass maintains a relationship to the outside while also inviting the mirrorlike reflection of the environment in the glass. Within this culture camp Philip Johnson built his "glass house" (fig. 4). While inside his "invisible" structure there is a remarkable connection with the environs: the time of day, weather conditions, season, and foliage dictate the mood of the house. The architectural commitment is made to the natural endowment of the site. The lack of architectural intrusions on the glass rectangular volume follows the Miesian canon of "less is more," and indeed the result is a remarkably rich structure.

There is a significant group of artists and literati who pronounce easel painting dead. I believe that their reasoning is ideologically tinged by the implausibility of a two-dimensional image within the twentieth-century context. The sculptor transmutes his notion of cosmic truth in his images. Alexander Calder's Mobiles, Marcel Duchamp's Machines, and Naum Gabo's Constructions were pioneering efforts. Calder set his designs into motion suggesting ever-changing relationships. Duchamp was a key figure in liberating art forms. He sought a new vocabulary appropriate for a machine age and both Gabo and Calder played with motorized motion, an element used frequently in the Kinetic art of the '60s. Gabo's brilliant experiments in volume with transparent materials had a variety of effects. It showed a new way of looking at things and a new set of things to look at. He also explored the materials of the new technology, liberating the sculpture from traditional materials such as metal, stone, or wood. Gabo issued the "Realist Manifesto" in 1920: "The realization of our perceptions of the world in space and time is the only aim of our pictorial and plastic art . . . we construct our work as the universe constructs its own, as the engineer constructs his bridges."

In the past decade an enormous body of work has been produced dealing with relationships in flux. I will mention only a few specific works by artists who have addressed themselves to the translation of the change and simultaneity that we popularly call the "fourth dimension." Yaacov Agam is a painter who changed the flat canvas in *Transparent Rhythms II* (fig. 2) by lining the surface with vertical stripes of V-shaped projections. His painting unfolds as you, the viewer, walk around it in a 180-degree arc. With each step the composition changes, because you see a different aspect of the painting. The powerful horizontal spectrum bands of color seen at one side are transformed into a dynamic composition of monochrome cubic forms in variation when seen from the center of the painting. This vision reverts to another brilliantly hued, chromatic spectrum at the other end of the painting, but these bands of color run vertically and are dominated by horizontal bars of an inky-black grid. Conceptually, you must move through space and time to "see" the painting.

In *Continual Mobile* (fig. 7), a relief, Julio Le Parc suspends in front of a large black rectangle a series of sixteen wires, hanging on each wire sixteen metal rectangles. The total of 256 suspended squares move 360 degrees as air currents cause a constantly changing pattern. Reflection also plays a role in this composition. The shiny surfaces of the metal squares project a series of satellite reflections depending on the light source or sources. The reflected images vary in form governed by the angles of projection and the surfaces on which they appear. The natural elements, air currents and light, dictate the changing forms of this work of art.

Light was the focal interest of many nineteenth-century artists, and it continues to be a consuming subject today. Whereas the Impressionists sought to create an ambiance of light and atmosphere within the pigment of a painted landscape, moderns such as Howard Jones create compositions dealing directly in light. *Skylight No. 1* (fig. 5) is a continuously changing pattern in concentric circles of lights. Beyond the mesmerizing flux in the light, the composition is a fascinating play of reflection and refraction on the brushed stainless steel background as you move around it.

Paul Matisse explores another possibility of change and movement in his *Kalliroscope* (fig. 6), made of liquid enclosed in a glass frame. Heat activates the liquid into flowing currents and patterns which are never the same.

Sound, considered in India to be the first element of creation, has been brilliantly programed into Jean Dupuy's *Heartbeat Machine* (fig. 8). A microphone, held to your heart, is connected to a drum sprinkled with colored powder; the drum responds to your pulse. As the *Heartbeat Machine* is tuned into your own life sounds, it provides an extraordinary spectacle: you watch the drum throw clouds of particles into the air within the box at the involuntary command of your electronically amplified pulse. Your life rhythms are revealed through the soaring dance of colored powder inevitably waving, cresting, dying, and resurging. It is a microcosmic version of Shiva's dance of creation, maintenance, destruction, and re-creation.

Another remarkable piece of sculpture, *Cybernetic Structure* (fig. 9), combining mechanical motion, light, and sound, was made by Tsai. It is a forest of wires topped with squares and planted in a metal platform which slowly rotates in a barely perceptible circle. A strobe light is focused on the wire columns, creating the illusion of a delicately beautiful dance of elongated curves. When sound, the third element, is brought into play, the·undulating columns dance in a more complex pattern.

Soft sculpture, using air as a positive rather than a background element, is illustrated by Andy Warhol's helium-filled, silver foil *Pillows* floating in a room according to temperature and currents. Otto Piene's monstrous plastic "flowers" in *Red Rapid Growth* grow, bloom, and die according to a cycle fixed by a motorized air pump.

A variety of Earth Works, such as trenches in the desert or a wheat field harvested in a pattern, represents yet another attempt to extend into the environment with a statement of form going beyond museum walls. The only limitations to their possibilities are the available earth surface and personal energy in digging.

Surely Earth Works represent a penultimate rejection of the "museum-object" view of art, and the Conceptual Artists lead the way to ultimate liberation. They have completely rejected conventional art forms—the object itself disappears as a work of art. Douglas Huebler, in *Water, November 1968,* took fourteen photographs at one-minute intervals of four styrofoam tide markers floating out to sea at high tide. The documentation of this act feeds your mind to where you project the possibility of the "work of art" being the unmonitored markers floating over and under the sea, relating to reefs, icebergs, continents, and islands. It is an infinite, constantly changing thing, with eons of possibilities.

While there may be some truth in the thesis that "easel painting is dead" and therefore the most meaningful contemporary art is being created in new forms, there is still some outstanding flat canvas painting being done which is definitely in step with new cosmic thinking. Painters such as Kenneth Noland, Jules Olitski, and Frank Stella have solved the spatial problems that plagued the Cubists by abandoning the goal of presenting an object in space on a flat canvas, and addressing themselves directly to unhindered color, relationships of form, and universal structure. Instead of trying to capture on the canvas an illusionistic image which appeared to be seen through a window, they use the canvas as if it were a trampoline, to launch or suspend their statements.

The universal vision extends throughout the texture of our culture transforming a lot of the paraphernalia of our daily life. Designers have rethought function in the reflected image of reality. From the boots to the martial cut of a space jacket, Courrèges' space-suit domesticates man's vision of himself in the world beyond earth. Rudi Gernreich's topless bathing suit destroyed the last vestige of Victorian decorum in dressing, to usher in an era of "see-through" garments. What is the appeal of the revealing costuming? Is it just blatant sexuality that leads society's debutantes and matrons to expose their bodies? Is it possible that, after fiercely liberating the torso from its former swaddle, there is an earnest yearning to reveal ourselves as we are? Is this new mode of minimal dressing related to the Women's Liberation Movement whose cause is dedicated not only to ungirdled freedom but to equality for women in a man's world? New attitudes of dress—or undress, as the case may be—are but another symptom of the revelation of who we are within a newly understood environment.

"See-through" furniture can be thought of as an expression of our newly extended vision (fig. 10). Plastic or glass tables and chairs allow the viewer to see through and beyond the object. The "invisible" object serves its function while encouraging a visual continuum of space.

Another approach to furnishing a house is to employ "built-ins." The interior space is thought out for its projected use: its functional definition is included within the master-plan of the house. Bench or pit, dais or divider, these elements mold the living space into patterns of spatial relations within the architectural setting.

It would be absurd to argue that our whole society has been completely transformed by this cosmological revelation; in a large measure we cling to the forms of the past, nostalgically trying to recapture an earlier era by evoking an old image. For many, grandmother's house represents a bastion of sanity midst twentieth-century perplexities; indeed, it was conceived to shut out the environment, to be an island of its own, a fortress of the past. But the effective forms of the twentieth century are those that reflect what we know to be true: the complexities of the universe in everchanging, never-ending relationships are measured in four or more dimensions.

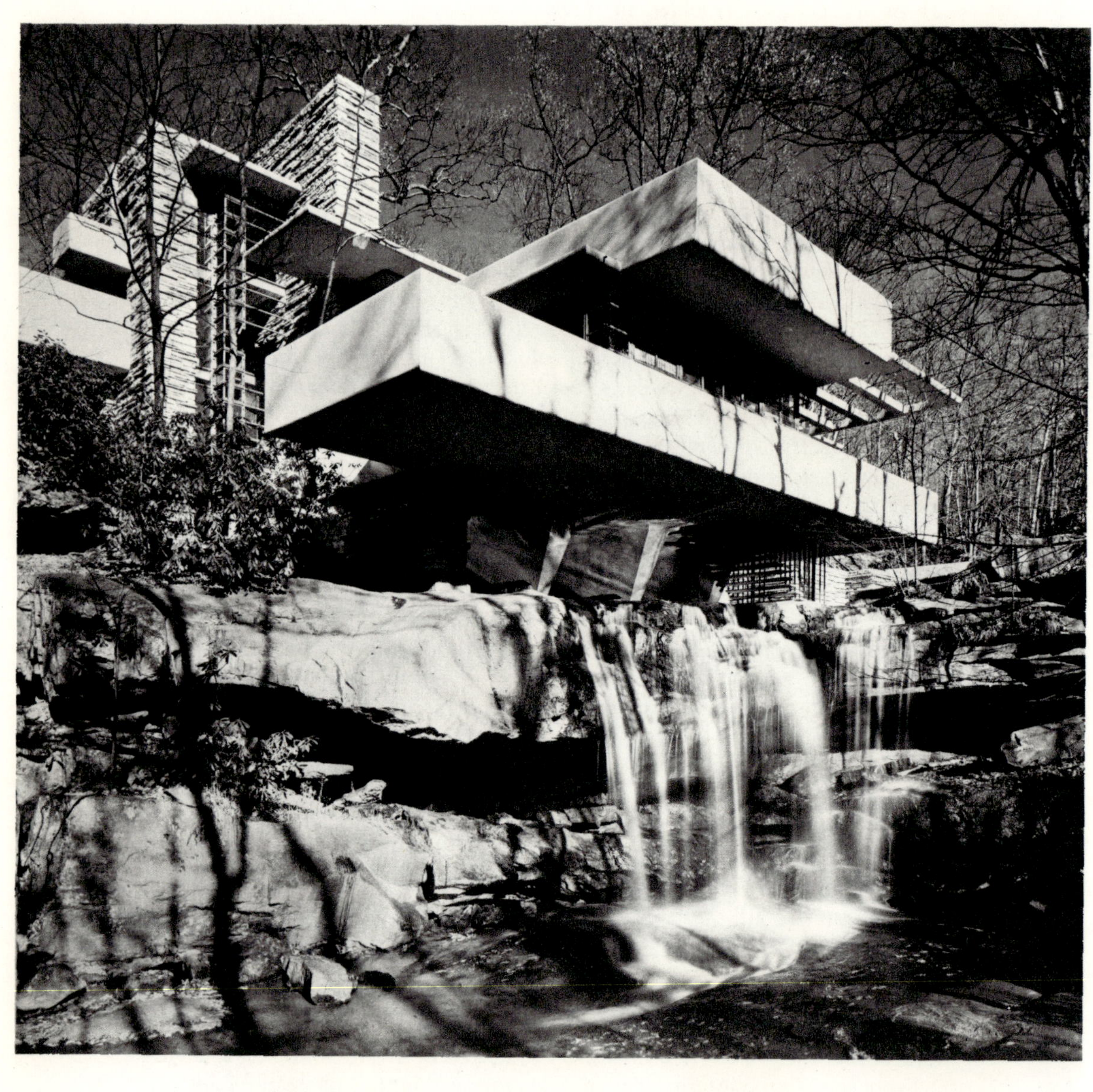

1. FRANK LLOYD WRIGHT. Kaufmann House, "Falling Water." 1936.
Bear Run, Pennsylvania

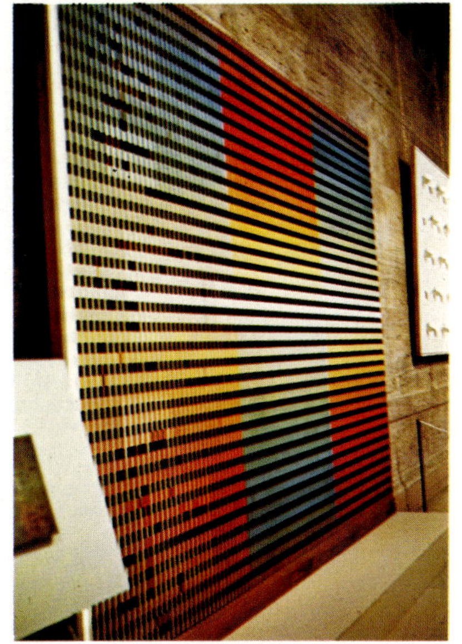

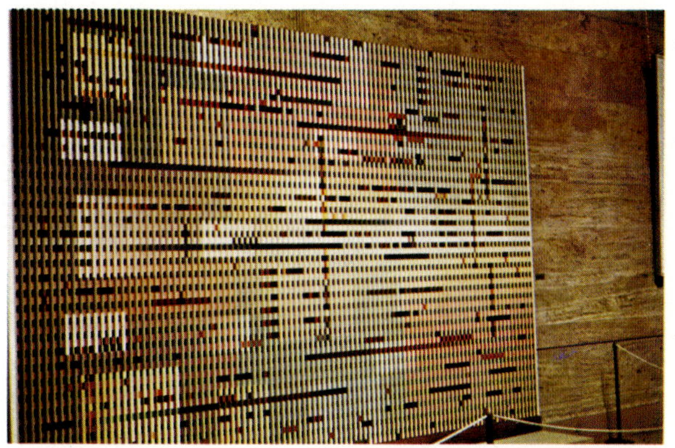

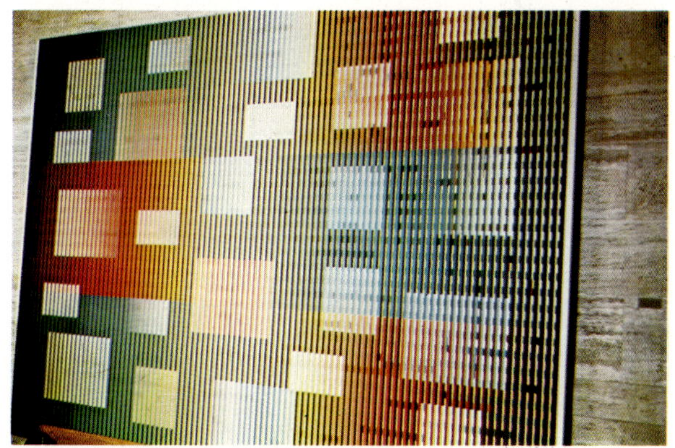

2. YAACOV AGAM.
Transparent Rhythms II,
views a–e. 1967.
Collection the artist

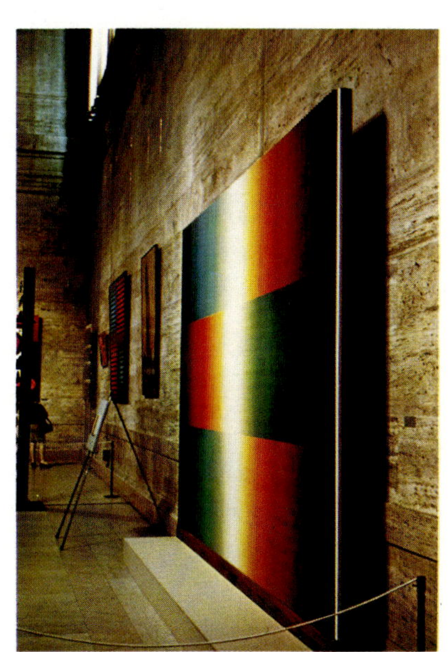

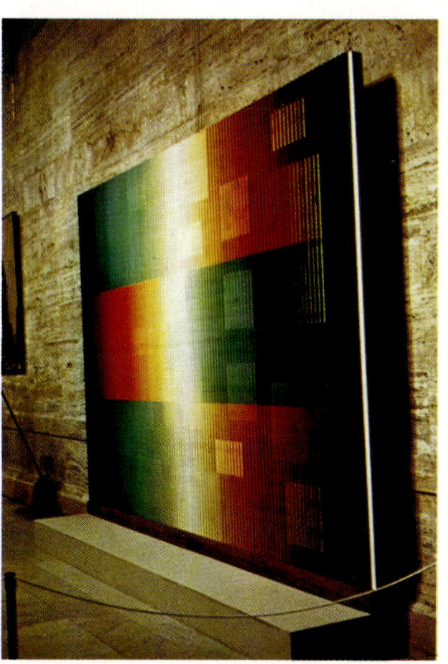

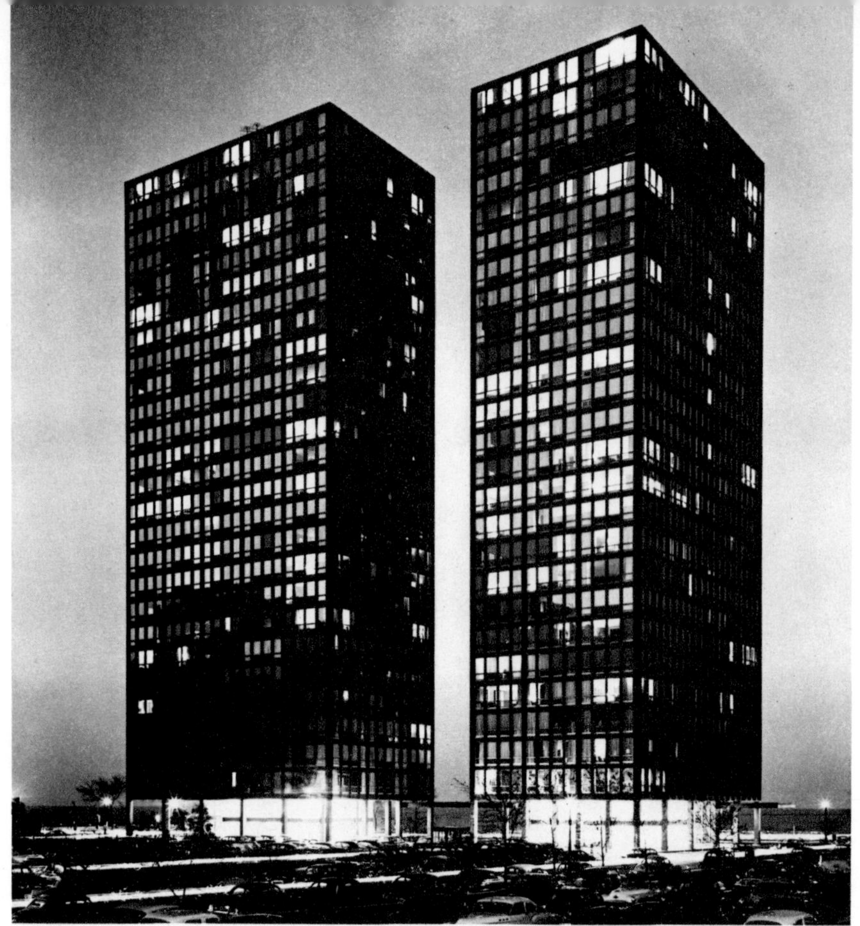

3. MIES VAN DER ROHE. Lake Shore Drive Apartments. 1950–51. Chicago

4. PHILIP JOHNSON. Glass House. 1949. New Canaan, Connecticut

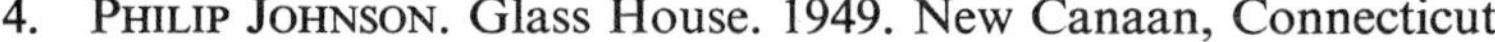

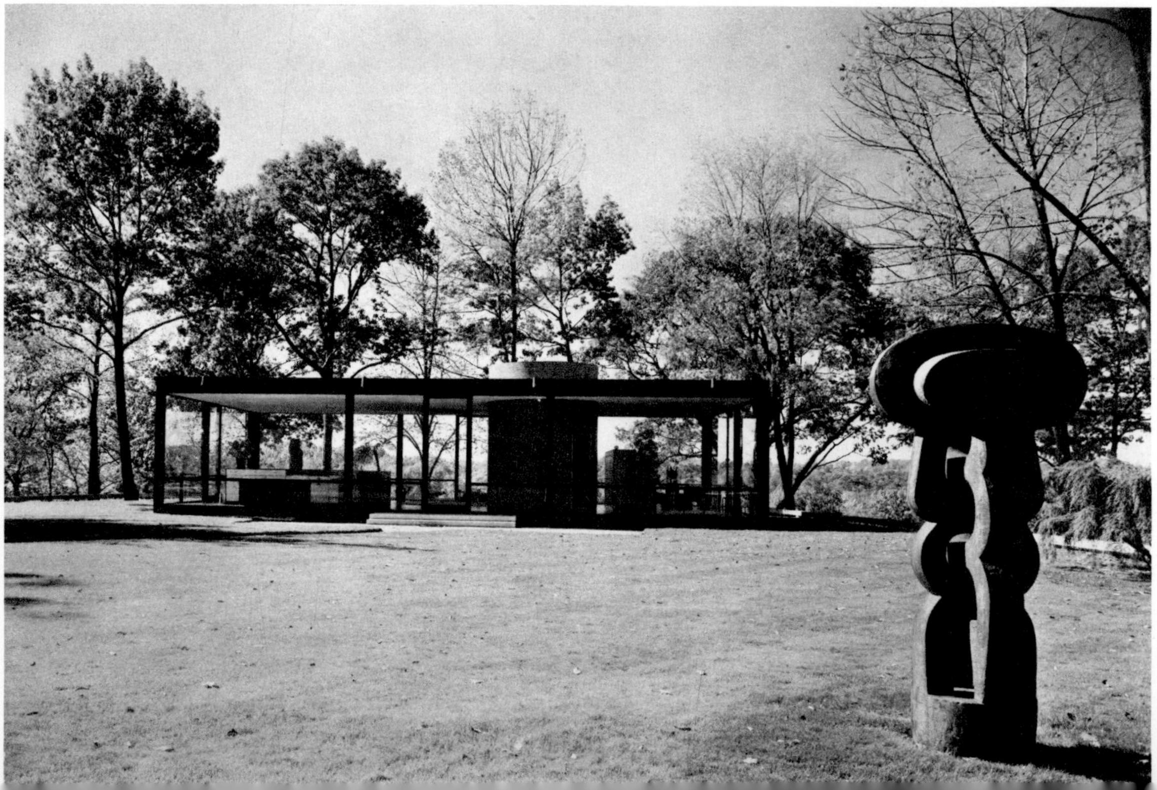

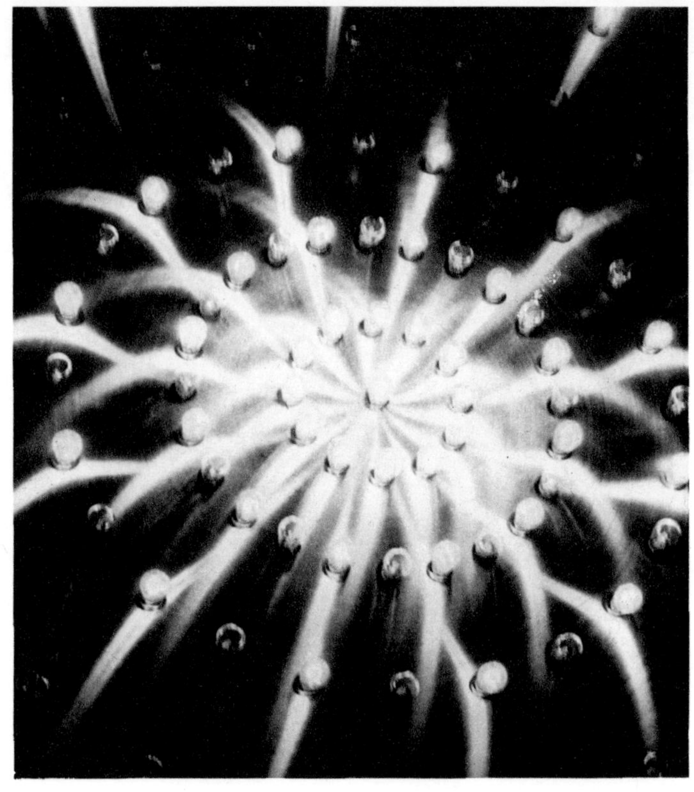

5.   HOWARD JONES. *Skylight No. 1*. 1968.
Formerly Howard Wise Gallery, New York

6.   PAUL MATISSE. *Kalliroscope*. 1967.
Formerly Howard Wise Gallery, New York

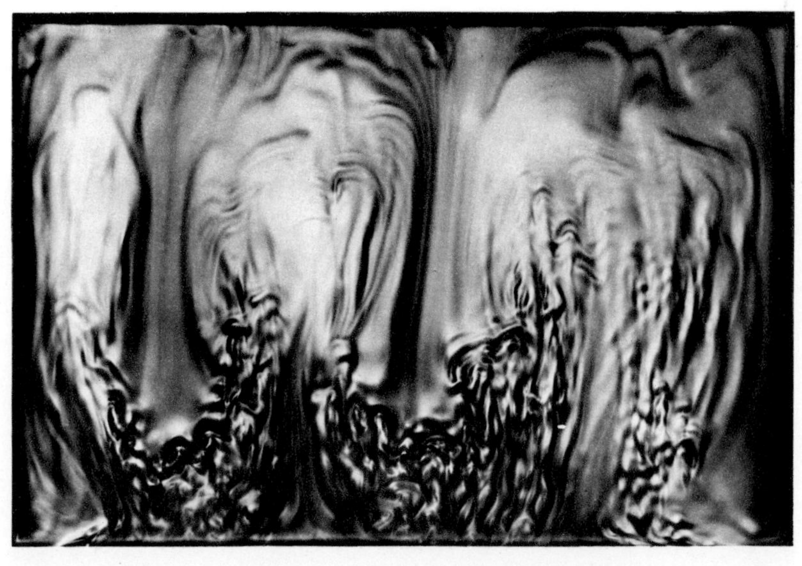

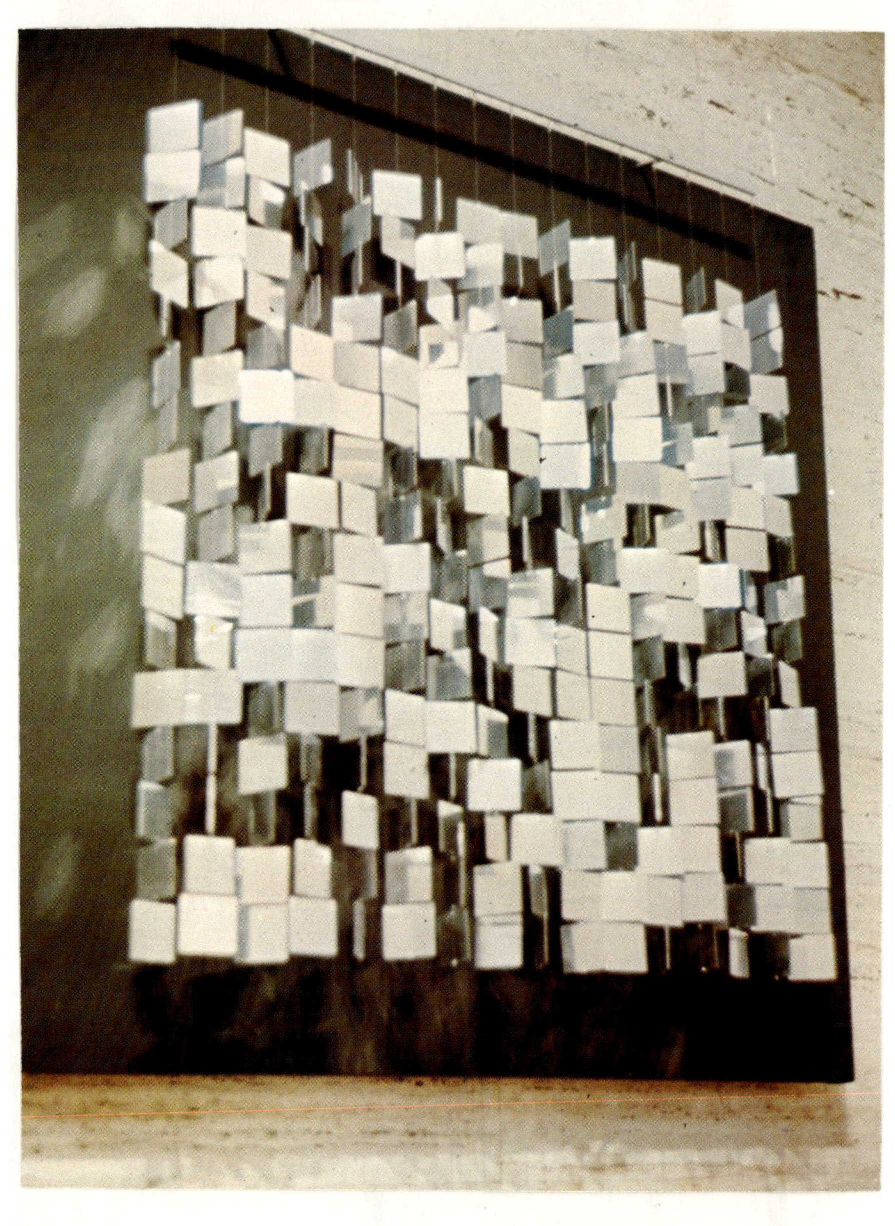

7. JULIO LE PARC. *Continual Mobile*. 1964. Private collection

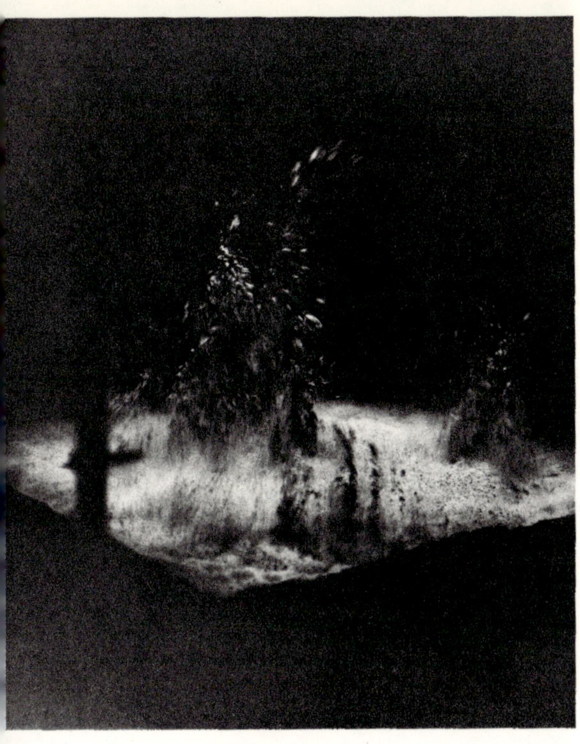

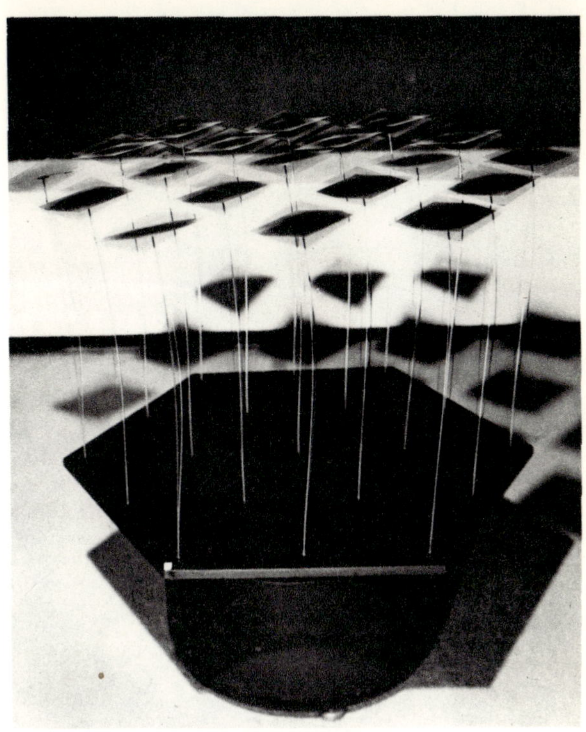

8.   JEAN DUPUY. *Heartbeat Machine*. 1969.
Formerly Howard Wise Gallery, New York

9.   WEN-YING TSAI. *Cybernetic Structure*. 1968.
Collection Siv and David Fox, Rye, New York

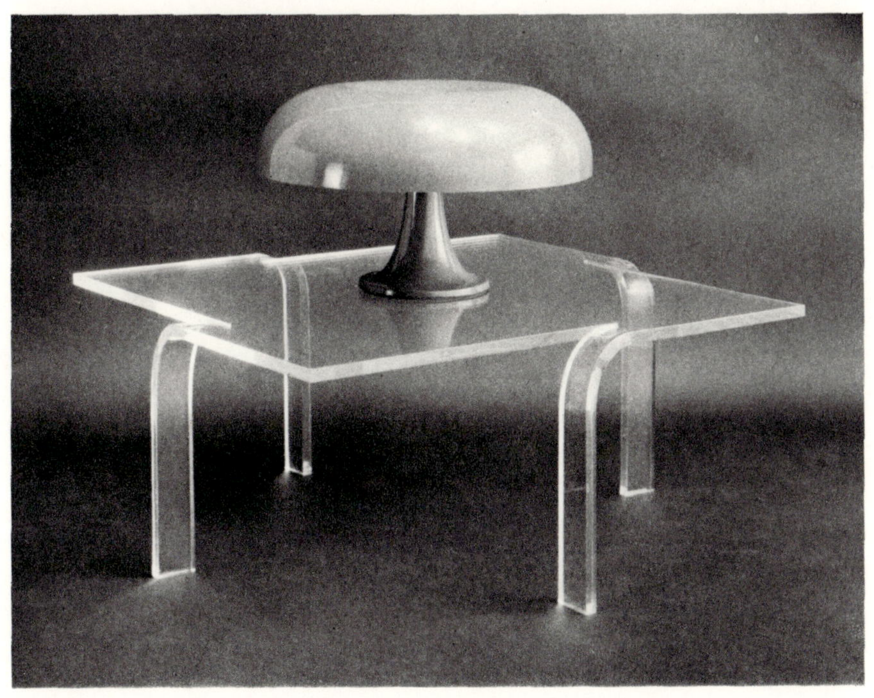

10.   NEAL SMALL. Cocktail Table. 1966.
The Museum of Modern Art, New York. Lily Auchincloss Fund

4

PIERRE COURTHION

La Notion de temps
dans la peinture moderne
(Rôle de la durée et de l'instant)

Chaque art a sa propre nature. C'est un lieu commun de dire que la peinture se situe avant tout dans l'espace, alors que le temps est départi à la musique en particulier.

Mais il y a des échanges d'un art à l'autre et d'une notion à l'autre.

La peinture s'est plus ou moins ouverte au temps depuis toujours, et, à certains moments, elle parvient à suggérer le passage du temps, c'est-à-dire l'avant et l'après d'une chose dans sa présence, comme le Janus des Latins, dont le double visage symbolisait à la fois le passé et l'avenir.

Plusieurs catégories de temps peuvent venir empreindre la peinture.

LE TEMPS CHRONOLOGIQUE

La première catégorie est le temps chronologique, celui qui apparaît au plafond de la Sixtine où nous voyons, conjugués par Michel-Ange, l'espace et le temps dans la création du monde. Puis, décomposés en heures du jour: matin, midi et soir, ce sont les éclairages temporels des marines et des scènes champêtres de Claude Lorrain qui nous conduisent à la plus saisissante irruption du temps dans la peinture quand, en 1844, dans *Pluie, Vapeur, Vitesse* (fig. 1), le peintre anglais Turner lance son train fou sur le viaduc, dans le brouillard doré de l'espace. Le temps chronologique se subdivise encore dans les instantanés des impressionnistes, ceux surtout de Claude Monet. Chez ce dernier, les heures sont à leur tour section- nées suivant le degré lumineux dont elles frappent la meule ou la cathédrale. Vers la fin de sa vie, le vieil enchanteur tenta—et réussit—à nous mettre devant les yeux la fuite même du temps, avec les nymphéas (fig. 2), ces fleurs que nous voyons glisser sur le miroir des eaux.

Ceci, c'est le temps qui nous est suggéré en dehors de l'acte même de peindre, c'est le temps extérieur, le temps hors de l'artiste, tel qu'il est divisé par le cadran solaire.

LE TEMPS DÉROULÉ

Un autre temps de la peinture, c'est celui qui consiste à juxtaposer dans l'espace comme sur les lames d'un éventail, les actes divers d'un personnage, les positions d'un objet, ou même d'une figure de géométrie. C'est le temps, par exemple des Cubistes qui rejoint la vision synoptique des Primitifs. C'est, avant tout, le temps de Picasso dont on peut voir des visages et des corps de femme à double et même à triple profils, où le mouvement s'inscrit rotativement, en toupie, dans l'espace, et où c'est au spectateur à rassembler les diverses phases du rythme que l'artiste a jumelées ou déroulées sur la toile. Ce temps, qui nous suggère les divers aspects d'un acte, c'est aussi celui de Marcel Duchamp quand il nous montre le *Nu descendant un escalier* (fig. 3) dans le tableau du Philadelphia Museum of Art; le mouvement fragmenté s'y déploie en une poussée entraînante. C'est encore le temps des Futuristes quand Boccioni et Severini peignaient le mouvement même de la danse ou la vitesse de l'autobus, et quand ils juxtaposaient et associaient dans une même toile des souvenirs visuels.

LE TEMPS MORAL

Il y a enfin un troisième temps, celui qui intéresse en particulier la peinture actuelle. C'est le temps inhérent à l'artiste lui-même, c'est-à-dire le temps moral, le temps de l'artiste au travail. La présence et l'action du peintre sont portées alors à notre regard par la seule peinture; car la durée de son travail fait partie intégrante de l'oeuvre. C'est une germination, une floraison qui s'opère là, sous les yeux, et selon l'intuition de celui qui crée. A cette phase de production, le temps chronologique extérieur et celui de la juxtaposition successive ne participent pas.

Ce temps appartenant à l'artiste, ce dernier cherche à le communiquer directement, dans un moment d'inspiration, à son geste de peintre qui voudrait laisser sur la toile ou le panneau l'empreinte même de sa perception interne et de sa vision en un mouvement cardiogrammé et, cela, à l'instant où il l'éprouve. Amplifiée et ramenée à l'acte de la personne même du peintre, cette saisie du mouvement est devenue le fait de ce qu'on a appellé la peinture gestuelle *(action painting)*, celle de Pollock et de Franz Kline (fig. 4). Mais, l'origine de cet art qui se voudrait générateur et transmetteur d'activité, on la trouve chez ceux qui, comme le Tintoret, Rubens et Delacroix, en faisant parler la touche et le tracé nous entraînent dans leur mouvement, cherchant à faire éprouver, de leur vivant et dans l'avenir à celui qui regarde ou regardera leur peinture, le geste profond qu'eux-mêmes ont accompli au moment du travail.

Par le fait qu'il appelle la collaboration passive du spectateur, ce troisième temps de la peinture semble bien être à la fois plus passionnant et le plus difficile à réaliser. C'est le temps de la grande création qui porte, de regard à regard, le jet de sang du poète, transsubstantié en une pâte colorée et mystérieusement agissante. Et, cela, n'est-ce pas le problème capital des peintres d'aujourd'hui?

LE PROBLÈME DU TEMPS, SON ACTUALITÉ

Depuis le Cubisme, la peinture s'est surtout occupée de l'espace, et d'un espace en épaisseur, d'un espace suggéré qui n'est plus celui de la perspective euclydienne. Ça été la grande préoccupation de Picasso, de Braque, de Klee. Aussi, n'est-ce pas tellement surprenant que le problème du temps hante de nos jours les recherches du peintre. Ce qui le préoccupe, ce n'est plus—pour employer une expression d'Henri Bergson—le *temps-longueur,* mais le *temps-invention.* Car, comme le dit le philosophe français: "Le temps est invention ou il n'est rien du tout." Mais, du temps-invention, la physique ne peut guère tenir compte. Nous arrivons ainsi à l'intuition créatrice qui unit le Soi aux Choses, et dont Jacques Maritain a reconnu (contrairement à Alexandre Baumgarten pour qui l'art était une gnoséologie inférieure, et à Hegel, qui annonçait sa fin dans l'esprit et l'intériorité pure), qu'elle est un moyen de connaissance supérieure. Ce temps de la création, s'il est paradoxal pour la raison logique ne l'est donc pas pour la raison intuitive et visionnaire; il émane des sources secrètes à l'intérieur de l'âme humaine. C'est une sorte de "folie d'en haut" qui précède l'acte créateur, le lequel se situe dans un temps qui échappe aux calculs les plus subtils.

Rien d'étonnant non plus qu'à l'époque du cinéma, de la télévision et des procédés mécaniques on regarde comme un Paradis perdu les peintures où le temps nous était suggéré dans une forme arrêtée comme, par exemple, l'*Aurige* de Delphes. Les oeuvres patiemment élaborées font doublement notre admiration en cette époque nucléaire où tout va trop vite. Autrefois, le temps était suggéré aussi par le sujet du tableau, comme dans *Les Bergers d'Arcadie* (fig. 5) de Nicolas Poussin où les pâtres, penchés sur un tombeau rencontré dans la campagne, en épellent du doigt l'inscription: *Et in Arcadia ego!* ("Et moi aussi, je fus en Arcadie"). C'était là une façon de renouveler le thème du *Dialogue du Mort et du Vif* dont la représentation était fréquente dans la peinture et la sculpture, vers la fin du quatorzième siècle: *Ce que tu es, je le fus,* dit le mort au vivant, *ce que je suis, tu le seras.* La patience que nous avons perdue, le temps pris pour l'exécution d'une peinture font comprendre le succès actuel de l'oeuvre de Vermeer. Le lait qui coule du pot de la *Laitière* nous semble couler toujours et pour toujours. Comme il le serait par un sablier, le temps est suggéré par le motif même du tableau, car le sujet était alors si bien intégré à la peinture elle-même qu'il en est devenu inséparable (ce qui ne serait plus valable de nos jours).

Dans Poussin et Vermeer de Delft, le temps est ramené à sa plus grande épaisseur, celle du passage de la vie. Aux dernières pages du *Temps retrouvé,* Marcel Proust a tranché la question quand il dit: "L'homme n'a pas la longueur de son corps, mais de ses années qu'il traîne avec lui quand il se déplace." Voilà, n'est-il pas vrai, qui peut laisser prévoir—si l'on revient à ce genre—des portraits futurs qui ne seront plus ceux de Monsieur Ingres.

On le voit: la question du temps se pose sans cesse d'une façon nouvelle aux yeux du peintre. Car celui-ci ne vaut, en définitive que si, non content de créer dans son oeuvre son propre espace, il y ajoute, sous une forme ou une autre, pour en augmenter la tension, la marque de son propre temps, le signe perpétuel de son passage, afin de porter à nos yeux, dans le présent de la sensation visualisée, le passé et l'avenir.

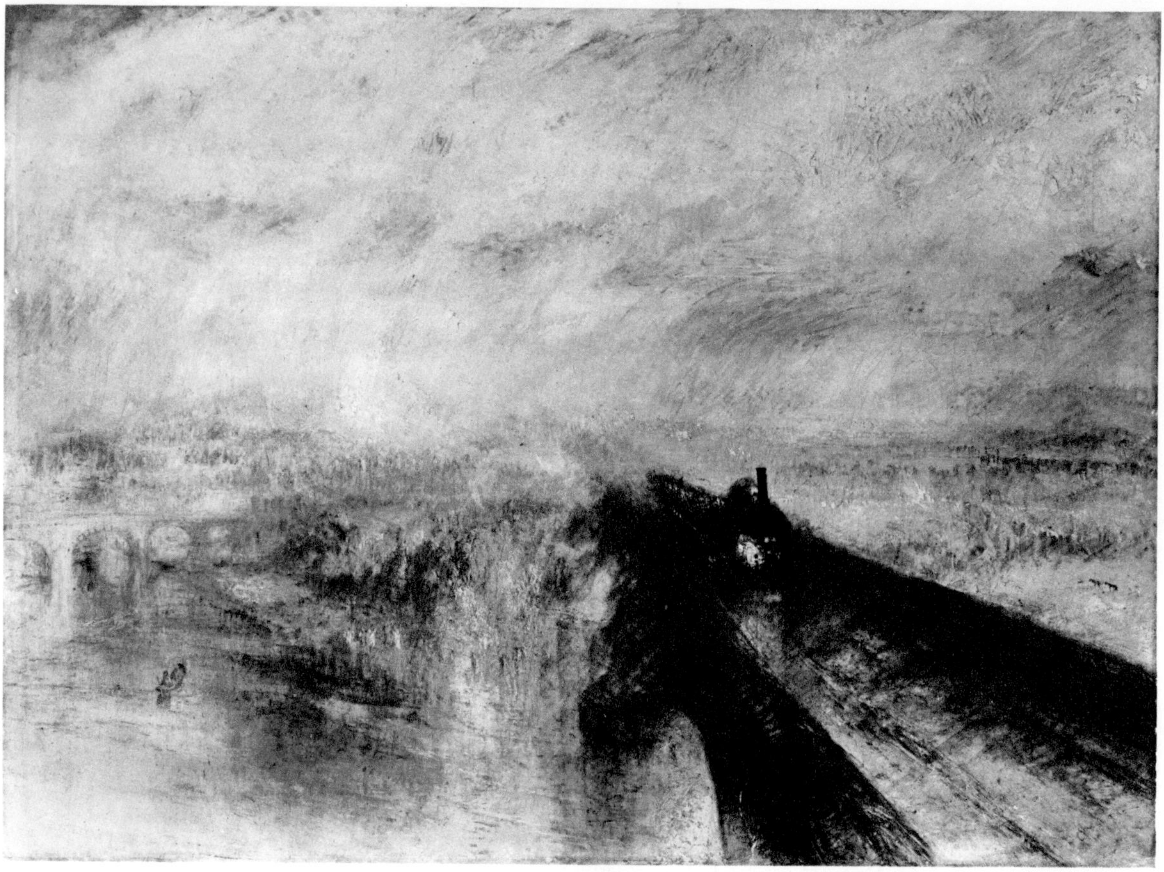

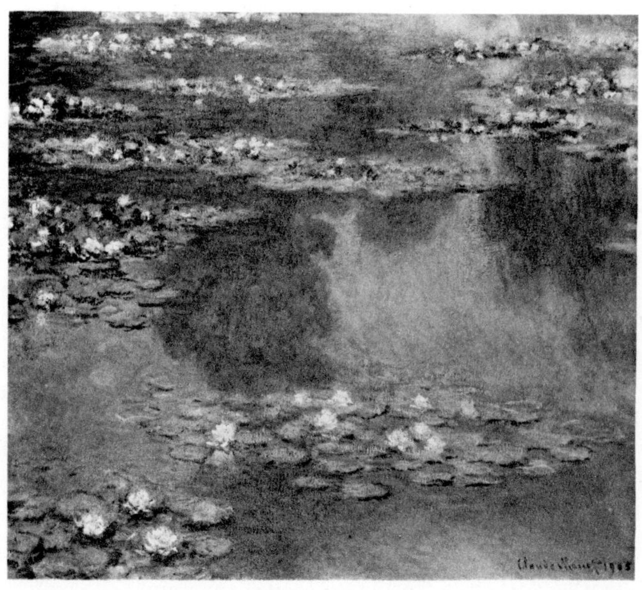

1. Joseph M. W. Turner. *Pluie, Vapeur, Vitesse (Rain, Steam, and Speed—The Great Western Railway)*. 1844. The National Gallery, London

2. CLAUDE MONET. *Les Nymphéas (Water Lilies)*. 1905.
Museum of Fine Arts, Boston. Gift of Edward Jackson Holmes

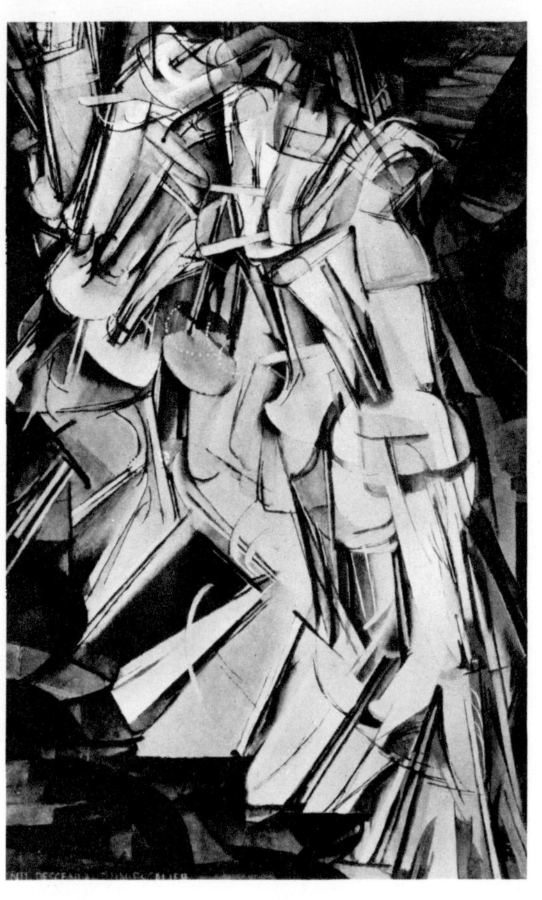

3. MARCEL DUCHAMP. *Nu descendant un escalier (Nude Descending a Staircase, No. 2)*. 1912.
Philadelphia Museum of Art.
The Louise and Walter Arensberg Collection

4. FRANZ KLINE. *Wanamaker Block*. 1955.
Collection Richard Brown Baker, New York

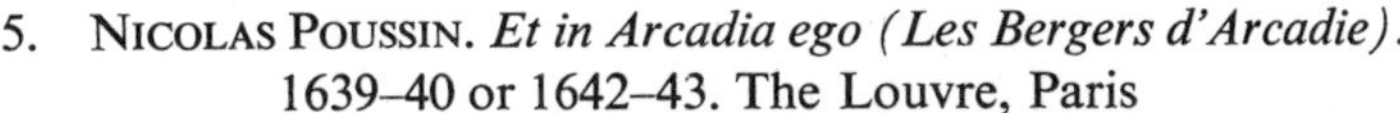

5. NICOLAS POUSSIN. *Et in Arcadia ego (Les Bergers d'Arcadie)*.
1639–40 or 1642–43. The Louvre, Paris

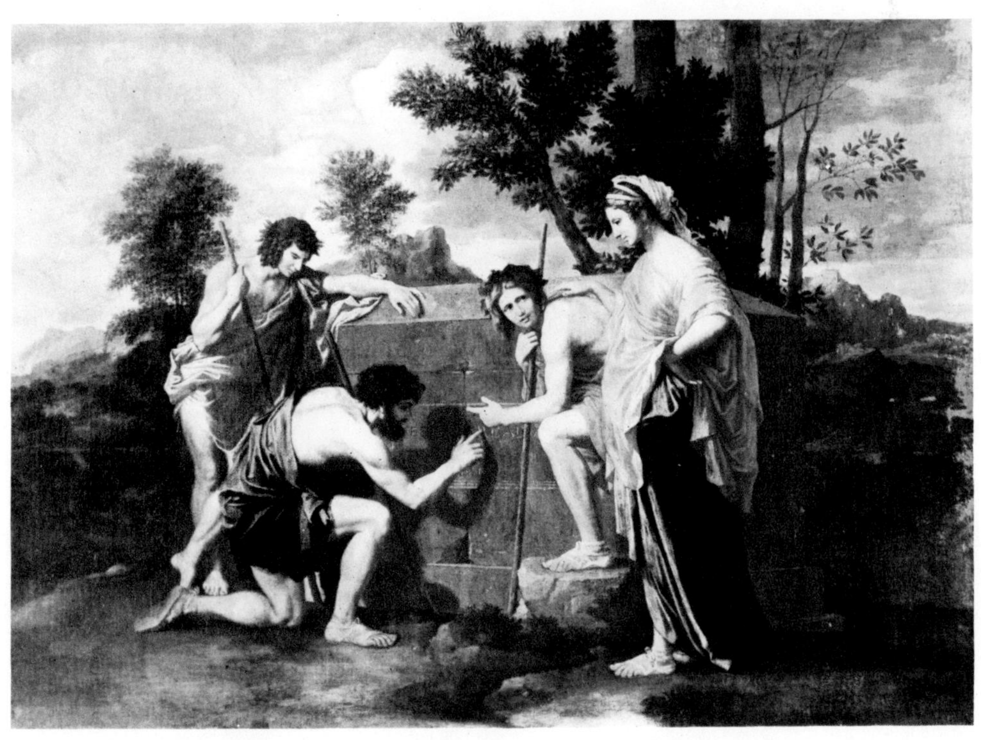

5

ABRAHAM DAVIDSON

Charles Willson Peale's
Exhuming the First American Mastodon:
An Interpretation

I have come to suspect that Charles Willson Peale's famous *Exhuming the First American Mastodon* of 1806–8 meant a great deal more to him than simply an extraordinary event elaborately depicted in his most ambitious painting (fig. 1). Certainly it was that. Nothing so ambitious, except for Trumbull's history paintings, had been done in America up to that time. The painting was unique. Historians like to observe that when American painting consisted chiefly of portraiture and a handful of landscapes and history pieces, here, *mirabile dictu,* was a genre painting,[1] or, as Larkin put it, a painting in the spirit of genre.[2] The *Exhuming* obviously became a more and more elaborate work. From Peale's letter of December 16, 1807, to Benjamin West, we learn that at one point that year the painting contained "upwards of fifty figures"—at completion the next year there were seventy-five—of which eighteen were portraits:

> Having the desire to represent the scene of getting up the Bones of the Mammoth, it being a very interesting article of the Museum, last summer I undertook a picture larger than one [of] which Rembrandt showed you [the] beginning when he was in London. This picture contains a great number of figures . . . my exertions excited the admiration of all the people for a considerable distance round that country. . . . Although I have introduced upwards of 50 figures yet

the number of spectators in fine weather amounted to hundreds—18 of my figures are portraits, having taken the advantage of taking most of this number from my own family.[3]

But for Peale the painting was more than the recording of a momentous event revealing the history of geological development in America. Begun when he was sixty-five, it was meant, symbolically, I believe, as nothing less than the visualization of the significance of his past life. As such, few subjects other than the excavation would have sufficed Peale, with his particular temperament, vision, and experiences—and, with the purpose behind his painting in mind, Peale could hardly have presented the painted scene in another fashion.

Familiar as the painting is, its subject has never been correctly assessed. At least, not fully. Every student of American art knows that an actual event is depicted and that Charles Willson Peale, always the realist, rendered certain details, such as the great wheel lifting water from the marl pit, the plank tool room in the middle ground, and the army tent for sleeping in the background, with remarkable fidelity. Yet, as only Peale scholars are aware, the *Exhuming,* completed seven years after the digging itself, is a highly imaginative re-creation. Of the many figures in the scene, only three had taken part in the digging on the upper New York State farm of a certain John Masten during the summer of 1801: Peale himself, who holds up the drawing of a bone and gestures toward the pit; his eldest son Rembrandt, who stands beside him and helps him hold the drawing; and John Masten, who in the foreground climbs out of the pit on a ladder.

What Peale has, in fact, done—and while this is known, it has surprisingly never been so stated—is to fuse two subjects: the scene of the digging, which is readily identified, and a very large group portrait of his family. Peale himself, writing in his autobiography in his curious third-person fashion, indicated this fusion as follows:

Peale wished to give the idea of the labour he had in getting the bones of the mammoth and at a leisure time while at the spot he made drawings, so that he would give a correct landscape and all the machinery as it actually stood. And as there was a great deal of company all the time, he made this occasion serve to give some resemblance of his family in groups of figures, and as it was mentioned in the relation of his going to Mr. Masten's and first began to make drawings from the bones. . . . Hence to complete the remembrance of it he has represented himself holding the end of the paper which shew [*sic*] one of the legs of the skeleton drawn on the scroll of paper supported by Raphaelle and Rembrandt, Mrs. Peale next to him [in the painting, however, Mrs. Peale stands beside Charles Willson], then Rubens' younger children, Sybella and Elizabeth, between Raphael and Rubens, his son-in-law Coleman Sellers in the next line and the wife of Raphaelle. Linnaeus and Franklin guides [*sic*] the floating cylinder —farther to the left is the mother of Linnaeus, Franklin, Sybella, Eliz'th and Titian, this boy, her youngest, she holds by the hand to retain him pointing to clouds of an approaching storm, and between them and the great wheel is Peale's brother James in an action of wonder at the exploring work. And a figure to the left standing alone with folded arms is Wilson, the poet and author of the American Ornithology. And near to Mrs. Elizabeth Peale [Peale's deceased second wife] and Titian is her sister Stagg and her husband—all the Personages named are Portraits and at the time when painted, esteemed good likenesses.[4]

I cannot be persuaded that the specific figures standing complacently before us in the *Exhuming* are "expendable," or could have been replaced by other figures not in Peale's family. While members of the family must have been at hand to provide ready models for the representation of the crowd that had been present at Masten's farm in 1801, most of the figures in the painting, it can be seen at a glance, are in fact posing for the spectator rather than participating in or in any way involving themselves with the digging. Standing in this way, the figures of the crowd, members of Peale's family, constitute a large group portrait.

In his *Autobiography*, Peale explicitly stated that the digging served as a pretext for rendering portraits of his family, and not vice versa: "And as there was a great deal of company all the time, he made this occasion serve to give some resemblance of his family in groups of figures. . . ." If Peale had wished only to preserve a visual record of the digging, why the careful recording of the appearance of specific persons, mostly members of his family who were in no way connected with the event, rather than a sea of generalized faces to suggest a great crowd? Conversely, if Peale wished to do a large family group portrait, as appears evident here (his last one had been painted in 1773), what is the purpose of the scene of the digging? Since Peale chose to juxtapose the two subjects in a single canvas—and it is to be kept in mind that the *Exhuming* was not born of a sudden impulse, but was three years in the making after a gestation period of four years—may we not presume that these subjects had come to take on, for the painter, some connection? It is my conviction that they do.

Peale was capable of using symbolism in his art. A prominent instance was his 1767 portrait of *William Pitt*. The Whig lord is surrounded by objects alluding to his liberal political beliefs, or those beliefs as Peale saw them: in the foreground the altar with a flame indicates Pitt's devotion to the cause of liberty, both in England and in America; the Indian placed, in Peale's words, "on the Pedestal in an *erect* Posture, with an attentive Countenance, watching, as AMERICA has done for Five Years past, the extraordinary Motions of the British Senate. . . ."[5] I do not argue a similarity of intention in the portrait of Pitt and in the *Exhuming,* but bring the *Portrait* to the attention of the reader to show merely that innuendo and indirect suggestion were within the scope of Peale's interests and abilities. In the Pitt portrait a specific object, such as the Indian on the pedestal or the altar with the flame, alludes to a political tenet or situation. In the *Exhuming* we are not confronted with a great variety of objects. I would suggest that the tangible reality of the large family group and the past event of the digging, rather than symbolizing things other than themselves, are complementary expressions of Peale's self-conception. If I do not offer unshakable proof of this interpretation, I expect the reader, in the end, to consider its validity seriously.

What did the uncovering of the mastodon bones mean to Charles Willson Peale? What significance did the event have for him, an unusually enterprising and resourceful American then, at the turn of the century, in the twilight years of his life? I would suggest that the answer might be found in certain presuppositions underlying interpretations of geological excavations in America around 1800.

Especially for those situated in the state of New York the mastodon must have epitomized the terrifying monsters of bygone geologic eras. Even before the discovery on the Masten farm in 1801, remains of mastodons had turned up frequently in the upper reaches of New York and elsewhere in the United States.[6] The Masten find attained unusual fame through Peale's painting. Moreover, the bones were in an excellent state of preservation, and Peale was able to construct two nearly complete skeletons and part of a third, one of which he set up in the southeast chamber of Philadelphia's Philosophical Hall,[7] and another he sent to Europe under the care of Rembrandt and Rubens Peale, who arrived in London in the summer of 1802 (four years before the painting had been begun).

In late eighteenth- and early nineteenth-century America, mastodon remains— or, for that matter, any fossil—would have been greeted by those who recognized the existence of fossils, and who thought within the framework of historical geology, under the presuppositions of the catastrophist viewpoint. I believe that catastrophism and the "great chain of being," with which I will deal momentarily, constituted Peale's theoretical framework in assessing the philosophical ramifications of the mastodon find. Peale must have held to this doctrine of catastrophism, simply because in his day everyone did who at least recognized that at one time there existed flora and fauna no longer in existence on the earth's surface.

Stated most simply, catastrophism was the interpretation of geological history as a series of sudden and violent changes, and until the 1850s, when the uniformitarian approach of Sir Charles Lyell[8] made a little headway here, there was not to be found in American geological circles the flimsiest challenge to the doctrine. In retrospect, the undisputed sway of catastrophism does not appear remarkable. On the surface it was eminently plausible and, as opposed to the gradualism urged by the uniformitarians, luridly colorful in the romanticism of its implied violence. Moreover, it was a doctrine able to bridge successfully the gap between the Biblical account of creation, which held that the world was but a few thousand years old, and recent excavations, which seemed to prove empirically that profound changes had occurred upon the earth since earliest times. Renowned humanists and clergymen such as Edward Hitchcock, President of Amherst College, followed closely the growing number of excavations, and accepted catastrophism as a first premise in all geological questions. Hitchcock was prominent among the clergymen who identified geological eras with the successive creative acts of God.[9] As one pores through the records of the geological expeditions around the time of Peale one finds that the interpretations offered for the changes which have occurred upon the earth's surface are invariably cast in a catastrophist mold. To offer quotation after quotation would be to work this irrefutable point to death. I cite only the following line of reasoning adopted in the early 1790s by one Benjamin De Witt, who counted along the shores of Lake Superior what appeared to him to be sixty-four varieties of stone:

> Now, it is almost impossible to believe that so great a variety of stones should
> be naturally formed in one place. . . . They must, therefore, have been conveyed
> there by some extraordinary means. I am inclined to believe that this may have

been effected by some mighty convulsion of nature, such as an earthquake or eruption, and perhaps this vast lake may be considered as one of those great "fountains of the deep" which were broken up when the earth was deluged with water, thereby producing that confusion and disorder in the composition of its surface which evidently seems to exist.[10]

Peale, then, was prepared to believe frightful things of the animal whose remains he had unearthed. For him, the creature was decidedly carnivorous, possessed claws and was not a mastodon, but a mammoth or, as he put it, a "carniverous [*sic*] elephant of the north."[11] Newspapers eagerly trumped up further sensationalism: *Poulson's American Daily Advertiser* dubbed the mammoth "the LARGEST of *terrestrial* beings" and claimed it had been buried since the Deluge.[12] Rembrandt Peale subscribed to the current catastrophist viewpoint by insisting that the animal had existed once in great numbers, but was destroyed at some point by an unknown cataclysm:

> How long these animals have existed, we shall perhaps ever remain in ignorance, as no judgment can be formed from the quantity of vegetable soil which has accumulated over their bones. Certain we are that they existed in great abundance, from the number of their remains which are found in America. We are likewise sure that they must have been destroyed by some sudden and powerful cause; and nothing appears more probable than one of those deluges, or sudden irruptions of the sea. . . .[13]

But the disappearance of the mammoth was a fortunate thing, Rembrandt insisted: "If this animal was indeed carniverous [*sic*], which I believe cannot be doubted, though we may as philosophers regret it, we cannot but thank heaven that its whole generation is probably extinct."[14]

In fairness to Charles Willson Peale, it must be mentioned that he was skeptical of the correctness of his reconstructions and tried diligently to learn the precise appearance of his "mammoth." He consulted with Thomas Jefferson, an avid geologist who had aided Peale materially during the excavation of the summer of 1801:[15] in a letter to Jefferson of April 19, 1803, Peale speculated that the beast may have been amphibious.[16] But it was, significantly, the French scientist Georges Cuvier to whom Peale turned for guidance and direction.

Cuvier (1769–1832), a superb paleontologist, was Europe's most eloquent proponent of the catastrophist viewpoint. His influence can also be traced in this country in, for example, the widely read *The Book of Nature* by John Mason Good. Good, following Cuvier, insisted that because fossil bones were usually not rolled or violently distorted, it followed "that the deluge must have been sudden, and overtaken them in their natural resorts."[17] Following the Scriptural account, Cuvier himself claimed that the human race was but a few thousand years old, and, as stated in Genesis, had survived the great Noachian Deluge. To account for the tremendous changes which the earth had obviously undergone, as he clearly learned from his studies, Cuvier came to maintain a theory of successive creations separated by violent geological upheavals. The curious disparities he found in fossils from the same time span he explained away by attributing them to the workings of an omniscient, but inscrutable deity.[18] Cuvier, moreover, had long taken a special interest in elephants: in a study of 1796, "On the Species of Elephants Living and Fossil," he had shown that the Siberian mammoth was different from known species of African and Asian elephants.[19] Peale asked Cuvier's help especially in reconstructing the "mammoth's" head, and wrote to Cuvier on July 16, 1802, that he was sending casts of the bones with Rembrandt.[20] Thereafter, communication between the two men seems to have broken down. Apparently Cuvier did not answer, or at least did not offer Peale an interpretation of the casts. For in a letter of April 21, 1808, Peale, asking Cuvier to sit for a portrait for Rembrandt, who had just arrived in France, confessed at the same time that he did not know whether the casts had been read until he saw them published in a periodical.[21] Yet Cuvier had taken great interest in Peale's reconstructions. Two years earlier, in 1806, probably unknown to Peale, he had concluded that the American mammoth was not a true elephant and was not carnivorous, but was part of a new genus to be called "mastodonts." Of the five species constituting this genus, the most imposing was Peale's animal—"le grand mastodonte."[22]

Before returning to the question posed earlier—why the fusion of the two subjects in Peale's painting—I would want to examine briefly one more of Peale's presuppositions. During the painter's day, many American intellectuals, among them Thomas Jefferson, held to the concept of "the great chain of beings," within the catastrophist framework. Each natural object was considered a link in a progressive chain, which began with the simplest of these objects, a rock or some sort of mineral, to culminate finally in man, seen as the highest form of life. Jefferson himself insisted that no link of the chain could be broken through the total extinction of a species and that somewhere, then, there must still be found a live mammoth.[23]

The American intellectual historian Daniel J. Boorstin writes that Peale through the exhibits in his museum demonstrated the indestructibility of the chain by placing his skeleton of the "mammoth" beside that of an Asiatic elephant.[24] Though Boorstin does not substantiate this statement, a reading of the *Scientific and Descriptive Catalogue of Peale's Museum* of 1796 would indicate that Peale, while neither leaving a systematic account of his views on the great chain nor claiming the indestructibility of its parts, as did Jefferson, did indeed affirm its existence:

> From the observations made on the various productions of the natural world, as they present themselves to our view, we find that nature gradually, and almost imperceptibly, passes from the most simple beings to the most compound; thus forming that chain or series of being, the parts of which, with their order and comely proportion, will continue to be the inexhausted subject of the researches of naturalists to the end of time.[25]

For Charles Willson Peale, then, the course of natural history was a meaningful and deliberate, rather than a haphazardly fortuitous process. But natural history meant still more to him than even this. In 1800, one year before he took part in the excavation on John Masten's farm and eight years before he completed the *Exhuming,* he concluded that the contemplation of the profound order encompassed by the chain of being ought to promote peace of mind and virtuous deeds. In a long, rambling address entitled *Discourse Introductory to a Course of Lectures on the Science of Nature; with Original Music, Composed for, and Sung on, the Occasion. Delivered in the Hall of the University of Pennsylvania, November 8, 1800*, Peale urged that:

> While we are fulfilling the duties which virtue dictates, there is no science that affords us as many lessons to aid us in trying scenes, as the knowledge of natural history; it is a solace producing a serene tranquility of mind amid the turmoils of our worldly concerns; to our youth (to whom all things are new) it is a source of infinite utility in [illegible word] them from destructive habits, for, if they enter with zeal into this pleasing source of meditation, they will not easily be seduced from the paths of virtue.[26]

Now again the question, why the juxtaposition of the two subjects in the *Exhuming?* Virgil Barker has written that relations and friends were inserted in the picture to "let them share in the honor of the great discovery" and this shows "a pleasing willingness in Peale himself to be agreeable. . . ."[27] But Barker's remarks serve, at best, only as an apparent solution. In his lifetime, Peale had seen and done many wonderful things, and the problem remains, why should the excavation in particular have been coupled with the large family group? Moreover, it ought to be kept in mind that the *Exhuming* was the most elaborate of all the paintings, and yet shortly before it was done, Peale, as he related in his letter to West,[28] had been considering giving up painting for his many other interests. So at that point there occurred not merely a renewed interest in painting, but the sudden immersion of Peale in the most ambitious painting of his career.

The meaning of the excavation, either from the very first or somewhat later, came to be related in Peale's mind to the idea of the family group. For Peale the course of natural history, as revealed through the manifest evidence of the existence of monsters of the past, such as the mastodon, was a series of cataclysms which were meaningfully ordered. The large family group, with three generations living and dead (including Peale's deceased second wife Elizabeth), was a convenient way for the artist to encapsulate symbolically the events of his life. It is to be remembered that when he began the *Exhuming* in 1806 Peale was sixty-five years of age, married to his third wife, and had sired seventeen sons and daughters. By including so much of his family, past and present, he must have been saying: this is the summation of my life. Through his wives and children and their children, he has represented the passage of generations in his own life; and through the scene of the digging, the passage of eons in prehistory. In the painting, as it stands, the two ideas become intertwined.

In his day there could have been but a handful of Americans as enterprising, remarkably inventive and universally productive as Charles Willson Peale. After careers as a saddler and watchmaker, he taught himself portrait painting, which he regarded merely as another useful trade. During the Revolutionary War, he crossed the Delaware with Washington, fought at the Battle of Princeton, and spent the dreadful winter at Valley Forge, where he did miniatures of some forty officers. He gained the intimate friendship of Washington, Franklin and Jefferson.

He patented a fireplace and a new kind of wooden bridge, perfected the polygraph (a kind of portable writing desk which could make several copies of a manuscript at once), invented a rude motion picture technique, began one of America's first museums of natural history, founded the Pennsylvania Academy of Art and wrote papers on engineering, hygiene and other subjects. Could not this life, which was a series of constant explorations and adventurous undertakings, have come to be linked easily with the scene of the exhumation and the concept of catastrophism it embodied? For catastrophism implied not necessarily disaster and calamity, but an ongoing process of eventful change, and it was such a process Peale must have known his life represented. This was change which was not blind and chaotic, but fulfilling and meaningful, just as the dynamic mechanism inherent within the entire course of natural history was teleologically directed in the great chain of being.

As mentioned above, the catastrophist viewpoint predominated in American historical geology at least until the 1850s, when slowly it came to be replaced by uniformitarianism and the gradualist approach of evolution. Moreover, from about 1810 till 1850 or 1860, catastrophism prevailed, too, in American painting as a major mood, or, better, as a recurrent theme revealed through various guises; and during this period, I suspect, the meaning of the *Exhuming* was recognized, to become forgotten toward the end of the century. Peale's painting, though not providing a subject or style which kept recurring, decisively influenced the course of American painting in the first half of the nineteenth century by setting forth catastrophism as a loosely structured theme which could be manipulated to fit a variety of expressions. The importance of catastrophism in American painting hardly needs elaboration. Allston's unfinished *Belshazzar's Feast,* dealing with the rise and fall of empires as does Thomas Cole's *Course of Empire* series, and Cole's *Voyage of Life* series, dealing with the abrupt changes within an individual's life span, are but the most famous examples. But Peale's *Exhuming,* by incorporating the family group portrait, became more than an embodiment of the catastrophist theme. Becoming more and more elaborate with the addition of more and more members of Peale's family, it came to represent, as well, the course of Peale's long life filled with a variety of events and accomplishments, all meaningfully part of an integrated scheme, as he believed the course of natural history to be.

NOTES

[1]   Richardson describes the painting as an "amusing record" of the excavation. See E. P. Richardson, *Painting in America: the Story of 450 Years,* New York, 1956, p. 119. Green calls it a "delightful genre piece." See Samuel M. Green, *American Art: A Historical Survey,* New York, 1966, p. 151.

[2]   Oliver W. Larkin, *Art and Life in America,* New York, 1960, p. 112.

[3]   Letter from Peale to West, December 16, 1807. Letterbooks of Charles Willson Peale.

[4]   Unpublished autobiography of Charles Willson Peale in Charles C. Sellers' Collection of Peale Documents, in Hebron, Conn. Photostat in Archives of American Art, Washington, D.C. (pages unnumbered).

[5]   Peale did a mezzotint bearing a description and explanation of the picture. This is reproduced in Charles C. Sellers, *Charles Willson Peale,* Philadelphia, 1947, I, p. 89.

[6]   The first mastodon find in the state of New York was recorded in 1705, letter of Governor Dudley to the Rev. Cotton Mather, July 10, 1706. For a fairly detailed listing of the many mastodon remains uncovered in New York until 1902, see John M. Clarke, "Mastodons of New York: A List of Discoveries of their Remains 1705–1902," *Report of the State Paleontologist: N.Y. State Museum Bulletin,* LXIX, 1902, 921–33. See also, with special emphasis on the Warren Mastodon, found in 1845 near the site of the Peale excavation of 1801, H. F. Osborn, "Mastodons of the Hudson Highlands," *Natural History,* XXIII, Jan.–Feb. 1923, 3–24.

[7]   For a detailed account of the exhibition see Sellers, *op. cit.,* II, pp. 137–48.

[8]   William M. Smallwood, *Natural History and the American Mind,* New York, 1941, pp. 246–47.

[9]   Stow Persons, *American Minds, A History of Ideas,* New York, 1958, p. 240; also, Smallwood, *op. cit.,* pp. 231–33.

[10]   Quoted in George P. Merrill, *The First 100 Years of American Geology,* New Haven, 1924, pp. 615–16. The source cited is a letter to the Philadelphia Academy published in the second volume (1793) of their *Transactions.*

[11]   Sellers, *op. cit.,* II, p. 138.

[12]   *Ibid.,* p. 144.

[13]   Rembrandt Peale, *An Historical Disquisition on the Mammoth, or Great American Incognitum,* London, 1803, pp. 90–91.

[14]   *Ibid.*

[15]   He ordered the Secretary of the Navy to lend Peale a pump and secured for him a few tents. See J. T. Flexner, *America's Old Masters,* New York, 1967, p. 224.

[16]   Letterbooks.

[17]   John Mason Good, *The Book of Nature,* Boston, 1826, I, p. 93. For competent summaries of American writings on naturalism and historical geology in the first half of the nineteenth century, see Smallwood, *op. cit.,* pp. 215–48.

[18]   For extensive summaries of Cuvier's views, see Zittel, *History of Geology and Paleontology,* London, 1901, and Geike, *The Founders of Geology,* London, 1905.

[19]   John C. Greene, *The Death of Adam,* Ames, Ia., 1959, p. 108. See *ibid.,* pp. 38–87, for additional up-to-date material on Cuvier and for an excellent review of the historical development of catastrophism from the late seventeenth century on.

[20]   Letterbooks.

[21]   Letterbooks.

[22]   Greene, *op. cit.,* p. 116.

[23]   Sellers, *op. cit.,* p. 125.

[24]   *The Lost World of Thomas Jefferson,* New York, 1945, p. 37.

[25]   Charles Willson Peale, *Scientific and Descriptive Catalogue of Peale's Museum,* Philadelphia, 1796. For the history of the concept of the chain as it developed from antiquity, see Arthur O. Lovejoy, *The Great Chain of Being,* Cambridge, Mass., 1936.

[26]   Philadelphia, 1800. Delivered at the University of Pennsylvania, November 16, 1799. Manuscript on microfilm at the Archives of American Art (pages unnumbered).

[27]   Virgil Barker, *American Painting: History and Interpretation,* New York, 1950, p. 319.

[28]   December 16, 1807, Letterbooks.

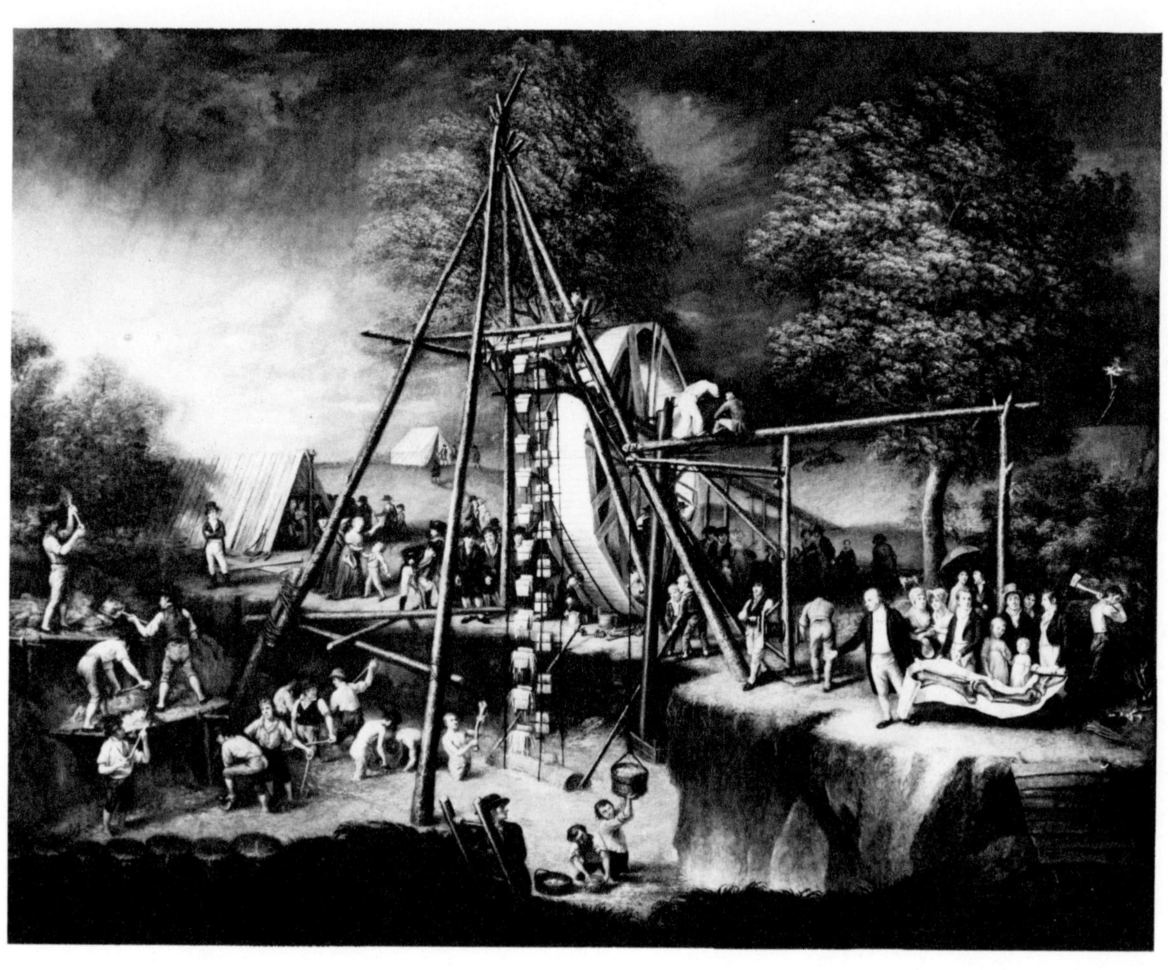

1.   CHARLES WILLSON PEALE. *Exhuming the First American Mastodon.* 1806–8.
Oil on canvas, 50 × 60½".
The Peale Museum, Baltimore. Gift of Mrs. Harry White

6

EDMUND BURKE FELDMAN

The End of "Art History"

For the purposes of this discussion let me define the history of art narrowly as the history of man-made imagery. And let me assume further that while images abound in our environment men are less and less involved in making them. Obviously, artists or designers are *responsible* for the images we see, but increasingly they do not *make* them. That is, they do not make them as the tradition of writing and thinking about art implicitly assumes images are made. I refer not only to the fact that images are duplicated and reproduced mechanically but also to the images that owe their distinctive forms to the processes of mechanical reproduction and electronic transmission. For example, a number of artists: Lichtenstein, Agam, Vasarély, Rosenquist, and Rauschenberg—mainly Pop and Op performers, but also Minimalists and the creators of primary structures, serial images, and systemic paintings—have been engaged in a radical reversal of the relations between art and technology: they have created handmade replicas of the imagery characteristic of mechanical reproducing processes. As a result, today's artistic creation exhibits a certain irony: the internal history of art is bypassed in favor of recording the marks left by tools originally invented to disseminate human marks and images. In other words, artists have decided to exploit a way of creating forms which devalues their biological heritage and their historical experience.

To understand this development theoretically, we must ask: What is the connection, if any, between the creation of art and the history of art? I think the con-

nection is, in Aristotle's sense of the term, a *necessary* one. That is, artistic creation—except in the most isolated communities, or at the very dawn of man's career
as *homo sapiens*—depends on the employment of a tradition of visual conventions
available in the form of models for artistic emulation and ideas about the way
useful objects ought to be shaped and experiences ought to be represented. When
I say that artistic creation relies on this tradition I am not referring, of course, to
art historiography—writing about art. Artistic creation which depends on writing
about art for its form as well as its content is a fairly recent development and not
necessarily one to be applauded. More about this later. Let it be said at this point
that image-making presupposes a tradition or "history" of image-making.

It can be argued that men make images spontaneously . . . because they possess
the equipment: eyes, hands, opposable thumbs, and a nervous system connecting
optical sensations with the same centers that govern their muscular activity. They
draw as they sing . . . because they have the vocal apparatus. But if this neuro-
logical-mechanical explanation seems plausible, it also conceals a hidden assumption that artistic imagery is an elaboration of motor activity, a more or less complex
type of gesturing with tools designed to leave the marks of gestures. To be sure,
scribbling seems to be pure motor activity, yet child scribblers give names to their
scribbles and adult scribblers write treatises about them. Both feel obliged to
explain the intent of the scribble, i.e., its relation to some convention for dealing
with visual experience. In other words, most creators of visual imagery believe they
are engaged in a linguistic endeavor—not a literary act but a cognitive one nevertheless. It appears that images—whether created by children or adults, artists
or amateurs—exhibit too many patterns, too many *semantic* implications to be
regarded as either random markings or the more or less complex traces of motor
activity. Even Abstract Expressionists tried for a "look," by which they meant
something re-cognizable—something that could be known and understood as well
as encountered and seen.

From the evidence of artistic creation one gathers that as an artist works he
waits for the *confirmation of his image,* its quickening, so to speak. That confirmation—that seemingly miraculous moment of creation—reflects his sense of
having joined his more or less guided forming activity with one of the immense
number of inherited and intuitive images he carries around inside him. My point
is that the images men carry within themselves—artists or not—constitute *the
latent history of art.* Historiography, or the written history of art, is something
else. For the most part, it is writing about ART, which is to say, about a com-
modity, or about the reputation of certain privileged objects. It is rarely writing
about images or visual experience. But there is a *biological* history of art recorded in
our genes by almost every scribbler, carver, and builder who ever worked since the
origin of the species. It is a distinguishing feature of our humanity; artistic seeing
and forming cannot be undertaken without reference to this "history." An act of
will is required to suppress this human history of art in favor of recording the
transactions and interactions among art objects apart from the persons and societies in whose experience the objects played a role. But many scholars manage the
task: the history of art separate from the history of vision and human feeling. Wölfflin understood the visual (not the expressive) dimensions of this problem and
began its solution, but few have followed his lead. That is why modern scholars

acting under humanistic auspices have to be reminded of the psycho-biological grounds they stand on: men cannot avoid perceiving images or trying to make new ones.

But lately artists have tried not to make images—that is, the old-fashioned images reflecting visual encounters with the world or the urgent projections of internal and imagined events. They use tools which are increasingly remote extensions of their eyes and hands. They employ workmen and assistants who are increasingly distant from their studios and who may be unknown to them personally. Or they devise ingenious ruses and stratagems not unlike the alibis of criminals —they claim to have been in another place when the artistic act was committed. In other words, they use tools, people, and ideas in the detached and anonymous way that a post-industrial civilization uses machines. And their imagery tends to reflect this impersonality, this lack of instant and continuous feedback through human organs of reception connected to a biologically evolved nervous system.

What I am describing is a development in art highly visible since Analytic Cubism—the progressive retreat of body imagery not only as a theme but also as a technical influence on the forms of painting, sculpture, and architecture. But is there any reason to regard the end of this sort of imagery as the end of art history? Do I merely take note of the obvious: the spectacular growth of geometric abstraction during the twentieth century; the emergence of a machine aesthetic; the employment of increasingly sophisticated technologies in place of the hand tools invented at the dawn of the Neolithic era? Is it not true that art history is operative so long as human intelligence and powers of decision-making initiate the processes which culminate in art objects and images?

Not quite. For one thing, a certain degree of technological determinism is always implicit in art forms, whether cave painting or "conceptual" art. This is to say that tools always endeavor to express *their* body imagery when they are put to work. The carver directs his tools with substantial awareness of where they want to go and where he would like to send them. The resultant work is very much a compromise. That it must be a compromise the carver knows at the outset; but he endeavors to control the shape of the compromise by invoking his personal version of the history of art. The direction of tools and the choice of alternative images from the profusion of technical possibilities that suggest themselves are guided by the artist's awareness of the possibilities inherent in his craft and his response to an inherited mode of seeing. However, when the strategies and protocols of artistic creation preclude the functioning of present perception as a factor in decision-making, and as they overlook those "inputs" based on memory and funded experience, we have a fundamentally new sort of process and product reaching us under the label "art."

"Art history" ends when the image is initiated by an act of will rather than visual intelligence modified by the contingencies of personal execution: the artist *desires* that an object shall come into being but he does not participate in *imagining* its forms; he starts the institutional and technical machinery whose collective result is either the display of an object or a record testifying to the fact that an object was intended. In this connection there is little point in citing the precedents of Rubens in his relations with Snyders, Van Dyck, and others of his students and assistants. The collectively executed paintings issuing from Rubens' workshop reflected *perceptual* controls at least, which is to say, imagery governed by visual conventions stored within human organisms, notably those of Rubens and his associates. Rubens presided visually as well as administratively over his workshop; it was a case of images managed by an image-maker.

It is no accident that the role of verbal language is enlarged in the presentation of art which has cut itself off from art history. To the extent that visual conventions are absent as formative influences on the creation and enjoyment of art, new contexts have to be established—new structures of meaning which can serve as connective tissue between naked form and unprepared perception. Art journalism, art writing, art teaching, and art publication constitute this connective tissue. Thus, as art writing proliferates, it functions for the new artist as the visual history of art functioned for the old. This is to say that artists find themselves responding to a verbal universe. They experience the history and criticism of art non-visually. Of course they have access to personal resources of imagery, but, as will be explained below, the circumstances of modern culture do not encourage them to repose confidence in visual imagery. Again, it is no accident that "minimal art" and "primary structures" are so completely cerebral—in whole or detail. They are created at several removes from the life of sensation, of directly seen and felt experience. The processes of abstraction entailed by the use of verbal or mathematical languages to direct the creation of visual forms lead to the development of an art whose overall structure depends increasingly on literary syntax.

The differences between visual and verbal syntax are obviously profound. They emerged prominently in the agrarian kingdoms of the Near East during the fourth and third millennia B.C. But we cannot doubt that these syntactical differences had been gestating for several thousands of years even then. Probably they reflected different types of neural organization based on the experience of hunters or cultivators whose merger in the city-states of the ancient world united the sensibilities of tribesmen guided by shamans, on the one hand, with the mentalities of scribes, on the other. Thus all men gained access to both traditions of language, both kinds of syntax, following the urban synthesis of food-gathering and agrarian cultures. However, the growing specialization of civilized life in the first urban kingdoms brought about two novel developments: first there was a polarization of the artistic or iconic functions, and the scribal or abstract-symbolic functions in social life; second, certain members of every urban population must have possessed, latently, both pictorial and literary powers of expression. These capacities were modified, elaborated, and recombined as urban civilization spread into the formerly rural areas of the earth and proliferated itself among semi-nomadic and pastoral peoples. The result for modern, post-industrial culture—some two hundred generations later—has been a vastly extended range of aesthetic sensibility with, however, a certain dilution of eidetic and imagistic gifts, and a deterioration in the capacity for heroic literary expression. Today, types like Hemingway and Mailer must virtually destroy themselves to achieve powers of literary vitality that were normal for members of the bardic castes which transmitted the oral traditions of Homer or the Bible. Similarly, the personal costs borne by contemporary painters and sculptors in their pursuit of authentic modes of visual expression are too well known to bear repetition. Modern artistic and literary types appear to represent more hybridized, less specialized, and more elaborately recombined versions of the human strains responsible for our original ability to create visual images and literary structures.

In the light of this analysis, what does the present retreat from art history—from the tradition of perceptual imagery—represent? At the simplest and most obvious level it represents the invasion of the realm of the visual by human types which are essentially scribal. Perhaps we should say "cross-pollination" rather than "invasion" because losses in iconicity are being repaid in enlarged thematic repertories and vast leaps in the cognitive ambition of art. This ambition, lacking the guidance of a conscious visual tradition, often exhibits what must be called formal or syntactic promiscuity—the association of images indiscriminately in an art which lives beyond its iconic means. The artist operating from a scribal base lacks access to an internal history of art; hence his reading of even the historiography of art tends to be inauthentic; literary intelligence distorts or obscures the phenomenal qualities of the images offered by art or life. Often the scribal artist prefers to deal with imagery at second or third hand—through the mediation of words, mathematics, or machines. The magical potency of sensory experience is often more than he can bear: hence it seems best to interpose a technology with its own built-in syntactics. His solutions to the problems of visual expression have to be founded on a weakened or debilitated capacity for managing sensations in their full vitality and shifting disposition. On the positive side, scribal art reflects an extraordinary capacity for discovering complex syntactical relations in exceedingly rudimentary visual structures. It makes strenuous demands upon the grammatical intelligence of viewers at the same time that it neglects their sensory capacities.

The discussion thus far may lead to a revision of our approach to the problem of simplicity and complexity in artistic organization or design. The formal structures I call "rudimentary" obviously support patterns of perception which seem very complex to those persons conditioned to examine art with the habits developed by reading or speaking. Verbal literacy places great stress on the *location* of signs in time and space. As anyone with a "bad" or scrawled handwriting knows, his script is legible because readers recognize the positioning of certain words, the repetition of familiar letter combinations, and the patterning of size relationships among common characters. If handwriters depended on accuracy and clarity in the shaping of letters, most could be read only with difficulty. The habit of reading inclines us to be more or less indifferent to the specifically visual qualities of images; we are interested not in their appearance but in the company they keep.

To exploit literary habits of perception, therefore, artists find they must simplify visual forms drastically; this is their accommodation to viewers who have lost the capacity to be stirred by the sensory, eidetic, and emblematic qualities of imagery. Complexity of syntactic relations has to compensate for the impoverishment of iconic form. The challenge to the eye becomes a literary challenge: the recognition of familiar combinations of marks, alertness to position and linear sequence, but indifference to non-discursive form, the immediate image. What is lost? The opportunity to rehearse optical victories over the incursions of reality. We lose confidence in our ability to confront the world with our personal organs of sensation and feeling; we require extensive prior preparation for the experience of art—the sort of preparation which is best afforded by the tradition of scribal literacy.

The dominance of scribal literacy over iconic intelligence in contemporary art might be regarded as temporary and cyclical if it were contingent only on the chance expression of certain genetic combinations. But, in fact, there are technical and ideological features of our present situation which militate against iconicity in art. First is our faith in computer technology not only as a superior type of intelligence but also as a source of economic and political power. This faith, seemingly vindicated by the computer's ability to keep track of immense industrial inventories and its usefulness in governing the flow of human and material factors in production, has encouraged artists to investigate the characteristic behavior of electronic devices with a view toward employing technocratic methods and cybernetic motifs in art . . . borrowing their magic, so to speak, since few artists understand the mathematical foundations of an electronic theory of mind. The scribal mentality, unacquainted with vision as a passionate mode of living, readily consents to the notion of using machines to see; it is even anxious to jettison eyesight in favor of electronic scanning. The electronic scanner seems to constitute a better model of visual perception than the human eye; it provides a superior way of "noticing" things regardless of their meaning or status. But, obviously, scanners cannot attend to visual forms as vehicles of human import: the scanner fashions its image by accurately locating interruptions in its visual field; objects are a type of interference—obstacles to the perception of pure nothingness. At a certain level, of course, this way of beholding also characterizes the most "sophisticated" types of drawing, painting, or carving. It corresponds to the second pole of Wölfflin's paired modes of perception; thus it acquires a spurious art historical legitimacy. Certainly Impressionist art, by converting all phenomena into functions of light and color, initiated the modern practice of cultivating indifference to the significance of objects;[1] thus it constituted the beginning of an electronic pictorial style. But art is too deeply implicated in the social character of existence for such a strategy to endure; it cannot operate exclusively on the basis of the human insignificance or even the physical neutrality of objects. A nullification of reality must ultimately be self-defeating—in art or in life; its very assertion invites a stylistic recoil. Hence reactions to the Impressionist dissolution of form were instituted, as is well known, in a number of late nineteenth- and early twentieth-century painterly repercussions. Artists could not indefinitely deny the physical character of reality, mainly because their art was rooted in artisanship, that is, manual operations performed with real materials—work. Some possessed innate capacities for re-inventing the magical-expressive qualities of art—qualities normally within the range of persons who have spontaneous access to an internal history of art. For others, it was a matter of received ideas. They heard or read about visual form as a vehicle of meaning, of the object as icon, of the image as symbol. But these ideas were often appropriated by artists with sensibilities unprepared for the visual implications of their discovery. As a result, we find ourselves today witnessing the operation of an artistic culture which at times resembles the barbarian occupation of an ancient and exceedingly wealthy city.

But there is an important difference: today's "barbarians" are literate. They instinctively translate their experience into lexical systems suitable for the computerized fabrication of art objects and, afterward, the code language of art journalism. They have an ideological commitment to ART and what they understand as the necessity of frequent stylistic change, notwithstanding a certain insensitivity to visual form itself. It almost seems that they worship ART the way barren women worship child-bearing. The spectacle of non-visual persons trying to create viable images is as pathetic as watching chickens trying to swim with ducks. This is because the scribe-as-artist perceives the image as an item in the history of ideas; he has to approach the immense resources of visual form the way media managers approach a newly nominated presidential candidate: The problem resolves itself into converting the man's residual humanity into the *lingua franca* of the masses who have become alienated from their own humanity. How can the real thing be dehydrated for convenient packaging and merchandising? Alas, the essential person rarely survives translation into the typical slogans of pop history, sociology, and economics.

Now, having separated themselves from the history of art in order to fashion concise narrative structures and unambiguous written records, the scribes and grammarians are again endeavoring to enter the realm of the visual, this time to fashion an electronic *oikoumene*. One recognizes here the agenda of erstwhile professors of literature become savants of communications science and theologians of the binary computer. Needless to say, a certain number of artists will go whoring after the gods of linguistic theory. It is not that they become votaries of false gods, but rather that they develop a false consciousness in adopting the rites of multi-media cultists. So, those of us who deplore, even while we endeavor to explain these developments, will have to live for a while amid the ruins of the art historical imagination, surrounded by shards of linguistic analysis, almost buried in the glut of electronic gadgetry, and regularly assailed by hosannas raised in the name of computer graphics. In time, perhaps, the rhetoricians of technocratic culture will discover their loneliness in a universe cut off from the life of the senses and the history of the human imagination. Then the history of art which lives in our genes will reassert itself; it does not atrophy, it only becomes recessive from time to time.

Note

1   In this connection, Max Friedländer shrewdly observes: "Impressionists avoid banality in that they see unsharply." One either sweetens the world or ignores it completely by homogenizing one's mode of seeing everything. *Reminiscences and Reflections,* New York Graphic Society, 1969, p. 89.

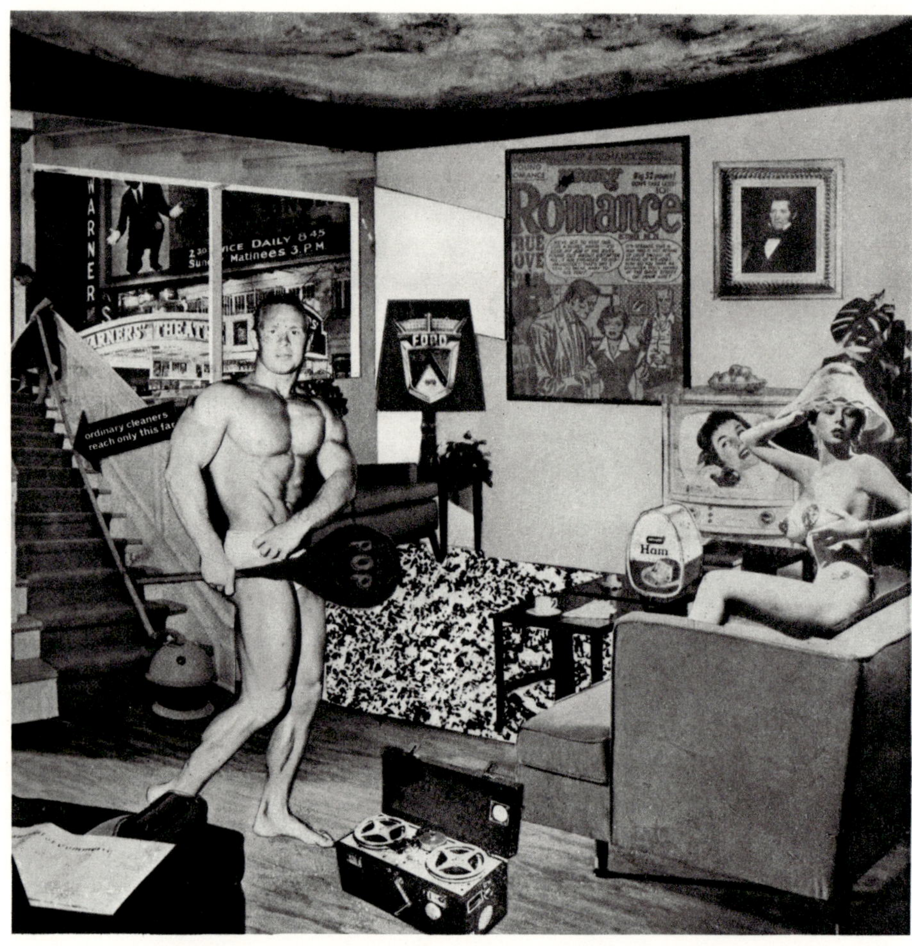

1.   RICHARD HAMILTON. *Just what is it that makes today's homes so different, so appealing?* 1956. Collage, $10\frac{1}{4} \times 9\frac{7}{8}''$. Collection Edwin Janss, Jr., Thousand Oaks, California

Silkscreened photographs on canvas organized according to a literary syntax which extends even to the heavy sarcasm of the title. Such works employ images as verbal counters, appealing to the viewer in his role as reader of socio-political texts. To deal visually with the ideas which are here invoked through the stereotypes of Pop culture would entail an organization of space, an arrangement of surfaces, and an invention of shapes such as would tax the formal resources of a Poussin. Nevertheless this imagery possesses visual weight. Despite the formal promiscuity of his work there is no way for an image-maker operating under literary auspices to avoid the optical connotations of his statement. Indeed, the visual disarray corresponds proximately with the literary idea. But if the artist wants to make an iconic statement about our squalid moral and aesthetic environment, he cannot rely so heavily on the documentation behind photographic imagery and what is essentially a lexical grammar. In other words, he must consult personally authentic resources of sensibility and experience; he must try to vitalize his access to the human history of form.

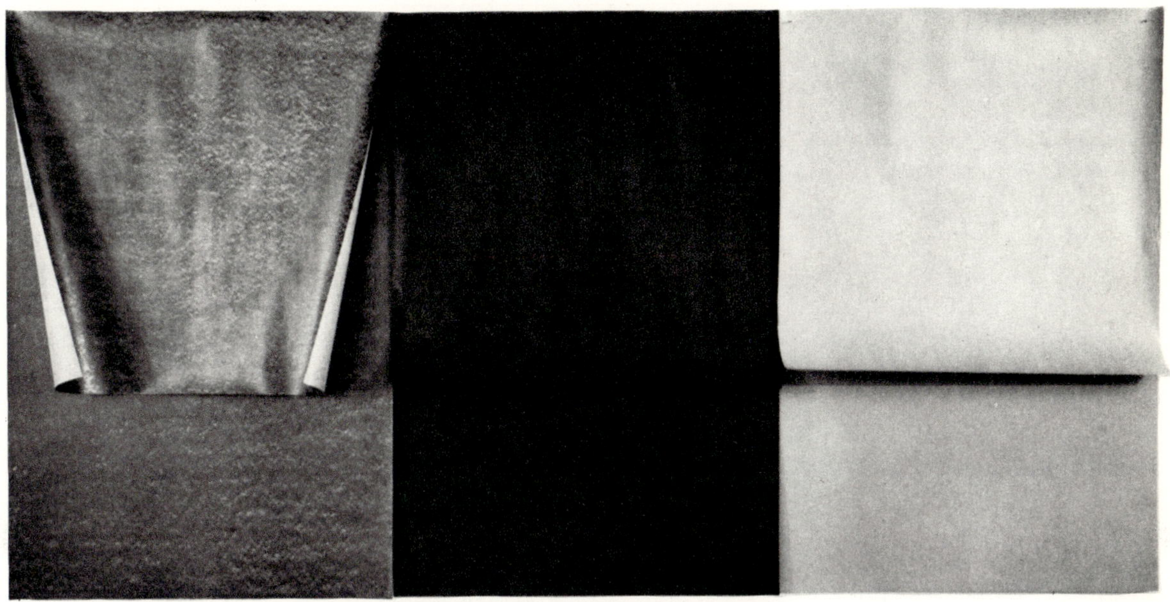

2. DOROTHEA ROCKBURNE. *Three.* 1970.
Paper, chipboard, graphite, nails; 60 × 120″.
Collection the artist

The artist writes, "Each element of the work is a sign functioning much as a letter does in language. Alone, the element is complete. In relation to other elements a logic is set up, interior to itself, in the way a grouping of letters makes a word. I designated the panels as A′/B, B′/B, and C′/B. I realized that when I put units together this way they ceased to be objects and took on the same qualities as functions in math." A remarkable statement, both as a description of the artist's strategy and as a frank avowal of the discursive character of that strategy. The meaning of the work as a whole requires that its parts be ordered successively, in a temporal sequence which the viewer is not free to rearrange insofar as he is guided by the logic of its design. By virtue of the viewer's unfreedom with respect to the order of his perception, the object acquires precision and economy of meaning—attributes of a scientific theorem more than a work of visual art. It may happen, of course, that viewers will attend to the work as an artistic rather than a logical statement, refusing to read it from left to right, for example. In that case, will they experience visual or pictorial rewards comparable to those accessible through a purely logical reading?

The translation of the form from wood to metal is only a minor logistical problem since the key decisions have been made. And that is the point: this is an art about which decisions can be made in advance of seeing, both from the standpoint of building the forms and experiencing the result. Most of the transactions can be "handled" conceptually. Perhaps we are approaching the condition described in the well-known joke about the convention of joke-tellers: they get laughs by shouting out numbers which designate jokes everyone at the convention knows. The story gives a fairly accurate account of a *linguistic* situation—one that is not unlike the discourse of a group of art historians who already know the iconography of, let us say, Van Eyck's *Arnolfini and His Wife.* But the analogy is inexact. Knowing the iconography of the Van Eyck is a most inadequate substitute for seeing the work. On the other hand, we suspect that knowing the dimensions, color, and material of Bladen's cube will eliminate many of the visual surprises the work can offer through its physical presence.

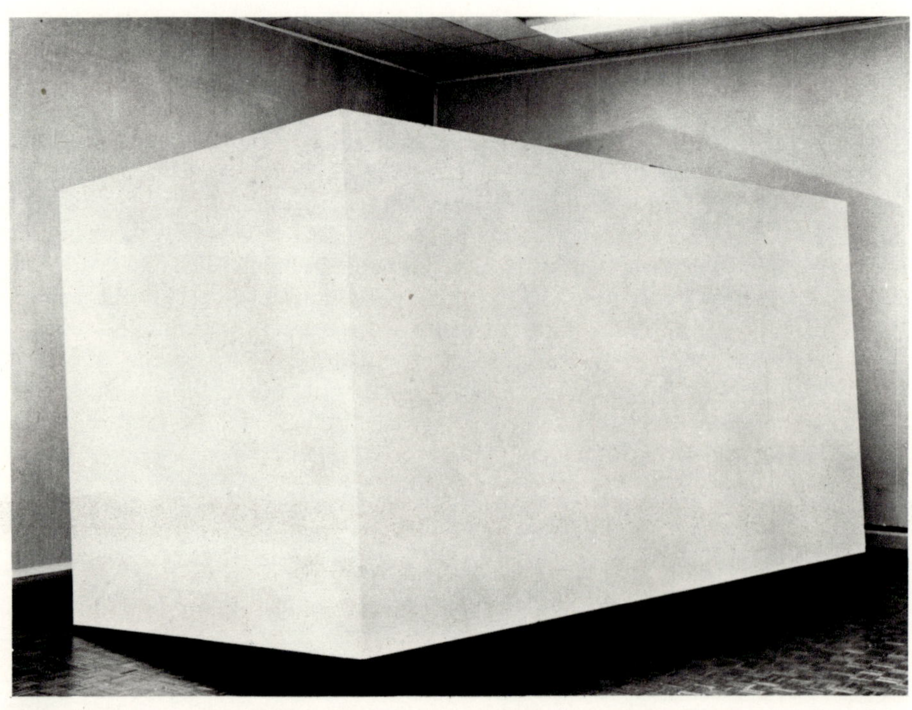

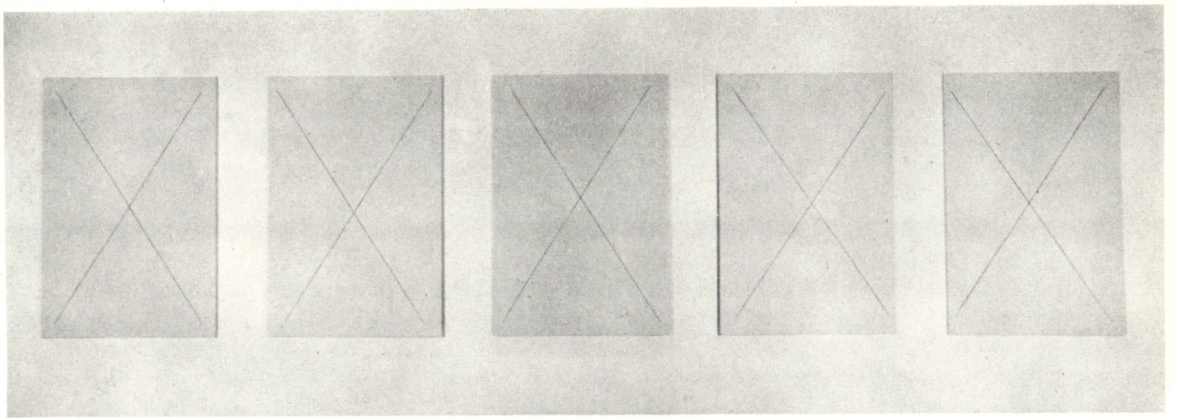

4. ROBERT MANGOLD. *X Paintings.* 1970.
Acrylic on canvas, each panel 60 × 40".
Collection Peppino Agrati, Milan

The five canvases are a uniform gray color; the X-es, graphite lines of equal weight, seem to be identical, but with the exception of the first canvas they do not intersect in the center. Initially, the viewer thinks the five canvases are alike in all respects; then, after a brief optical comparison of the X-es, he sees slight differences in their points of intersection. Perception of these differences lays open the visual content, what we might call the *iconography,* of the work (which is, of course, a single entity, not five separate paintings). We have to conclude that the visual reading, which calls into action a few, very low-order perceptual skills, results in an aesthetic experience of virtually no vividness, intensity, or imaginative scope. And that is because there is so little room for the mind's free deployment of symbolic processes. It is only as a logical statement that the work makes any serious claim on our attention. But it is not yet a cognitive statement because no conventions of vocabulary and syntax have been established which can give us the meaning or logic of the sequence of shifts in the location of the intersections. So, lacking conventions of language, almost wholly divorced from sensory experience, and reluctant to exploit any tradition of pictorial imagery, the work is neither presentational nor discursive, to use Mrs. Langer's terms. But if we cannot say what the work is, we *can* describe what it is becoming; its direction is clear: it moves away from the image and the history of images toward linear language—mathematics, symbolic logic, and writing.

7

CREIGHTON GILBERT

Art Historical Period Terms as a Lens for Looking at Dante

Dante's poem is obviously intended to be complicated, and has perhaps a larger bibliography of commentary than any other book, aside from the various Bibles of the world, so that an amateur can make remarks about it only with acute nervousness. It is equally unjustifiable to rely on the inevitably obsolete handbooks, in the hope of safety by following the expert, or to take a naïve spontaneous viewpoint, in the hope of being intuitively right. My refuge will be to speak of what is so conspicuous that it would, I trust, appear in all approaches.

Among the greatest works of literature the *Divine Comedy* must be the most insistently and neatly systematic. Neither Shakespeare nor Homer, not even Joyce, divides his work so thoroughly, first by three, then by a hundred; among the poems that have survived among the great ones, no other poet invented a rhyme scheme and a structural scheme that was then carried out with such endurance. In the terza rima the most special quality, of course, is that it is interlocking or interweaving, rather than simply sequential. The rhyme sound of each line ties across the ones before and after it so that a force is created like the weaving over and under that makes cloth out of threads. And each canto is simultaneously part of two systems, three-part and hundred-part. This is rightly called a structural or even architectonic approach.

Before working this metaphor too hard, I would like to justify it by recalling another quality in the *Divine Comedy* that seems unique in great literature, the great value given to the places where things occur. They are different for each event; as we go on the journey, new places are constantly described. The scenes have more meaning than in any play, certainly more than in Shakespeare's fixed sets, more even than in nineteenth-century plays where a few sets must make do for a series of events. Secondly, the environments of the *Comedy* are always of a constructed, even architectonic kind: the people walk along ledges, over bridges, in ditches, through tunnels, as against the possible alternatives of hills and fields. Thus the ostentatiously strong presence of an environment is associated with its artificial quality: man-made or man-imagined kinds of places fill the elaborately made poem. To find an equally emphatic ostentation of constructed locations in literature, we could perhaps only turn to science-fiction movies, which reflect Dante in their tendency to be about the way other worlds reward and punish men. This brings us to a related but distinct element, the tendency of the constructed environment to influence strongly the people's behavior. They do nothing but climb, scrabble, wade, or look for resting places; they never behave in ways relatively unconnected with their particular locations. There is a not so small literature of the restriction of human activity by environment; it finds one classic form in *Robinson Crusoe,* another in *Erewhon,* another—combined with the journey— in *Around the World in Eighty Days,* in which we devote all our time to managing the changing environments. But in every one of those cases it is an unusual aspect of nature that makes the quality of the environment; the hero's ingenuity is exercised by islands, jungles, deserts, and oceans. It is much less common for the effect of environment dominating action to be linked with an artificial, closed-in kind of environment; the best instance is perhaps in shipboard literature, but this does not seem a very apt analogy to the *Comedy,* since in such writing, from the *Seafarer* to *Moby Dick* to Katherine Anne Porter, the preference seems to be a concentration on the isolated human being himself.

Despite the fallacy of parallels between the arts, it does seem plausible to make a link between the exceptional constructedness in the verse form of the *Comedy,* and the exceptional constructedness in what it describes, considering that these are in the same poem (and no doubt specialists have tried out this approach). With this doubly prepared springboard, we can jump with a little less than the usual vagueness to a parallel with the kind of structure that the great builders of Europe had developed in the generations just before Dante. The analogy between the poem and the Gothic cathedral is a cliché, of course. A cliché has as much chance to be true as a proverb does, and this one seems at least to have usefulness. I may here be able to evade some of its commonplaceness by starting from the art historian's specialty rather than the more usual Dante specialty, and by evoking both the kinds of structures in Dante just mentioned. As a classic average Amiens may be used, built about fifty years before Dante was born but still a standard for new and sophisticated building methods in his lifetime. To begin at the beginning, the analogy at Amiens with a structural poem is not simply that it is a building, and hence a structure. It has a particular kind of structure different from its own predecessors, and it is the qualities that change from those of its predecessors that are its parallels to Dante; they may reasonably be called interlocking. The nave wall is perhaps the most typifying element of a High Gothic structure, and certainly one of the favorites for analysis. Where the round Early Gothic column had its quickest relationship with its neighbor column—a sequential procession like a human procession down the nave—the High Gothic column is most quickly seen in its internal interrelationships, its articulated subdivisions, the pieces of columns around its circumference that allude to the other similar arcs and vertically allude to the diverging arcuated supports of the vaults they carry. The earlier column alludes to such support, but inclusively, the single drum hiding in its imposing mass all the live cylinders of thrust. Thus between Early and High Gothic, there is a new presentation of the tying of threads to make an articulate expression of construction, as everybody knows, which is the most emphatic in the human history of building. Of course this development happens in partial fits and starts, and it is true that in the earlier shafts the upper portions are articulated, and in some instances the shapes appear in the whole height of the column, but perhaps the reader will be willing to agree that these are marking off the sequence, not interlocking.

It appears that this High Gothic pattern has been satisfying to later generations, to judge from the copies made of Gothic in every subsequent century in western Europe, either in simple repetitions of its external shapes or, indirectly, in structures like the Eiffel Tower. On the other hand, later poets did not find it often desirable to imitate the articulation of interlocking structure in the *Comedy*. If this is so, the quality may be considered primarily an architectonic one, once extended to poetry as an analogy, a form of relationship which indeed the choice of the label "structural" implies from the start.

If this means that the *Comedy* is an architectonic sort of poem, that suggests that it is illustrative of the theory that in history one art is ahead of others at particular epochs, and gives the others their period qualities. Such a notion has a certain amount of evidence in its favor, more it would seem than most of the usual hypotheses about parallels of the arts. The most famous instance, and perhaps the most attractive, refers to modern art from the nineteenth century on, with a focus in Walter Pater's soft epigram: "All art aspires constantly to the condition of music." It is not very difficult to find modern paintings that illustrate the association, literal instances from Whistler to Klee and to Mondrian's *Broadway Boogie-Woogie,* or broader and probably more interesting suggestions from Van Gogh to Picasso and Pollock, in which the paintings heavily depend on rhythmic and harmonic pictorial techniques, designed to transmit a feeling directly, while they shy away consistently from the religious, the story-telling, from modeling and especially from effects of air, from three dimensional mass—all non-musical qualities and all pivotal to much painting in earlier centuries. Less strongly, modern literature can sometimes be seen becoming musical; obviously poetry, from Whitman and Hopkins, both un-Dante-like in this aspect of their work, to Dylan Thomas or Allen Ginsberg; even some novelists, from Joyce to Faulkner, show a sense of order based less on interlocking construction of parts than upon temporal continuity, rhythm, and reverberation.

If Pater's formula has, then, some use in the age of art for art's sake, the notion of art led by architecture may have as much or more in the age of art for the church, in the masonry as well as the institutional senses of the term. When we start to look at medieval painting it is noticeable that for the most part it is not painting at all, in the sense of being produced with paint, though we must call it such for convenience. It is mosaic or enamel or stained glass, and the remnants of medieval frescoes in French and Italian churches are the exception to prove the rule, for they betray themselves as meant to be cheap substitutes for more desirable mosaic. Mosaic itself, enamel, and glass share not only their greater luminousness, but their greater demands on careful craftsmanship—a notorious medieval specialty— and their greater dependence on systematic arrangements of small sections. They also share the interesting quality of not being autonomous objects, but parts of larger physical things, the mosaic and the stained glass part of a building, the enamel part of a reliquary box or the like, undetachable, separate only in being a subdivision distinguishable by the diversity of media applied. Though we may call them painting by courtesy, we cannot call them paintings, which would mean— in a change so basic that we rarely give it thought—things that are autonomous and movable. The one great vehicle of medieval painting that is in part made of paint, the illuminated manuscript page, is an undetachable (except by vandals) portion of a book, and its artistic form always refers to this fact. Only very small medieval pictorial objects, approaching the quality of jewelry, such as an enamel crucifix, can be autonomous and movable; and the same is true of sculpture, as in small ivories. These objects prefigure separable post-medieval painting and sculpture, but differ from the later culture, and seem to belong to their own, in being conditioned by their highly particular shapes—such as a crucifix—and thus by the structure and the non-pictorial purpose they serve, as much as the larger ones are conditioned by their contexts.

Architectural sculpture, weak and sparse in Byzantium and also in the early Middle Ages in the west, later becomes there surely the most tremendous triumph of any architecturally dependent other art. In looking at the sculptural series of a French cathedral façade, we seem indeed to be looking at something that is *like* the *Divine Comedy,* sharing underlying assumptions with it. These façades, so familiar to us today after a century of pilgrimages, were being painted by Monet while Tchaikowsky was composing and Rodin modeling motifs from Dante, all of them paying the homage of musical arts to something they found marvelous, and which seemed, however hazy, to mark a clear accomplishment in a trivial modern world.

As an example of these façades, Reims may be taken as a classic (fig. 1), in the sense of being a complete illustration. We know the three doors, the central one just slightly wider and deeper, the arch above containing the rose window in turn containing the stained glass, the side bays whose lancet arches hold, on a first level, glazed windows again, on a second monumental sculpture, on a third open windows through which the bells are heard. All this is the interlocking structure cited before at Amiens, and in fact seems a bit less elegant here. We are aware in this case that the entrance porches are like sheds, projecting in front of the building. They seem to mark an abnormal growth of one element beyond the point of equal balance with the rest, the element of the sculpture; thus the Gothic structure seems a little loose. This is confirmed by the slightly less than exact relationship in the rose window between the circle and the arch (fig. 2), where the circle connotes among other things the religious and human imagery contained in it. Coming closer, the sculptured figures in the thickness of the doorway and the fired figures in the glass make us say, first of all, how architecturally conditioned they are, fitting just so the rows of columns and the window frames. And yet they have free personalities, they are not bound slaves in cages. This becomes more obvious in a comparison with similar sculpture a hundred years older, on the front of Chartres (fig. 3), where, however vital and rhythmic, the figure action is constructed and also constricted; the rhythm is the stylized one of builder's blocks. The Reims figures have another point of departure, the organic reality of the person. At Reims the factor of the individual feality and the factor of the structural pattern almost coincide, but not quite; there is a factor of gap or tolerance which the shed porch may measure for us, and which is then seen again in the loosening of the people from their columns. Earlier, in the tympanum at Chartres, if ever, the pressures of individual reality and orderly pattern are entirely identified with each other; the aliveness of the winged lion is not merely harmonious with the curve of the arch, but can be regarded equally well as the product of either the pattern maker or the image maker, without the slightest tremor of exception. In the Christ figure the abstraction of the supernatural immortal seems in absolute harmony with the fleshed reality of the man, indeed, each of these presumably antagonistic expressions seems to reinforce the validity of the other. This can occur because of the relation between the building structure and the mind's message. Christ is placed just here, in the mandorla, in this scale, fitted beside the four beasts of the Evangelists in smaller scale, followed by the angels in the arches, the apostles sharing their canopies yet also making a group, and below them the larger column figures of the ancestral kings and queens. Related, as the product of a person working within his culture, to feudal society, to scholasticism, these sizes, positions, and frames are a main vehicle of a convinced statement about the most important meanings. They occur not only in single figures but in scenes. The tympanum represents a Last Judgment, a fact that we may not recall because Chartres is, with respect to dramatic interrelationships, a little primitive, as we see again in the Nativity groups nearby: the balance of meaning with structure is not fully realized in the case of multifigural events. For that we should turn a little forward again, and may at Amiens look at a part of the sculpture that I particularly like, the scenes of the Labors of the Months (fig. 4). Inside each quatrefoil the action is so fresh and easy, even loose, that it is in tension with the rigid and complex confinement of the frame. But the tension is equal on both sides, evoking vibration and life; as we step back, it makes us aware that the events are a related set, the activities of people typical of all people at the specified times. As the figure is to the frame, so is the action to the whole of active life.

At this point I may justify a very familiar presentation by applying it, unfamiliarly, to the *Divine Comedy,* in what I hope is a rich and evocative way. At first I only compared the terza rima system to the Gothic column system, a matter of formal order. After that I suggested the unusual role of structures in the story told by the *Comedy,* and we can now add to that description. It is not just that the people of the poem constantly have to cope with structure, with ledges and tunnels: it is the greater fact, so obvious it is not discussed, that it is very important on what ledge they are, in boiling lake or formal garden. This placing is a chief tool the poet uses to bring us his moral message, a peculiar tool in literature but a normal one in medieval visual imagery. A person in the *Comedy* is to be read by us through the usual means, and, in addition, by the place he belongs to, and, further, by being in that place in relation to the whole map of other places in the total *Comedy,* such as the fourth circle of the second canticle. Thus the *Comedy* is architectural poetry in three distinguishable senses: first, in its emphasis on its own rhyme structure, where the interlocking quality is unusual; second, in the emphasis on structures as affecting the behavior of the dramatis personae; and third, the use of place definition to allude to the whole organization of places through the poem, and through it to the organization of life, death, and judgment. Of these the first and third are not merely architectonic but in particular Gothic. The *Comedy* and a Gothic cathedral porch can both be described in the following terms: there is an expert web of structure, itself noticeable, and serving to embed human beings; these carry significance to us, readable by many devices of which an important one is the point on the web at which each is plotted; what we read thereby is both its hierarchic and its dramatic statement. The other structural quality of the poem, which is not especially Gothic, the influence of buildings on the people's behavior, might be thought simply an overflow token of the poet's zest for construction, but I think it has a further implication, to which I will come back shortly.

At this point the careful reader may wish to complain of sweeping generalizations and needed qualifications, beginning with the obvious discrepancy that the cathedrals and the *Comedy* are not the products of one culture in any but a rather broad sense: the cathedrals are a hundred years older and far to the north of Tuscany. One might cure this by citing Dante's respect for older French culture, concretely for Provençal troubadour lyrics, and adding that Provençal church façades of the twelfth century have some similarity to what we have been discussing. But it seems more hopeful to explore the reverse relationship, not with earlier French poetry, but with later Tuscan sculpture. This is promising, first, because in the generations later than Amiens and Reims, toward Dante's own time, this sculpture was indeed productive of great artists, and they had an intelligent admiration for their French predecessors. In this way they altered the traditions of earlier Italian carving, making it distinct and modern. Nicola Pisano's first great pulpit in Pisa (fig. 5), of 1260, has a status—the more secure because not often dwelt upon—of being the first monument leading to the Italian Renaissance, tacitly agreed upon in rare unanimity. His second great pulpit is of 1265, the year of Dante's birth, and fifty years nearer Dante than Amiens as well as so much closer in space. It is standard and true to speak of Nicola's inspiration from ancient Rome, but this occurs literally, at particular points, thus in the form of quotations, and it seems proper to invoke the paradox that what an artist takes in quotation form is not what he has felt most deeply. Neither Roman nor derived from local tradition is the design of the whole pulpit; it differs from preceding pulpits, I suggest, in the direction of being interlocking, in having a noticeable masonry system that does double duty as a frame for the sculptural narratives. It is a dramatic revision of a normal local kind of object, the carved pulpit, on the basis of a foreign feeling, from French Gothic.

If this suggestion seems questionable when presented so simply, it may be strengthened in detail by looking at another later Tuscan pulpit by a great sculptor who happens to be the earlier one's son, Giovanni Pisano. This one, for Pisa Cathedral (fig. 6), was finished in 1310, and thus at last we are at the moment of the *Comedy*. I would like to think of it as a brilliant late Gothic architectural design, an approach which is unusual because we don't think of pulpits this way nor of Tuscans as late Gothic, and also because the pulpit was taken down and has been reconstructed. In plan it is a circle, subdivided by eight columns. Each one-eighth segment is a panel and holds a story; since these are curved, projecting convexly toward us between their columns, they have the effect of being held in compression like barrel staves. In fact, the strong projection of the columns makes the segments appear not tô make a pure circle, but a melon form, each segment a bigger curve than a pure circle would produce, but that is probably an illusion. The circle, a new shape, was clearly much on Giovanni's mind; the one large building inside one of his scenes, the *Presentation in the Temple,* is also a circle divided around its circumference by columns. And the inscription at the base of the work, Giovanni's poem—"the most revealing statement in medieval art," as Michael Ayrton rightly observed—begins with the word *circuit:* "John here has circled the rivers and the parts of the world." This novel form is a supremely elegant illustration of a Gothic principle which has been most elegantly defined as maximum articulation with maximum continuity. Because the articulation is the traditional element, the series of panels, and the continuity is new, their circularity, the continuity acquires a special swiftness, of rushing around the circumference. This in turn is in keeping with the carved figures, Gothic and un-Roman, who express high-keyed emotion through the elasticity of stringy arms, hunched shoulders, sucked-in rib cages and clawing fingers. Desperation, the need for making things right again, is the unanimous mood of this congested world, whether progress toward this aim seems to be being made or lost—and all this within the interlocking frame: the pulpit is my candidate for the one best equivalent of the *Comedy* in the visual arts.

I would like in two asides to support this rather odd presentation of Giovanni Pisano as a French Gothic architect. The first is that he probably did go to France, aside from being directly affected by recent sculpture there. The second, which like the first makes this a literal, not a figurative, formulation, is that he was literally an architect in the sense of the period, in which an architect is best defined as a trained sculptor or painter who has become the foreman of a job. His spectacular work in this line is Siena Cathedral, something utterly new in Tuscany, with its façade made of monumental statues. Its damaged present state sets up the missing link we need with Reims and the rest. If the Pisa pulpit seems an unsuitable parallel because of its ridiculously smaller scale, we may expand it imaginatively, without being historically improper, to the measurements of this façade. The ruined large sculptures by Giovanni for this work, and for the Pisa buildings, are little-known masterpieces which do show a monumental but not divergent restatement of the pulpit's people. And they are Dantesque. This general quality can perhaps be suggested best in an intuitive way, by opening the *Comedy* at random and reading a few lines: O proud Christians, poor wretches, infirm of sight, of mind, who yet have faith in your backward steps, do you not perceive that we are worms, born to form the angel butterfly, that flies to justice with no screens?

> O superbi Cristian miseri lassi
> Che, della vista, della mente infermi,
> Fidanza avete ne' ritrosi passi,

Non v'accorgete voi che noi siam vermi
Nati a formar l'angelica farfalla,
Che vola alla giustizia senza schermi?

If this parallel between the *Comedy* and sculpture seems odd, it is partly because the commonplace analogy is with painting, by Giotto. I would like in the last part of this essay to suggest why sculpture seems a better analogy. The first reason is that it seems to have attracted Dante more. Contrary to a popular impression, he never discusses painting. In the famous reference to Giotto, Dante is conversing with a painter, Oderisi, and mentions Giotto as another. He does, on the other hand, come upon two sets of sculptures, in the well-known passages in *Purgatory;* they are cut into the wall of the cliff. I quote a part describing an Annunciation. "I became aware that the cliff was bright marble, and adorned with such carvings that nature would be shamed, not only Polycleitus. The angel, who came to earth with the decree of peace, so many years wept for, to open heaven from its long bar, appeared so truthful before us, carved there in a gentle action, that it did not seem an unspeaking image. One would have sworn he was saying, Hail, because she was shown there, who turned the key to open the high love. And it had stamped that phrase in action, Behold the handmaid of the Lord, just the same way a figure is sealed in wax." Yet this evocation of the Gothic, in its fluid and realistic aspect, less indeed like the Amiens Labors of the Months than like a fresco in the Arena Chapel, is as a description of a work of art less intrinsic to the poem than a metaphor given us a little later in this same canto, describing the motion of a person as if he were a sculpture. The sinners punished for pride are humbled under heavy loads they carry. And "just as we see a figure sometimes, for holding up a ceiling or roof, whose knees touch its breast, which makes true distress arise in the observer from the untrue, just so I saw these people." Dante is calling to our mind a particular kind of sculpture, and even more our psychological response to it. Occurring both in Romanesque and Gothic, it is a perfect example of architecturally dependent sculpture. I did not cite it before as an example of that quality, because it is an extreme rather than an average example. It is the more fascinating that it is Dante's most intimate consideration of a work of visual art, and it is even richer in that the sinner who is walking like a sculpture is none other than Oderisi, the one painter whom Dante meets on his journey.

Giovanni's sculpture, in the pulpits and the figures applied to the buildings, is more powerful than the architectural framing. A Romanesque figure in a French door may be more affected, though not always, by its architectural locus than its internal forces; at Chartres, as I suggested in adopting an old analysis, these forces are in balance. Then soon the figure emerges a little from the frame, as at Reims. In Giovanni it is even a wrench for us to think of him as an architect or of his sculpture as architectural; we detach it in our illustrated books. On such a graph-line of evolution, Dante connects with a rather early stage. From the frame of the terza rima, of the canticles, of the circles, pits, and bridges, the figures do not emerge at all; that was after all our first postulate. This requires us to label Dante's art as less modern than the visual art of his contemporaries, and more medieval in his use of the structural frame for his imagination. This is the deduction toward which I have been moving, and I hope it will seem real even if not of the greatest significance. It may be reinforced if, as a control, we do for once compare the *Comedy* to Giotto, the usual analogy though in my view the less interesting one. It is generally done not only because they are of the same age and town, but because they are two grand historic personalities, Giotto having had more effect on the world's painters even than Dante on its writers.

Let us look at Giotto's largest surviving work, the Arena Chapel frescoes in Padua of about 1305, from the standpoint of Gothic structure. Until lately this was done not at all; today the framing of the stories and their painted buildings have been analyzed by several interesting writers, but I would emphasize something a little different, the frame system as a metaphor of carpentry. We soon see why the effort is not made. The real walls of the chapel are unarticulated, presumably left neutral for the painter (who perhaps was the builder). The existence of windows on one side and not the other seems to have no symbolic or design significance. Giotto relates to this asymmetry by painting five scenes on one wall and six on the other, which seems a merely practical and comfortable arrangement. The top level of scenes curves a bit with the vault but does not adjust to it. The emphatic character of the frames seems to belong to their character as borders of the scenes, proscenium arches for the tableaux (fig. 7). Within, as he concentrates on the physical truth of the figures and on their drama, he is like Dante, but the exclusive value given to the people, in a one-directional time sequence that is non-systematic, is revolutionary by negative exclusion. Giotto is like us in throwing a lot away within the scene, all Dante's interlocking and constructing frame, as he reduces it to an elementary guideline outside the scene. It is often noticed that a great revolutionary art that establishes the habits of an age is elementary, anticipating much that will later be worked out in detail, but bearing down on the basic. Giotto does this as much as the Cubists of 1909, or David in his first Neoclassic works, or Wordsworth in his first Romantic poems. Dante does nothing of the sort; in this respect he appears to be the last and most elaborate of great medieval artists. Perhaps we should make our analogy between him and painting by using Giotto's predecessor Cimabue, whose astonishing art does something our categories have found to be impossible; within the traditional stylized shapes of Byzantine types he creates individual human feeling. Perhaps Giotto's literary analogue is Dante's great successor of the next generation, Boccaccio. If this seems an unusual approach, it is not a new one; Lanzi's view was that "Giotto was the father of the new painting as the father of the new prose was Boccaccio." Boccaccio, to be sure, wrote his greatest work with a framing system of ten stories in each of ten days, but perhaps did so only out of retained respect for Dante, since this structure does not penetrate the meaning of particular stories, their tone, or even their length, which is randomly diverse. And Boccaccio of course is elementary and unsystematic in the most basic way, by writing in prose. The *Decameron* is rightly, I believe, described as the first prose masterpiece in any modern European language, and it is thereby realistic, casual, and non-structural in contrast to the poem. Dante in this context may be one of those artists typified, in a remote age, by Bach, who works with all the impediments of the unmodern, using style habits that would have seemed no longer valuable to artists. Dante does not emerge from the medieval frame; we do, led by Giotto. This may tell us something helpful about them or about ourselves.

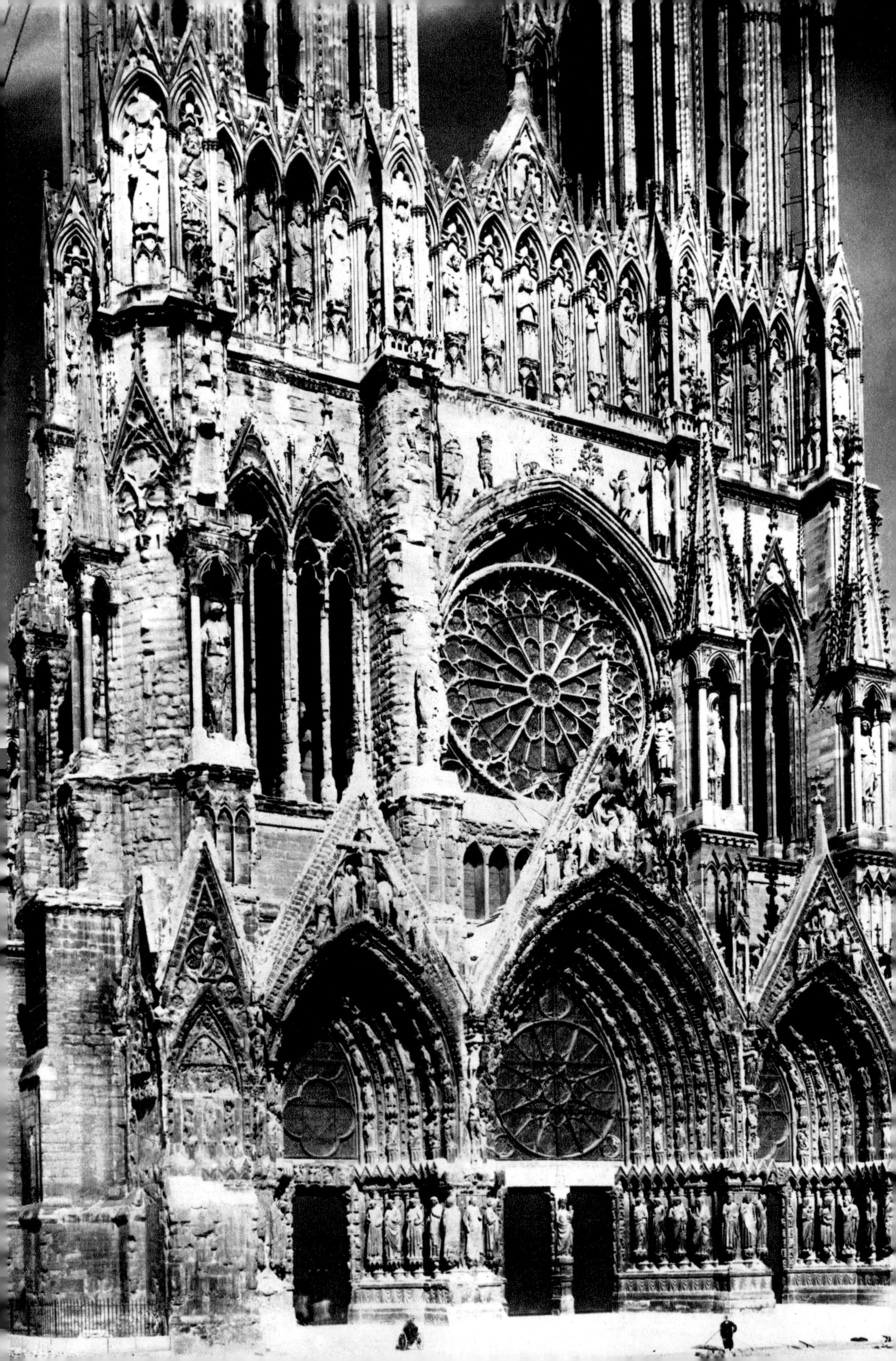

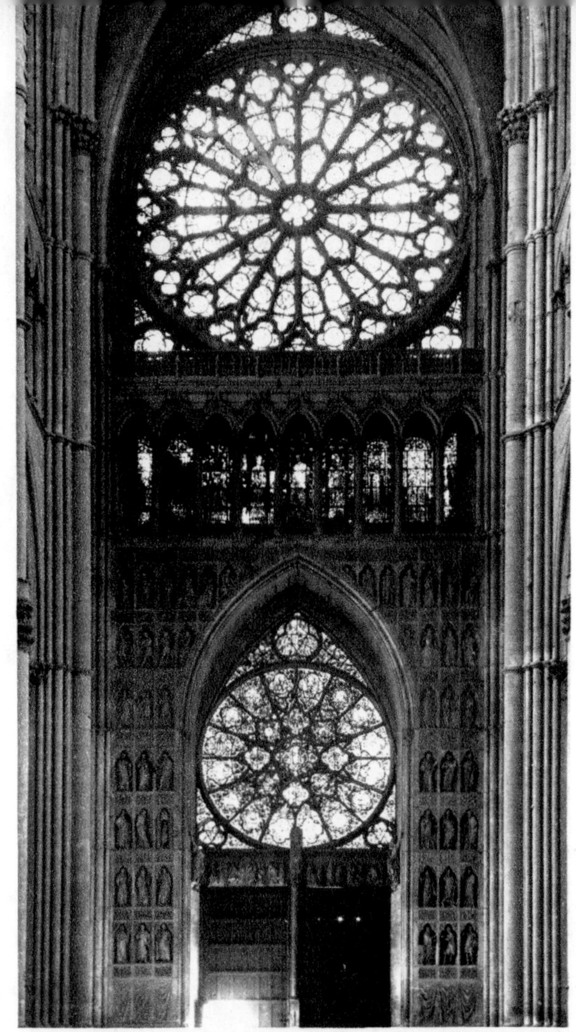

◀1. Reims Cathedral.
Façade

2. Reims Cathedral.
Interior, transept

3. Chartres Cathedral.
Central portal, façade

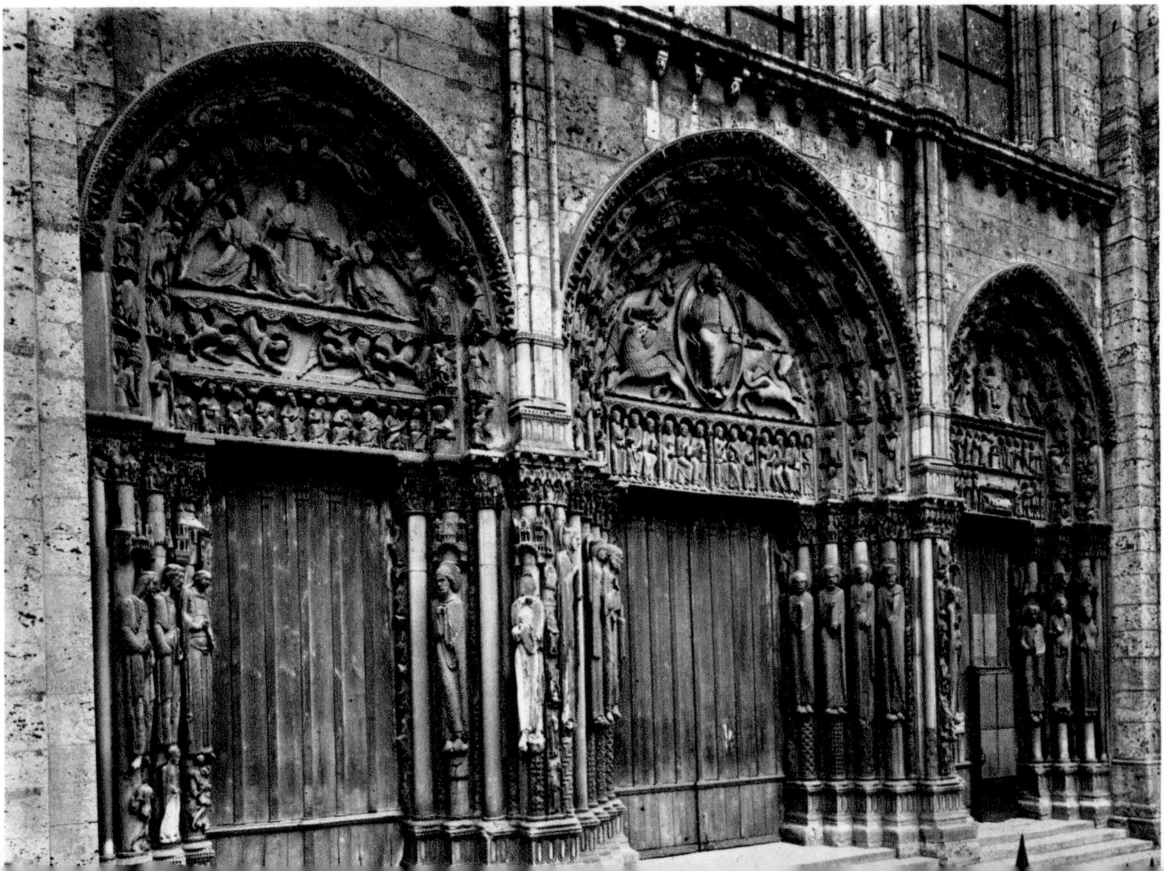

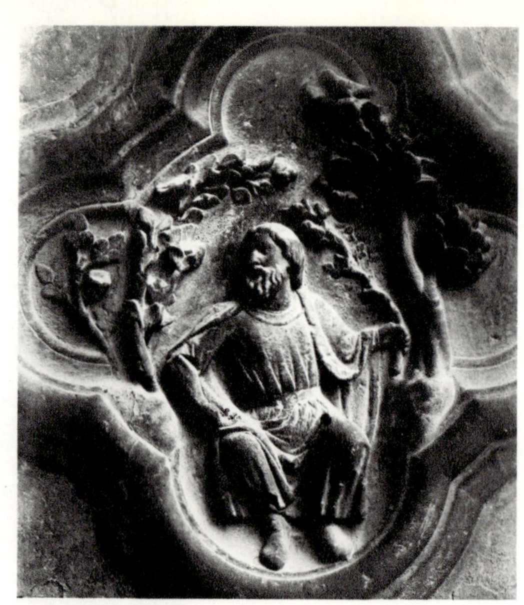

4. Amiens Cathedral.
Quatrefoil with month of May

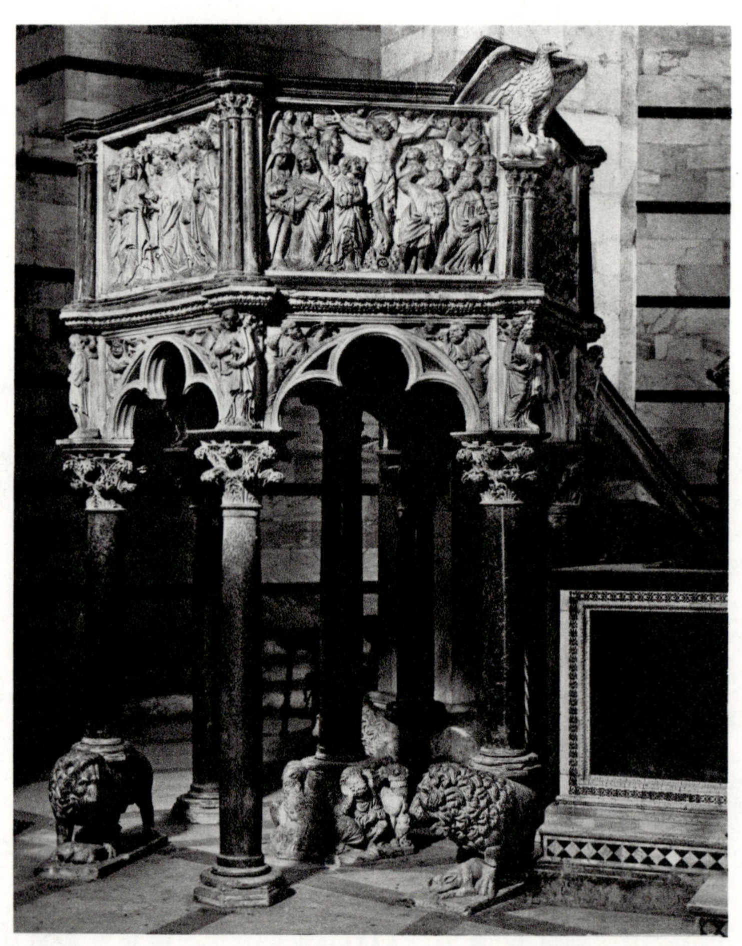

5. NICOLA PISANO. Pulpit. Baptistery, Pisa

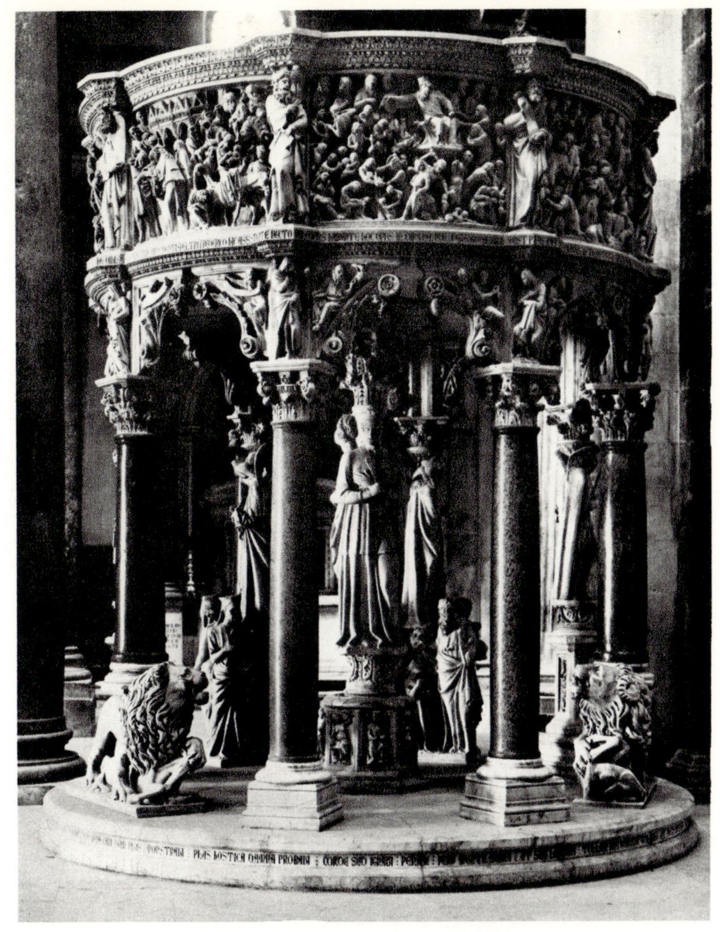

6. GIOVANNI PISANO. Pulpit. Cathedral, Pisa

7. GIOTTO. *The Mocking of Christ*. Arena Chapel, Padua

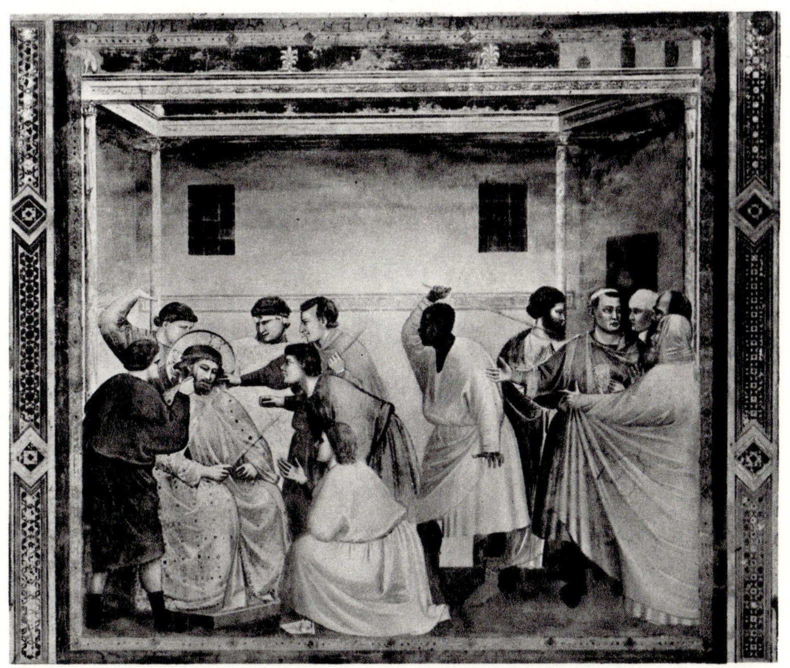

8

FREDERICK HARTT

Thoughts on the Statue and the Niche

The observation that the niche for Michelangelo's statue of Giuliano de' Medici (fig. 1) is "too narrow and too shallow to accommodate him comfortably"[1] states a fairly instinctive modern reaction to a disturbing relationship between enclosure and enclosed, neither of which seems to be fulfilling its proper function. Yet Vasari was under the impression[2] that Michelangelo himself directed the placing of the statues in their niches before leaving Florence forever in 1534. Although no documents corroborate this statement, recent students of Michelangelo's sculpture have universally taken Vasari's remark at face value, and all interpretations of the meaning of the Medici Chapel start from the assumption that the statues of the Dukes are placed more or less as Michelangelo intended them to be seen. After all, even the earliest prophets and sibyls on the Sistine Ceiling (fig. 2) also protrude somewhat beyond their thrones, and the latest, noticeably uncomfortable within their narrow and shallow spaces, overflow them entirely (fig. 3).

It has been correctly noted[3] that High Renaissance statues often protrude from their niches. One could even state somewhat more baldly that they were generally intended to. Raphael's beautiful drawing at Oxford for the statues on the right side of the architectural background of the *School of Athens* (fig. 4) proves this point quite clearly. At the left he has drawn Minerva standing at the very edge of her niche, but with her right hand holding a spear projecting well beyond the frame. At the right he has studied three of the four statues in the niches lining the central nave of his imaginary barrel-vaulted structure (who appear to the left of Minerva in the actual fresco), precalculating the effects of arms, legs, and faces protruding from their enclosures as if their owners were engaged in conversation across the intervening architectural masses.

Apparently Raphael thought that ancient statues did indeed emerge partly from their niches. Although niches containing statues were a standard feature of Roman Imperial architecture, and although we possess many ancient statues known or presumed to have rested at one time in niches, very rarely does an ancient statue still stand in its original niche to give us an insight into how, in classical times, statue and niche were interrelated. A conspicuous example is the statue seated serenely in a square niche in the left side of the Monument of Philo-pappos in Athens, dated 114–16 A.D. (fig. 5), which accommodates it comfortably enough. Plenty of space remains around the statue, yet the right foot and its foot-stool nonetheless slightly overlap the lower edge of the frame, producing a restless effect, as if the figure could move about within its enclosure. Even more striking, the neighboring female bust protrudes sharply from its arched niche. By such means as these the second-century sculptor has established a spatial rapport between his sculptures and the observer.

I know of no example in Italy of an ancient statue still in its original niche. Could Raphael have seen examples now lost to us? We have no way of knowing, save that in all surviving Renaissance drawings which attempt to portray the remains of ancient buildings with any degree of credibility, the niches are empty; the reasonable assumption is that by Renaissance times the statues had long since fallen or been pulled down. It is much more probable that the great masters of the Renaissance recalled a tradition preserved in Roman relief sculpture, whose smaller size permitted relationships of a freedom less likely to have been possible in monumental sculpture on a grand scale. In the little relief from the Tomb of the Haterii near Rome, for example (fig. 6), several statues appear to project from their niches. And in the Asiatic sarcophagus of the second century representing a wedding scene flanked by the Dioscuri, now resting alongside the south portal of the Baptistery of Florence (fig. 7), all the figures emerge vigorously from and at times overlap their richly ornamented enclosures. This sarcophagus was one of several which in the Trecento surrounded the Baptistery, and must have been known two centuries later to both Raphael and Michelangelo.[4]

No one who has ever listened to the lectures of Meyer Schapiro on medieval art can fail to be sensitive to the new relationship between figure and enclosure which, beginning in the early Middle Ages, comes to a climax in the Romanesque period—nor, in fact, to recall many examples. A striking early instance is the beautiful *Archangel Michael,* a leaf of a sixth-century ivory diptych now in the British Museum (fig. 8), the figure seeming to float over the flight of steps—far too small for the enormous feet to rest on—and the right hand carrying the cross-surmounted orb of power and the left holding a staff projecting far beyond the niche, much in the manner of the spear-bearing hand of Raphael's *Minerva.* Equally well known, and typical of scores of seated figures in Romanesque manuscript painting, is the *St. Mark* in an eleventh-century Gospel Book from Corbie, now in the Municipal Library at Amiens (fig. 9). Here the seated Evangelist, in excited dialogue with his symbolic lion shown floating upside down, seems literally to burst from his frame.

With the revival of large-scale sculpture in Italy the dynamic relationship between statue and niche is carried to a new plane of monumental grandeur, and clearly related to the forces of the surrounding architecture. Benedetto Antelami's majestic *King David* on the façade of the cathedral of Fidenza (fig. 10) only appears to be a free-standing statue; in fact, the figure is little more than a high relief, approximating quite closely in all its major projections the original surface of the block, or rather slab, from which it was carved. Extremely important for our theme, however, is the fact that the statue stands, not on the floor of its niche, but on a ledge which emerges well beyond the confines of the niche as, at the apex, do the little domes above the group of the *Presentation in the Temple*. A strong vertical axis is thus established, subordinating the niche to the forces of the figures, and in turn uniting them with the verticality of the façade.

It is this Romanesque tradition from which the statue-niche relationships of the Italian Renaissance sculptors derive. Donatello's epoch-making *St. Mark* of 1411–13 for Orsanmichele (fig. 11) is an early and powerful example.[5] The statue seems to draw backward and upward within the niche, gathering weight and momentum as it moves. Seen from the street below, the major divisions of the body—foot to knee, knee to waist, waist to shoulder—appear to be aligned with the three horizontal divisions of the marble paneling inside the niche. Although the cushion on which the figure stands is flush with the lower moldings of the plinths of the pilasters and colonnettes, it protrudes beyond their socles, as if to prepare a suitable support for the upward movement swinging from knee to hip to shoulder, and for the intense outward glance of the eyes at the center of the niche, just above the cornice.

This essential relationship between figure and niche may go far to explain the insistence of Donatello that the statue be set in place before being judged, in the famous incident recorded by Vasari:[6]

> This figure was wrought by Donatello with such judgment that, when on the ground, its quality not having been recognized by those who had no judgment, it was about not to be permitted by the consuls of that guild to be placed on the building; whereupon Donato asked that they let him put it up, that he wanted to show that, working about it, it would turn out to be another figure, and no longer the same. This done, he screened it for fifteen days, and without otherwise having touched it, he uncovered it, filling everyone with wonder.

We can see what must have disturbed the good consuls if we compare the statue seen from the side without its niche (fig. 12) with the *St. James* (fig. 13) attributed either to Niccolò di Pietro Lamberti or to his son Pietro di Niccolò,[7] probably finished in 1410. In the *St. James* they could see from three sides just what they were getting: a conventional piece of Gothic sculpture in the round, fully finished up to the juncture of the back with the niche—and not a whit advanced beyond the sculpture of Amiens Cathedral in the opening decades of the thirteenth century, in case that mattered. More important to the Linen-weavers and Pedlars must have been the fact that every inch of visible drapery was neatly delineated. Yet to modern eyes these folds are delicately deployed about nothing more than an inert column.

Donatello's statue was doubtless the first Renaissance figure to display the masses and the forces of the human body operating freely in the manner of classical sculpture within the envelope of drapery.[8] It comes as a shock, therefore, to see how the statue would have looked to the consuls of the guild when they could walk around it at eye-level.[9] Seen from a point of view from which Donatello thought it would be forever concealed, the *St. Mark* looks unexpectedly weak and flabby, the masses of the body are far from clear inside the drapery, and—worst of all, doubtless, in the eyes of the Linen-weavers—the surface of the drapery, once one got around toward the back, was left unfinished because Donatello knew that it would be securely hidden by the engaged colonnettes of the niche. In fact, Renaissance statues from Donatello onward rarely have finished backs unless they were intended to be free-standing, and some monumental bronzes are no more than open shells.

The niche for the *St. Mark* may or may not have been designed to please Donatello, but it is likely that his instructions were followed for that of the *St. George,* especially as both plinth and gable are decorated by his own marble reliefs. This niche differs from all others at Orsanmichele in that the simple blocks of *pietra forte* of which the building was constructed are left unrelieved by marble incrustation within the niche (fig. 14). Until the statue's removal to its present position in the Bargello the frame of the niche functioned as a window into indeterminate space, quite in harmony with the two *schiacciato* reliefs, rather than as an enclosing niche.

Donatello's final niche at Orsanmichele (fig. 15), designed by him and executed together with Michelozzo in 1422–25, escapes entirely from the Gothic tradition, a departure made possible by the facts that the niche was commissioned by the all-powerful Parte Guelfa, that it was centralized on the short side of the building facing the central Corso degli Adimari (the present Via dei Calzaioli), and that the statue was completely gilded. Obviously Donatello, in command from the start, equilibrated his figure of St. Louis of Toulouse with the major elements and proportions of the Brunelleschian niche within which it seems to tower because it is so much taller than the flanking Ionic columns. The figure is placed so that its face corresponds with the level of the blank frieze. The hanging fold of the saint's cope and the knuckles of his left hand are at the level of the apex of the convex fluting of the pilasters, exactly one-third the height of the pilasters including capitals. The second third is marked by the molding between architecture and frieze, which coincides with the saint's mouth. The proportions of the Corinthian capitals are roughly equal to those of the saint's face.[10]

It is unnecessary to go into such detail with the niches by Nanni di Banco and by Ghiberti, both undoubtedly influenced by Donatello although quite individual in the ways in which they interpreted the relation of statue to niche. Nanni's *Four Crowned Martyrs* (fig. 16), although protected like Donatello's *St. George* by the blessing figure of the Lord in the gable, are—in keeping with Nanni's overriding concern with mass and enclosure rather than perspective and atmosphere—enshrined in the pregnant space of their niche as in a draped sanctuary. How little sense the niche and the enclosed statues make apart from each other is easily demonstrated by the accompanying photographs (figs. 17, 18, 19): the empty niche has drapery in the background, carried out only where it would be visible between or above the figures; one separate statue and two linked ones show movements which, without those of the accompanying figures and the drapery at sides and back, are clumsy, weak, and ineffectual. Yet together, confronted on their crescent-shaped base—the direction of their heads toward each other reinforced by the beautifully proportioned cusps of the surmounting arch, their drapery echoed and abutted by the hangings so opulently displayed on the flanking pilasters—they form one of the grandest compositions of the Early Renaissance, which must have provided the nucleus for Masaccio's *Tribute Money*.[11]

Ghiberti's feelings about the interrelation of statue and niche are embodied in the presentation drawing in the Louvre (fig. 20) by an assistant[12] for the *St. Stephen,* whose head is so carefully aligned with the frieze of the niche that its dark stripe passes behind his eyes. In time the layer of the frieze has come to show through the face painted over it, giving the unintended effect of a robber's mask.

Photographs of the *St. Matthew* of 1419–22 without its niche, of the niche without the statue, and of the statue in its proper place (figs. 21, 22, 23) show how exquisitely this most classicistic of Ghiberti's sculptures in the round was equilibrated with its surrounding elements and how much it loses without them. First of all it may well be suspected that Ghiberti would have preferred at this point to design a round-headed niche, in keeping with his newly espoused Renaissance principles and with the round arches that appear throughout the architecture in his relief sculpture.[13] Ghiberti's two niches are roughly coeval with the earliest Renaissance buildings of Florence, Brunelleschi's Barbadori Chapel and Sagrestia Vecchia started in 1418, and Loggia degli Innocenti and Palazzo di Parte Guelfa in 1419, all under conspicuous construction at the moment. They also bracket in time the fully Renaissance niche by Donatello and Michelozzo for the *St. Louis of Toulouse.* The compromise between pointed arch and Corinthian pilasters may have been offered by the sculptor to harmonize with the adjacent Gothic niches, or it may have been forced upon him by the guilds in the interest of conformity. In any event, every line of the drapery of *St. Matthew,* classical orator though he is universally acknowledged to be, is calculated to harmonize with the taut beauty of these still-Gothic curves, just as much as with the elegance of the slender Corinthian pilasters, and indeed to reconcile these apparent opposites with each other.

The shapes of the arch are repeated in the folds playing about the torso, just as the hanging folds are scaled to the fluting of the shell, on the pilasters, and on the paneling of the jambs. The half-springy, half-relaxed stance of the figure is so proportioned within the niche as to produce a beautiful ascending rhythm of alternating lighted and shadowed spaces. The foliate cusps harmonize with the curly locks of St. Matthew's hair. Even the handsome statuettes serving as acroteria for the gable—seldom mentioned but worthy of study—are proportioned and weighted to go with the *St. Matthew.* Beautiful as the figure is, its shapes seem curiously empty when stripped of the rich linear, formal, and tonal fabric of the interacting niche which echoes and sustains them. (Glancing back at the empty niche, it may be noted how even the harmonious and gentle Ghiberti placed the base of his statue so that it protrudes well beyond the upper moldings of the bases of the flanking colonnettes and pilasters, and therefore violates the plane established by the frame.)

Few will complain that Donatello's *Prophets* were not replaced in their niches on the Campanile after World War II (why are such protective measures in Florence always taken so late?), but it must be admitted that something vital has been lost now that the *Zuccone,* for example (figs. 24, 25), no longer stands silhouetted in its rose marble space, its rawboned, angular forms compressed by the narrow Gothic niche, the white mass of its bald head asserting itself against the narrow trefoil arches. Exhibited hardly above eye-level in the Opera del Duomo, the *Zuccone* and its companions are still great statues, but we miss the element of conflict between man and his surroundings that was an essential part of Donatello's view of human existence—indeed that of the embattled Republic whose struggles for survival he symbolized in a series of heroic statues.

In the later Quattrocento the dynamic, sometimes dialectic, equilibrium between statue and niche is relaxed, as in Verrocchio's *Doubting Thomas* (fig. 26), placed in 1483 in the niche from which Donatello's *St. Louis* had, by an odd trick of fate, been recently evicted. In fact, as the expanded group spills over the outer and lower edges of the niche, along with the dissipation of compression there goes a dissolution of mass itself into innumerable pockets and facets of substance, light, and shadow. How relief-like the group has now become may be seen in the figure of St. Thomas alone, taken from half-right, so shallow that it is unable either physically or aesthetically to stand by itself (fig. 27). The culmination of this dispersive tendency in the later Quattrocento appears in the riotous abandon of simulated statuary and reliefs in the backgrounds of paintings by Botticelli and Filippino Lippi—the *Calumny of Apelles* (fig. 28), for example—whose sculptural decorations have well-nigh escaped from their architectural enclosures. (The helmeted figure at the center, incidentally, gives us a suggestion as to how Donatello's *St. George* originally looked, with his great sword jutting out above the passersby in the street.)

After this brief glimpse of the sculptural and pictorial tradition from which Michelangelo comes, we may return to the Medici Chapel and its statues. The two *Capitani* now appear somewhat less uncomfortable in their niches—or rather their discomfort seems more acceptable in that it derives from a millennium and a half during which the statue and its niche were considered to be in a state of dynamic, sometimes even hostile, interaction, especially intense in the artistic generations immediately preceding Michelangelo's own. Whichever of the various recent interpretations of the meaning of the Chapel may eventually gain common acceptance, it cannot have been foreign to Michelangelo's understanding of the purpose of the seated statues, as embodiments of the triumph of the departed Dukes over the defeated Times of Day, to depict the figures as emerging forcefully from their niches. The great sculptor-architect, who invariably defined the settings down to the tiniest detail before completing the statues to go in them, must have intended the liberation of the *Capitani* to contrast visibly with the imprisonment of the *capitelli* in the corners of the Chapel (fig. 29).

NOTES

1   H. W. Janson, *History of Art,* New York, 1969, p. 361.

2   Giorgio Vasari, *Le vite de' più eccellenti Pittori, Scultori ed Architetti,* Florence, 1568 (Life of Montorsoli), ed. G. Milanesi, Florence, 1878–85, VI, p. 634.

3   John Pope-Hennessy, *Italian High Renaissance and Baroque Sculpture,* London, 1963, I, p. 21.

4   *Firenze e dintorni, Guida d'Italia del Touring Club Italiano,* Milan, 1950, p. 72.

5   H. W. Janson has published most revealing photographs of Donatello's *St. John* taken from the side (*The Sculpture of Donatello,* Princeton, 1957, I, pls. 12a, 12b), but they do not concern our theme directly since the niche in which the statue was placed no longer exists.

6   *Op. cit.,* II, p. 403.

7   Charles Seymour, Jr., *Sculpture in Italy 1400 to 1500,* Baltimore, 1966, p. 60.

8   As pointed out by Janson in a justly celebrated passage of art-historical analysis, *op. cit.,* p. 19.

9   This idea occurred to me only when the appropriate passage of my *Donatello, Prophet of Modern Vision,* New York, 1973, was already in page proof and no further alteration was possible. It does not change but rather reinforces and amplifies my conclusion that Donatello had calculated the optical distortions inevitable when his statue was seen from the street below, and that he had insisted that it be elevated to its final destination before being judged so as to prove to himself that the proportions would indeed look right once it was in place.

10   Also, the plinth without its supporting corbels equals the width of the entablature; with corbels, the height of the pediment. A line drawn tangent to the inner volutes of both Ionic and Corinthian capitals passes through the center of the roundel in the base of the niche.

11   See Hartt, *History of Italian Renaissance Art,* New York, 1969, p. 159.

12   See Richard Krautheimer, *Lorenzo Ghiberti,* Princeton, 1956, p. 97, n. 19, with bibliography, including discussion of Berenson's opinion (*Drawings of the Florentine Painters,* Chicago, 1938, I, p. 327, note 1; II, p. 310, no. 2391B) that the drawing is neither by Ghiberti nor for the *St. Stephen,* but "has much more affinity with Nanni di Banco's Philip . . . and may be a sketch for it by Rossello di Jacopo Franchi." It is hard to disagree with Krautheimer, in view of the apparently original inscription in Gothic gold lettering on the base: SCS STEFANUS MAR. On the other hand the proportions of the figure and the morphology of both face and drapery suggest that Berenson's tentative attribution to Rossello is correct. The most reasonable solution may well be, as Krautheimer proposes, that Rossello was called in by Ghiberti to do the presentation drawing.

13   With only two exceptions: the Gothic tracery (still enclosed by round-arched windows) in the *Last Supper* on the North Doors of the Baptistery; and the pointed arches in the side-aisles of the Temple in the *Marriage of Solomon and the Queen of Sheba* on the Gates of Paradise, a possible reference to the partly Gothic, partly Renaissance Cathedral of Florence.

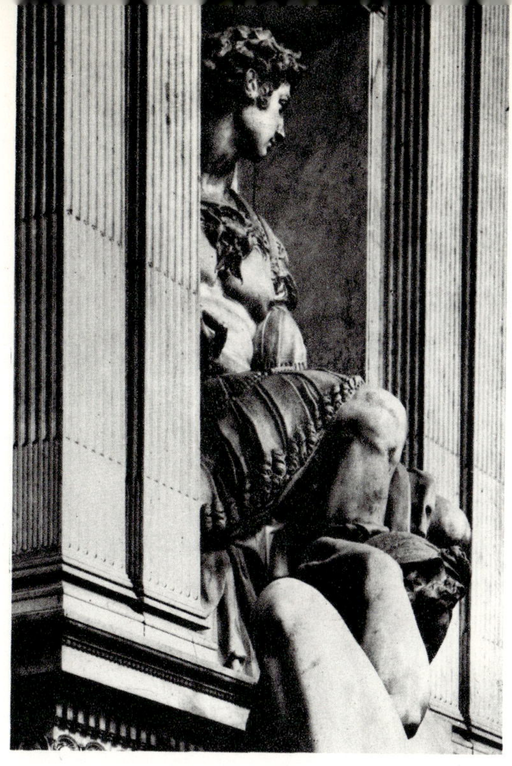

1.   MICHELANGELO.
Tomb of Giuliano de' Medici.
San Lorenzo, Florence

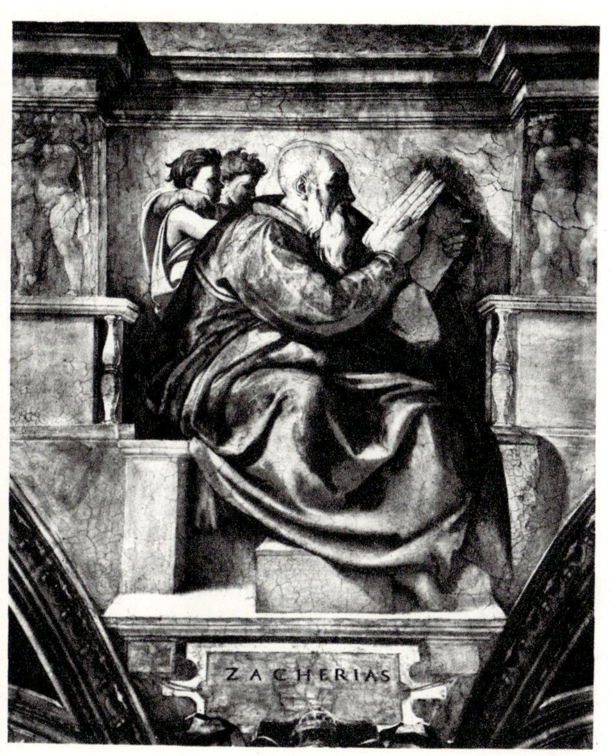

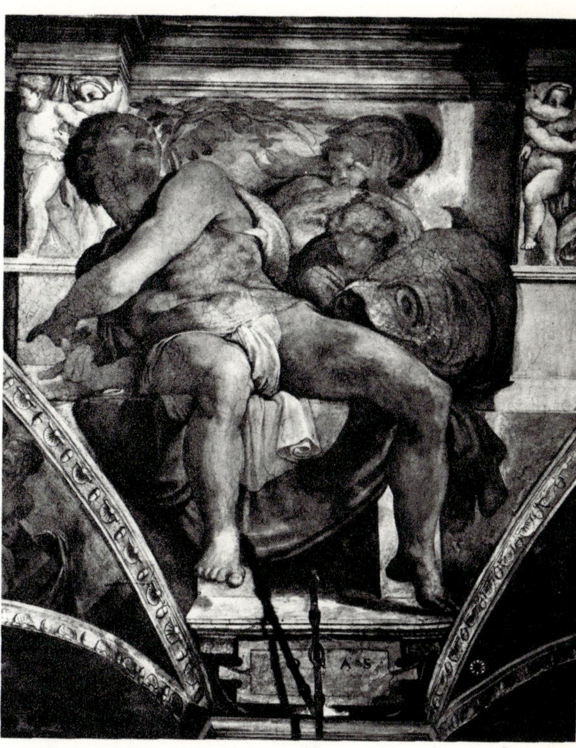

2.   MICHELANGELO. *The Prophet Zachariah.* Sistine Chapel, Vatican

3.   MICHELANGELO. *The Prophet Jonah.* Sistine Chapel, Vatican

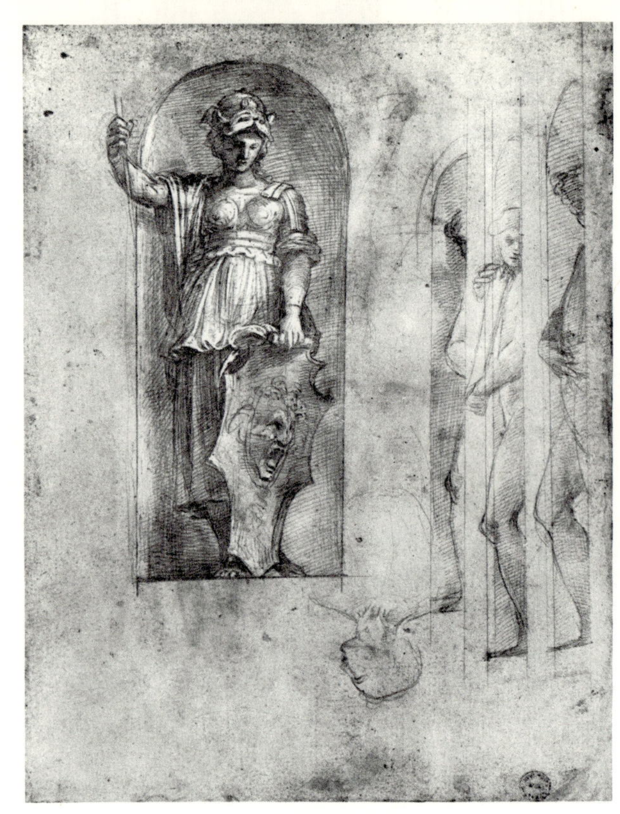

4. RAPHAEL.
Studies of Minerva and
other statues for
the *School of Athens*.
Ashmolean Museum, Oxford

5. Monument of Philopappos. 114–116 A.D. Athens

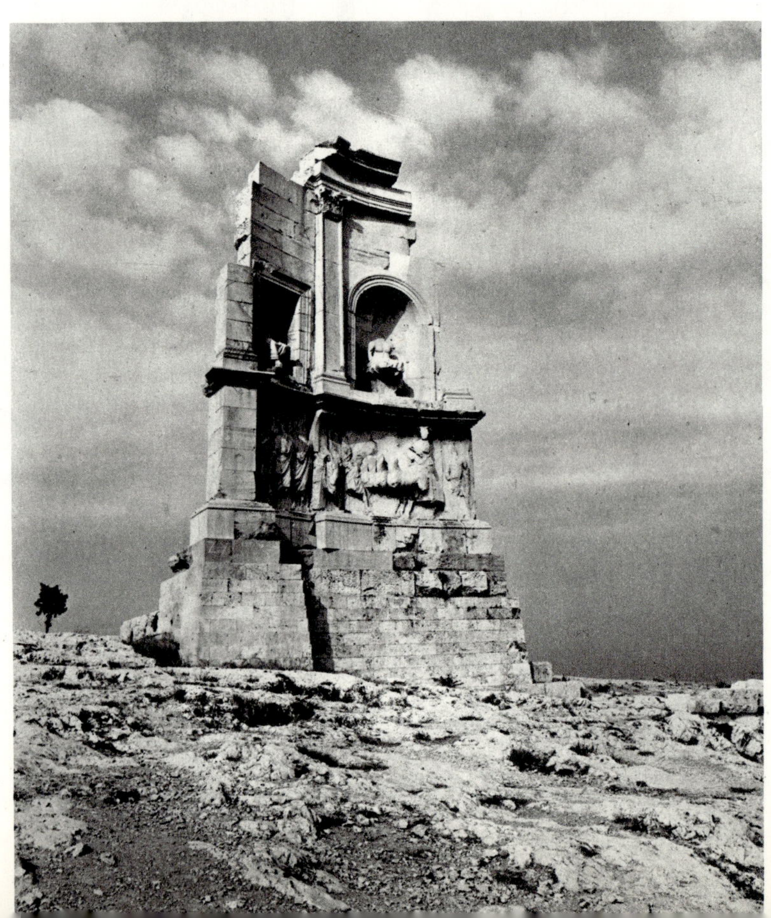

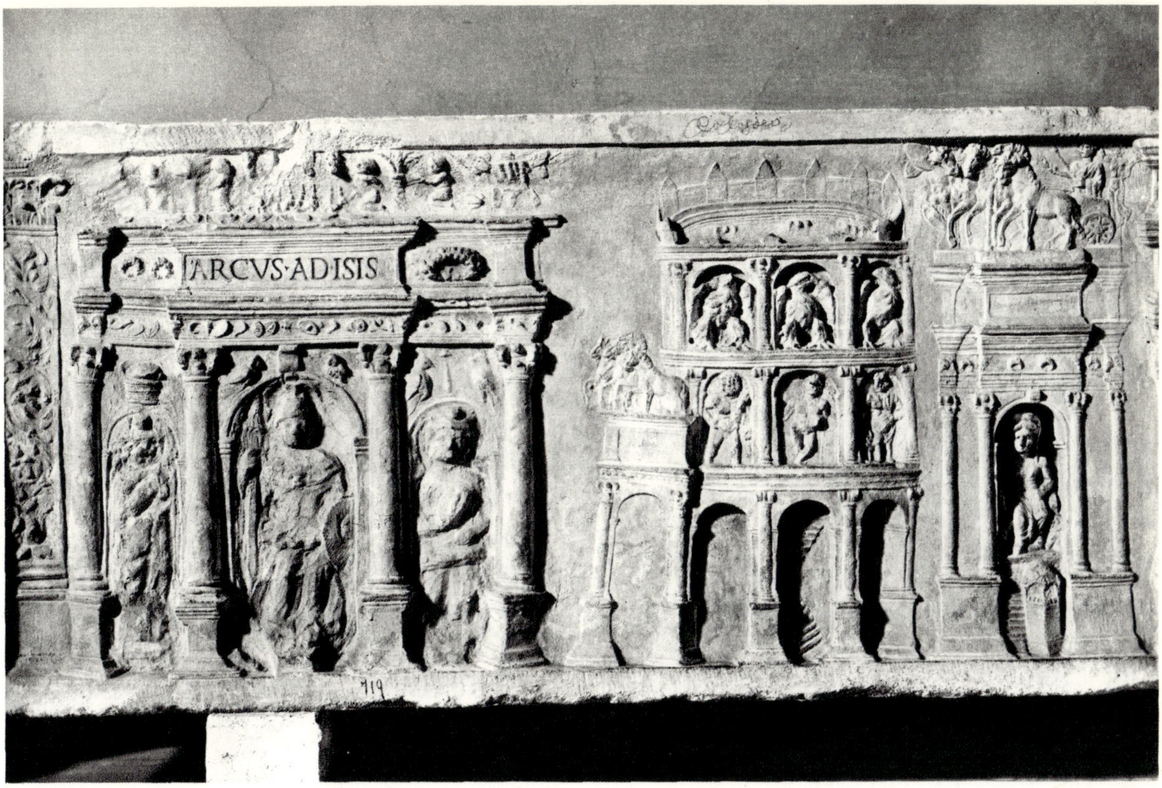

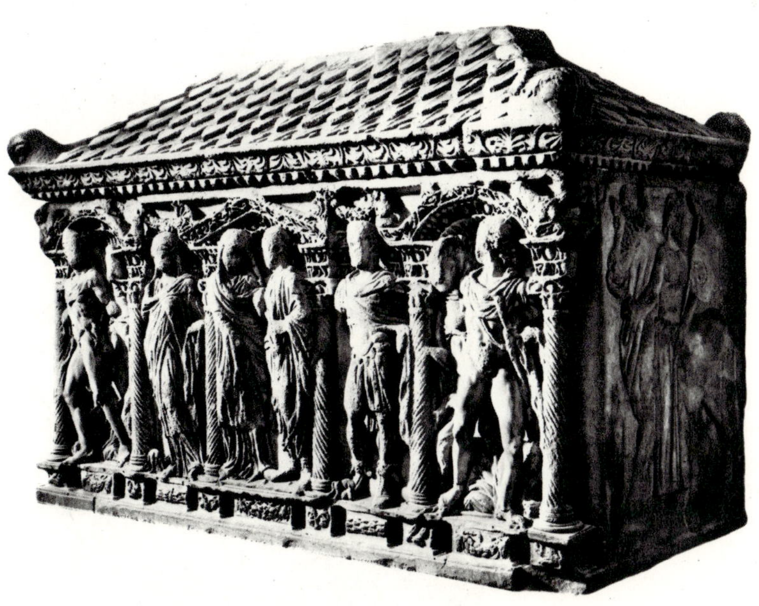

6.   Relief from the Tomb of the Haterii. Late 1st–early 2nd century A.D.
Lateran Museums, Rome

7.   Asiatic sarcophagus showing wedding scene. Second century.
Baptistery, Florence

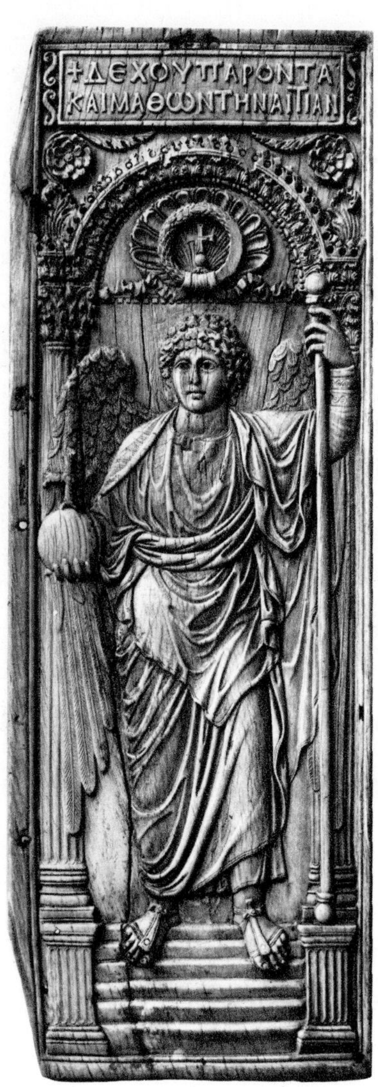

9. *St. Mark.*
From a Gospel Book
produced at Corbie,
c. 1020–50.
Municipal Library, Amiens

8. *The Archangel Michael.*
Leaf of an ivory diptych, early 6th century.
British Museum

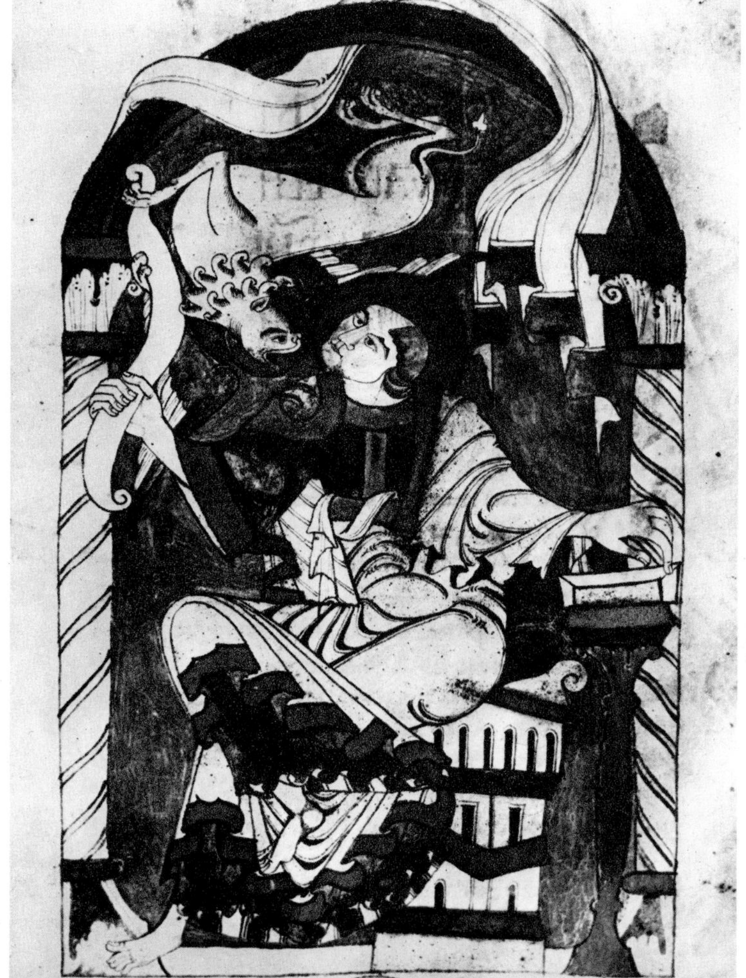

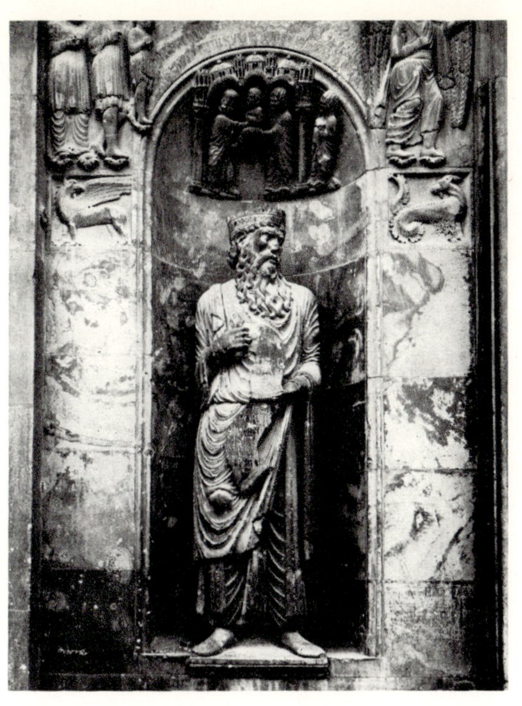

10. BENEDETTO ANTELAMI.
King David. c. 1180–90.
West façade, Cathedral, Fidenza

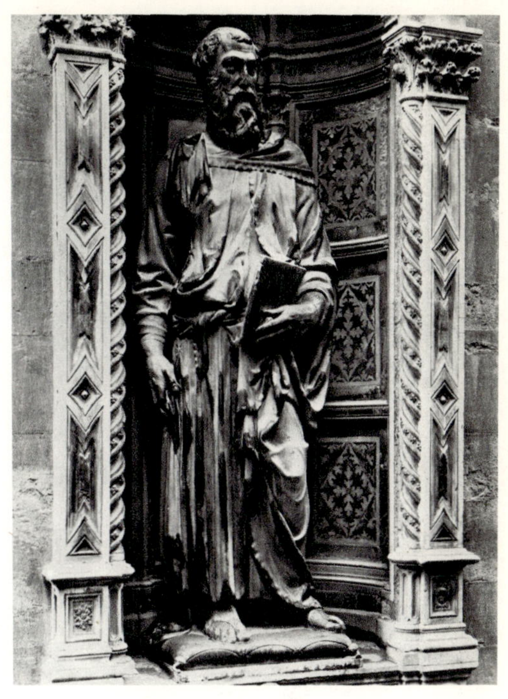

11. DONATELLO. *St. Mark.* 1411–13.
Orsanmichele, Florence

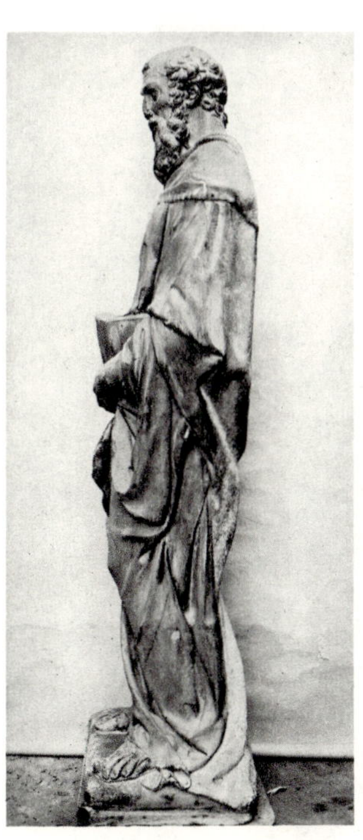

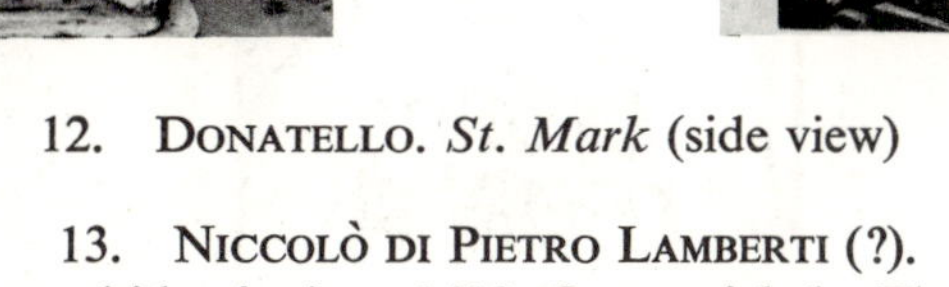

12. DONATELLO. *St. Mark* (side view)

13. NICCOLÒ DI PIETRO LAMBERTI (?).
St. James (side view). c. 1410. Orsanmichele, Florence

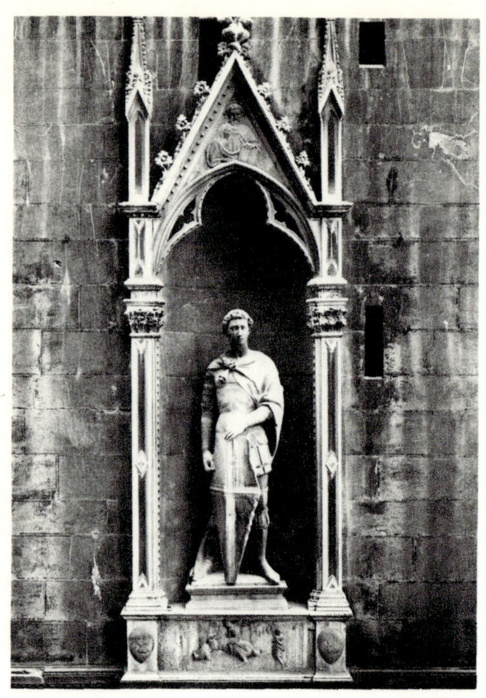

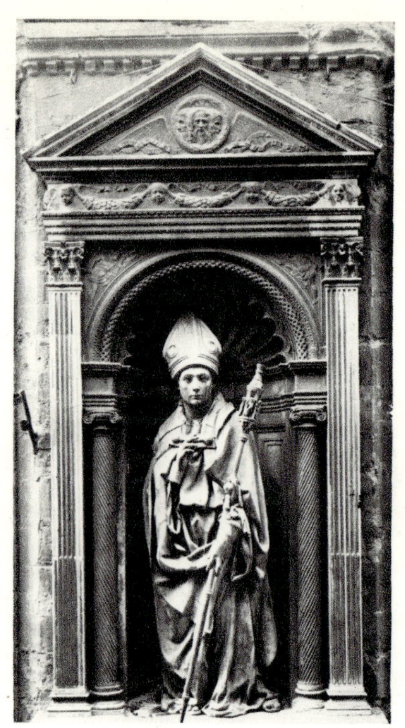

14.   DONATELLO. *St. George,* in original niche. 1416.
Orsanmichele, Florence

15.   DONATELLO. *St. Louis of Toulouse,* in original niche.
1422–25. Orsanmichele, Florence

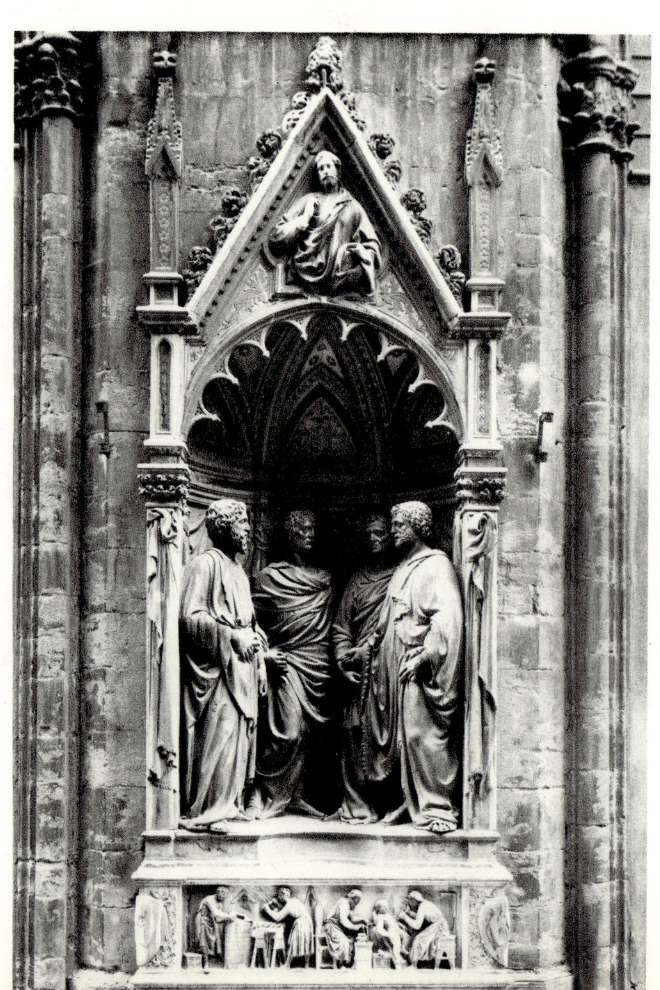

16.   NANNI DI BANCO.
Four Crowned Martyrs,
in niche. c. 1413.
Orsanmichele, Florence

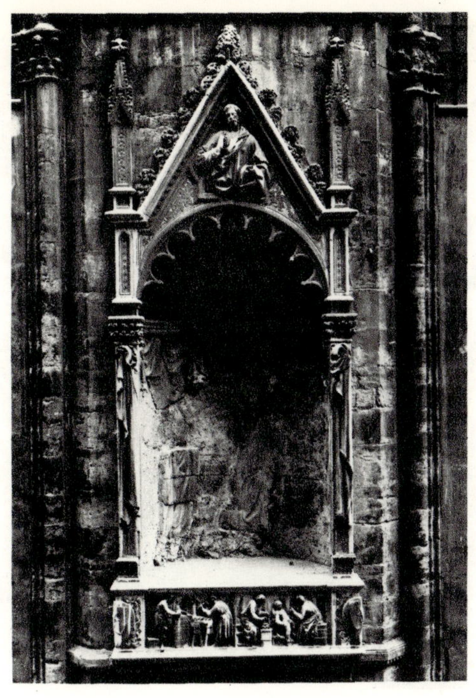

17. NANNI DI BANCO. Niche for *Four Crowned Martyrs*

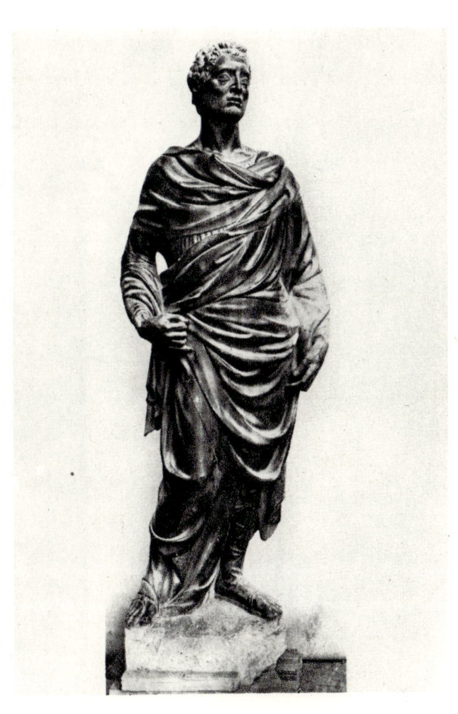

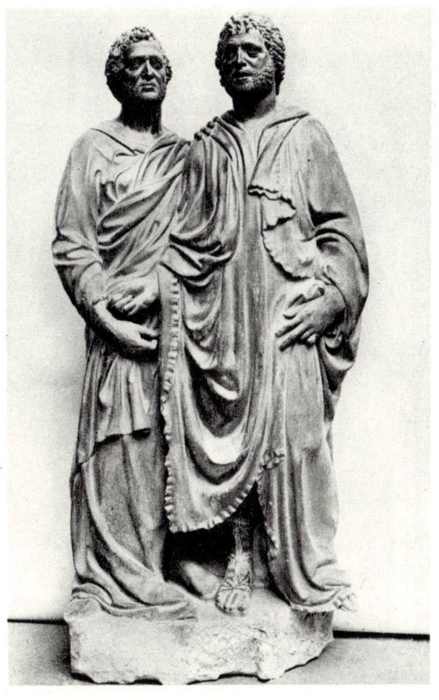

18. NANNI DI BANCO. One of *Four Crowned Martyrs*

19. NANNI DI BANCO. Two of *Four Crowned Martyrs*

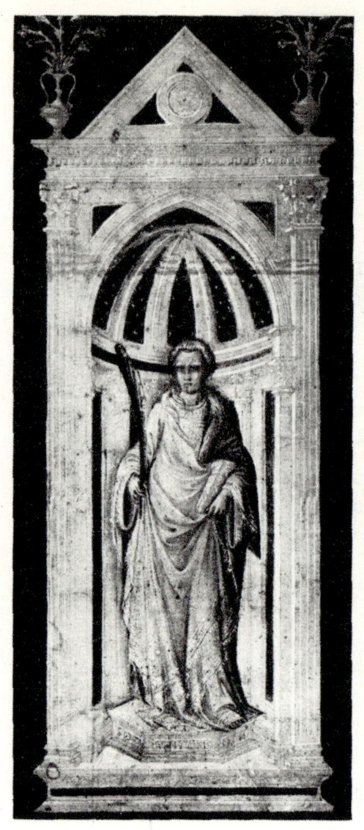 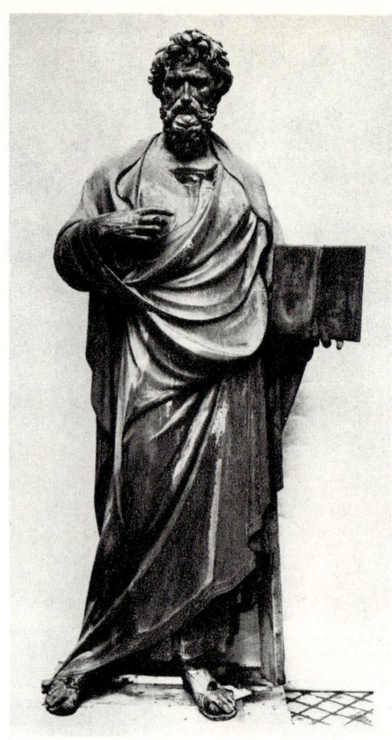

20.   LORENZO GHIBERTI (workshop). Presentation drawing for *St. Stephen*. c. 1426. Cabinet des Dessins, The Louvre, Paris

21.   LORENZO GHIBERTI. *St. Matthew*. 1419–22. Orsanmichele, Florence

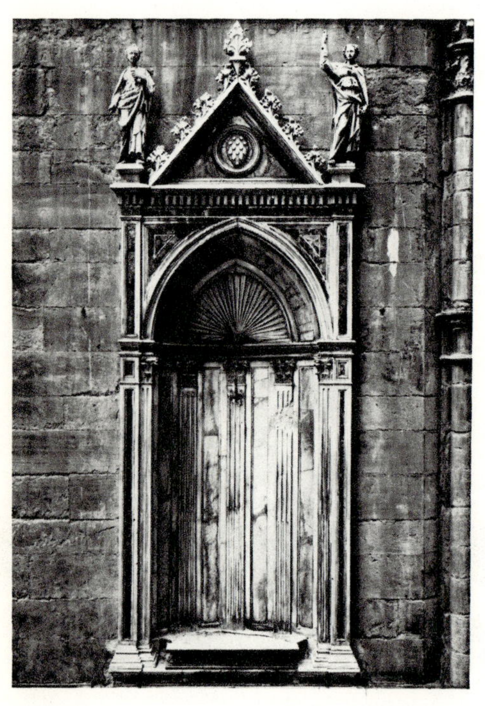 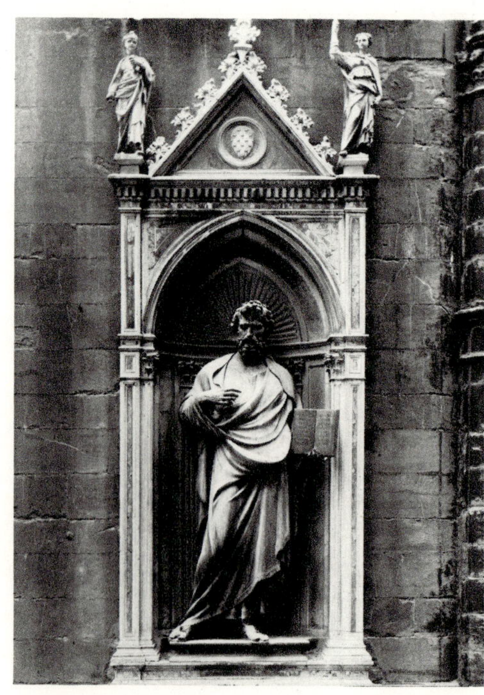

22.   LORENZO GHIBERTI. Niche for *St. Matthew*

23.   LORENZO GHIBERTI. *St. Matthew,* in niche

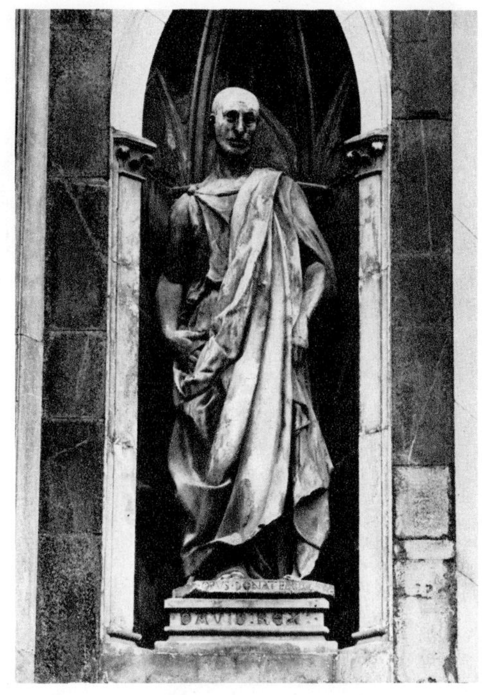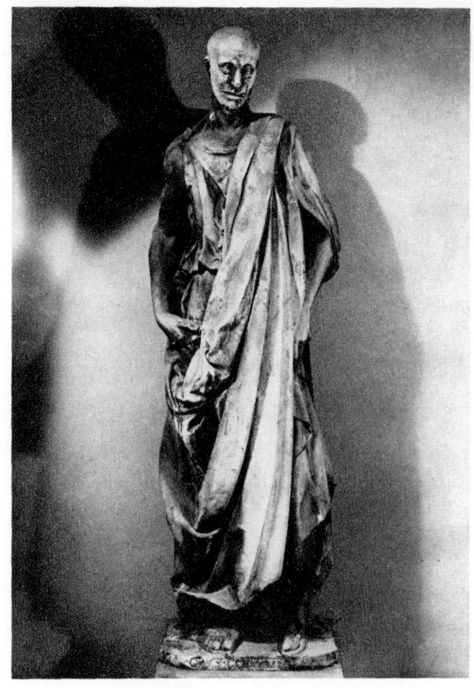

24.   DONATELLO. *Zuccone,* in niche. 1423–25. Campanile del Duomo, Florence

25.   DONATELLO. *Zuccone.* Museo dell'Opera del Duomo, Florence

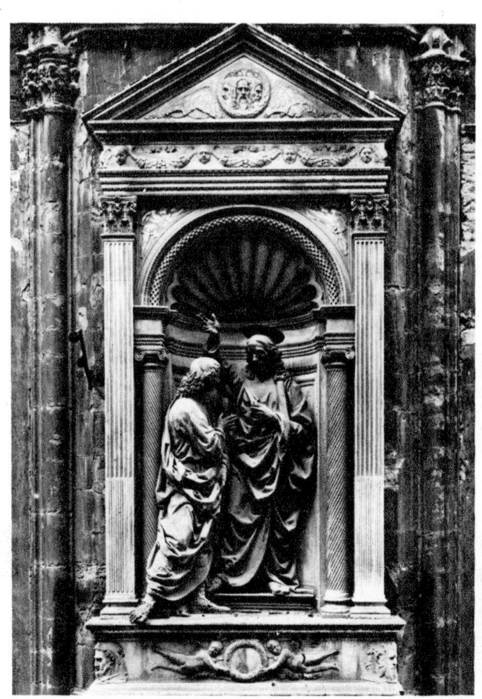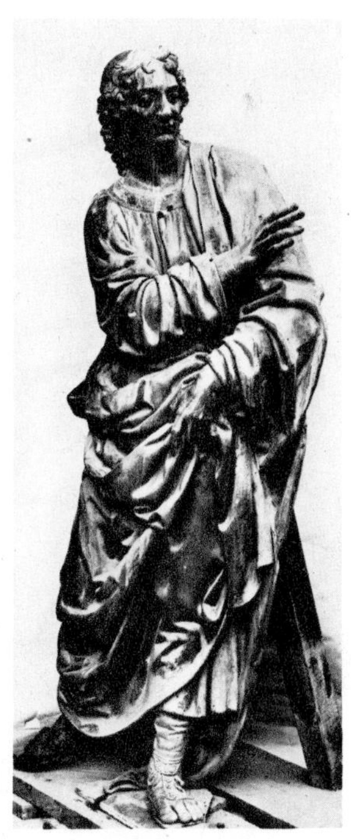

26.   VERROCCHIO. *Doubting Thomas,* in niche. 1483. Orsanmichele, Florence

27.   VERROCCHIO. *Doubting Thomas.* Detail

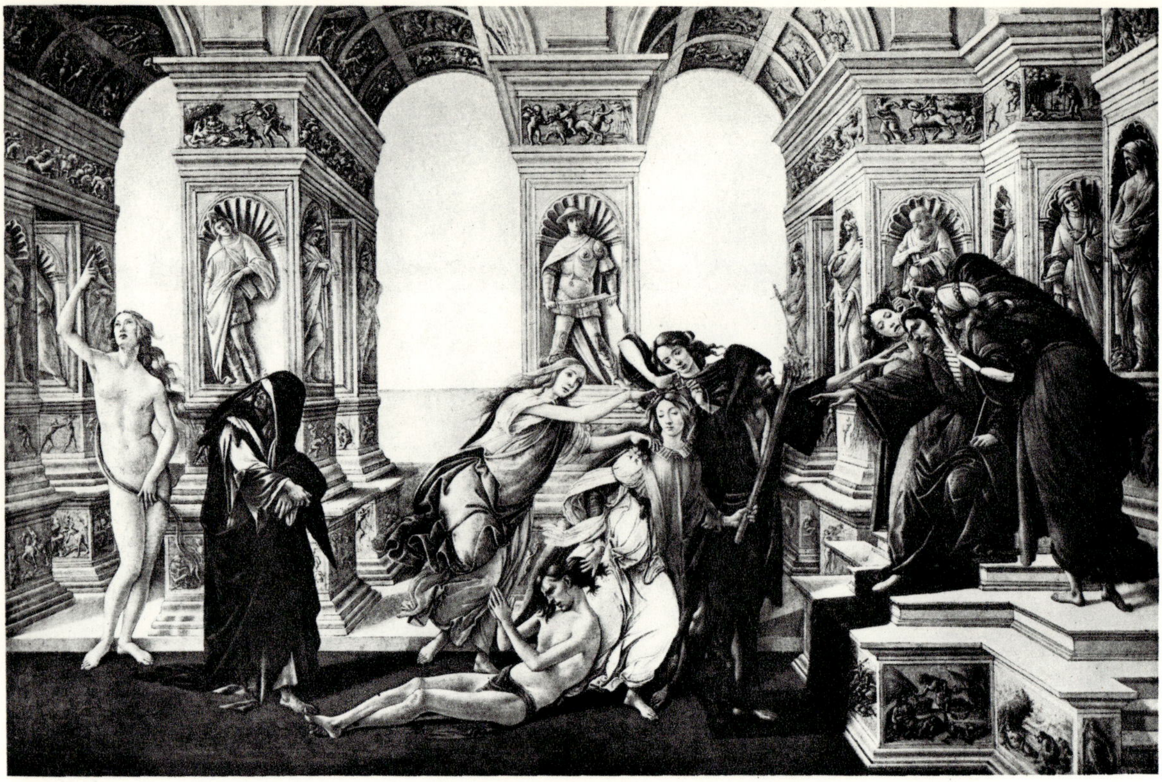

28.   BOTTICELLI. *Calumny of Apelles*. 1497–98(?). Uffizi, Florence

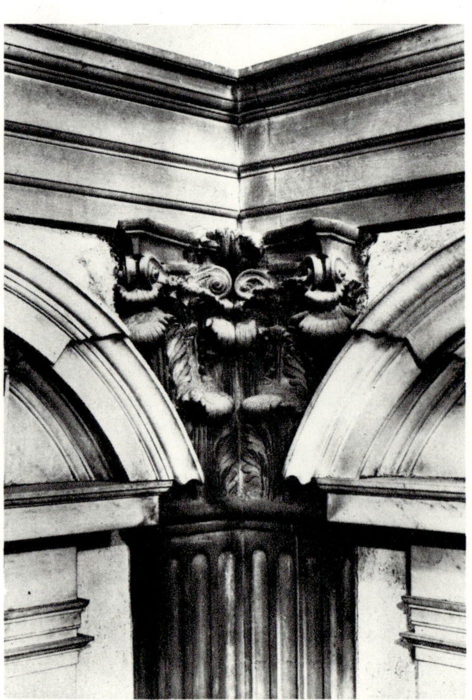

29.   MICHELANGELO.
Medici Chapel, 1524–34.
Corner pilaster capital

9

JULIUS S. HELD

Gravity and Art

The paper offered here to the memory of Milton Fox is the text of a lecture given its final shape about fifteen years ago, when flight beyond the earth's gravitational field was just beginning. The sentiment voiced in the last sentence—not surprisingly expressed by many others since—has not lost its sting, even though man's travels in outer space have succeeded beyond anything one could have expected in the late 1950s.

Since echoes of that old lecture have found their way into print (see "Giotto e il suo tempo," *Atti del Congresso Internazionale,* Rome, 1971, p. 368), I decided to submit it now unchanged to a still larger audience, this despite my suspicion that there are ramifications of the problem of which I am unaware, and that there probably is much literature in other areas—aesthetics, psychology, and linguistics —with which I am unfamiliar. At any rate, it is precisely the "non-historical" and somewhat speculative nature of the paper that might justify its inclusion in a volume dedicated to a man whose own activity was guided more by aesthetic sensibility and free-ranging associations than by a strictly historical method.

As a lecture, this text was naturally accompanied by slides. They were often chosen at random and others might have served as well. In fact, it is quite possible that the central idea presented here comes through with more impact if the reader is not diverted by hunting for a particular illustration.

One of the most hackneyed formulas about art maintains that it is a kind of language. The teaching of art history, indeed, has often been made palatable to faculty committees and school administrations on the grounds that art is an *international* language. Unfortunately, when it comes to art, a great many people seem to be poor linguists, and modern art, particularly, appears to be a rather esoteric idiom.

Modern art, indeed, has served to make us aware of the differences between art and language. A real language uses conventional sounds and symbols, and organizes them into intelligible sequences. When we say "tree" or "railroad" or "hummingbird" we conjure up, with a few simple sounds, images and associations that are differently charged for each of us but nevertheless adequate for the normal needs of communication. The principle of language, in other words, is an agreement among a large number of people to associate more or less definite meanings with more or less articulated sounds or sequences of sounds. There have been times when art created visual signs or symbols that were generally accepted and understood, and little changed over hundreds or even thousands of years. Yet in art we are now committed to look for, and to admire, not the conventional but the personal, not the traditional but the unique, not the familiar but the novel. Thus, if we were to insist on the formula that calls art a language, we would also have to admit that each artist tries to make up a language of his own, surely not a practical device for having an intelligent conversation.

The situation, however, is perhaps not as bad as it seems. It is clear, first of all, that language itself is not an arbitrary creation (artificial languages have never made real progress), but that language grows out of and incorporates a great many phonetic elements from pre-logical conditions of our nature. Spoken language, furthermore, makes use of additional elements, such as pitch, inflection, volume, gesture, and physiognomic expression, most of which are universally understood. If we want to put a baby to sleep, we do not yell at him, even if we may sometimes feel like doing so. Although some people may act differently, we generally raise our voices when we are angry, we speak softly and tenderly when we are in love, and we are more precise and grammatical on the lecture platform than at the breakfast table.

It is evident that similar formal elements are used in art for the sake of communication of expression. In a work of art light and dark, color combinations, various compositional patterns, and not least, the physiognomic elements in the widest sense of the word (not only facial expression) convey to us specific meanings. Some of these devices are based on fundamental aspects of life and human behavior. Others are associated with specific cultural patterns which we understand either because they are still ours or because we have learned to understand them through a study of the history of human civilization.

What I mean by these cultural associations, and how the same objects can mean something very different to a being unfamiliar with them, can be illustrated by the following incident. In the entrance hall of a building in Barnard College there stood a bronze figure (now placed outside) of a young woman in a short skirt who is running with a burning torch in her outstretched hand, apparently ready to pass it on to a partner in a torch relay race. I can describe the work in this particular way because I am familiar with Greek traditions in sports and costume and with the survival of some of these traditions in an annual athletic contest, the so-called Greek Games of Barnard College. Some time ago I walked into that corridor accompanied by my dog. When *he* saw the figure, he growled, and even barked at it, his hair bristling in intense excitement; after we had left the building, he still turned around apprehensively, ready to defend himself. I cannot explain his reaction otherwise than by assuming that what *he* saw was a very big figure with a stick in its hand, whose lunging pose threatened him with an imminent attack. The dog's reaction was emotionally charged because the work of art appealed to a sphere of experience that is not unfamiliar to dogdom. We may ask whether my more or less indifferent acceptance of the correct or at least intended meaning of the piece was as adequate a reaction as the intense emotion of the dog—which was actually based on a misapprehension.

Art historians generally pay little attention to fundamental reactions, like those of my dog, though they admit their existence. Panofsky, in *Meaning in the Visual Arts,* distinguishes three levels of meaning in a work of art, the first and lowest of which he calls the primary, or natural, subject matter. The identification of that subject matter he somewhat derisively calls pre-iconographic description and pseudo-formal analysis. As he puts it, "everybody can recognize the shape and behavior of human beings, animals, and plants, and everybody can tell an angry face from a jovial one."

Yet there are scholars to whom precisely this level of experience, even in a work of art, is full of problems and mystery. It is primarily writers on aesthetics and the psychology of perception who have investigated Panofsky's first level of meaning. In doing so they have not overlooked the problem I plan to examine here, the reflection in art of our attitude toward physical gravity. René Huyghe, for instance, has made some observations along similar lines. Yet no one, I believe, has explored the question in all possible directions, and this essay, too, is only an outline of what might be further elaborated in a systematic study.

How gravity actually functions even the physicists do not know, but its effects were formulated into a law by Isaac Newton: any two bodies in the universe attract each other with a force which varies directly as the product of their masses, and inversely as the square of the distance between them. While there are in consequence all sorts of gravitational fields around us, and while there is even a center of gravity in every one of us, there is only one center of gravity of overriding importance for our lives, that of the earth. It is one of the basic conditions of all human existence. If the earth's attraction did not hold us down, we would simply not be here. Theoretically, we should be as grateful to the earth's gravitation as we are to the light of the sun that makes things grow and sustains our lives as well.

Actually, if we examine the question more thoroughly, we see that the contrary is true. Subconsciously, man is resentful of the gravitational pull. Although this is by no means unknown—and I might quote Robert Frost's last poem, where one parenthetical (and surely punning) line reads, "Our gravity has been our major curse"—I still believe that the importance of this fact has not been sufficiently recognized. Our relationship to this unseen, unknown, but ever-present power is profoundly charged with emotion. Man's life on earth, though conditioned by, and adapted to, gravity, is actually a constant battle against it. It is a battle we wage from the moment we are born, when we stretch out our arms, kick our legs, and finally raise up our bodies. The battle is carried on daily until we are too tired. It is recessed while we sleep and gather strength to renew the fight the next morning. There are times of retreat, for instance, while we are sick. Then our weight is felt heavily, and we have moments when we are too weary to go on. But on we go, as long as we live, until the end—and it *is* a bitter one—for no matter how gallantly we struggle, it is a tragic and hopeless task. As we get older our bodies bend downward, like wilting flowers. Death means the ultimate victory of the forces of gravity. In death we are overcome by its pull, and our burial is the fitting recognition of this defeat. In burial, we are finally given back to the earth that has coveted us so long. It is perhaps the expression of a desire to snatch a last victory from defeat that some religions insist on the burning of the body so that it may symbolically rise again in the flames. (We may also quote Cassirer's *Essay on Man,* which stresses that "myth and primitive . . . religion . . . deny the very possibility of death. In a certain sense the whole of mythological thought may be interpreted as a constant and obstinate negation of the phenomenon of death.")

Our fear of death, of annihilation, determines our attitude to the subconsciously felt force of gravitation. By the same token, man's upright walk is a mark of his defiance of gravity. Plato realized this unique quality in man when he defined him as a featherless biped, since he saw that, except for birds (or pseudobirds, like the ostrich), there is no other animal that tries to walk on two legs. His definition was already ridiculed in antiquity, when Diogenes produced a plucked rooster, saying "This is Platonic man." Yet walking upright is not the only way for man to express his scorn of gravity. When we watch with bated breath the performance of a tight-rope walker, we do not admire his sense of balance. Rather, we are elated because he gives us the illusion of a triumph, even if precarious and momentary, that he is gaining over the sinister pull of gravity. Man's eternal desire to fly, wishfully fulfilled in occasional dreams, is another expression of this desire to be unhampered by gravity. Held down by gravity's pull, we yearn to escape from it. The myth of Daedalus and Icarus characteristically combines both the motifs of flight and of ultimate defeat. It is precisely the awareness of the futility of all previous efforts of the kind that made the introduction of true flying machines such an exhilarating experience. And it seems not impossible that the worship of the phallus, so common in primitive societies, has been aided by the realization that in the exercise of its most vital function, the male member also seems to overcome the pull of gravity. (See S. Freud, *The Interpretation of Dreams,* Modern Library Edition, p. 266, with reference to the "winged phalli of the ancients.")

Since gravity is manifested in the directions of up and down, the whole emotional load that is associated with gravity is also projected into these directions. This is easiest to grasp in the metaphors of language. The direction of "down" is charged negatively: we are *down*hearted, *down*trodden, or plain *down,* not to say down and out. We turn *down* an offer, and no more telling gesture of doom has ever been invented than the "thumbs down" of the Roman Circus. Conversely, when we feel great we are *up*lifted, *up* to a thing, *up* to somebody's tricks, or we have the *upper* hand, and while, unfortunately, we may on occasion be hard-up, we are really in bad shape only when we break down. Some people look *down* on inferiors, but try to keep *up* with the Joneses. Words formed with the Latin prefixes *sub* and *super* have similarly opposed associations, such as sub-human, sub-standard, and on the other hand the hucksters' awful "superfine." (And is there not somehow a certain contradiction in the fact that a man whom we call *super* often lives in the basement?)

Endless are the associations which we make with the concepts of high and low, but almost invariably things high are good and desirable, while those low are not. Admiration (if not also envy) shaped the expression of *high* society, contempt that of the *lower* classes. We speak of *high* ideals and of *low* opinions, of *high* spirits and a *low* morale, of a *high* court and a *low* comedy. (Synonyms of low, characteristically, are abject, mean, degraded, coarse, vulgar.) In allegories of Hercules at the Crossroads, Virtue points at a narrow road up a steep mountain, while Vice invites the hero to take the easy road downhill. In a chart Professor Gombrich published in his *Meditations on a Hobby Horse,* he printed the "good" scale on a rising line, the "bad" on one descending.

A special problem is posed by the traditional use of the words high and low for sounds of high or low frequency. I wonder whether the explanation may not be found in the fact that in moments of a heightened vital stimulation—be it fear, joy, or anger—the human voice is apt to produce sounds of high frequency, while in repose and moments of reduced vitality our voices are "low."

Cicero already had realized that bodily motions are expressive of psychic life (*De oratore,* III): "Each motion of the soul has its natural physiognomic expression, sound and gesture." Now it is easy to see that we attach very specific meanings with motions in the *upward* or *downward* directions.

Falling is one of the words that immediately bring to mind unpleasant associations. Original sin caused man's *Fall,* a conquered city *falls* to the enemy, and the Roman Empire *fell* when its power was exhausted. To the Victorians, a woman who had lost her honor was a *fallen* woman, no matter how upright she walked. But when we accept a challenge, we *rise* to the occasion; our spirits *rise* when we take courage. We "get a lift" and may even be in the clouds—an expression which, incidentally, is surely connected with the observation that clouds themselves do not seem to be subject to the tug of gravity. And there is the charming saying that you can't keep a good man down.

Kneeling and bowing are actions expressive of submission; crawling and groveling signify abject surrender. The serpent in Paradise originally walked upright, but after it led Adam and Eve to their doom it was condemned to the eternal degradation of having to crawl on its belly. It could never again get the feeling of uprightness, both in the physical and moral sense. Is there a finer expression of the association of upright existence with life and moral worth, in contrast to the helplessness of the horizontal, than that of the song telling us that John Brown's soul goes marching on, while his body lies a-mould'ring in the grave?

Many are the patterns of human interaction that are invested with meanings that reflect our experience of gravity. When we think of violent conflicts, we imagine the victor above, the vanquished below. In medieval imagery, personifications of virtues stand on those of vices. In the illustrations by Renaissance artists of Boccaccio's cyclical triumphs, the wheels of each triumphal chariot roll over the erstwhile victor, now vanquished by a superior power. In Indian art, the god Shiva dances his dance of life and death on a reclining dwarf, the symbol of evil. The old metaphorical image of the Wheel of Fortune shows the man of success on top, "at the height of his power," while the one out of luck is underneath.

Inevitably, we are led to pursue the projection of man's subconscious experience of, and hostility to, gravitational forces into the sphere of theology and metaphysics. The mean earth-gods of the early Greeks were superseded by a much more cheerful crowd that selected a high mountain, Olympus, as its residence. In the Judeo-Christian tradition God resides in Heaven, that is, above us, and believers everywhere point upward to indicate His realm though they actually will point in an opposite direction if they happen to be antipodes. Down below may be either an underworld, the realm of shadows, or downright Hell. As a matter of fact, I am inclined to think that the Devil, whose habitat is below us, is primarily a mythical condensation of man's subconscious fear and hatred of gravity.

This is perhaps the moment to state that there are other experiences which we invest emotionally as we do the up and down, such as light and dark, given to us most tangibly in the alternation of day and night. Of the two, it is day, and light, with which we associate positive qualities, while night, and dark, are charged negatively. (This may be connected with atavistic recollections from primitive ages, when hunting and food-gathering was done during the day, while the dark was a time of danger. Darkness, however, may under special conditions be associated with security, if connected with an appropriate place for hiding, such as caves.) There are "dark" dreams, "dark" plans, "dark" crimes, and the Devil, appropriately enough, is the Prince of Darkness. It is he and his evil companions who pull or push us down. (A medieval legend about the Virgin tells how a painter, after making a portrait of her on a church façade, painted a scene involving the Devil higher up on the wall. His portrait of the Devil was so repulsive that the Devil was offended, and came to persuade the painter to portray him more handsomely. The artist refused, and was pushed off his scaffold by the furious fiend. Yet as he fell, he passed by his painted image of the Virgin, and this image swiftly shot out an arm into space grabbing the painter in mid-air and holding him there until he could be rescued. Thus, for a few moments, the Virgin, acting through her painted image, suspended the earth's gravity which the Devil had counted on to do his work.)

There is one phenomenon given to us in our daily experience that seems to link our feelings about up and down with those about light and dark in such a way that they seem to support each other beautifully; this is the apparent motion of the sun. We do know, of course, that what we see as the sun's motion does not exist in this way, but we still share the happy sensation of primitive man for whom the welcome light came at the *rising* of the sun, while darkness was the result of its setting or going down. (German: die Sonne *geht auf* und *geht unter*.)

Perhaps the most characteristic expression of man's abhorrence of gravity as connected with both death and Devil is his belief in a final resurrection. Just as Christ rose on the third day, rendered by the so-called Grünewald as a magnificent upward soaring, so all bodies will *rise* on Judgment Day, pushin away the lids of their coffins to be selected either for eternal life in Heaven or eternal damnation in Hell. In that final chapter a new metaphysical force makes its appearance, against which the old fiend—gravity—is helpless, a power that attracts or pulls upward, just as the Virgin was carried upward in what appropriately has been named her Assumption. The elect are attracted by a new center of gravity that lies above us rather than below. (The "Anziehungskraft" of this force is still suggested in Goethe's "Das ewig-weibliche *zieht uns* hinan"—all but lost in the lame translation "the woman-soul *leadeth us* upward and on.")

Not all religions think of man's ultimate fate in terms of death and resurrection. Yet the problem of gravity is of concern in other beliefs, too. In Buddhism's Nirvana, the body's weight, symbol of its subservience to a power outside us, is suspended in the experïence of a perfect state of mental and physical equilibrium in which man also abandons all striving and ambition.

Of the several arts, the one most directly concerned with the problem of gravity, quite naturally, is the dance. In her theory of art, Suzanne Langer states, "free dance movement produces above all, for the performer as well as the spectator, the illusion of a conquest of gravity, that is freedom from the actual forces that are normally known and felt to control the dancer's body." She also cites another author: "The ballerinas seek to demonstrate that the earth's gravitation has practically no hold upon them." Graceful ballerinas seem indeed to float through the air, and the enormous jumps of their partners jubilantly defy gravity. Yet not all dance is ballet, and escape from gravity is not necessarily involved in every dance. Arnheim quotes experiments in which college dancers were asked to improvise on themes such as "sadness," "strength," and "night," and we are not surprised to learn that in a dance on sadness, for instance, "the body seemed to yield passively to the forces of gravitation." He also comments on the form of the weeping willow, where "the branches convey the expression of passive hanging" that evokes an association with sadness. (R. Herrick, "Divination by a Daffodil": "When a daffodil I see,/Hanging down his head t'wards me;/Guesse I may, what I must be:/ First, I shall decline my head;/Secondly, I shall be dead;/Lastly, safely buryed.") You may have seen Marcel Marceau in a piece that symbolizes in a few minutes all of human life. It consists of a slow upward growth of an originally hunched figure until he seems to walk forward in the fullness of strength and mature size, only to slowly lose force again, gradually sinking down into the earthbound passivity of death.

What is expressed by modern dancers and mimes has long been visualized in art. In Giotto's Arena Chapel in Padua, *Hope,* of which we still say that it springs eternal, soars, its arms extended, upward, while *Despair,* having hanged herself, sags downward heavily, a helpless victim of gravity. *Inconstancy,* however, is shown as a figure teetering on a wheel in a position of unstable equilibrium that symbolizes its inherent insecurity. I have said before with reference to Plato's man that by his uprightness man proudly asserts his opposition to gravity, which constantly tries to claim him. No matter whether our body was made for a vertical existence (and there is justified doubt that it was), we consider verticalism our natural axis. In an overwhelming number of cases, idols of primitive people and drawings of children show people upright. Artists trying to express physical strength, self-assertion, and fearlessness show man standing straight, feet apart, for greater security. We find such figures in Egyptian tombs, on Renaissance murals, such as Castagno's *Pippo Spano,* and in fifteenth-century German painting (K. Witz). In Oroszco's Dartmouth College mural the figure representing Victory is a plain soldier standing upright in a tumbling world. It is for the same reason that guards in front of palaces must stand. A guard sitting down, unless he sits on a standing horse, would be an unthinkable concession to gravity.

The sense of strength we gain from the experience of our own vertical bodies is transferred, almost metaphorically, into different contexts. The invincibility of a whole army is strikingly visualized in the massed verticals of lances in a sixteenth-century woodcut, long before Velazquez repeated the pattern in his *Surrender of Breda.* Likewise, the grand sequence of columns which Maderno gave to the façade of St. Peter's in Rome is symbolical of the power of the papacy revived in the period of the Counter-Reformation. Upright walking, with wide steps, is also a sign of a vigorous condition, of unimpaired vital energies (Munch's *Bathers,* and Baizerman's *Man with a Spade,* a monumental piece although it is only a few inches high).

These examples show a calm, sure determination, the possession of all the physical and mental qualities that enable man to maintain himself in his vertical position. There are just as many examples that stress a mood of exuberance by increasing the odds, as it were, and by suggesting an actual upward motion. The simplest form is a raising of arms, as seen in *Dancing Girls* painted on the wall of an Egyptian tomb. When we raise the arms we raise the center of gravity, thus creating a greater danger to our stability. By doing so we suggest a kind of joyful abandon, though the relief of the Egyptian chorus line is still rather sedate. In Seurat's study of a circus rider, the upward motion is more emphatic and more suggestive of freedom from gravity because the body is capable of sustaining itself in an oblique position. Still bolder are poses also found in Seurat, where legs are kicked upward, accompanied here by upward curling mouths, moustaches, locks of hair, and ribbons. Seurat had developed a theory of expression in which upward, downward, and horizontal movements had functions not unlike those we ascribe to them here, but in which the central problem of man's emotional relationship to gravity was not taken into consideration. At any rate, long before Seurat the dancers of yet another Egyptian tomb, in Saqqara, had far outdone in acrobatic agility and high-stepping *joie de vivre* the somewhat precious night-club performers of Seurat's canvas.

In Giotto's *Allegory of Despair* we have seen how the downward motion is negatively charged, as it were. A *Foolish Virgin* from Strasbourg Cathedral, holding her extinguished lamp in a limply hanging hand, seems to sag downward, devoid of the strength that is needed to oppose gravity's pull. Rodin's *Icarus* tumbles downward, all the more a symbol of failure as some of his wings still adhere to parts of the body. Lehmbruck's unforgettable figure of a man close to the ground, arched over forward and resting what little weight he has on arms, legs, and even his head, is a moving expression of lassitude and ultimate defeat. Nadelman's *Bull,* done in 1915, catches a similar feeling as it shows the potentially forceful animal in a state of helpless collapse, its thin legs buckling under it and its nose nearly touching the ground. With Barlach's *Beggar Woman,* we have forms that hug the ground, suggestive of infinite weariness or grief. The will to live, to act, even to stir, seems to have gone from the figure.

In the many *gisants* of French Gothic and Renaissance sculpture, as, for instance, of Cardinal Jean de Lagrange, Avignon (1402), gravity has finally taken its toll.

The horizontal position, in physics called neutral equilibrium, can convey many meanings depending on the general context, but it is always charged with suggestions of giving in, of passivity, of inertia. Munch's *Morning After* conveys the extreme exhaustion of dissipation, all the more depressing as the axis of the body is tilted downward in the direction of the head. The very life of the figure seems to drain into the unchecked flow of her dark hair across the sheet of the bed. With Pieter Bruegel, to lie on the ground is to be associated with the sin of sloth. The man snoring under the tree in *The Harvesters* in the Metropolitan Museum most certainly alludes to the Biblical saying: "He that gathereth in summer is a wise son: but he that sleepeth in harvest is a son that causeth shame."

In the *Land of Cocaigne* three lazy men are stretched out on the ground around a tree converted into a table. They have achieved the pipe-dream condition of all slothful gluttons, to become inhabitants of the land of plenty where pies grow on roofs and fried pigs and boiled eggs walk about, ready to be eaten. These people, too, have given in to gravity but have earned the artist's scorn in the bargain. And it is Bruegel again who shows blind beggars stumbling and falling, symbolic less of their human frailty than of the spiritual blindness that makes them put their trust in blind leaders, thus missing the true church of Christ that stands in the background. Where the downward forces prevail, evil qualities that are always potentially present may come out into the open. Jealousy is symbolized in Munch's picture, not only through the extremely low position of the brooding man, but also through the additional weight of rocks whose size increases toward the bottom. The downward motion so overpowering in Rubens' *Fall of the Damned* in Munich (and so appropriate for the expression of punishment to sinners) is made visually convincing by the huge weights that mark the lower end of the long chains of tumbling bodies. (Those adhering to the vice of gluttony are probably providing these weights.) The power of gravity manifested in the theological situation of punished sinners was unfortunately active not long ago, when a madman attacked this very picture to call attention to some crackpot theories; this self-appointed savior of mankind threw a bottle of paint remover against the panel and the chemical, following the law of gravity, ran down the front of the picture and destroyed the painted surface all along its downward path.

Particularly rich in expressive potentiality are the motions suggestive of unstable equilibrium such as seen already in Giotto's *Allegory of Inconstancy*. The earth's attraction is felt powerfully in Rubens' *Drunken Silenus,* not the least because of the bulkiness of the bodies involved. Yet, except for the satyr woman on the ground who has practically passed out, the energy lent to man by the gift of Bacchus still sustains the staggering figure of Silenus and stimulates the animated crowd around him. Drunkenness is rendered by bodies in oblique positions, but so is the ecstasy of love—as in Correggio's *Io*—when the ingrained struggle against gravity is momentarily swept away by the powerful stimulus of passion. An oblique position may also be used to signify an aristocratic and fashionable inactivity (Boucher), an existence devoted to graceful leisure. The plight of refugees is visualized by Barlach, by showing two heavy figures inclined towards one side, as in fatigue, bringing to mind Emma Lazarus' "Give me your tired, your poor, your *huddled* masses yearning to be free . . . " When Delacroix painted Christ at the Mount of Olives in His one moment of human weakness, he gave to Him a pose similar to those of the pathetic figures of Barlach. Brooding, melancholy, and mental disequilibrium are most frequently associated with oblique positions: they are states of mind which lack strength and self-assurance, but are not yet a complete physical and mental capitulation. Delacroix's *Michelangelo* reclines moodily among his sculptures, temporarily inactive and in need of physical support but still concerned with creative dreams and visions. We also see it in Géricault's *Portrait of an Artist,* who rests his head on his hand, crosses his legs, and thus assumes a pose which, despite its aspects of elegance (reminiscent of Boucher's *Madame de Pompadour*), suggests a moody, depressive personality. It is most revealing to see that seven hundred years before Géricault, a Spanish Romanesque painter of the twelfth century (Tahull) hit upon a similar pose when he wanted to convey the idea of poor Lazarus sitting or leaning outside the palace of the rich man, the very image of suffering and misery.

We encounter it again in Delacroix when he shows Tasso, the poet, in the madhouse; the slouching pose he gives to the poet is the most telling indication of his unbalanced mind. In our own century Klee followed this use of the oblique position when he painted the grotesque little figure of a collapsing marionette as a touching symbol of frailty and futility.

It is obvious from the foregoing that the limits neither of time nor of geography have any influence on principles of expression that take their cue from such a basic condition of life as is found in gravity. All the examples I have shown, no matter when they were done, have in common that they acknowledge the existence of gravity. The figures maintain a strong verticalism in defiance of its threat, or they yield to it submissively, or yet are seen in a precarious state, wavering, as it were, between the two poles.

There is, however, a final possibility, one which I feel is particularly significant in our own time.

When we look at the kings and queens on the west portal of Chartres we must admit that they cannot be classified as belonging to any one of the gravitational types listed above. These figures do not stand, though they have been provided with little bases under their feet; they do not fall, either, nor have they momentarily lost control. The artist shows them quasi-suspended, attached to the columns; he gives us the impression that gravity simply did not exist for them. Their gowns also do not fall, but cling to the slender shafts of their bodies. The figures of Chartres seem to be weightless and thus do not share in the normal conditions of human life. They are vertical, but not because of any effort of theirs. Whatever life they have is obviously one of a world which is not ours.

Although gravity never ceases to affect our actual existence, the privilege has long been given to us to imagine a state where it is completely absent—and not only in dreams. In Chartres the denial of its existence may be linked with the notion of a kingdom of eternal life in which both Devil and Death, the personifications of gravity, have lost their power. For very different reasons the eighteenth century was fond of imagery which, while not exactly denying the existence of gravity, plays down its significance. Watteau's *L'Indifférent* is a figure who looks as if he could take off from the ground with the greatest of ease. In this period we often find images of people on swings held by long ropes (Fragonard), and swinging, indeed, appears to have been an exceedingly popular pastime of the period, especially in the upper layers of society. People on swings forget for a few dizzy moments that they are earthbound. Normal relationships of up and down are lost sight of, the world around us unexpectedly appears to be in motion, possibly out of joint. It is tempting to establish a connection between this pictorial and, in the physical act of swinging, *actual* escape from gravity with an attitude of recklessness and frivolity that may have been, to use a modern psychological term, a kind of escape mechanism from ever more urgent social problems.

It is when we come to modern art, however, that we are confronted with a veritable flood of artistic expressions in which the very existence of gravity appears to be denied. While Fragonard's girl is still living in the framework of the concrete forces that make up our physical world, Chagall's lovers float across the river, carried away on a bunch of lilacs and presumably engulfed in its heavy and sweet fragrance. In many pictures by Chagall, people float through the air or walk upside down (houses even stand on their heads); in *Homage to the Eiffel Tower* a figure with flowers wings its way through a window, and trees grow horizontally across the picture from either side. In prints by Redon strange forms hover in midair, messengers from a world that is part of our experience but not of our waking existence. The study of dreams (begun scientifically at about that time and culminating in Freud) opened up new possibilities for an imagery in which physical laws are ignored with one great jump of the imagination. Dreamlike floating is also the theme of Max Ernst's *Beautiful Flowers*—accompanied by a breaking up of bodily coherence and by the creation of transparent shapes. That the modern trend in art favors the minimizing of gravitational relationships even in fields where they still function unimpaired is seen in our lovely bridges that seem to have no weight at all. The span of the Whitestone Bridge jumps across the water with one effortless leap, and at the 1958 Brussels World's Fair one could see many structures that seemed to be weightless or ready to float. How pervasive is our love of the weightless form, how much we seem to associate with it a positive and desirable value, I saw in one of those insipid art reviews of which our newspapers are full:

> Two solid sensuously rounded black shapes, wrapped in mystery and no longer lumpish and inert, float on a cloud of light-color. Their sense of movement and their weightlessness give this picture a monumental buoyancy.

But what else is the meaning of Calder's mobiles if it is not the free movement (floating) of its components in space? The same thing is true of Miro's or Klee's charming and gay configurations, in which brightly colored areas of whimsical shapes have emancipated themselves from the laws of gravity, using the field of the canvas for their carefree gamboling. There are innumerable works that show these qualities but possibly none in which the principle itself is reduced as clearly to its barest minimum as Malevitch's *Red and Black*. While the black square, by echoing the horizontal and vertical extension of the canvas itself, contains at least a memory of gravitational relationships, the red square, by the simple device of its higher position and its sideways tilt, seems to float weightlessly—though without the metaphysical associations of the figures of Chartres West.

Brancusi's famous sculpture, finally, called *Bird in Space,* could—in the light of our present experience—be called just as aptly *Bird of Space,* for it brings to mind nothing more vividly than a space missile, delicately poised on its launching platform. Indeed, long before scientific technicians constructed such missiles an artist created here a powerful visual symbol of soaring, free from any gravitational impediments.

If the emancipation from physical reality, and especially the denial, or at least disregard, of gravity are among the most striking aspects of modern art, we may ask indeed if there is not a link between this phenomenon and the achievements of modern technology. In modern art, forms and colors often seem to float and a gravitational orientation is so meaningless that some modern artists do not even care whether their pictures hang right side up or upside down. Is it completely accidental that such an art has been created at a period when man's age-old dream of flying has been realized (and, mind you, one can fly upside down—as in Chagall's paintings—though not for long), an age in which we are now approaching the threshold of weightless flight outside the earth's gravity? We may turn the question around, of course, and ask whether modern technology, with its promise of an escape from gravity, does not derive some of its fascination and appeal from the fact that in our subconscious mind we are equating escape from gravity with escape from all sorts of human predicaments, including death? The large seventeenth-century literature on Travels to the Moon is a literature of escape. In these books, the cosmic traveler enjoys a state "without hunger, thirst, weariness —all ills resulting from the effect of gravity" (Marjorie Nicholson).

Are perhaps our modern space dreams also signs of escapist tendencies? Is the "conquest of space," of which we hear so much, tied up with a wish to escape *into* space—getting away from all our troubles down here? However that may be, let us always remember that there never will be a remedy against gravity, no more than there is one for death, and that the problems of our existence will not be solved anywhere if we cannot also solve them down here on our earth.

10

GORDON HENDRICKS

"Let's Keep 'Em Ignorant..."

The need for serious work in the history of American art is often lamented. My own experiences have shown that this lack is not always the fault of the historian. Institutions from which one must ask assistance—chiefly museums—often have operating practices that so discourage a worker that the job may not get done at all. The following vignettes are examples of recent experiences in researching biographies of Albert Bierstadt, Thomas Eakins, and Eadweard Muybridge. They are not typical of every institution I visited in the United States. But I believe that they are at least not uncommon, and even frequent.

It is often desirable to visit one museum while on the way to another. If you are writing about Eakins, why visit Milwaukee? Yet a trip to Chicago is a must, considering the Art Institute's Eakinses, and if you are also working on Albert Bierstadt a side trip to Milwaukee is indicated, to see the excellent Bierstadts there. (The following remarks, incidentally, have nothing to do with the Milwaukee staff, which was very pleasant and gave me the most cheerful and enthusiastic cooperation.)

So you call the museum long distance (which can become a considerable expense), assuming, as cannot be assumed, that the person to whom you should speak is availadle and can be lured to the telephone from the social whirl which is so often part of a museum attaché's life; a frequent, even customary, response is,

"You've picked a bad week—we're putting up our Picasso show"; or, "We're just into the process of moving and everything is a mess"; or, "Mr. Smith is no longer with us." Or perhaps Mr. Smith has left his job to take another—in the chessboard manner of museums—and his successor, if there is one, is not familiar with the collection and therefore cannot perform the vastly complicated task of unlocking a vault and showing you a picture. All this in an institution which may keep its records so poorly that no one knows where some pictures are, or, indeed, if they are still in the collection. And from staff members whose principal concern seems to be to suppress any show of enthusiasm for the art they handle, lest you think them unsophisticated.

Several years ago I visited the museum of an historical society of a large Eastern city in quest of a lost Eakins portrait. It was not hanging on the wall, and I was not allowed to look at the portraits in storage—even with a staff member watching me —because, as I was told later, I had a beard. (This was before bankers, lawyers, and stockbrokers began to blossom.) Had I been able to identify the portrait, incidentally, it would have meant no less than a hundred thousand dollars to this shoe-string institution.

I had planned while in that city to look at the reverse of another Eakins portrait in the public museum. I called them no less than ten days ahead and was told it was a "bad time," that no one would be available to take the picture off the wall, or merely to hold it forward so that I could look at the back. Nevertheless, after arriving in the city I decided to take another look at the front of the portrait.

At the museum I stood before the painting, the only visitor in a hall in which three custodians ambled about. On my way up I had passed the door to staff offices and seen at least three staff members sitting at their desks, sipping coffee and chatting amiably about what were doubtless serious museum matters. Returning to my hotel I called the director of the museum, who told me I would not be able to see the back of the painting until the following spring—it was then fall—"when things got straightened out"; I must then write a letter for an appointment and travel 150 miles for my few minutes' work. It was, I confess, with considerable satisfaction that I later came to believe the picture was not an Eakins after all.

The conservator of a large metropolitan Eastern museum, when cajoled into showing me the reverse of another Eakins work, asked, "And what do you expect to find, Mr. Hendricks?" She knew well what I might expect to find, and that a good-sized book could be written about what one might find on the backs of paintings.

In another case I asked to see the reverse of an Eakins watercolor hanging in a large Midwestern museum, and was told by the registrar, "That's asking too *much*." When I recounted this experience to the curator of a still larger Eastern museum I was told, "It *is* asking too much."

While traveling through the Far West, hoping to see whatever Eakinses I could wherever I went, I called a large museum in one city and asked the director if they owned an Eakins. He replied that he thought not, but at my request he would check to make sure. After some time he came back to the telephone to say that he was indeed correct, they did not own an Eakins. But the idea rankled and I went to the museum the following morning. There it was, hanging boldly on the wall, an

Eakins portrait. Moreover, the only catalogue they had ever published contained a full-page reproduction of it. This director went on to greater glories in another large city, but has now landed in a backwater; recent contact with him has revealed the same knowledgeable enthusiasm for American art.

One large collection in the West requires three local references before a researcher may even enter its library. If you do not know three such people there—defined as persons known to the collection's authorities to be "responsible, solid" citizens— you may be quite excluded from examining the collection; this in the course of work which might substantially benefit the collection, both in value and prestige. If most of your work has been done in one part of the country, it often takes considerable persuasion to effect an exception to the rules when visiting another part. Some- times, if one of the ubiquitous class of languorous museum staffers is in charge, it may not be possible at all.

Recently I was forced to travel several hundred miles out of my way, and to spend several hundred dollars of slim advances, to do a piece of work which, once at the museum, I accomplished in an hour. The work could have been done as quickly for me by a staff member, a number of whom were walking about when I arrived. It may or may not have been a coincidence that the director of this museum, who had denied me this information by mail, was a well-known specialist in the same field in which I was working.

There is a pervasive obsession with the concealment of enthusiasm in these establishments. We are dealing with Art, you know, and Art—even American art —is too serious for us plainly to like it. As a result museums are replete with staff members moving about in heavy languor, weary under their burdens of Apprecia- tion and the Responsibility of caring for the Treasures entrusted to them. This trust often comes to seem ownership, with museum people regarding the art as their very own and behaving, when asked to show it or give information about it, much like the bookkeeper who hands you your wages as if he were taking them from his own pocket. "Do not touch *our* works of art," one very large museum warns (italics mine). "Every work of art," the director of this museum recently announced, "is entirely owned by the trustees."
A recent visit to the museum of a large, prestigious Eastern university to look at nineteenth-century American paintings elicited from the German-born, German- trained curator the intelligence that "anything worth looking at is on the walls." The only "worthy" American paintings were those showing European influences; properly petitioned, she would show you a Benjamin West, a Washington Allston, or a William Leslie.
This same museum, incidentally, when furnishing dimensions—along with some of the poorest photographs of art ever taken—gives them in full meters only, not even centimeters, forcing translating scales on whomever wants to know the equivalent in inches. "We must keep them ignorant. Otherwise they'll get too smart and we'll be out of a job."

Museum directors will often answer objections to this sort of practice by pointing to a lack of funds, and to the difficulty of finding "good people" at such low salaries. But people most often considered "good" are those with experience in similar museums, or freshly graduated from some college specializing in art history, or museum training, or both.[1] In these institutions the very giants of American art receive scant attention, while the lower right-hand figure of the left-hand panel of a third-rate triptych in a fourth-rate European city may be given weighty analysis.

One answer to the problem of getting "good people" at museum salaries might seem to lie in the enlistment of volunteers, and museums do swarm with these. They are often *cast*—not hired—for the very qualities that make these volunteers so like the professionals: ennui, snobbishness, and disdain for the public and for much of the art, at least the American art, around them. Museums may draw personnel from the social register, justifying their practice on the grounds that many of these Seven Sisters' alumnae are rich—and may be richer some day: everybody knows that museums need money. Trustee pressure can, of course, be a substantial factor in this procedure, and too often trustees have been appointed for their knowledge —or possession—of money, more than for their knowledge or enthusiasm for art.

Getting information which should be routine often proves less than that. A letter to a registrar or curator asking for a description of markings may be answered that the work in question is "signed and dated." A rough calculation of the different ways in which a painting may be signed and dated comes to 1152! Thomas Eakins, for example, used a number of variations, and these may be crucial in documenting his work: Thomas Eakins 1899; Thomas Eakins 99; Eakins 1899; Eakins 99; Thomas Eakins/1899; Eakins/99; Thomas Eakins/99; Eakins/1899; EAKINS 1899; EAKINS/99; EAKINS/1899; EAKINS 99; etc., etc. And when other punctuation is added, the possibilities become dizzying and correspondingly frustrating.

In answer to a letter stating that a work is "signed and dated," a follow-up letter may properly ask *where* it is signed and dated. Back comes the information that it is "signed lower left"; this leaves you to wonder whether the "and dated" in the first letter was an error, or its omission in the second letter an inadvertence. So you try again: is it signed *and* dated? and if so, *how* and *where?* The responses, particularly to the "how," often muddy the waters further. Time, patience, or both run out; the worker is left to use his imagination, and he must not be blamed for exercising it willy-nilly.

Titles of paintings can be equally troublesome. One museum will write that the official title of a work is *Mrs. John Smith;* another letter from another staff member —or a later one from the first—says *Portrait of Mrs. John Smith;* another states that the title is simply *Mrs. Smith,* and another that it is *Portrait of Mrs. Smith.* When spelling variants are taken into account—a recent conglomerate produced three spellings for the same name—the final choice may cause the museum to take umbrage at your use of what they call an incorrect title. The historian and the publisher may have received different versions of the same information, leaving both worried about which is the "correct" form to put finally into print.

A museum may deliberately withhold information. This is particularly true when you are venturing into a field where a staff member has been grazing contentedly for some time, perhaps known as the institution's "Hudson River man," or "still-life man," or "contemporary man." It matters not how charged the scroll may be with his threats to publish—published his work often is not, and his dog-in-the-manger attitude may endure for years. It is outrageous, both from a scholarly and an ethical viewpoint, and if the museum receives tax money or tax concessions—and what museum does not?—it is also illegal.

One delaying technique is to promise material but never deliver it. Recently a supernumerary of a large Western collection agreed to send along critical information, but when I got back East, unable to afford a return visit, the agreement was reneged upon. The reneging was couched in luxuriant library jargon, but it was effective and incontrovertible. It rarely pays to go over the head of the staffer involved; he will never forgive you, and will meanwhile make life miserable for the colleagues who challenged his authority. Often you must wait—generally beyond your deadline—for a change in regime or his demise.

When museum personnel are faced with questions they are not sure of handling gracefully, they may resort to grotesque statements. I recently questioned the authenticity of a Worthington Whittredge that had been on the rounds from runner to dealer to museum. Asking a museum director, to whom I knew the painting had been shown, if she thought it was a real Whittredge, her reply was, "I didn't look at it with that in mind."

When a museum decides it doesn't like one of its paintings—sometimes, one suspects, simply because it is by an American artist—the usual technique in beginning to dispose of it is to cast doubts on its authenticity. Such a process is relentless. But after the elaborate "deaccessioning" has been accomplished, the picture may, to general chagrin, be proved genuine. The blame for the error is rarely faced squarely: it was the fault of a preceding regime, or it was done on the basis of an "authoritative opinion" (scrupulously unidentified), or it was gotten rid of because it was "in *such* bad condition."

Another practice which discourages historians, particularly those who plan to publish, is the widely varying and often exorbitant prices charged for photographs. One institution may charge as much as $15.00 for a print from an existing negative, another only $1.50 or thereabouts; the average now runs about $3.00. In my own work I have often needed a photograph of a photograph; whenever possible I try to acquire or borrow a negative and have the print made by someone of my own choice, with whom I can work to make the reproductive quality as high as possible. The price may be a very fair two or three dollars or it may be as high as twenty-five, the institution keeping the negative you have paid for out of your pittance and making for you what is often an unprofessional print.

I pointed out to a curator that the New York Public Library made excellent photographs, and threw in the negative as part of the deal; his museum charged as much for the print as the Library charged for both print and negative. His response was, "Ah, but they don't have what you want, and we do."

This unfortunate situation is made worse by reproduction fees. One leading Eastern museum charges fifty dollars for this, no matter how small the illustration will be or how limited the circulation of the book. Many charge high prices because they think publishers will pay whatever is asked; but unfortunately, a book contract often calls for the author to pay these fees. Though publishers may be rich, authors are nearly always church mice.

Private collections, in return for the right of reproducing a work, routinely ask for two copies of the book: one recently asked for three. This request is not often enforced, and indeed enforcing it would be difficult. But like the laws against adultery, the stricture makes us all dishonest when we sign the agreement to deliver the free books, knowing in our hearts that we will not do so. Nowadays an art book often costs forty or fifty dollars, and the agreement becomes absurd as well as dishonest.

Photographs can also be sold aggressively. Some museums routinely send them —and bills—in answer to requests for information. In assembling my recent books I ended up with thirty-five extra photographs from twenty-two museums, and I had ordered none of them; I already had my photographs, and had written only for details of size, support, etc. In addition to unresponsive answers, I often got another photograph and another bill. An occasional such lapse may be ascribed to a dreaming staff member, hurrying through the unglamourous part of a job in time for tea. But the photographs arrive so regularly that it is difficult to believe the practice is not encouraged—and even directed. The fees for two or three hundred unordered photographs per year can comfortably supply tea for everyone in sight.

The casualness with which many museums keep records is matched by their zeal in guarding their treasures against unauthorized use. One museum requires an applicant for reproduction rights to fill out a questionnaire containing thirteen items; the same museum supplied incorrect information about medium and support of the work for which it wanted these commitments. In another case, it took nine months to produce photographs, and then only after three letters and unnumbered telephone calls.

Both the registrar and the assistant curator of a large museum preeminent in modern art recently gave me incorrect information, when asked what examples they owned of the work of a now out-of-fashion contemporary painter. The museum actually owns nine drawings by the artist, but each staffer, firm in his conviction that American art began with Jackson Pollock, told me there were six. I also encountered another common roadblock for importunate scholars: one drawing was "in the vault" and could not be seen for a month. Everyone was too busy to show it.

Museums sometimes ignore letters for months; one great Midwestern museum has still to answer an inquiry first made five years ago. Such unprofessionalism can result from carelessness or boredom, but more often it comes from an exclusionist, obscurantist personality on the staff.

In my work on Albert Bierstadt I was curious to know how a painting in a large Midwestern museum had gotten its title. Was it written on the back? if so, was it in the artist's hand? I wrote the curator, and after waiting several months for a reply I wrote a second letter. That was also ignored. I then wrote the director, with whom I had some acquaintance; he spoke to the original addressee, who replied to me within days: he was sorry, he had not received my letters . . . but now he sent me his reasons for believing the painting's title to be correct. (For discretion

I will use Ohio place names because Bierstadt, as far as I know, never painted anything in Ohio.) The museum called the Bierstadt *A View of the Ohio River from Cincinnati* because they had a letter from a man who knew Lake Erie well and was certain that the painting was a view of Lake Erie from Toledo. *Sic.* This syllogist now holds a more prestigious job in a more prestigious museum.

To write hundreds of letters and make as many more telephone calls for the material in a single book, and to receive on an average not more than one reply in five that contains the information you asked for, is to make the project discouraging. I can count on the fingers of one hand the American museums that produce truly responsive letters. "Excellence dwells among the inaccessible rocks," someone wrote, "and a man may wear his heart out trying to attain it." Wear out his heart indeed—and his patience and his purse—and, at the end, might give up the whole thing as a bad job.

NOTE

[1]   In the United States these have been principally two: Harvard's Fogg Museum, and New York University's Institute of Fine Arts. Neither institution offers a regular course in the history of American art.

11

MADELEINE HOURS

Réflexions sur la critique d'art et ses transformations par les méthodes scientifiques

Au coeur de Paris, entre les deux ailes du Palais du Louvre, réunies autrefois par le chateau des Tuileries se situe un parterre dont les statues de Maillol jalonnent l'ordonnance; c'est dans ce lieu que débuta il y a près de dix ans un long et amical dialogue entre Milton Fox et moi.

Milton maîtrisait la langue française, aimait profondément le Louvre mais de son bureau de New York ou de son logis des rives de l'Hudson, il méditait sur l'art avec une ampleur de vision qui lui était personnelle. Il avait une vision de géographe assortie d'une grande sensibilité.

Pour nous français, notre position est bien différente: plus familiers de l'histoire que de la géographie, plus attachés à une exploration en profondeur, à une vision circonscrite, nous avons de la critique d'art, une autre conception.

Par contre, nos tentatives d'analyser techniquement l'oeuvre d'art pour une finalité esthétique furent immédiatement admises par Milton Fox. Alors que ce mode d'analyse suscitait des réticences bien explicables de la part d'historiens ou de critiques dont les méthodes étaient essentiellement subjectives; l'intrusion de critère objectif devait suivant une réaction bien naturelle soulever des obstacles, analogues à ceux que Laennec, le grand médecin français, inventeur du stéthoscope rencontra en son temps.

Il n'est point dans nos vues de soutenir que la part qui revient aux méthodes d'analyse scientifique doit être prépondérante, mais comme en médecine, le diagnostic doit s'établir pour une part, sur des éléments scientifiques.

C'est au XVIIIe siècle le moment clef de la Critique. Le Moyen Age s'était attaché au problème de l'étude de la technique de la peinture (*Schedula diversarum artium* du Moine Théophile). Ces notions de technologie survécurent dans le nord de l'Europe: alors qu'avec la Renaissance, l'individualité de "l'homme artiste" est exaltée au détriment de l'information technique; c'est l'époque où les vies d'artistes, à l'imitation de celles de Vasari prendront leur plein essor. Le XVIIe siècle français conservera cette attitude, plus historique que critique, cependant qu'au XVIIIe siècle, par le biais de l'observation scientifique les encyclopédistes tenteront de mieux connaître, de mieux reproduire l'oeuvre d'art; ce sont les buts reconnus des travaux du physicien Alexandre Charles, de Chaptal, de Niepce lui-même qui, en inventant la photographie cherchait à mieux reproduire l'oeuvre peinte.

Mais malgré des recherches sporadiques conduites tout au long du XIXe siècle, c'est à notre temps, et non sans bien des réticences, que l'on doit le mérite de voir l'analyse scientifique s'inserrer entre les deux grandes voies: celle de l'histoire et celle de la poésie.

Nous nous sommes mis d'accord sur le fait qu'il y avait jusqu'ici deux voies pour aborder l'oeuvre d'art: l'histoire et la poésie. Il est incontestable que la sensibilité poétique peut permettre de percevoir et d'analyser l'oeuvre d'art ou le fait artistique, sans le secours de la méthode historique; les textes de Baudelaire ou ceux de Paul Valéry sur Corot ou Houdon, pour n'en citer que quelques uns, en sont des bons exemples.

La seconde voie, la voie traditionnelle est celle de l'histoire, elle a maintenu sa prééminence de la Renaissance à nos jours.

Si l'on admet que l'analyse scientifique du fait matériel qu'est une oeuvre d'art peut conduire à une perception du fait spirituel qu'est le message de l'artiste, c'est alors que l'on peut considérer cette démarche comme une voie indépendante des deux précédentes. Le plus souvent ces méthodes nouvelles d'analyse sont complémentaires de l'histoire.

Ces méthodes scientifiques et techniques que nous évoquions qu'elles sont-elles? Ce sont celles qui utilisent le pouvoir des radiations électromagnétiques: d'éclairer, de pénétrer, d'analyser la matière et également la manière de l'artiste.

Au premier plan de ces radiations, la lumière naturelle ou artificielle, diffuse ou condensée, exalte les pouvoirs de l'oeil. C'est une analyse non destructive qui permet, grâce au relais de l'appareil photographique, de conserver un témoignage permanent d'une observation fugitive (fig. 1).

La lumière tangentielle, rasante, dirigée, permet une analyse de surface mettant en évidence les caractéristiques de la surface, la forme de la touche, son rythme, les empâtements et les glacis, le support originel (fig. 2).

L'analyse globale, en opposition à l'analyse ponctuelle devra être poursuivie de la surface de l'oeuvre jusqu'à son support s'il s'agit d'un tableau ou d'un document plan, jusqu'à son noyau s'il s'agit d'une sculpture ou d'une oeuvre en ronde bosse.

Les radiations ultra violettes filtrées ou la fluorescence de ces mêmes rayons, révéleront les altérations chimiques de surface; tandis que le pouvoir pénétrant des radiations infra rouges situées sur l'autre côté du spectre, facilitera la lecture des textes, mettra en évidence un état intermédiaire entre l'esquisse et l'oeuvre achevée (figs. 3, 4); tandis que les radiations X, plus pénétrantes encore, révéleront les repentirs de l'artiste, les caractéristiques de l'état du support et parfois celles d'une esquisse conçue par l'artiste différente de l'oeuvre achevée—ce fut le cas de la *Bethsabée* de Rembrandt et du *Saint Mathieu* (fig. 5)—révélant ainsi les caractéristiques de la technique, les marques d'une écriture personnelle, les stades jusqu'ici invisibles de l'élaboration de l'oeuvre d'art.

La radiographie a un rôle primordial à jouer dans l'histoire de l'art, à condition toutefois que les documents soient exécutés dans des conditions constantes et que le mode d'obtention soit normalisé. Il est à noter que la normalisation que doit s'imposer le technicien des radiations X au stade de l'élaboration, ne doit pas être ignoré de l'utilisateur qui doit en tenir compte dans la critique du document.

Ces documents, les images nées de ces recherches, ont un dénominateur commun. Elles sont comparables avec l'oeuvre achevée dont elles restituent les étapes successives. Ce sont les images de l'invisible et les images du passé de l'oeuvre d'art. L'interprétation de ces documents peut être effectuée par l'historien d'art lui-même après une rapide initiation. Cette interprétation, cette exploitation du document doit se faire sur deux plans : verticalement et horizontalement.

La radiographie du tableau de Gustave Courbet *L'Homme à la ceinture de cuir* illustre admirablement les propriétés de cette technique (figs. 7, 8). Le document révèle non seulement la structure interne de l'autoportrait mais révèle également une première composition jusqu'ici invisible : une copie par Courbet de *L'Homme au gant* du Titien.

C'est donc non seulement les aspects de l'élaboration de l'oeuvre de répartition des lumières, l'analyse des matériaux, mais aussi la confirmation d'une supposition : l'influence des Vénitiens et de Titien sur Gustave Courbet.

Ces documents révélant des étapes de la création doivent être exploités verticalement. J'entends là, une étude comparative entre l'oeuvre d'art et le document exécuté d'après elle, afin d'en noter différence ou concordance sur le plan esthétique : transformation de la composition, changement d'expression ou d'écriture sur le plan technique.

Le document doit ensuite faire l'objet d'une exploration horizontale. Il s'agit d'une étude comparative des documents entre eux ; radiographies des oeuvres du même maître ou d'une même école, afin de noter l'évolution d'une écriture ou d'une technique—les ressemblances ou les divergences étant sources d'enseignement (figs. 9, 10).

Aux documents nés de ces méthodes d'analyse globale, il faut ajouter ceux qui sont le fruit d'analyses localisées sur un point de surface.

Le microscope permet d'étudier en surface un point précis, la succession des observations permet de percevoir des anomalies, fruits d'une falsification ou d'une altération de la surface, de préciser la technique, le broyage du pigment. Le microprélèvement de quelques microns carrés permet d'obtenir en un point donné une analyse stratigraphique qui confirme les observations faites par des méthodes globales et fournit en outre des informations sur le métier de l'artiste, son tempérament.

Une coupe microscopique exécutée sur le tableau de G. Courbet *L'Homme à la ceinture de cuir* (fig. 6) vient confirmer les observations, les découvertes obtenues par les radiographies.

Dans le cas, Courbet, l'analyse de surface globale se trouve confirmer par l'analyse ponctuelle, l'exploitation des microprélèvements peut être conduite par diverses méthodes, le microscope, l'inclusion et la coloration des coupes. Des méthodes physiques peuvent permettre de dissocier et d'analyser les constituants des divers prélèvements. La détermination des pigments par la microsonde de Castaing, permet une analyse précise sur des surfaces de l'ordre du micron. Elle peut aider à l'étude des pigments. Il en est de même de l'activation neutronique. Les analyses, les graphiques obtenus par ces méthodes ne peuvent pas être directement interprétés par l'historien. Elles nécessitent le relais du spécialiste, physicien ou chimiste, mais elles sont riches d'enseignement tant sur l'étude de l'histoire des techniques, que révélatrices du métier et du comportement de l'artiste.

Nous pensons avec Lukas que "la valeur de toute oeuvre est réflétée dans sa structure." L'étude du "détail" du "fait singulier" est un des stades indispensables de l'histoire. Il l'est plus encore selon nous en histoire de l'art.

Depuis peu, la Critique d'Art ne cesse d'évoluer, elle a subit l'influence du structuralisme, dans son concept littéraire, c'est un fait certain, mais ne négligeons pas pour autant les recherches nouvelles conduites en France, celles de l'Institut d'Esthétique et des Sciences de l'Art et plus particulièrement les travaux de René Passeron sur la Poïétique qui tendent à attirer l'attention sur le concept négligé jusque là au profit de l'esthétique. "Comment le domaine de l'art serait-il délimité sans référence aux conduites qui instaurent les oeuvres" ainsi que l'écrit René Passeron.

L'oeuvre d'art c'est l'insertion de la création dans le réel. L'analyse des faits matériels permet à l'historien d'adapter son intuition au réel, seul le poète peut s'en passer.

BIBLIOGRAPHIE SOMMAIRE

Roger de Piles, *Abrégé de la vie des peintres,* Paris, 1699

Jean Baptiste du Bos, *Réflexions critiques sur la poésie et la peinture,* 1719

L. Venturi, *Histoire de la critique d'art,* Bruxelles, 1938

S. Sulzberger, *Le Langage pictural,* Office de Publicité, Bruxelles, 1949

"Problèmes du structuralisme," *Les temps modernes,* no. 246, Novembre 1966, Paris

La Poïétique, d'après Paul Valéry, Variétés, *Oeuvres,* L. I, Paris, p. 1342

René Passeron, "La Poïétique," *Revue d'esthétique,* no. 3, Paris, 1971

Bernard Berenson, *Esthétique et histoire des Arts visuels,* traduction et preface de Jean Alazard, Albin Michel, Paris, 1953

Madeleine Hours, *Annales du Laboratoire de Recherche des Musées de France,* Ed. des Musées Nationaux, Paris, 1971, pp. 2–17

———, *Les Secrets des Chefs d'Oeuvre,* ed. Robert Laffont, Paris, 1964

———, *Secrets of the Great Masters,* Putnam, New York

———, *Les méthodes scientifiques au service de la critique d'art,* publié par l'Académie des Sciences de Hongrie, Budapest, 1972

Suzy Delbourgo et Lola Faillant, "Autoportraits de Courbet," *Étude au Laboratoire de Recherche des Musées de France,* Ed. des Musées Nationaux, Paris, 1973, pp. 17–22

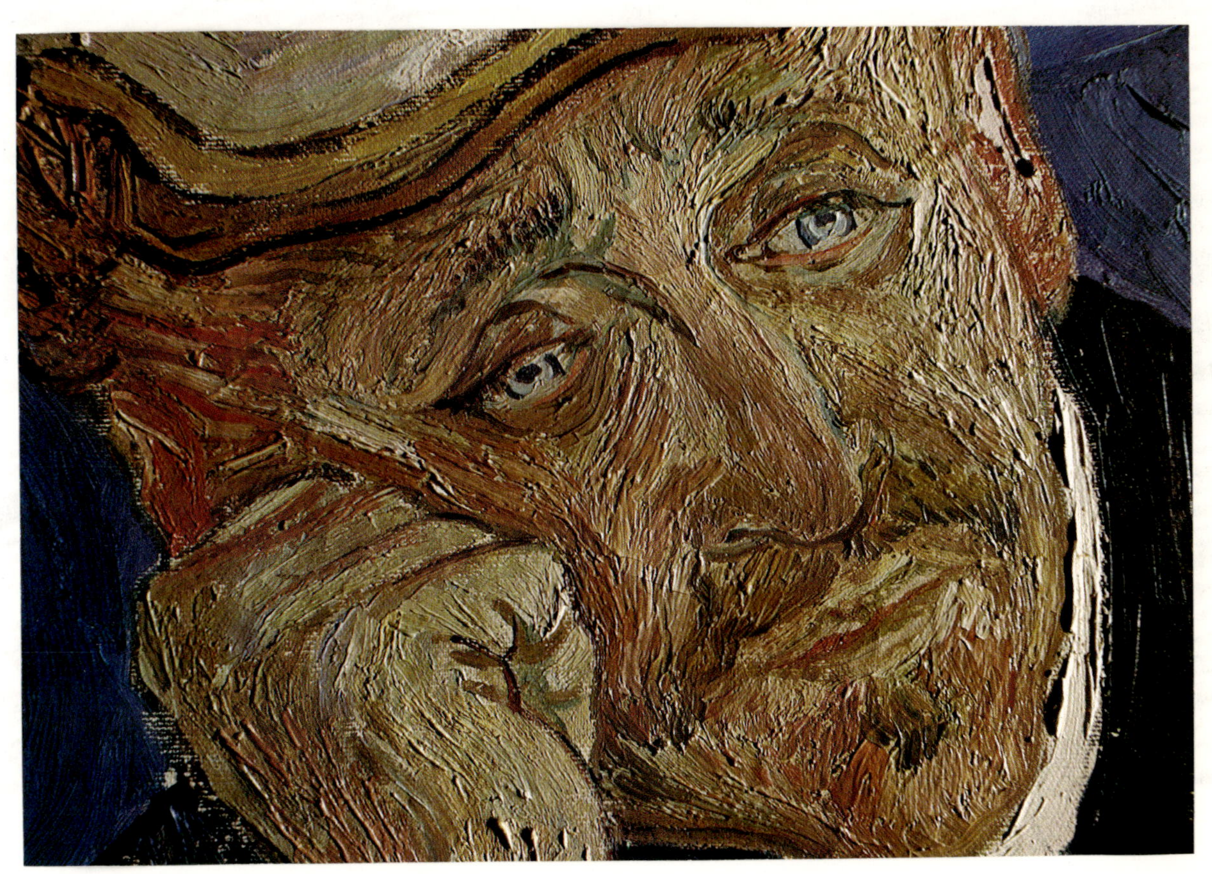

1. VINCENT VAN GOGH. *Portrait du Docteur Gachet*. Detail. The Louvre, Paris

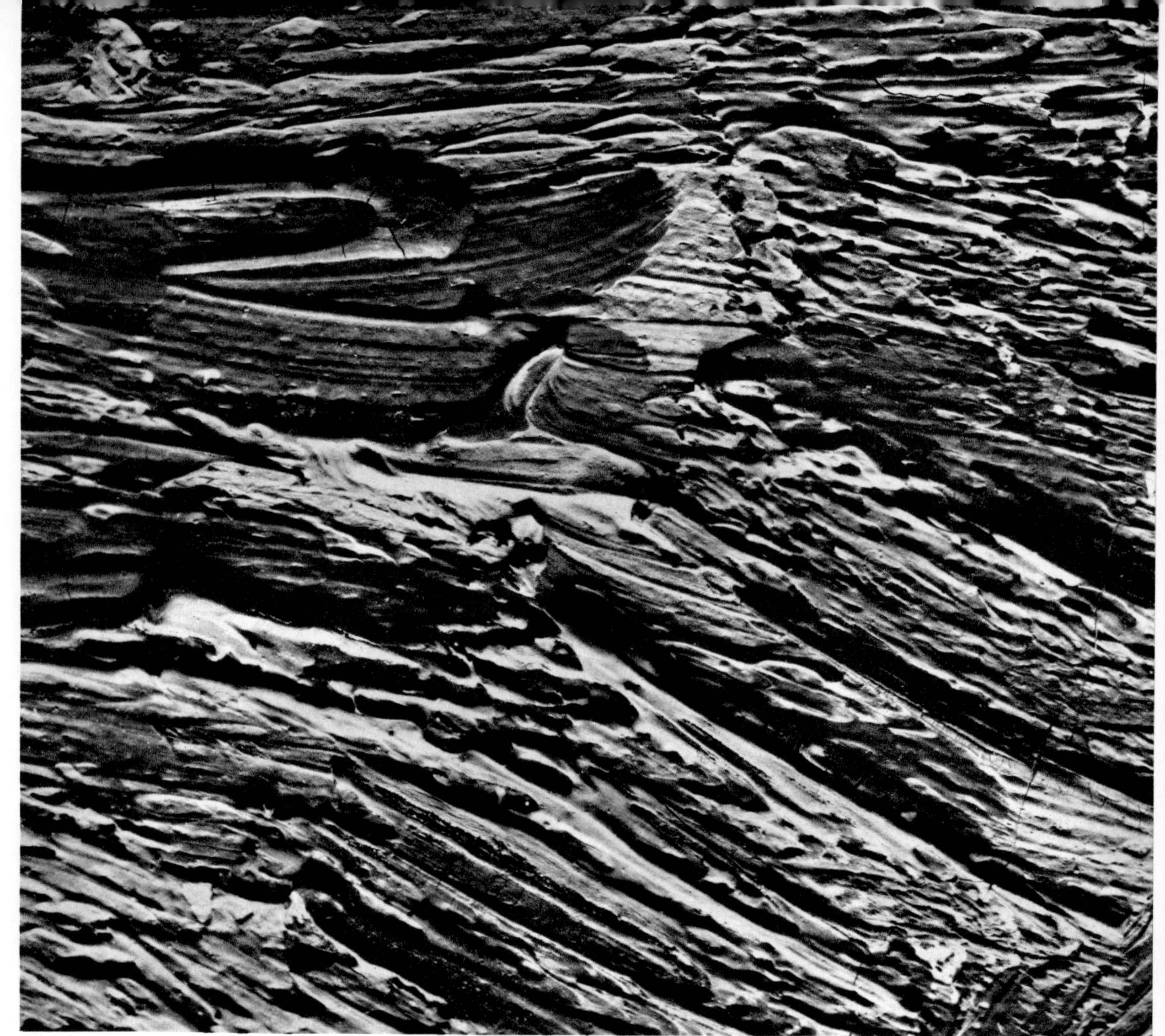

2.   Vincent van Gogh. *Portrait du Docteur Gachet.*
Detail (macrophotograph in raking light)

La touche du peintre, isolée, découpée par l'objectif, est mise en évidence sur cette macrophotographe obtenue d'après le *Portrait du Docteur Gachet* par van Gogh. Ce document souligne le caractère cosmique de l'écriture du peintre, la pression violente et impulsive qui vient de la main même de l'artiste. Cette technique photographique a le mérite d'exalter la qualité de la matière picturale, le rythme du pinceau, et témoigne de l'individualité même de l'écriture de van Gogh.

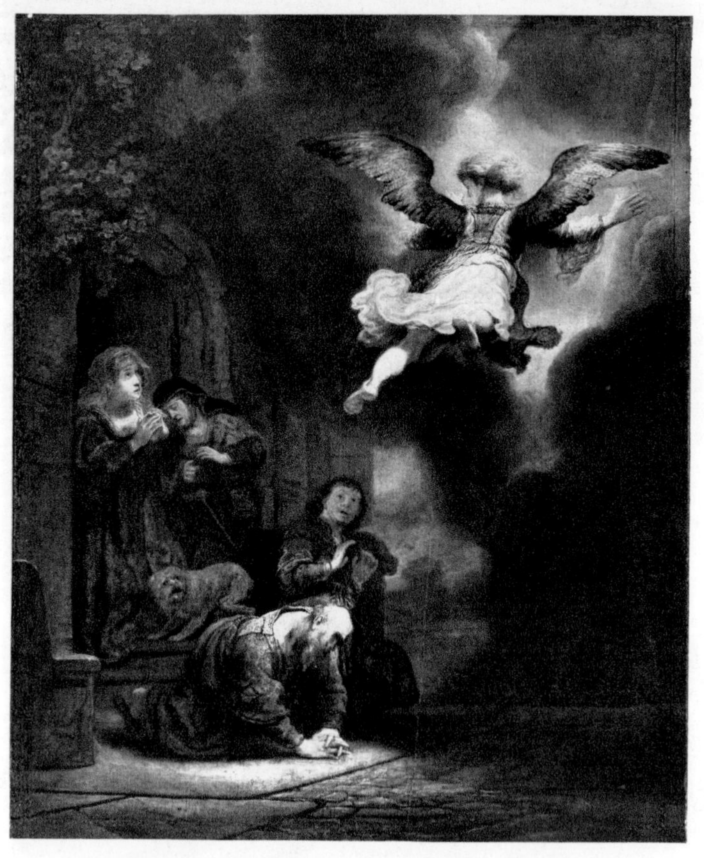

3. REMBRANDT. *L'Ange Raphaël
quittant Tobie*
(photograph in direct light).
The Louvre, Paris

En traversant les couches superficielles d'un tableau, les rayons infra-rouges révélent une étape intermédiaire de la création artistique; ils ont mis ainsi en évidence une technique picturale toute particulière à Rembrandt. *L'Ange Raphaël quittant Tobie* apparait sous ce rayonnement dans ses moindres détails, composé, dessiné. Les grandes surfaces sombres, les accents lumineux ont été ensuite apposés par l'artiste sous forme de glacis transparents; ils donnent au tableau cette profondeur intense caractéristique de l'oeuvre du Maître.

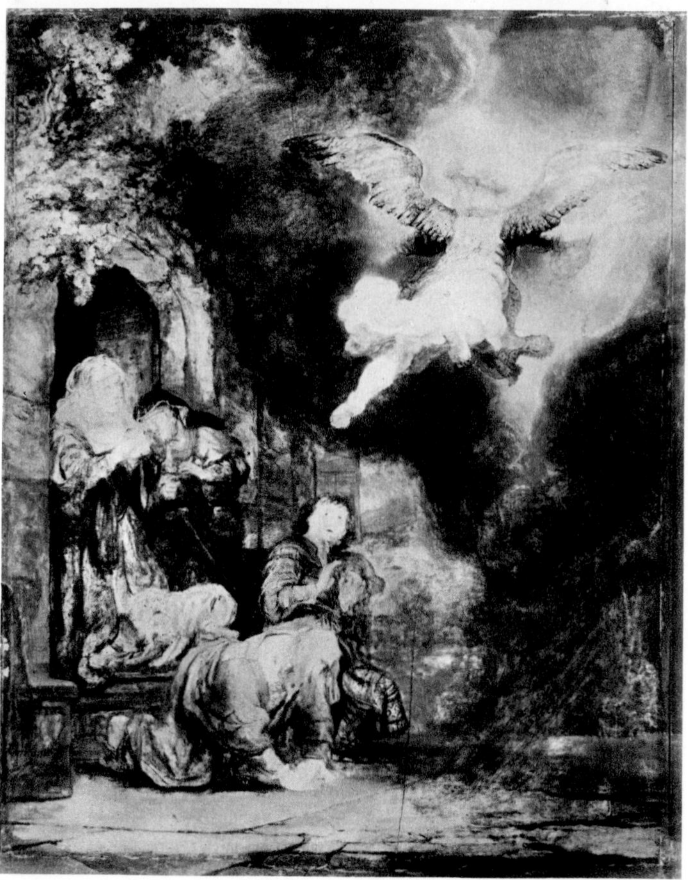

4. REMBRANDT. *L'Ange Raphaël
quittant Tobie*
(infra-red photograph)

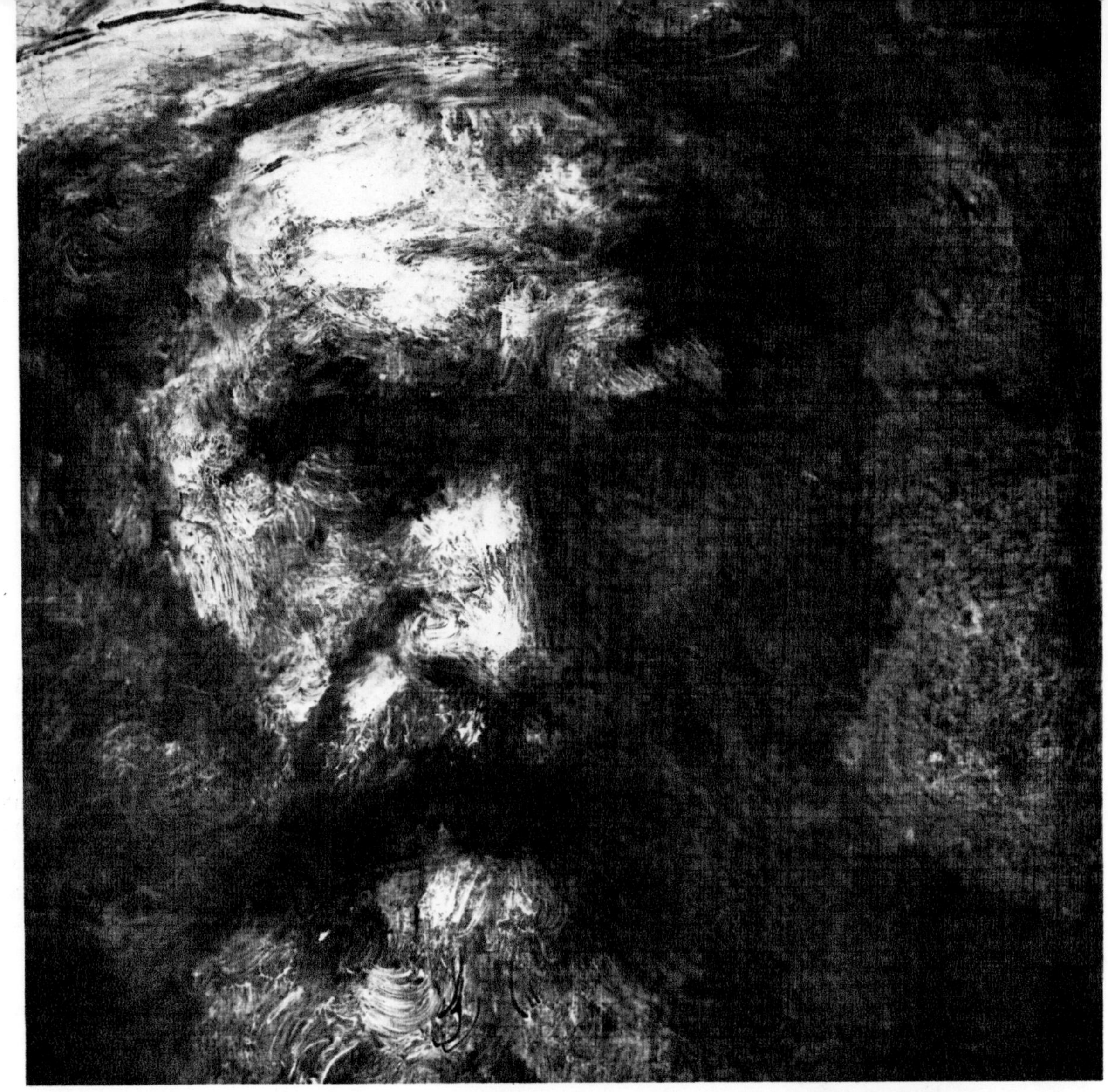

5. REMBRANDT. *Saint Mathieu et l'Ange*. Detail (X-ray photograph).
The Louvre, Paris

La radiographie du visage de St Mathieu obtenue d'après le tableau de Rembrandt *Saint Mathieu et l'Ange* n'est pas une image sélective d'une étape dans l'élaboration de l'oeuvre, mais elle met en évidence une technique familière à l'artiste: la moitié du visage seulement est travaillée avec des couleurs de masse atomique élevée; les yeux sont modelés dans l'ombre; la vigueur de la brosse et la maîtrise de l'écriture sont nettement visibles.

6. GUSTAVE COURBET. *L'Homme à la ceinture de cuir*
(microphotograph showing layers of paint)

Un microprélèvement effectué sur le poignet gauche de *L'Homme à la ceinture de cuir* a permis l'étude stratigraphique en profondeur de la matière picturale. Un fort grossissement a mis en évidence une superposition de couches de couleurs brune, jaune, rougeâtre, brun foncé, gris, chair, résultant du premier et laborieux travail de Courbet copiant *L'Homme au gant* et de la deuxième composition finale.

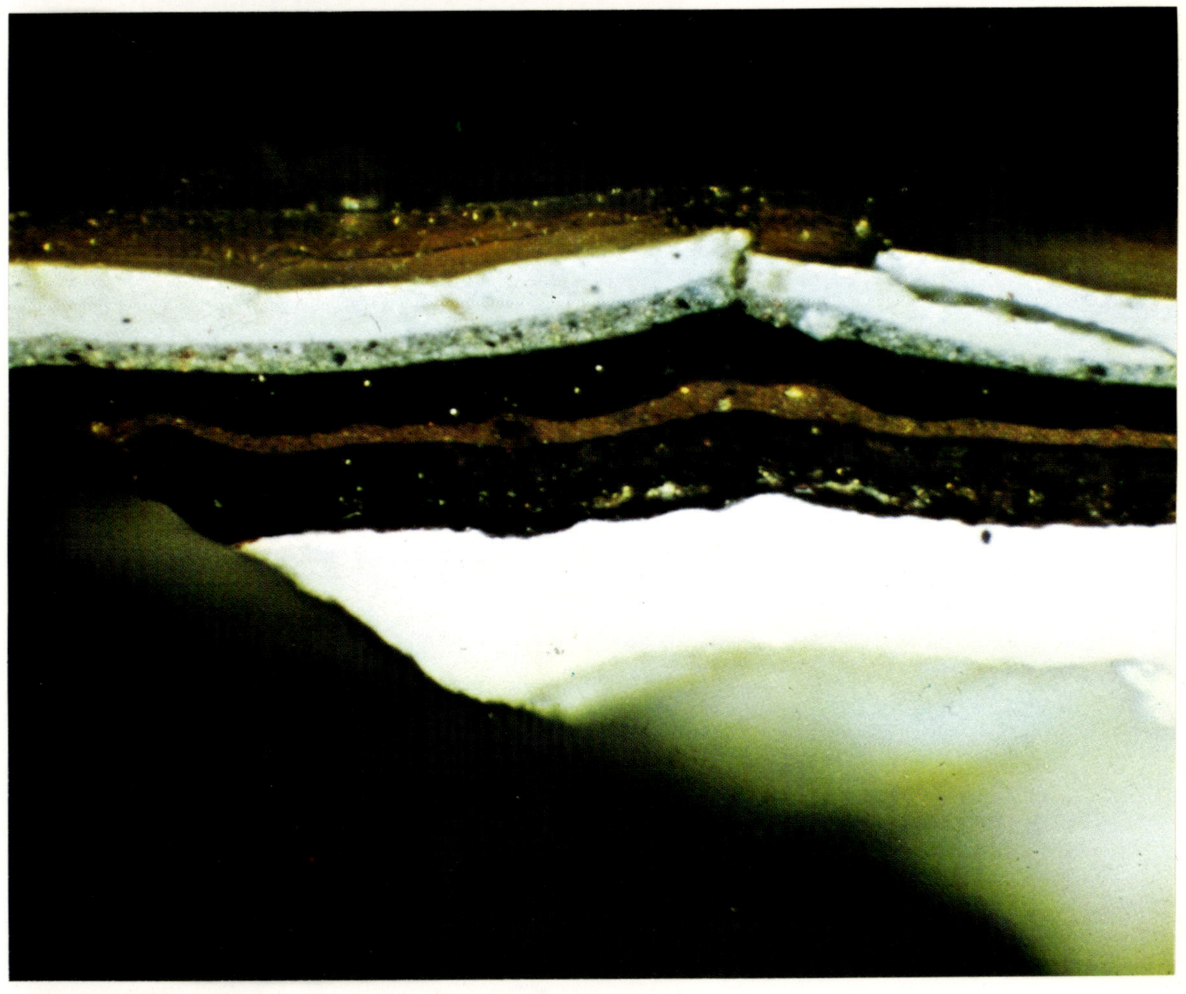

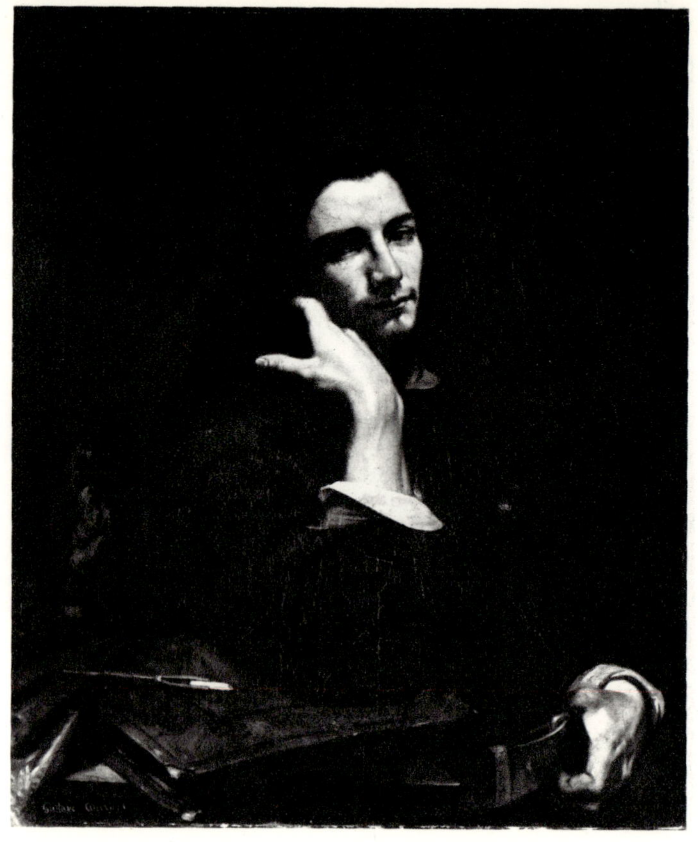

7. GUSTAVE COURBET.
L'Homme à la ceinture de cuir
(direct light).
The Louvre, Paris

Les rayons X ont révélé sous le portrait de Courbet *L'Homme à la ceinture de cuir* une copie du célèbre portrait de Titien *L'Homme au gant*. Cette copie, assez faible, a été réutilisée par l'artiste qui y peignit "tête-bêche" le portrait que nous admirons aujourd'hui. La substructure de cette seconde image est d'un modelé vigoureux, le visage et la main droite du personnage ont été travaillés avec des couleurs de forte densité. Courbet les a placés dans l'axe de la première étude de *L'Homme au gant,* utilisant ainsi les blancs de la chemise du premier modèle pour servir de fond à la main et au visage du second.

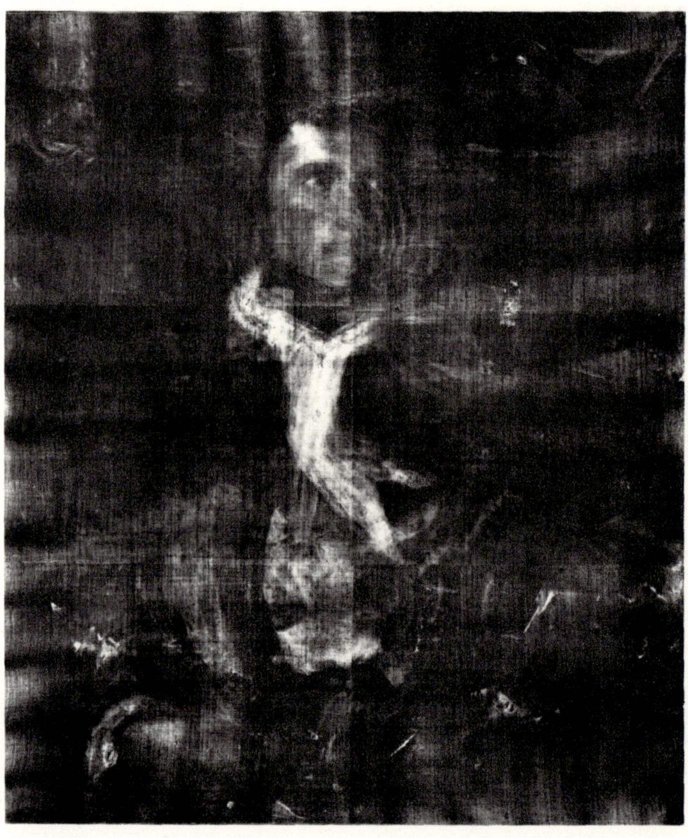

8. GUSTAVE COURBET.
L'Homme à la ceinture de cuir
(X-ray photograph)

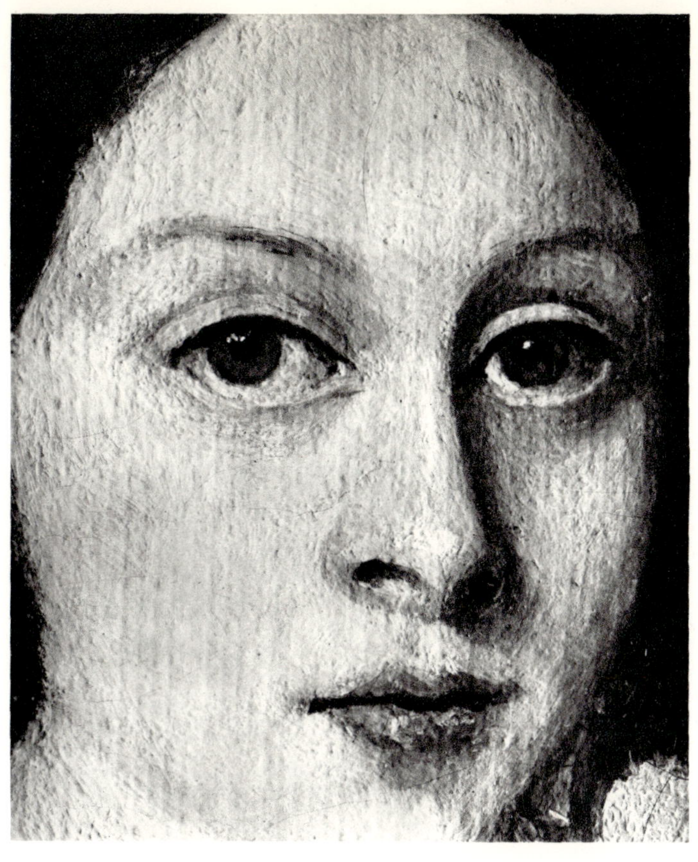

9. CAMILLE COROT.
Portrait de Madame Charmois.
Detail (macrophotograph
in direct light). The Louvre, Paris

La macrophotographie permet de suivre
l'évolution de l'écriture et du métier de
Corot. La touche est lisse, délicate, les
contours bien dessinés dans le visage de
Madame Charmois. Vers cinq ans plus
tard, lorsqu'il peindra *Saint Sébastien,*
Corot fait preuve d'une technique qui
annonce déjà celle des impressionistes:
la brosse est large, souple, vibrante, les
contours semblent s'estomper dans la
lumière. L'artiste est parvenu à une
parfaite maîtrise de la matière. C'est là
un bon exemple de la méthode "horizontale" basée sur la comparaison de
documents executés dans des conditions
comparables.

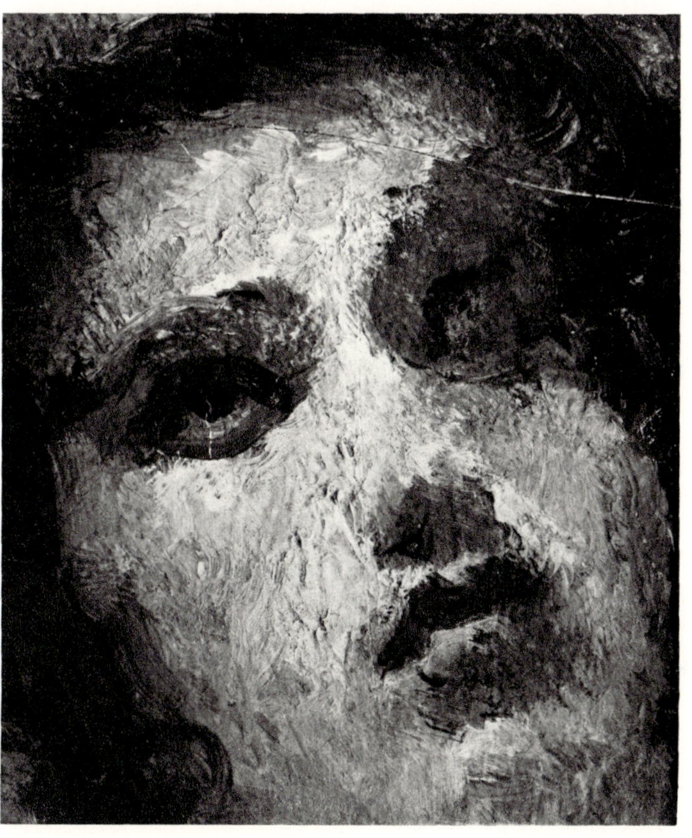

10. CAMILLE COROT.
Saint Sébastien. Detail
(macrophotograph
in direct light).
The Louvre, Paris

12

SAM HUNTER

Chryssa

The artist Chryssa is a dark, handsome, and mercurial woman so dominated by her sense of artistic mission, to the exclusion of all other considerations, that it becomes difficult for an observer to reconcile her theatrical personal style with the cool, controlled objectivism and technical precision of the exquisite light boxes on which her artistic reputation rests. Everything about her carefully constructed neon sculptures testifies to esthetic sobriety, finesse, and a fanatical patience. Yet she is known as an artist who can make strong workmen and artisan assistants blanch by her eruptions of cold fury, especially when some fabricated sculpture element she ordered does not meet her exact specifications. She demands in others the same perfectionism she has come to expect of herself. With less provocation, she frets and fumes at the frustrations of urban life in New York, and often overreacts to the petty rivalries, real or imagined slights, and internal politics of the art world. Since 1961 she has had a number of New York dealers representing her work, and all of them were exceptional in taste and intelligence, and generally effective promoters of vanguard art. Yet she has restlessly, almost compulsively, changed dealer representatives, on rather flimsy pretexts, whenever she sensed that their commitment to her work was less than total. As a result of her occasional temperamental indulgences and moodiness, apocrypha and legend seem to collect around her name.

Yet, while Chryssa is clearly hypersensitive to criticism, and strong-willed, her reputation as an *enfant terrible* is quite undeserved. Her personality, indeed, can best be understood against the background of her European origins and culture. An ingrained ambivalence about American life and mores is compounded equally of ecstatic affirmations and mistrust. Essentially Mediterranean in her simplicity of outlook, she finds the headlong pace and anonymity of American life still somewhat unsettling after nearly twenty years of residence.

She was raised and educated in Athens, left Greece to study art in Paris in 1953, and then came to live first in San Francisco, and then in New York two years later. The bustling energy of this city, the highly visible drama of popular culture played out in public places, especially in the spectacle of commercial signs, combined with the new eloquence of emerging American art in the '50s to directly form her own sculpture, which is unmistakably a cultural product of the New York experience. Nonetheless, Chryssa has never been able satisfactorily to identify with American existence as a whole, and the pastoral landscape of her youth always seems to beckon like the dream of some departed golden age. She maintains her traditional, European affiliations and manages to restore her spirit and equanimity by making frequent trips abroad. The occasion may be professional, or simply pleasurable, and most often it is a combination of the two.

Chryssa stands apart from the art "scene" and maintains a certain reserve, and even suspicion. This pose of being on guard unfortunately tends to obscure her natural warmth, gregariousness and considerable wit. One could not guess, from her grave mien and guarded manner on public occasions, that she is a gifted raconteur and mimic capable of stripping the self-important characters in her professional circle—eminent artists, museum officials, influential collectors—of their pretensions. It is this hidden, playful side of her personality which makes her such an intense delight to her friends, with whom she relaxes from the tensions of work.

When Chryssa began her pioneering experiments in the new mode of "luminist" sculpture early in this decade, she found herself laboring under the double penalty of pioneering in unfamiliar esthetic territory, and directly challenging the sacrosanct technical procedures of a variety of conservative but indispensable artisans, electricians, glass blowers, and shop managers not in the habit of responding to fresh initiatives on the part of outsiders. Unlike some of the Minimalist sculptors today, she is not able to proceed on the assumption that her designs will be fabricated into a satisfactory artifact by anonymous workmen, without her attentive and continuous intervention. Her eye and touch are required at every stage of the creative process to assure the requisite intricacy of structure or circuitry, and appropriate levels of color and light intensity. While her neon sculpture distills something of the visual delirium and throbbing urgencies of nocturnal Times Square, within a highly refined and transforming artistic idiom, the message is by no means simple, or necessarily compatible with elementary commercial signs whose style and forms have been appropriated. The commercial sources of her work provide a facade masking a complex artistic order, and a decision-making process over which the artist, given her natural inclinations, agonizes from the moment of conception to finished execution. The coherence and clarity of the end product is a measure of her profound knowledge of and total immersion in the technological process.

Chryssa began producing accomplished work some nineteen years ago, at the rather tender age of twenty-two, and she has remained a significant and consistently innovative figure in the art world ever since. After a brief study period in Paris and a short-lived residence in San Francisco, she came to live in New York, and it was here in 1955 that her first distinctly personal work emerged in her so-called *Cycladic Books*. These undetailed, virtually featureless reliefs in clay were marked only by vertical and horizontal divisions, forming a wide T. The tablets ambiguously recalled the vague, flattened masks of Cycladic sculpture.

Given the irresistible logic of her artistic growth, and her responsiveness to milieu, both artistic and social, it required only a short step to progress from the raised tablets and subsequent plaster reliefs of individual letters with their shadow play, to her more direct "homages" in neon to Times Square, a locale which epitomized for her so much of America's raw power and vitality. Chryssa later summarized her feelings on this score in an interview in 1968 in *Women's Wear Daily:* "America is very stimulating, intoxicating for me. Believe me when I say that there is wisdom, indeed, in the flashing of the lights of Times Square. The vulgarity of America as seen in the lights of Times Square is poetic, extremely poetic. A foreigner can observe this, describe this. Americans feel it."

Recalling her first New York years with nostalgia, Chryssa remembers herself as "utterly alone, broke and very happy," a solitary seeker after novel artistic meanings who haunted the anonymous city streets as well as the museums and galleries of the city, and was already magnetized by the spectacle of popular culture. With her Greek background, she still tends to look for classical references everywhere in contemporary experience. "I was naturally drawn to Times Square," she reminisces. "Times Square I knew had this great wisdom—it was Homeric— even if the sign-makers did not realize that." In the inexhaustible fantasy and nocturnal blaze of New York's most enthralling "light show" Chryssa discovered her inspiration. The "spiralic" form and "flat linear approach" of the commercial neon sign-makers made contact across the ages, she believes, with her Byzantine heritage and an interest in El Greco's serpentine flicker. Whether or not she conceived of "low" and publicly available art in such exalted terms and with such reverence at the time, she did embark boldly on a new series of compositions using junk signs and metal word fragments in 1959. By 1962, in a pioneering work entitled *Times Square Sky,* she had introduced a delicate thread of neon script spelling the word "air," as a kind of grace note within a scrambled assemblage of fractured metal letters. The illuminated word was not merely inventive flourish or *tour de force;* it became a source of personal liberation and represented nothing less than an influential advance for American art. The next year she committed herself more decisively to neon and light works with one of her most important and ambitious compositions called *Americanoom.* Here, an even larger, more emphatic panel of neon letters acted in strong visual counterpoint against an identical band of word fragments in metal, as if to demonstrate that solid and insubstantial form possessed equal artistic prerogatives, and were alternating aspects of each other. It took only another short step to compose in neon tubing exclusively. With great originality and conviction, Chryssa thus managed to give definition and structure to the least nameable of substances, hitherto considered inaccessible to art: colored light and air.

Significantly, Chryssa feels that the distinguishing feature of her works, their illumination, is not an absolute, defining necessity, and urges that they be understood as a form of sculpture independent of the historical accident of their contemporary technological existence. "When the sculpture lights up," she has remarked, "it is only one aspect of 'how it works.' When the box is *not lit* it is the same thing . . . 'how it works.' For me it is like breathing, whether in or out.

"The dark interval is never long enough for me. I do not expect or want anybody to wait for the moment when the sculpture lights up. I never do that myself when I have my works around me. I look *through* it all the time. That is how I communicate with these light or dark intervals."

In a period when the word "major" has been devalued by the extravagance of critical rhetoric, it is just as well to refrain from assessing for posterity the career of an artist in her early forties. It does seem safe to hazard the opinion that Chryssa is one of the more significant woman artists of her generation. Even if her claim to fame rested only on one work, she would probably have a secure historical niche, by reason of her magnificent *Gates to Times Square* (fig. 1). This superlative work absorbed most of her energies over a two-year period, and must rate as her most ambitious venture to date. The construction takes the form of an open three-dimensional triangle with a steeply sloping, roofed form supported by a monkey-puzzle grid of stainless steel and diagonal sheets of aluminum. These provide a framework for a honeycomb of stacked, vertical rows of massive metal letters interspersed with illuminated neon script, the latter housed in plexiglass boxes. *The Gates* is architectural in scale and represents a *summa* of Chryssa's formal and imagistic preoccupations since she first began to work in neon.

Chryssa's recent work has been among her most extraordinary, renewing familiar themes and testing new grounds. One of the most brilliant and satisfying of her light boxes is *Automat* of 1972 (fig. 2), a slim, five-foot-high dark plexiglass box, not quite two feet wide, which houses letters well known to all New York streetgoers who have ever eaten at the ubiquitous Horn and Hardart's self-service cafeterias. The word "Automat" is spelled out twice in banks of half-letters which are completed by their echoing reflections in the dark glass, glimmering like an illusionistic mirage. The two rows of half-letters also complete each other, like their own reflections. And the end views through the glass are perhaps most astonishing in their ruby-red, baroque tangle of over-laid letters, a latter-day Celtic interlace in neon, formally related to the earlier *Analysis of the Letter B.* For ecstatic, burning brilliance of light-effects, and formal resolution, the ensemble is unsurpassed. Like so much of Chryssa's work, a simple and coherent scheme is made just sufficiently intricate to give one the sense of richness without suggesting any involved problem solving. The alterations in letter positions and angles of vision, and the interplay with reflections completing the tangible neon form recall the paintings of Jasper Johns and his interest in lettered forms and common signs, with their esthetic potential both for expressive ambiguity and crystalline clarity. Yet all the intellectual content of the work, with its varied modes of representation, would only be sterile, if it were not for Chryssa's mysterious, effective ability to achieve sensuous beauty. Indeed, it is the light intensity of the work, veiled by the dark plexiglass, which has the potential of ecstasy as the controlling rheostat is adjusted to its highest pitch of brilliance.

Curiously, other artists in Europe and America who worked in neon have almost without exception been limited by the popular character of their art, and soon run out of formal invention when the impact of their imagery palls. Since Chryssa's letter variations are essentially abstract ciphers despite their obvious allusions, and are governed by a complex artistic evolution, her individual line of development continues to nourish itself on the same sources which sustain the vital non-objective art of our time.

Today, one applauds in particular her courage as an artist of sure inventive capacity willing to undertake ambitious ventures; her finest moment was probably *The Gates of Times Square,* one of the truly impressive sculptures of the American post-war period—a work surely that belongs in a museum where it would be accessible to young artists, and take its place in the evolving order of contemporary sculpture (donated to the Albright-Knox Gallery, Buffalo, by Mr. and Mrs. Albert List). Her more recent attempts at monumental scale in the recent *Boogie Woogie* and other studies for large-scale, perhaps for the moment only visionary, constructions, as well as the heroic character of the only moderately large *Automat,* indicate that Chryssa's ambition and willingness to take risks are undiminished. Just past forty years of age, at the peak of her creative powers, and once again prolifically working with the kind of intensity that produced her finest shows, Chryssa, indeed, seems perhaps the only "light" artist in America who has managed to transcend both the limitations of Pop imagery and the technical seductions of her chosen medium.

However, Chryssa tends to take a dim view of her recent triumphs. "All those pieces," she complained recently, "have been for me a disaster, financially and in every way. When I do work on a large scale, I must invest everything I have materially, and my entire existence, my health, in my work. I live by the most inhuman schedule . . . I sleep in my clothes." Like many contemporary sculptors, but perhaps even more so than most, she finds that the materials, technology and special fabrication which her work entails are extremely costly. Even her moderate-size light boxes require expenditures of thousands of dollars. Nor is there any assurance that the large works of the past such as *The Gates,* or her newer ventures on a comparable scale will find a willing purchaser at the sometimes stunning prices she feels she must ask, which in turn reflect astronomical manufacturing costs, quite apart from the work's intrinsic artistic worth. While she is not indigent, and collectors and museums continue to seek her new work out in her studio, one does get the impression that her normal state of anxiety and creative tension has more validity now than usual. But one also entertains the suspicion that Chryssa generates crises purposely, although unconsciously, if only to provide a motive for then dispelling them—through the catharsis of work. For most of us, a state of emergency as an habitual ambiance would be too hard on the nerves to be long endured. Chryssa seems to thrive in a high-risk environment, though, and her best work flows out of a continuing sense of drama and crisis.

Not long ago she received a visitor in her crowded, narrow floor-through apartment-cum-studio on the upper East Side. The apartment serves both as living and working space, small and cramped though it is. Large mechanical constructions are fabricated elsewhere, of course. As she spoke about her work, her expressive, sunshine-and-showers face momentarily screwed itself into a frown: her landlord was threatening eviction, since her lease was nearly up—an old story! She needed all her wits and powers of concentration to complete her newest group of sculptures, but life was an unending series of costly, taxing interruptions—the latest in the form of crated work arriving from an exhibition just terminated. In the meantime, there was the phone, ringing incessantly. Her small living room which consists mainly of a couple of couches, chairs and a large 10-foot-square table under a Noguchi lantern, piled high with unopened letters, drawings, albums of installation photographs, jammed ash trays (for she smokes incessantly), discarded clothes and remnants of distant meals, was an indescribable mess. The disorder, one was assured, represented only a momentary aberration, about to be cleared up just as soon as she was released by the demon of work, the relentless demands of the phone, and was permitted to "breathe again." However harassed Chryssa may appear to be, beset though she is by hostile forces which include landlords, deadlines, unfinished projects, logistical problems and other distractions, the continuity of her work and her immense productivity do seem to remain miraculously unaffected.

She is fortunate in her loyal and concerned friends, who range from anonymous Greek countrymen living quiet, private lives in New York to the affluent and powerful of this world. They do what they can to make her American existence more bearable, but it is unlikely they will succeed in significantly calming her anxieties, or appeasing her *wanderlust*. Like many artists, her preferred condition is nomadic. She resembles her work in that she can never quite come to rest, or accept any simple or obvious solutions, like staying rooted in one locale for a long, unbroken period of time. "For the creative person," she solemnly declares in her most characteristic sibylline manner, "life is like a play—you continue until you reach your destiny."

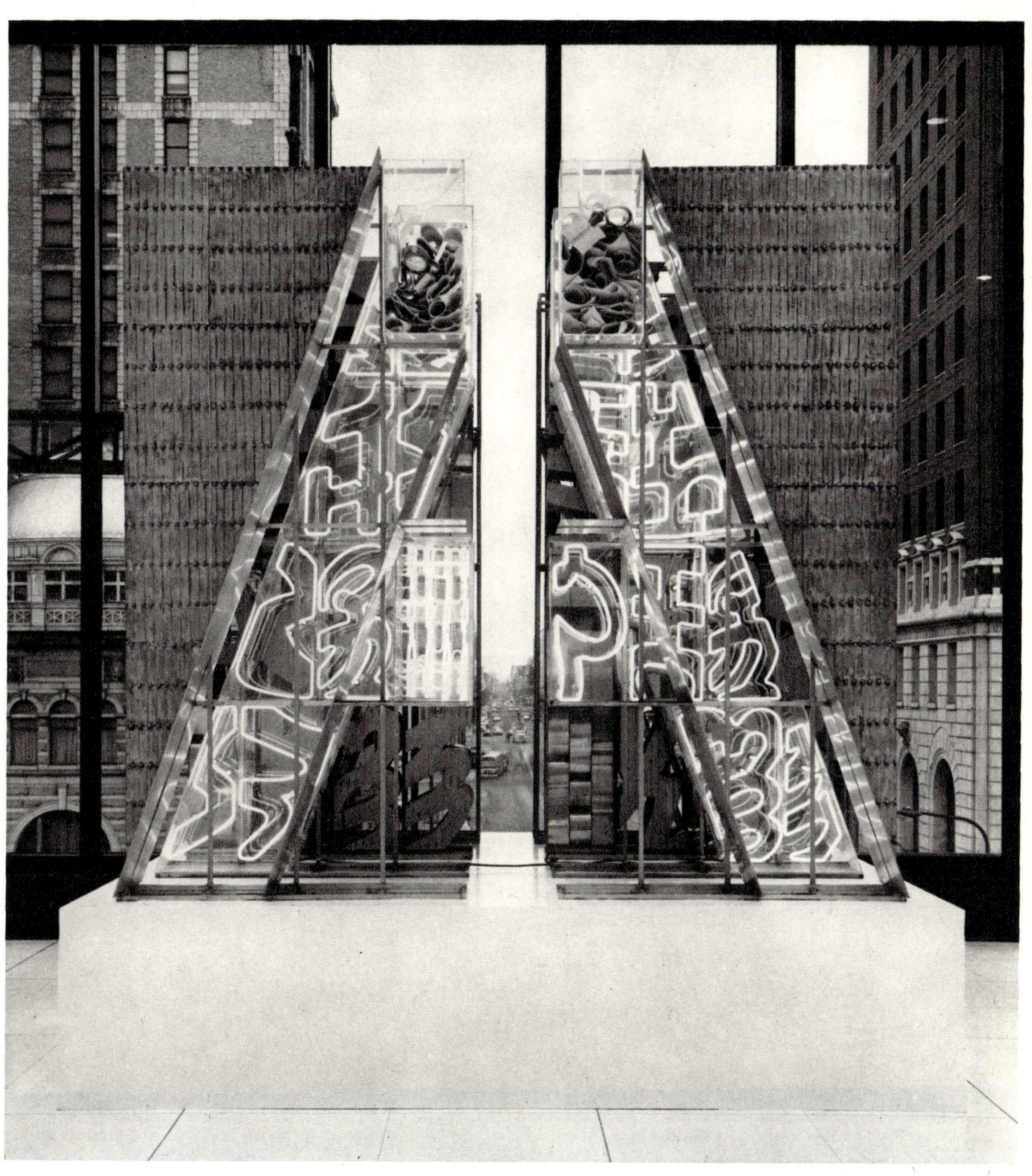

1. CHRYSSA. *The Gates to Times Square.* 1966.
Albright-Knox Art Gallery, Buffalo, N.Y.
Gift of Mr. and Mrs. Albert A. List

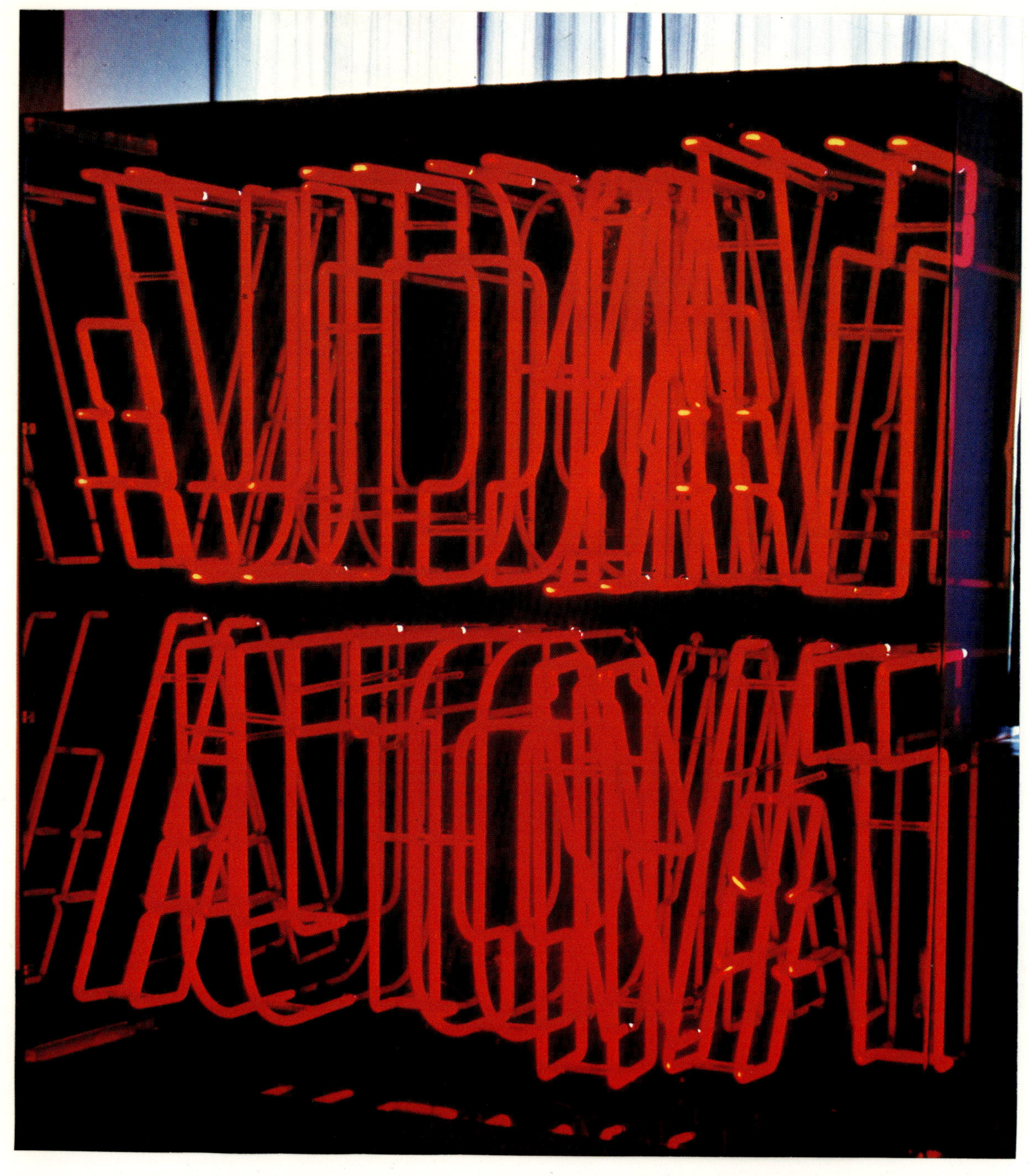

2.   CHRYSSA. *Automat*. 1972. Harry N. Abrams Family Collection, New York

13

HANS L. C. JAFFE

The Visual Arts:
Their "Industrial Revolution" and
Its Consequences

In 1928 Paul Valéry, the French poet who very often has foreseen the essential changes of our modern civilization and has worded his prophecies in marvelously suggestive and succinct language, published an article on "The Conquest of Ubiquity" (La conquête de l'ubiquité).[1] In this short essay he forecast the triumph of television and the possibility, arising from the very recently developed faculty, to distribute every aspect of perceptive reality to the home of anybody willing to receive it. The surprising precision of his language makes it preferable to quote parts of his essay in the original text: "Comme l'eau, comme le gaz, comme le courant électrique viennent de loin dans nos demeures répondre à nos besoins moyennant un effort quasi nul, aussi serons-nous alimentés d'images visuelles ou auditives, naissant et s'évanouissant au moindre geste, presque à un signe. Comme nous sommes accoutumés, si ce n'est asservis, à recevoir chez nous l'énergie sous diverses espèces, ainsi trouverons-nous fort simple d'y obtenir ou d'y recevoir ces variations ou oscillations très rapides dont les organes de nos sens qui les cueillent et qui les intègrent font tout ce que nous savons. Je ne sais si jamais philosophe a rêvé d'une société pour la distribution de la Réalité Sensible à domicile." After having explained that this distribution has already become a fact as far as sounds are concerned—music, speech, etc.—and that it has become possible to "make audible, at any point of the globe, on the very moment, a musical work executed wheresoever" and "on every point of the globe, at any moment, to restitute, at one's choice, a musical work," he continues: "Nous sommes encore assez loin d'avoir apprivoisé à ce point les phénomènes visibles. La couleur et le relief sont encore assez rebelles. Un soleil qui se couche sur le Pacifique, un Titien qui est à Madrid ne viennent pas encore se peindre sur le mur de notre chambre aussi fortement et trempeusement que nous y recevons une symphonie. Cela se fera. Peut-être fera-t-on mieux encore et saura-t-on nous faire voir quelque chose de ce qui est au fond de la mer."

Valéry's prophecy has become true within a quarter of a century. Images at any point of the globe can be distributed everywhere, and even the images drawn from the bottom of the sea have become visible all over the earth. And what is even more important: Valéry has touched upon the main problem of modern mass-media, the problem of ubiquity. Modern mass-media—not only television, but videotape as well—have made it possible to fulfill the demand (which he already formulated for the world of sound and auditory experience) for visual perception: the witnessing by persons living far away of any event on a remote spot of the globe, and the reconstruction of any visual fact, anywhere on the globe, at any moment and according to the choice of the individual. Modern mass-media have indeed extended to a maximal degree our visual dictionary, in the sense that Baudelaire gave to this word when he wrote "La nature n'est qu'un dictionnaire," explaining his thesis by the following phrase: "Tout l'univers visible n'est qu'un magasin d'images et de signes auxquels l'imagination donnera une place et une valeur relative; c'est une espèce de pâture que l'imagination doit digérer et transformer."[2]

The most relevant fact about this enlarged visual dictionary is that now, by the evolution of modern technique, it is at the disposal of almost everyone: that is to say, that the dialogue with "Perceptive Reality" (the "Réalité Sensible" written in Valéry's capital letters) no longer calls for the intervention of the artist, but gives access to the vocabulary of visual facts to mankind in its largest extent. This is indeed the "industrial revolution" of the fine arts, which started with the invention of photography, but has reached its second and decisive phase with the development of television. The fact that television makes every citizen of the world a potential witness to any event on the globe contributes to a large degree to the authentication of visual facts: every human being who has access to modern mass-media, wherever he lives, can see things happen elsewhere, and no longer depends on a reporter or other eyewitness for the veracity of facts, for he has become an eyewitness himself. He still depends on the "reporter" and a possible bias of vision only because the man handling the television camera chooses the point of view (in the most literal and metaphorical senses of the word) for his machine, and is therefore capable of manipulating the statements of the actual eyewitnesses.

The influence of the "industrial revolution" of the fine arts has been profoundly treated by Walter Benjamin in his masterly essay, "Das Kunstwerk im Zeitalter seiner technischen Reproduzierbarkeit."[3] Benjamin, whose article was published in 1936, had not then taken into account the possibilities of television, and oriented his research mainly on the capacities and resources of the cinema. Though he quotes from Valéry's essay, he could not yet stress the point of ubiquity as can now be done. Yet he sees clearly the importance of a growing democratization of the visual images: "Er beruht auf zwei Umständen, die beide mit der zunehmenden Bedeutung der Massen im heutigen Leben zusammenhängen. Nämlich: die Dinge raümlich und menschlich *näher* zu bringen, ist ein genau so leidenschaftliches Anliegen der gegenwärtigen Massen, wie es ihrer Tendenz einer Überwindung des Einmaligen jedes Gegebenheit durch die Aufnahme von deren Reproduktion ist";[4] and, a few phrases further, "Die Ausrichtung der Realität auf die Massen und die Massen auf sie ist ein Vorgang von unbegrenster Tragweite sowohl für das Denken wie für die Anschauung."[5]

These trends of thought have recently been taken up in a more apologetic plea for life-photography and the authenticity of the image by K. Pawck in his "Das optische Zeitalter"; they have also turned the memory of several authors to another French quotation that deals with another industrial revolution in the fine arts—or, to use Benjamin's words, "thinking and viewing" (Denken und Anschauung); this is Victor Hugo's phrase on the birth of the printed book: "L'archidiacre considère quelque temps en silence le gigantesque édifice, puis étendant avec un soupir sa main vers le livre imprimé qui était ouvert sur sa table et sa main gauche vers Notre-Dame, et, promenant un triste regard du livre à l'église:— Hélas, dit-il, ceci tuera cela."[6] This prophecy, which in retrospect dealt with democratization as well, has become true only to a small degree: indeed the printed book has become, from the sixteenth century on, the major source of information, but the fine arts have not been killed by the book. They have survived, but they have been able to survive by accepting the printed book as a challenge, that is to say, as a revision of the boundaries of their realm. In the same work from which the prophetic phrase on the printed book is quoted, Victor Hugo writes: "Que ce soit fatal ou providentiel, Gutenberg est le prédécesseur de Luther."[7] As a matter of fact, the depiction of visual reality—portrait-painting, in the broadest sense of the word—preceded Gutenberg's invention.

Today we may ask in our turn if the fine arts are indeed to be killed by what seems the successor of the printed book: visual information. There can be no doubt that the invention of photography, film, television, and videotape, combined with radio and gramophone records and tapes, constitutes as important an industrial revolution as the invention of the printed book was in its time. The new facts provide access to information for an ever-increasing number of people, without the restrictions caused by language barriers: the dictionary offered to our contemporaries is open to all tongues. It is world-wide indeed, and limited by only one important characteristic: the visual perceptibility of the facts contained in the dictionary. Here the phrase of Gustave Courbet, coined for the fine arts, comes up again in a new context: "La peinture est un art essentiellement concret et ne peut consister que dans la représentation des choses réelles et existantes. Un object abstrait, non visible, non existant, n'est pas du domaine de la peinture."[8] This exclusive and rigorous formula—which may now be taken up again by the philosophy of the mass-media—has been considered a challenge to the art of our century. Courbet, who wanted his art to be as faithful to visual perception as photography could be—much as Balzac wanted to "faire concurrence à l'état civil"—achieved his magnificent work by starting out from an axiom that in his period was self-evident: the congruity of sensual perception and reality (fig. 1).

But since Courbet's time—the epoch of positivism—this axiom has been questioned and even denied: discoveries, scientific theories, and the conclusions derived from them for our vision of reality have shown that sensual perception does not render a totally true and valid image of reality. Science has opened domains, inaccessible to perception, which give a deeper, more essential insight into reality. Psychology has made us understand that beneath the phenomena registered by our behavior there are forces pertaining to the essence of our human existence. And new facts have changed our vision: speed and the conquest of space have altered the old, stable point of view, the fixed position of the eye. Not only has our vision changed since the middle of the nineteenth century—the period of the first "industrial revolution" in the visual arts—but reality has changed as well, and so has the relation between perception and reality. It is here that the results of the new visual inventions make themselves felt: the birth of abstract art is one major consequence of this industrial revolution, and the invention of photography and its subsequent developments—film, television, etc.—have had a fundamental effect.

The most important example of this change is the portrait. Before photography was invented anyone wanting to perpetuate the likeness of an object, to retain its external form, could find help only from the artist—painter or sculptor. The portrait in the most extensive sense of the word, the rendering of the appearance of a man, a house, a ship, or a well-laid table, was the task at which only the artist worked. Now, since the invention of photography, anyone can find a photographer or do the work with his own camera. The "industrial revolution" within our visual possibilities has thus changed the boundaries of the visual arts: the whole domain of portraiture, which for centuries had belonged to the realm of artistic communication, has now been split off and relegated to that of factual information. This change in the boundaries of its territory has been one of the challenges to modern art that led to the new relation between perception and reality. The new attitude, entirely opposed to Courbet's peremptory and exclusive statement, was first put into words by Vincent van Gogh in a letter to his brother about a portrait he was doing (fig. 2): "I should like to paint the portrait of an artist friend, a man who dreams great dreams, who works as the nightingale sings, because it is his nature. He'll be a blond man. I want to put my appreciation, the love I have for him, into the picture. So I paint him as he is, as faithfully as I can do, to begin with. But the picture is not yet finished. To finish it, I am now going to be the arbitrary colorist. I exaggerate the fairness of the hair, I even get to orange tones, chromes and pale citron-yellow. Behind the head, instead of painting the ordinary wall of the mean room, I paint infinity, a plain background of the richest intensest blue that I can contrive, and by this simple combination of the bright head against the rich blue background, I get a mysterious effect, like a star in the depth of an azure sky."[9] The problem he poses—to render visible in painting his feelings and thoughts which cannot be perceived by the eye—became a program for the following generation. And when Cézanne postulates "une harmonie parallèle à la nature"[10] he stresses not the outer appearance of nature, but the laws of its creation—which cannot be perceived by the human eye, but only by the human spirit: geometry tells us more about nature than our senses do. Odilon Redon, who belonged to the same generation, painted his images of nightmares and fantastic apparitions even before Freud had discovered the realm of the subconscious—images which man can only perceive when he closes his eyes, but which enlarge our understanding of our human existence. In all these works, created late in the nineteenth century and under the spell of the "industrial revolution" of the visual arts, painting has taken a course almost opposed to its traditional scope since the Middle Ages: it has been guided, not by the "vis imitativa," but by the "vis cognoscitiva" which had been already closely related to the visual arts by St. Thomas Aquinas.[11] Paul Klee has clearly formulated this thought in 1924: "Kunst gibt nicht das Sichtbare wieder, sondern macht sichtbar."[12]

Only in the twentieth century have the visual arts resolutely broken away from perception: abstract art was born, partly as the capacity to render visible a new image of the world, partly as an answer to the challenge of the industrial revolution. When Mondriaan—perhaps the most consistent artist in the chain of abstractionists—defines the scope of his art as "a clear vision of reality"[13] he does not aim at rendering a perceived reality, but considers it his task to build a visual model of reality, of the laws and rules which are not accessible to perception (fig. 3). The visual arts have become, during the last fifty years, a means not to render reality but to approach its comprehension, its structure, its laws. Indeed, the visual arts have undertaken a task similar to that executed by scientific research: to build a model of reality which makes comprehensible the facts of perception, which makes them fall into a pattern. This important change in the direction of the visual arts can be seen as a direct consequence of the "industrial revolution" of our visual experience: technique—that is to say, photography, film, television, etc.—has taken over the old task of the visual arts to perpetuate the appearance of reality, to make its outward likeness accessible to perception, and has thus directed them toward the discovery of a yet unexplored domain: the structure of reality.

This task, this range of new possibilities, had already been foreseen in 1852 by another French writer, Gustave Flaubert, when he said in a letter: "La beauté deviendra peut-être un sentiment inutile à l'humanité et l'Art sera quelque chose qui tiendra le milieu entre l'algèbre et la musique."[14] An art, therefore, that partakes of cognition—as mathematics—and of delectation—as music—but that is based, by its two sources, on numbers and on mutual relations. In opposition to the new media which have brought forth the "industrial revolution" in the visual arts, abstract art and its relatives in the family of arts do not aim at information, but at comprehension. Mondriaan can be quoted again: "Art—though an aim in itself—is, as much as religion, again a means by which the universal can be known, that is contemplated in plastic essence."[15] A dialectic process has changed the course of the arts, as the industrial revolution has done in so many domains of human life: walking through nature, the only way of transport in the earliest centuries, was replaced first by the horse-drawn carriage, then by automobiles and airplanes; walking through nature has now become a form of recreation, a means toward feeling contact with surrounding nature. A similar dialectic process has split the realm of the visual arts, and of human visual existence, into two fields: the domain of perceptible forms, on one side, and the domain of their structure, their construction, on the other.

What does this change, this shifting of the boundaries, mean for the visual arts and for our view of the world? We may assume that it is symptomatic of a very gradual, almost unconscious return toward a more universalist conception of the world. In any case, the arts of our century seem to have broken away from the dominating tradition of nominalism that reigned for centuries and placed the individual object at the center of artistic ambition: *universalia sunt nomina*—the general concepts are merely words, and it is only the objects, the individual facts of reality, that contain the truth on which the arts can build their works. Now, the thesis seems reversed: *universalia sunt realia*—the general concepts have become reality indeed, and the individual facts of creation are only arbitrary phenomena, variations which cannot serve as a foundation for a "true vision of reality." It seems that most artists of our century base their vision of the world on these general concepts, these "universalia"—the general laws and basic principles of reality which are inaccessible to direct perception, but are nonetheless "really existing things," as Van Gogh terms it. In any case nominalistic perception and universalist conception exist side by side, and together they form the realm of our visual capacities.

At the beginning of abstract art—in 1912—Kandinsky was already conscious of this double possibility of visual expression and communication (fig. 4). In his article "Über die Formfrage," published in *Der Blaue Reiter*,[16] he states that there are two poles in the conveying of a visual message: "Diese zwei Pole sind: 1) die grosse Abstraktion; 2) die grosse Realistik. Diese zwei Pole eröffnen zwei Wege, die schliesslich zu einem Ziel führen."[17] He describes the second objective by writing: "Die erwähnte, erst keimende grosse Realistik ist ein Streben, aus dem Bilde das äusserlich Künstlerische zu vertreiben und den Inhalt des Werkes durch einfache ('unkünstlerische') Wiedergabe des einfachen harten Gegenstandes zu verkörpern."[18] The definition of the first pole is: "Der grosse Gegensatz zu dieser Realistik ist die grossen Abstraktion, die aus dem Bestreben, das Gegenständliche (Reale) scheinbar ganz auszuschalten, besteht und den Inhalt des Werkes in 'unmateriellen' Formen zu verkörpern sucht."[19] And he unites both tendencies by stating: "Und hier sind diese abstrahierten oder abstracter Formen (Linien, Flächen, Flecken, usw.) nicht selbst als solche wichtig, sondern nur ihr innerer Klang, ihr Leben. So wie in der Realistik nicht der Gegenstand selbst oder seine äussere Hülle, sondern sein innerer Klang, Leben wichtig sind."[20]

Only both aspects together—the factual reality and the comprehensive contemplation—can form our vision of reality. The "industrial revolution" of the visual experience has given mankind the means to bring forth an adequate expression of the two aspects of one reality.

NOTES

[1]   Valéry, P., "La conquête de l'ubiquité," *Oeuvres complètes,* Bibl. de la Pléiade, Paris, 1962, II, p. 1284.

[2]   Baudelaire, Ch., "Salon de 1859," *Oeuvres complètes,* ed. Crépet, Paris, 1923, Curiosités esthétiques, p. 283.

[3]   Benjamin, W., *Das Kunstwerk im Zeitalter seiner technischen Reproduzierbarheit* (reprinted, ed. Suhrkamp, Frankfurt, 1963).

[4]   Benjamin, *op. cit.,* p. 18.

[5]   Benjamin, *op. cit.,* p. 19.

[6]   Hugo, V., *Notre Dame de Paris,* III, ch. 1.

[7]   Hugo, *op. cit.,* V, ch. 2.

[8]   Courthion, P., *G. Courbet raconté par lui-même,* Geneva, 1950, pp. 205–6.

[9]   *The Complete Letters of Vincent van Gogh,* Greenwich, Conn., 1959, III, p. 6 (letter no. 520).

[10]   Gasquet, J., *Cézanne,* Paris, 1926, p. 131.

[11]   St. Thomas Aquinas, *Summa,* I, qu.5, a.4. ad.1.

[12]   Klee, P., *Das bildnerische Denken,* Basel, 1956, p. 56.

[13]   Mondriaan, P., *Plastic Art and Pure Plastic Art and Other Essays,* New York, 1945, p. 15.

[14]   Flaubert, G., *Correspondance,* III (1852–54), Paris, 1927, p. 18.

[15]   Mondriaan, P., *De Stijl,* I, p. 52 (reprinted, Amsterdam 1970).

[16]   Kandinsky, W., "Über die Formfrage," *Der Blaue Reiter,* Munich, 1912 (reprinted Munich, 1965).

[17]   Kandinsky, *op. cit.,* p. 147 (82).

[18]   Kandinsky, *op. cit.,* p. 154 (83).

[19]   Kandinsky, *op. cit.,* p. 154 (84).

[20]   Kandinsky, *op. cit.,* p. 155 (85).

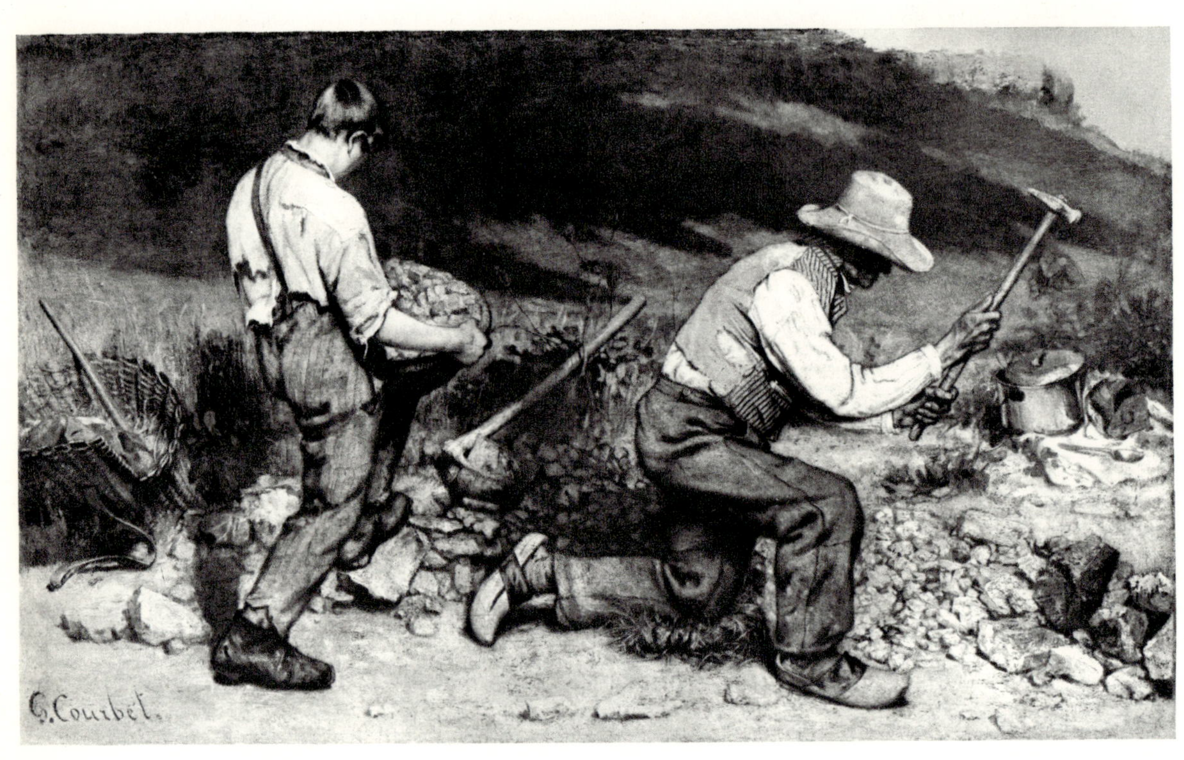

1. GUSTAVE COURBET. *Stone Breakers*. 1849.
Formerly State Picture Gallery, Dresden. Destroyed 1945

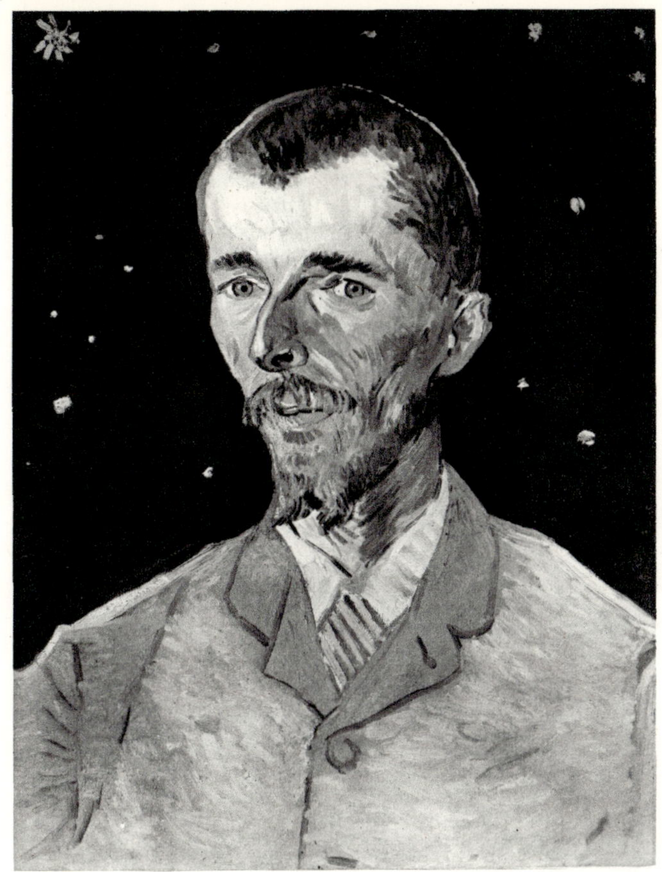

2. VINCENT VAN GOGH.
Portrait of Eugène Boch.
Jeu de Paume, The Louvre, Paris

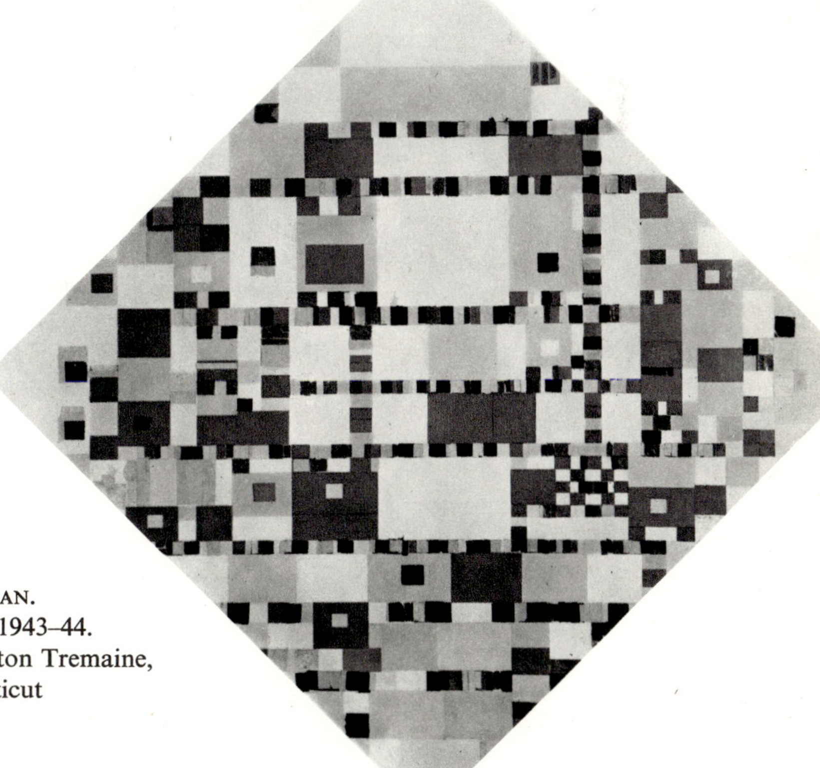

3. PIET MONDRIAAN.
Victory Boogie-Woogie. 1943–44.
Collection Mr. and Mrs. Burton Tremaine,
Meriden, Connecticut

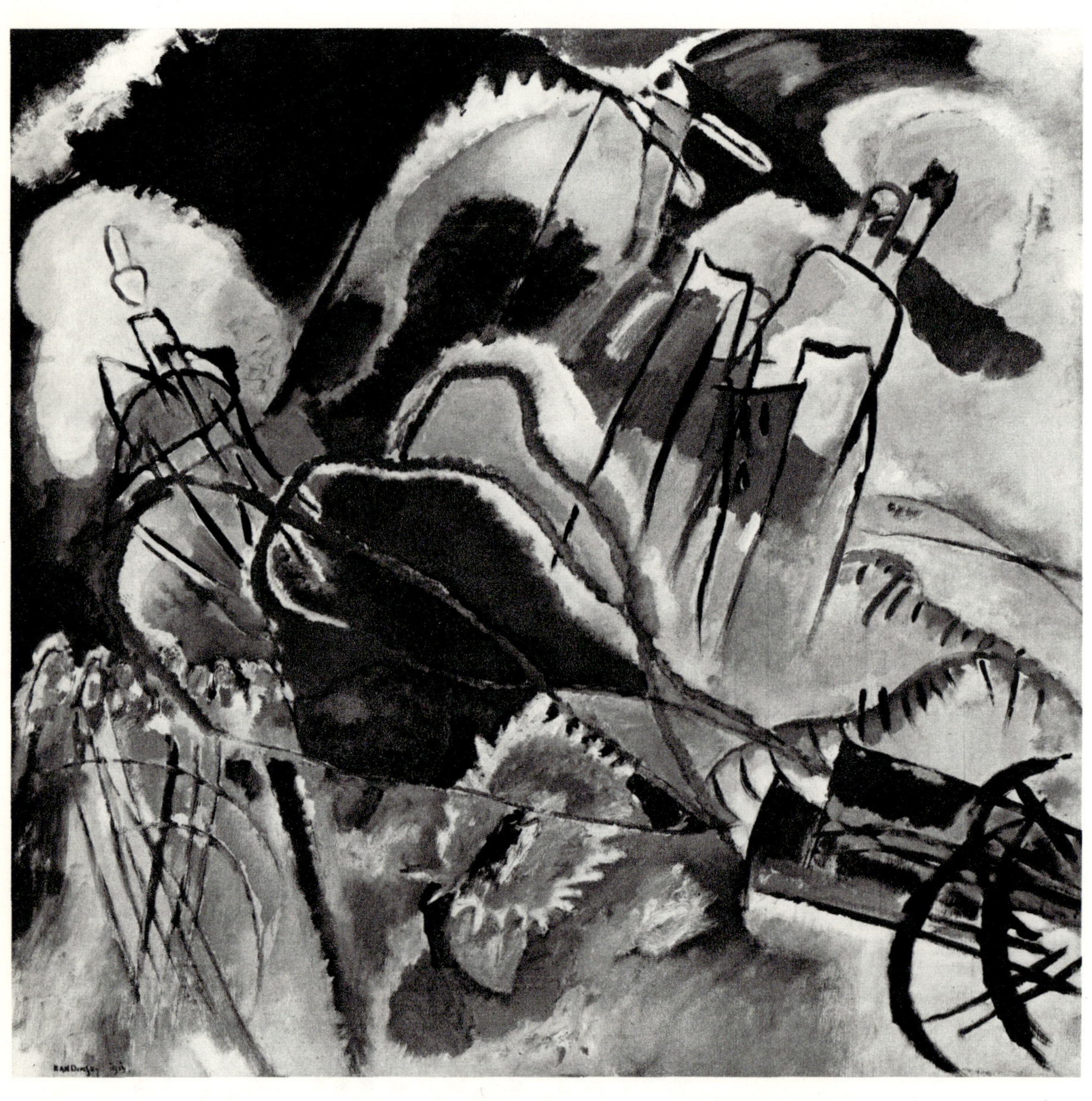

4. VASSILY KANDINSKY. *Improvisation 30 (Cannon)*. 1913.
The Art Institute of Chicago

14

H. W. JANSON

The Myth of the Avant-Garde

The 1960s, in retrospect, may well be looked upon by cultural historians as the Decade of the Death Wish. It was the time, our grandchildren will be told, when theologians announced the death of God, historians declared the death (or at least the irrelevance) of history, sociologists denied the possibility of social science as distinct from political action, and art critics mourned the death of the artistic avant-garde.

I am not prepared to appraise the reports of the death of God. They may, in the words of Mark Twain, turn out to be greatly exaggerated. As for the death of history and the death of sociology, these fields seem, if judged by the attitude of their less patient practitioners, to have fallen victim to our widespread wish for instant gratification—a wish perennially denied by the contemplative life and held out as the proverbial unreachable carrot by the active life (and aren't we all tempted to be "activists" these days?).

The death of the avant-garde is a more complicated matter. There must be something to it, otherwise we could not have had, in 1969–71, Ralph Ginzburg's expensive but vulgar coffee-table magazine called *Avant-Garde*. More importantly, we have by now a small body of writings by serious and knowledgeable people dealing with the phenomenon. The earliest to announce the death of the avant-garde seems to have been William Seitz, in an article that appeared, somewhat surprisingly, in *Vogue* in 1963. There are, as we shall see, some implications in the author's view of the subject that the avant-garde has to do with fashions, intellectual if not sartorial. Not long after, Harold Rosenberg began to write of The Death of the New, which is another way of saying "the death of the avant-garde." Professor Donald Egbert of Princeton analyzed "The Idea of the Avant-Garde in Art and Politics" in a long essay in the *American Historical Review* in 1967. And more recently Professor James Ackerman of Harvard has pursued the demise of the avant-garde in an article significantly subtitled "Notes on the Sociology of Recent American Art."

Except for Professor Egbert, who clearly states that his concern is with the *idea* of the avant-garde, all the authors I have named seem to take it for granted that there actually was, until very recently, such a thing as an artistic avant-garde. Their writings are in the nature of obituaries, detached yet tinged with a genuine sense of regret. No one, so far as I know, has inquired into the relation between the avant-garde as an idea and as a historic reality. My remarks are intended to be a first step toward such an inquiry.

We must begin by taking a closer look at the prevailing explanation of the death of the avant-garde as set down, or suggested, by the Messrs. Seitz, Rosenberg, and Ackerman. The latter has summed it up with his usual felicity of phrase: "The avant garde is a phenomenon of the past, because [today] the entire army—and a good part of the civilian population—has moved up to join and surround it." In other words, the avant-garde was choked to death sometime between 1950 and 1955 by its own success. Let me elaborate a bit on this view by paraphrasing Seitz and Ackerman: according to them, the avant-garde demands as a condition of its existence a social environment sufficiently set in its traditions and taste to be disturbed and offended by works of art that abandon accepted standards in the search for new form and meaning. From the Romantic era (i.e., the early nineteenth century) to the 1950s, significant innovation in art enjoyed the stimulus of just such a social environment: at first, any significant innovation was massively rejected by an enraged middlebrow audience but accepted by a handful of artists and critics; only much later was this art widely appreciated and celebrated in the mass media. Since this pattern repeated itself again and again, Ackerman tells us, it promoted and justified the artist's increasing sense of alienation and thus became a stimulus to innovation. Before 1800, in contrast, there was no sense of alienation among artists, because the public was more sympathetic; but just because in those earlier days the artist respected his public, he was more cautious in trying innovations that might offend it. The official rejection that came to be the artist's fate from the early nineteenth century on produced suffering as well as freedom, and the avant-garde artist depended on it in articulating his attitude toward his work. What, then, broke the pattern? It was the acceptance by the public of the New York School of painters in the years 1955–60. These artists— Pollock, de Kooning, Klein, Rothko, etc.—had struggled in obscurity during the 1930s and '40s until they arrived at a mature statement in the years immediately after the end of the Second World War. This mature statement, a difficult and esoteric art, at first met the usual response: the large public was scandalized and accused the artists of either fraud or incompetence. But suddenly and surprisingly the tide changed, and within less than a decade after their first exhibitions these artists were eagerly bought by museums and private collectors. How did the artists respond to this unexpected drop in the "pressure of rejection"? According to Ackerman, the effect was catastrophic. Their art could not support the embrace of the public, and within ten years nearly every surviving member of the group had passed his prime and was producing works of lesser quality.

What accounts for this shift of fashion, from a public posture of rejection of the avant-garde to one of acceptance? Ackerman denies that it represents a maturation of general taste and comprehension. He sees it, rather, as a sociological phenomenon and insists that the new attitude of acceptance is just as indiscriminate as the older attitude of rejection. The galleries, quick to sense the change of climate, soon shifted attention toward other novelties, especially Pop Art; and Pop Art found acceptance even faster than had the Abstract Expressionists, only to have its own crisis of style within a few years and to be displaced in public favor by a quick succession of still more recent movements—Hard-Edge, Shaped Canvas, Color Field, and what have you. Change, titillation, had become a positive value in itself.

This, then, is what Ackerman means when he says that today the entire army, and a good part of the civilian population, has moved up to join and surround the avant-garde. Clement Greenberg, the critic whose career and convictions are most completely identified with the New York School painters of the 1950s, has noted the same phenomenon. In a lecture, *Avant-garde Attitudes,* delivered in 1968 and published the following year, he denounces what he contemptuously refers to as the "nominally advanced art of the sixties" and concludes that "variety within the limits of the artistically insignificant, of the aesthetically banal and trivial, is itself artistically insignificant." In other words, he sticks to his critical guns of the 1940s and '50s—nothing that has happened since the demise of the New York School is artistically significant, and the true avant-garde attitude remains that of the artists he championed back in the good old days. Had Greenberg been willing to use the terminology of Seitz and Ackerman, he would have said that the avant-garde is not dead but simply in abeyance for the time being because nothing significant is being produced. To accept the notion of the death of the avant-garde would, for him, be tantamount to claiming that no significant art will ever be produced again, that art itself is dead.

To me, there is a deep and somehow touching irony in Greenberg's critical stance. His refusal to acknowledge that anything at all of artistic importance has been achieved since the 1950s, and the implication that art today is, if not dead, at least in a state of torpor, recalls the pessimism of every conservative critic since the seventeenth century. The impending death of art has been proclaimed any number of times in the course of the past three hundred years, though usually in terms of "art will die unless . . ." ; that is, unless we follow the Carracci and not Caravaggio, Poussin and not Rubens, Ingres and not Delacroix, Matisse and not Picasso, Picasso and not Marcel Duchamp. In much the same way, Greenberg enjoins us to follow the Abstract Expressionists and not Pop Art, because Pop Art is not—*cannot be*—avant-garde.

Although Ackerman agrees that Pop Art is not, and never was, avant-garde, he does not love it on that account. He calls its vocabulary familiar and its message simplistic. Yet he sees the anti-avant-gardism of Pop as a positive value. The traditional role and self-image of the artist as the "outsider," the alienated avant-gardist, can only nurture an art world that forces the artist into a demeaning dependence on tastemakers, publicists, and exhibitors, Ackerman says. And he welcomes a new (albeit as yet hardly defined) role of the present-day artist that makes him an "insider," something akin to the teacher and the scientist, and assigns to him a public role.

At first glance, this attitude may seem optimistic, positive, forward-looking as against Greenberg's pessimism. But actually Ackerman finds only one promising trend among younger artists today: the striving for the colossal in size, which makes it almost impossible for museums, let alone private homes, to display the works of such men as Donald Judd, Robert Morris, and Tony Smith. It might be argued, Ackerman admits, that by frustrating the conventional channels of exhibition and communication this new art is seeking through sheer size the sort of avant-garde isolation formerly gained through far-out content and form. But he prefers to see in the new trend toward the colossal an indication of the artist's acceptance of a public role: such work, he maintains, is designed for the scale of our cities—the square, the campus, the skyscraper, the airline terminal lobby— so that the artist now addresses the public directly rather than through the channels of the dealer and the museum. And he holds out the promise that what has been lost in terms of isolation can be gained in terms of collaboration for the attainment of common goals, without restricting innovation in art.

Unlike Greenberg, who maintains the partisan stance of the critic to the bitter end, Ackerman claims to have arrived at his appraisal of the current situation as a historian, whose analysis of the new condition of post-avant-garde art does not constitute a qualitative judgment. It would not be difficult, I think, to get him to agree that in proclaiming the death of the avant-garde he has been acting, in the current phrase, as a "committed historian" with very definite value judgments of his own. The only difference between Greenberg and Ackerman in this respect is that Greenberg's values are clearly visible (they are those of the New York School of the 1950s) while Ackerman's are not, since they are anticipated values of the future. And, I may add, a utopian future. Now, it is clearly not the historian's province to construct utopias. Utopias have their uses, but none conceived so far has turned out to anticipate the future except perhaps in a few details. Thus we may take comfort in the thought that Ackerman's artistic utopia is not likely to come to pass, either. A future that no longer knows any relationship between the artist and the individual patron, where all art has the impersonality of industrial products, does sound a bit bleak, after all. At the bottom of this vision there seems to be a kind of McLuhanite fallacy. The death of the Gutenberg Galaxy is another report that is likely to be greatly exaggerated. Television, I venture to say, will no more replace the printed word than the invention of printing wiped out handwriting. Media of communication tend to complement each other as they multiply, and much the same may be said of artistic media and styles. Photography, after all, did not wipe out painting, although there were those who feared this a hundred years ago. There is no reason why impersonal and personal artistic techniques and styles should not continue to exist side by side in the future.

But to return to the problem of the avant-garde. In proclaiming its death, Ackerman and his predecessors obviously imply that it once was alive, that it was a historic reality rather than a myth. And that is precisely what I wish to question.

Myths of course are in themselves historical realities, insofar as people's beliefs shape their behavior. I readily concede this kind of reality to the idea of the avant-garde. But that is not the same as Greenberg's and Ackerman's conviction that avant-gardism was the motive force behind the development of Western art between, roughly, 1800 and 1950. I would submit that such is a narrow, partisan view, which befits the critic who wants to influence events according to his own conviction of what is desirable, but does not befit the historian who is trying to find out what actually happened.

The title of Professor Egbert's paper, "The Idea of the Avant-Garde in Art and Politics," suggests the origin of the term. He found its earliest use, in our sense, in Saint-Simon's *Opinions littéraires, philosophiques, et industrielles* of 1825, where an artist, in a dialogue with a scientist, proclaims: "It is we, the artists, who will serve you as avant-garde. . . [i.e., as the prophets of future events]." Saint-Simon had been a soldier, Egbert points out, rising to the rank of major in the forces of the young American republic, hence the military simile came easily to him. It suggests an army on the move, with the main mass preceded by a picked few who reconnoiter the road and guard against enemy ambushes. If the idea of the avant-garde is transferred to politics or to art, it implies that history moves like an army: everybody in the same direction, toward the same goal, with the brightest and most venturesome in the lead—but not in command, since the command is provided by the supposedly inevitable goal of history, which the avant-garde must know but cannot determine. The Hegelian or Marxian supreme commander is invisible somewhere far to the rear, his existence to be inferred only from the movement of the army under his authority. To accept the idea of the political or artistic avant-garde, then, we must be willing to believe that man's history has a goal, and that it is our duty to "cooperate" with this goal even though it will be reached whether we do so or not. We must, in other words, believe in the inevitability of historic events.

This is not to say that we must necessarily accept every sparrow's fall as inevitable. But we must at least accept the notion of historic "progress." And it is, I believe, the notion of progress in the development of art that ultimately lies behind the concept of the artistic avant-garde. Oddly enough, the idea of progress as applied to artistic events appears to be much older than the idea of progress with respect to history in general. Pliny the Elder, our main literary source for Greek and Roman art, constantly describes artistic events in terms of progress: this painter, he will say, was the first to use colors instead of monochrome; that painter was the first to master the three-quarter view, surpassing his predecessors who knew only front and side views. And yet the Ancients saw no progress in human history as a whole. How then did the idea of progress enter into their view of art? Once we start reading Pliny, the reason becomes clear at once. Pliny was no art historian, in fact the very notion of art in the modern sense did not exist in his day. All he knew were "the arts," and these were not distinguished from the crafts or technical inventions. Now, the one area of human endeavor which by common consent demonstrates progressive development is that of crafts and technology; even the most cursory view of the past reveals that our tools and our ways of using them have improved over the centuries. For Pliny, the use of colors and of the three-quarter view represented progress in this technical sense—progress toward an ever more perfect rendering of the visible world. And the Renaissance notion of progress in art, as Professor Ernst Gombrich has pointed out, is a revival of the Graeco-Roman concept as enshrined in Pliny and other ancient authors.

Antiquity and the Renaissance, however, are separated by the Middle Ages, a thousand-year interval during which the notion of artistic progress was forgotten. In its place, the Middle Ages had the concept of progress, or at least of a goal, for history as a whole, a goal determined by the inscrutable will of God and revealed in His plan of salvation as set down in Scripture. The acknowledged purpose of art was to celebrate this divine plan, hence art could not have any goals of its own such as the perfection of realism. With the advent of the Renaissance, art did not suddenly lose its religious purpose when the humanists revived the ancient idea of progress toward an ever more perfect mastery of nature. There arose, moreover, a further complication, since nature to the Renaissance could mean two different things: nature as we know it from direct observation, and nature of an elevated, perfected kind as exemplified in the works of art of Antiquity. How were these conflicting claims to be reconciled? The demand that art celebrate the glory of God was broadened into the demand that art must elevate the mind of the beholder. This implies, however, that art is not for Everyman but for a select audience which has the right kind of understanding; Petrarch's remark on Giotto, that his work "does not appeal to the multitude but is greatly admired by the experts," may be the earliest expression of this attitude. As for representing nature-as-we-all-know-it, it could be argued that to do so was to praise the glory of God, since nature was after all His creation. This is the ultimate justification of Renaissance realism, even of the tradition of *saper vedere,* from Piero della Francesca to Leonardo, which asserts that analytical seeing is the most reliable way to gain knowledge of the phenomenal world. The argument for the representation of ideal nature, or nature perfected, as the goal of art runs as follows: ideal nature and nature-as-we-all-know-it coincided only in Paradise, before the Fall of Man. Ever since then, nature has "run down," deteriorated, so that in Antiquity nature was still a good deal closer to what God had intended it to be than it is today. Hence we must strive to imitate the original beauty of nature rather than its warts and blemishes. Even Winckelmann still claims that nature in ancient times was superior to that in his own day.

Such, broadly speaking, was the framework of Renaissance art theory until about 1700. At that time, a further conflict developed: the assumption that art must elevate the mind and thus appeal to the connoisseur, the small select audience, came under fire. In the French Academy of Painting and Sculpture there arose a "laymen's faction," the Rubénistes, who argued against the idealistic style of Poussin and against the primacy of design on the grounds that art ought to appeal to everybody and that this could best be accomplished through the sensuous appeal of color. Toward the end of the eighteenth century, this notion had hardened into the attitude exemplified today by the slogan, "I don't know anything about art but I know what I like." On the other side of the controversy were Winckelmann, the ideologue of Neoclassicism, and the early Romantics, with their worship of the Sublime. The lay faction insisted that *vox populi vox dei,* that true values in art were simply what the layman liked. And the layman liked *trompe l'oeil,* the closest possible approximation of everyday reality. This new insistence on realism provided the pressure behind the invention of photography in the early nineteenth century. Neoclassicists and Romantics, on the other hand, continued to proclaim the aristocratic concept of art, the pursuit of the Ideal, of the Sublime. But the notion of aristocracy was hopelessly tainted by now; it symbolized the "old regimes," the traditional monarchies that were to tumble under the assault of the French Revolution and its less violent counterparts elsewhere in the Western world. So a new aristocracy was invented: the aristocracy of the mind, the avant-garde. What made this particularly easy and tempting was the fact that the artist at this point could be, and often was, deeply involved in the political issues of the day. The vanguard of the French Revolution included not only the intellectuals of the Enlightenment but also artists such as Greuze and David, whose works may not have had a political propaganda purpose from the start but were so interpreted by Enlightenment critics. A new goal for human history as a whole emerged at this point: the triumph of Reason among rationalist thinkers such as Voltaire, or the realization of the original goodness of man as projected by Rousseau. The early avant-garde among artists was linked to this general goal of history. In Communist Russia, with its doctrine of art's subservience to politics, the link is still officially enforced. But even there the old conflict between "raw nature" and "nature perfected" persists; Russian artists are not allowed to show the warts on the face of the admittedly imperfect present state of society, only the perfect ideal toward which society and history are assumed to be striving.

In the West, meanwhile, art had achieved a kind of autonomy. Its own purpose proved ever more difficult to link with the goal of history as a whole. The mastery of nature was accomplished with the invention of photography, hence the direction in which the avant-garde was leading us had to be redefined. This redefinition may be summed up in the famous phrase of Walter Pater: "all art constantly aspires to the condition of music." In other words, the goal of art is the direct expression of the emotions. In this perspective, it becomes clear why Herbert Read, one of the great propagandists of Modern Art between the two world wars, could claim that representation itself was a fallacy, an alien "literary" element that ought to be eliminated altogether from painting and sculpture. But this goal could, of course, be reached only by stages. The first step was the devaluation of the traditional range of subject matter; it was in part achieved by Delacroix, the leader of the Romantic avant-garde in France, whose notebooks are full of analogies between painting and music and who valued his subjects more for their exoticism, geographic or historical, than for the content they traditionally conveyed. Courbet, the next hero of the avant-garde, went a step further: he remained a Romantic in personal temper but insisted that art must be concerned only with present-day reality ("I cannot paint an angel because I have never seen one"). From then on, the primacy of the "how" over the "what" of art becomes ever more evident until we arrive at Abstract Expressionism, which really does represent a terminal point in this line of development. If we believe, as Clement Greenberg does, that this is indeed the goal of art in modern times, his despair at the state of things since 1960 becomes entirely understandable.

But are we really compelled to read the history of art since the collapse of the Renaissance tradition at the end of the eighteenth century in avant-garde terms? Since about 1960 a younger generation of art historians, such as Robert Rosenblum and Albert Boime, has been taking a new look at artistic events during the past two hundred years and has proposed new evaluations of many phenomena that used to be regarded as insignificant, reactionary, or in any event not avant-garde. Who, for instance, was the avant-garde around 1825—was it Delacroix or Ingres, Turner or Constable, Caspar David Friedrich or the early Nazarenes? The same question could be asked at any other moment in the nineteenth or twentieth century, and would yield equally perplexing answers. There never seems to be only one avant-garde but several, striking out in as many directions at once. The problem is further complicated by the fact that at any given time there are artists at work who belong to several different generations. Monet, for example, was still vigorously painting in the heyday of Cubism. Was he *vieux jeu* during those years? Many would have said so at the time, but his late work was rediscovered with considerable fanfare in the 1950s and suddenly looked very avant-garde because of its kinship to certain aspects of Abstract Expressionism. Must we then place Monet among the avant-garde in both 1865–75 and 1910? If we ask who was the avant-garde around 1865, the obvious conventional answer is Manet and the pioneers of Impressionism. But if we ask the same question as of 1885, we can no longer say "the Impressionists" (after all, Manet had died, and had been received into the Legion of Honor shortly before); our answer must now include Gustave Moreau, along with Cézanne, Seurat, and Van Gogh. But at this point we are likely to recall that in 1865 Moreau was already painting pretty much as he did twenty years later. How is it possible, then, for him to have belonged to the avant-garde of pioneer Symbolists in 1885 but not yet in 1865? Can it be that in 1865 (as at other times) there were several avant-gardes striving in different directions? Once we acknowledge this state of affairs, we can continue to employ the term avant-garde only in rather watered-down fashion as a synonym for artists whose work is in some sense exploratory, regardless of the direction it takes. Why, then, should we be tempted to use it at all? Perhaps because the traditional concept of "period style" does not seem applicable to the nineteenth and twentieth centuries, so that we tend to think of Modern Art in terms of movements rather than as a chronological succession of styles. Yet "avant-garde," too, assumes—unless we are careful to specify which movement we mean in using the term—that at any given moment art has only one goal (or "advances in a single direction"); and that is exactly what we have such difficulty discerning in modern times. Wölfflin's categories or even Riegl's *Kunstwollen* prove useless here. As a matter of fact, they have turned out not to be very illuminating with respect to earlier centuries, where period styles used to be taken for granted. On closer examination, avant-garde as an art historical term is no less difficult to apply to, let us say, the seventeenth century than to the nineteenth or twentieth. Poussin, Pietro da Cortona, and Georges de La Tour were all born within three years of each other; would anyone claim that they represent a single avant-garde advancing in a discernible common direction, or are they rather three separate avant-gardes? The question seems absurd, for the obvious reason that nobody has proposed such a projection of the avant-garde approach into pre-modern times. Still, our example ought to caution us not to confound myth and reality when we speak of the avant-garde in more recent art.

Bibliographical Note

William Seitz' article appeared in *Vogue,* September 1, 1963, pp. 182 ff.; Donald Egbert's paper was published in *The American Historical Review,* LXXIII, 1967, pp. 339–66 (see also the same author's *Social Radicalism and the Arts,* New York, 1970); James Ackerman's essay was printed twice during the same year, in *L'Arte,* 6, 1969, pp. 5–17, and (with a preamble) in *Comparative Studies in Society and History,* 11, 1969, pp. 371–84; Clement Greenberg's lecture was published by the Power Institute of Fine Arts, University of Sydney, Australia, in 1969; Ernst Gombrich's paper on the idea of artistic progress in the Renaissance is to be found in his *Norm and Form,* London and New York, 1966, pp. 1–10.

15

A L L A N   K A P R O W

Easy Activity

Loss would have been called a Happening a few years ago. But "Happening" has come to mean in the public ear almost anything, from a political campaign, campus uprising, hit song, to a chancy occurrence; and to the arts world, of course, it is a type of art. In none of these, not even the latter, do I recognize what I do.

There is a sense, nevertheless, in which this confusion was inevitable and I am partly responsible for it: since the late '50s, in both my Happenings and writings, I've emphasized the blurring and removal of distinctions between art and whatever was non-art up to a particular moment. As this mythology was spread and simplified by the press and as artists began to produce increasing numbers of their own Happenings, Happenings which were in any case quite different from mine, it isn't hard to understand how all sorts of popcult reactions followed along with serious acknowledgments in art books and anthologies. Both contradiction and paradox are the result.

Yet my choice of the word "Happening" was intended to neutralize art and to suggest the possibility of a consciousness and mode of action unencumbered by associations with either any art or other profession. Once I saw that it acquired stereotypical meanings which only got in the way of that consciousness, I adopted Michael Kirby's word "Activity" as an alternative. This is probably futile (as are most intentions and most aliases) but for better or worse, the following is an Activity.

LOSS

drinking an amount of water
boiling an amount of water

waiting for an amount to be:
urinated
or
evaporated

telephoning someone doing the same:
being telephoned by someone doing the same:
to drink that amount of water
or
to add that amount of water
to the water boiling

continuing:
drinking
boiling
urinating
telephoning

until the bladder is empty
until the pot is empty

Loss was prepared as an event for some friends on the occasion of a short visit of mine to New York City in the winter of 1973. It was to be easy to do, and was to take place primarily in the friends' respective homes. Including myself (I took part with Peter Moore at his house), fourteen persons participated on a rainy afternoon, January 27th.

The group met first for a half-hour briefing at the apartment of participants Martha and Henry Edelheit.[1] This customary meeting was necessary to discuss the program printed above, regarding both its practical details—that is, who does what and when—and some of its larger implications. The program's terse form, echoing the simplicity of the actions described, was a verbal shorthand or code that benefited from clarification on the spot rather than in written notes. It was a functional stage in a particular involvement of human beings.

The briefing, therefore, was an essential part of the larger form in process. Logistical questions (some that I hadn't foreseen) were raised and worked out, among them the group's decision to limit the Activity to three hours (4:00 P.M. to 7:00 P.M.), in order to allow for individual needs such as dinner appointments, and a return gathering at the Edelheits at 9:30 P.M. that evening to discuss what had happened; this discussion also was a part of the whole, a parallel evolving of real-time events and a verbalization of their import. I emphasized the inseparability of these features, suggesting that a language of "thoughtful" activities was being created. Put another way, we were *doing thought*. Attentiveness to how this was taking place was necessary to communicating with the language and perhaps using it to some advantage.

After exchanging names and telephone numbers, everyone returned to their apartments (the heavy rain made this an appealing prospect and seemed to allude to the water theme in the event); on arrival each person drank an amount of water and put some on the stove to boil, both measures a matter of personal decision. By about 4:30 P.M. the phone calls began. Besides conveying the necessary information, that is, how much water was to be swallowed or added to a pot, there was much friendly banter among the participants, questions about how things were progressing, humorous remarks over not being able to drink any more, or to urinate, and speculations about who was calling whom for what reasons.

More than that, other social and business calls were made, children were fed their dinners, nonparticipants arrived and left, and normal life went on. Sometimes it was exasperating to find that the telephone lines were constantly busy (with whose calls?) or that no calls came for a long time, causing half-anxious worries that communication was frustrated or that one was being deliberately ignored. (In fact, lighthearted games like this *were* being played among the group, as it turned out in the later discussion, although it was impossible to know that at the time.)

To some extent, as I said, the friends had been prepared to see in these mundane acts a potential of implication not ordinarily apparent. At the briefing I had spoken of certain key ideas in the Activity—some evident in reading the program while others were probably less so—ideas that in any case might be introduced into the actual undertaking. The condensed wording of the program (a "telegram" style) spells out tasks to be accomplished but leaves unspecified the details of execution. Hence, given the fact that the program was to be *done,* not just read, considerable freedom had to be left to the individuals and the group. And this factor, if nothing else, virtually invited speculation about its broader associations.

One of these is structural and present in the written form of the program, a kernel or metaphor of the larger form in practice. "Structure" is not used here simply as an esthetic arrangement of parts into a whole but as a syntax of meaning. I didn't speak of that at the briefing except in passing because it seemed too analytical and lengthy for the occasion, but in retrospect and for this commentary it may be of interest.

Loss is composed of five parts (call them A, B, C, BC, AD). There is a simple, loose symmetry involved in which A and AD are related as a start-stop or intake-output pattern. Within it B is similarly connected to BC. In both, the second term of the symmetry is added to by attaching a previous part, i.e., A to D before it and B to C after it. C, a clear middle, separates the "start" from the "stop" parts with B and BC acting as passages between them. The effect of this is almost circular, namely, that the latter part is like the earlier part with small accumulations of what was prior, their order altered to make that fact apparent. In other words, to paraphrase an old French saying, things don't change much though they seem to. In our case, it was consciousness that may have changed more than the physical conditions of our lives. And while this is the most important change of all, it can't be quantified in the way that A, B, C, BC, AD can. This irony is built into the structure of the five parts.

To go on: these five parts contain 2 lines, 4 lines, 6 lines, 5 lines, 2 lines, respectively; and five of the lines have 5 words each, concentrated in the first and last pairs, thus reenforcing the near symmetry. This points up the differences between the actual structure and our experience of it: the printed program appears sequential, encapsulated in a clear shape, which begins and returns to its beginning; we ended up pretty much as we began, with little or no water. Yet the process of doing it was a random overlay of occurrences in no perceptible order! This feeling was buttressed by the discussions before and afterward, which acted literally as introduction and summary (closing the situation off) while they also were transitions between our lives preceding and following *Loss*.

Shifting from internal structure to that of the subject matter used, *Loss* brought into play two parallel ways of containing and losing water. These were commonplace cycles: a body system and a domestic system, both natural in obeying physical laws. A person consumes water; the body burns some of it off depending on its exertions, retains some of it, and excretes the rest. A pot of tap water boiled (say) for tea loses some of its contents into the atmosphere depending on the heat of the flame, and what remains is partly drunk, with the rest saved or poured down the drain.

Loss was also a mock attempt to align two arbitrary and possibly different measuring systems, namely, whatever method(s) a participant would choose to account for the loss of urine and vaporized water. While most persons chose the same measures for both losses (for example, an ounce), this was initially unforeseeable, and in almost all cases they were distinct for each individual. So the correspondence that might exist between the human and non-human cycles could not be measured; what *was* measurable by subsequent reports was everyone's *differences*.

In the process, *Loss* assigned to each person the function of a measuring instrument—an instrument, however, that *experienced itself*. At the same time the participant was also a measurer, using standard instruments like cups, pints, and quarts.

As measurers, certain estimates could be made beforehand with regard to the time needed to carry out the first steps of the Activity. For instance, from experience we know that at high heat a quart of water in an average-size pot will completely boil off in about forty-five minutes; and that a cup of water swallowed will be excreted in about one hour. Multiplying these estimates by greater amounts of water would give a rough idea of how long each in the group might be involved.

But no one could predict the variations in rates of digestion and excretion within the group, the amounts of water that would be used, the effect on vaporization of wide- or narrow-mouth pots, the degree of heat that would be applied, the delays or frequency of phone calls . . . Hence the time spent (or "lost"), while quite real, was as wildly indeterminate as the real amounts of water consumed or added to each pot.

In theory, of course, the Activity could have extended to several days, but since all measures were arbitrary to begin with, the total time could be arbitrarily fixed by group decision in acknowledgment of real-time-needs, such as dinner, or the unlikelihood of anyone wishing to stay near the phone day and night. As mentioned above, the limit set for *Loss* was three hours.

In this respect, the telephone linkup had an important function. As the invariable conduit between parties, it increased the number of variables in the carrying out of the event. Like the coupling of expected and indeterminate aspects throughout, its common physical presence and relative availability contrasted with the surprise effects of the information (or instructions) it conveyed. Most important, while the participants were isolated they were in contact through both their shared project and this telephone medium, exactly as a telephone normally brings those separated closer to each other. That is to say, the participants communicated about themselves *indirectly* by instructing each other to *add* to their respective activities what had been lost. Each person's "loss" became another's "gain"; but since there was an exchange both ways, such words were ambiguous.

What exactly was "lost" when it meant to *relieve* oneself, or to make room for more water in the pot, in anticipation of a call to add to it? Sometimes it was difficult to drink as much as was ordered, or the pot would not hold any more water; such "gains" were burdensome. At the briefing I mentioned that the title *Loss* by itself often suggested human pain, yet there was little in the Activity that evoked this feeling. Instead, it was light in mood, almost uninflected in its moment-by-moment proceedings; there were no appreciable frustrations throughout, no climaxes. Although there was the philosophical absurdity that nothing was really lost, there may have been a profit of sorts: that of humor. The title emerged in a mood of witty irony.

When most of the group reassembled that night (some were unable to do so and this too was understood as a vital part of *Loss,* a "loss"), there were other friends invited to the gathering who hadn't taken part in the Activity during the afternoon. Yet they intersected with the review session, and in that way they also became involved in what had occurred and was still occurring. For instance, one of the participants acknowledged that she tended to retain water longer than most and had just gotten rid of what was certainly part of the afternoon's intake; the newcomers' occasional visits to the bathroom thus became laughingly linked with a pattern of events they hadn't until then been aware of.

This observation was made when a question was raised as to how much of that day would carry over into the future; would we remember what had happened every time we drank water, boiled it, excreted and measured it, and every time we telephoned someone in that approximate context? Would that special focus we had gotten on the commonplace affect our lives henceforth? And would it extend beyond our immediate circle? Would it communicate? Though unanswerable, it was an appropriate issue to the participants and the newcomers. For myself, the question triggered new thoughts about how degrees of noncommunication might become the language mode of other Activities.

Note

[1]   The others were Rhett and Robert Delford Brown, Letty Eisenhauer, Mark Gabor and Edie Solow, Jane and James Gollin, Victoria and Michael Kirby, and Nam June Paik.

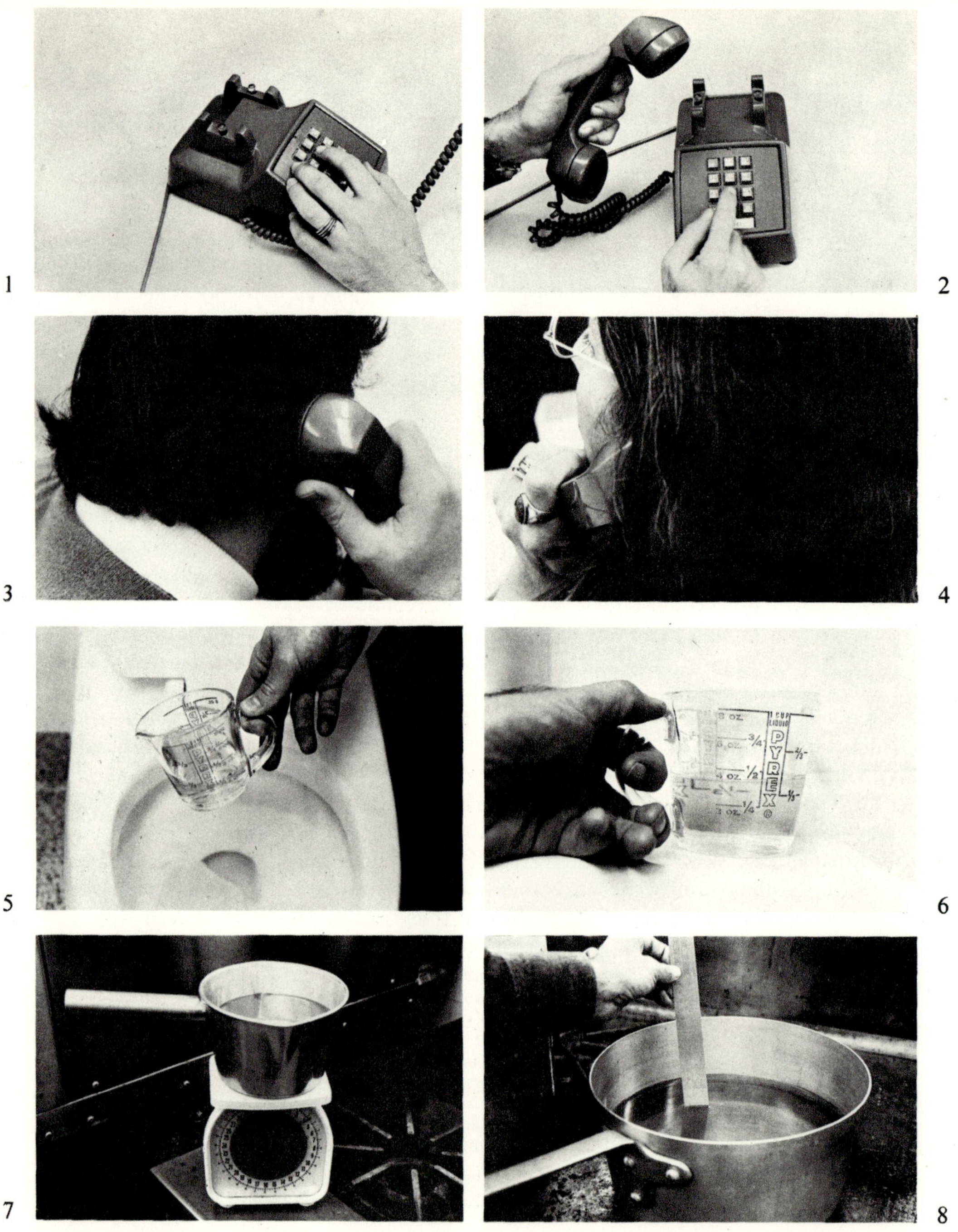

1–8. *Loss*. The eight shots included here were posed and taken some weeks after
the Activity. They are intended to be *illustrations* rather than documents.
Like the text of this article, they both explain something and mythify it,
thus becoming a part of the evolving form of *Loss*. That is, what is lost by
faulty memory is replaced by words and pictures.

16

RICHARD KOSTELANETZ

Numerical Meditation

Mirror. 1973. Reproduced on following pages

1111111111111111111
12222222222222221
1233333333333321
123444444444444321
12345555555554321
123456666666654321
12345677777654321
1234567888887654321
1234567899987654321
1234567890987654321
1234567899987654321
1234567888887654321
12345677777654321
123456666666654321
12345555555554321
123444444444444321
1233333333333321
12222222222222221
1111111111111111111

00000000000000000000
09999999999999999990
09888888888888888890
09877777777777777890
09876666666666667890
09876555555555567890
09876544444444567890
09876543333334567890
09876543222234567890
09876543212234567890
09876543222234567890
09876543333334567890
09876544444444567890
09876555555555567890
09876666666666667890
09877777777777777890
09888888888888888890
09999999999999999990
00000000000000000000

17

SHERMAN LEE

Two Cheers for Irrelevance

If one is committed to so gross and inappropriate a title as this, one owes, if not a panoply of apologies, at least an explanation. The words are a paraphrase of the title of E. M. Forster's collection of essays published years ago—*Two Cheers for Democracy*. The motivation for the title is to be found in the essay "What I Believe," where Forster says:

> So Two Cheers for Democracy: one because it admits variety and two because it permits criticism. Two cheers are quite enough: there is no occasion to give three.

The substitution of the word "irrelevance" for "democracy" may seem to some an action bordering on insolence but the choice was made with, if you will, malice aforethought. How could an art scholar, or worse, a connoisseur, presume to offer his remarks on democracy, the state of the world, or the uncertain future, to a motley (that is: composed of diverse parts) audience? How could one, *anyone,* add more words to those already issued on the catastrophic, pressing and depressing, relevant issues of our times? Obviously this writer could not; thus, his choice of the word "irrelevance," dictated by the nature of the subject of his discourse—the arts—hopelessly irrelevant in the midst of the grinding forces of contemporary dilemmas.

Before we tackle "irrelevance" we had best, in classical as well as dialectical tradition, define our terms lest we fall from the wall of reason like Humpty Dumpty in *Through the Looking Glass:*

> "When *I* use a word," Humpty Dumpty said, in rather a scornful tone, "it means just what I choose it to mean—neither more nor less."

> "The question is," said Alice, "whether you *can* make words mean so many different things."

> "The question is," said Humpty Dumpty, "which is to be master—that's all."

I assume good will on the part of all parties using the word relevance or its derivatives. Both the Webster and Oxford dictionaries agree on *timeliness,* on the applicability *to the case in hand,* as lying at the heart of the definition. In this temporary quality, changeable from minute to minute, hour to hour, year to year, depending upon the case in hand, "relevance" shares kinship with a word much used in the vocabulary of art—"fashion," as opposed to "style." Fashion changes, as it should, and as relevance should; style is more constant, if not eternal; and is therefore far less relevant than fashion. And style is the essence of art; both are far less relevant than fashion.

Perhaps an extreme example may be relevant here. The famous, at least in France, *petit bourgeois* collector, Lacaze, donor to the Louvre of a collection worthy of a prince, found one of his finest paintings by Chardin through its being used to keep a cobbler's feet warm. This use was relevant to the cobbler at the moment, but who would deny the meaning and delight offered by Chardin's painting to successive generations of the public visiting the Louvre? Clearly the irrelevance of art has something to do with its continuing power to move men to thought and sheer delight.

The Library at Alexandria was irrelevant to those who destroyed a good part of the literary heritage of antiquity. The Parthenon was more relevant as a munitions depot to the Turks, and hence its partial destruction by a Venetian shell in 1687. The irrelevance of the Gothic sculptures of Notre-Dame-de-Paris, of the cathedrals of Laon and Clermont-Ferrand, dictated their destruction in the cause of the Cult of Reason during the French Revolution. Perhaps the classic literary explosion against the irrelevance of art is that of St. Bernard, commenting upon the marvelously rich and inventive sculptures of Romanesque France:

> And further, in the cloisters, under the eyes of the brethren engaged in reading, what business has there that ridiculous monstrosity, that amazing mis-shapen shapeliness and shapely mis-shapenness? Those unclean monkeys? Those fierce lions? Those monstrous centaurs? Those semi-human beings? Those spotted tigers? Those fighting warriors? Those huntsmen blowing their horns? Here you behold several bodies beneath one head; there again several heads upon one body. Here you see a quadruped with the tail of a serpent; there a fish with the head of a quadruped. . . . In fine, on all sides there appears so rich and so amazing a variety of forms that it is more delightful to read the marbles than the manuscripts, and to spend the whole day in admiring these things piece by

piece, rather than in meditating on the Law Divine. In the name of God, if men are not ashamed of these follies why at least do they not shrink from the expense?

We can at least, at this remote distance, perceive that St. Bernard "doth protest too much." He has obviously studied these irrelevant sculptures with much care and describes them far better than any modern historian of art. One cannot say the same for the man on a recent TV news program, interviewed about the desirability of saving a row of rare trees in a Los Angeles suburb, who summed up the know-nothing attitude on both right and left with a succinct "To hell with beauty, the leaves get on my lawn."

Unfortunately, if one troubles to follow historical precedent, it appears that much of mankind, whether reactionary or liberal, escapist or extremist or middle-of-the-road Philistine, always has and still does consider the arts to be irrelevant. And so they are, for in this is their nature and their strength. Again, I fall back on E. M. Forster, in his essay on "Anonymity." Here he makes the point, incontestable it seems to me, that in the long line of what one can call literature, running from the purely informational "stop sign" to the lyric poetry of a Donne or a Shelley, the literature that needs a signature, a specific origin, is that at the informational end of the line. Who tells us to stop? Where? When? and ultimately, Why? But the line "A slumber did my spirit seal" has no use, no relevance at all. Only the Modern Language Association worries such irrelevancies to death with endless elucidation, exegesis, and research, as if they were dealing with information, a kind of "stop sign" from the past. One obsessed with, or even interested in, poetry would still read the line, and others, regardless of its anonymity of person, place, or time.

No, the cry for relevance in the arts is a peculiarly modern and Western product of the related systems of *laissez-faire* with its concept of progress applied to everything, and historical determinism with *its* concept of inevitability leading to perfection. Reflection on the question, fortified with the historic insights to be found in non-Western cultures, leads us rather to a social mosaic of relevance and irrelevance, of short-term and long-term interests. What one wants, to use a relevant term, is an "ecological" balance—the lion *and* the lamb. The insistence that all art, whether historic or contemporary, be relevant is fundamentally antihuman, a superimposition of technological concepts of usefulness upon the nontechnological parts of man's humanity.

The virtue of irrelevance is detachment, or truly free, uncommitted observation and creation, insofar as that is humanly possible. The odd fellow, the hermit, the outcast, the silent watcher, the artist, poet, musician, and all their peers, as well as the institutions dedicated to them and their creations, occupy a place so important *and* irrelevant that no social order can be without it, however perfect or perfectible that social order may claim to be.

Art is made truly relevant only where men are not free. The irrelevant artists, pursuing the inherent nature and order of their art, become, in the words of Hitler,

> . . . degenerate artists, I forbid them to force their so-called experiences upon the public. If they do see fields blue, they are deranged and should go to an

asylum. If they only pretend to see them blue, they are criminals, and should go to prison. I will purge the nation of them, and let no one take part in their corruption—his day of punishment will come.

Or, to paraphrase Comrade Mao, "Political criteria come before artistic ones. The function of art and literature is to serve the revolution."

In the just society, technology, politics, transportation, food distribution, distribution of wealth, and many other factors are properly judged by their relevance to the members of that society, changing according to its needs and its development. But two cheers for irrelevance in the arts, only two, not three, for total irrelevance is quite impossible in any living society, good or bad.

One could end there, but I prefer to close with the words of a Greek intellectual, Anastasios Peponis, imprisoned by the Colonels and then, in 1968, deported:

We cannot be hopeful, nor can we give up hope. Thought can still function, and under any circumstances the mind, in order to survive, must find outlets toward freedom and claim its responsibilities. We cannot accept art pressed into the service of this or that political expediency. As long ago as 1945, Severis [his compatriot] wrote: "The sound craftsman is one of the most responsible beings on earth. . . . Out of the human experience that rages or lies still around him, what shall he save? What can he save? . . . In dreams begins responsibility."

18

DOUGLAS NEWTON

Kubru Shields: Style and History

Certain art styles, at first glance homogenous, are in fact composites of mutually incongruous elements, which are in themselves sometimes described by archaeologists as "styles." This is particularly true in the Sepik district (New Guinea), and here the shield-designs of a single village, Kubkain (or Kubru), are examined from this point of view. The designs, said to be specialized to individual clans and the clans' mythology and traditions of origin, are compared with shield-designs and traditions of neighboring areas. Kubru claims about the origins of both clans and designs are shown to be confirmed by the contemporary distribution of styles. Small-scale immigration, for the elucidation of which oral tradition is a useful tool, was probably the process by which local Sepik art styles were formed.

I. Style and History

"Style" is a commodious and vague word which not only refers to no single reality, but has the peculiar property of being adaptable to the large number of definitions which have been packed into it; witness to which is the quantity assembled by Meyer Schapiro (1952). Most of them exist in the area between "style-as-trait" and "style-as-gestalt." Style-as-trait is useful as a working tool: as Schapiro says, "For the archaeologist, style is exemplified in a motive or pattern, or in some directly grasped quality of the work of art, which helps him to localize and date the work and to establish connections between groups of works or between cultures." Style-as-gestalt, or (Schapiro again, in his general definition of style) "the term

. . . applied to the whole activity of an individual or society," could also be called the system of relationships which links the irreducible traits into a whole recognizable as unique in itself, and therefore also irreducible. But the "unique" whole cannot be truly unparalleled, since if it were it would bear no relationship to anything else in the world, and would therefore be truly intolerable. Thus the same linkage must extend over a number of things and form the style common to all of them. Style then is a unificatory factor, and thus one which makes the representatives of it subject to classification. If it is this, it must also have a quality of predictability.

As a simple example, let us propose a graphic style in which the elements are invariably two pairs of short parallel lines intersecting each other, with nine circles and crosses (always either four or five of each sign) arranged in the spaces and angles formed by the lines. These elements could be arranged in a finite but enormous number of combinations (and are, whenever two people settle down to play noughts-and-crosses), but each variant would be more like the other variants than like anything else. Given knowledge of the elements involved, it would be possible to predict the range of the style. It would not be possible from this experience to predict the range of another set of graphic designs: one could not, for example, predict from the noughts-and-crosses style the possibilities of the crossword-puzzle style. Given the existence of the grid, the optional black squares, and those somewhat rococo flourishes, the square-numbers, the range of the crossword-puzzle style is also reasonably predictable. But however many the variants, the crossword-puzzle and the noughts-and-crosses remain as much different "styles" as dogs and cats are different species of mammals.

While there is no explanatory, evolutionary link between such "styles," it is possible for them to undergo evolutionary developments independently of each other. It is also possible for the styles to be grafted on to each other, in response to some necessity of the society or of the artists. In some cases the graft takes, and a complete coalescence of styles results. In others the graft remains unassimilated, and only the skill of the artist gives his work a semblance of unity.

Cases of this second sort seem to abound in the art of the Sepik River area; the famous *yipwon* and related figures from the Karawari River are an excellent example. This combination of naturalistic heads with the systems of totally abstract "opposed hooks" as a stroke is successful enough, even though it seems to be so owing to an almost perverse ingenuity. But in themselves the naturalistic style and the abstract hook style are polar opposites, each with its own tradition and possibilities.

Another such situation, though a less obvious one, is exemplified by the art of Kubkain, an upper Sepik River village. In point of fact, not very much that can be called art from Kubkain exists today; it is possible the people never were very productive. Their work, however, was both distinctive and accomplished, and there is satisfactory evidence that it was made in the village, not imported from elsewhere. Of the extant work, the most important objects are shields carved in low relief. It is these that we should examine for evidence of a style which could be specifically that of Kubkain.

The shields are a distinct group in that they are all single-plane carvings in low relief of practically uniform size and shape. Further, a superficial examination shows another factor the shield-designs have in common: all are built up out of a standardized set of motifs. More than this, the individual shields can be divided into several easily recognizable sub-groups, each of which has an almost identical overall design. Apart from their motifs, the whole corpus of shields has several features in common: one is a particularly bold use of long dentate borders, the other narrow ridges of an elegant sinuosity. The motifs are arranged on symmetrical plans, with an unusual degree of density, so that they cover most of the surface to be decorated. These borders and ridges, this combination of boldness and sinuosity, give a peculiar texture to the shields which one feels is the unmistakable signature of a local style. This is all the more true because the same combination can be found on other objects as well; having discerned it, one would be prepared, even without documentary evidence, to assign other works to the same set of hands. Superficial as this description is, it might therefore stand as the beginning of a definition of Kubkain style.

But if style is a unificatory quality, is there really a stylistic consistency here? That one can stress certain qualities as pervasive does not necessarily mean that they are fundamental. They may, just as well, be a veneer which serves to disguise the true nature of the basic material; and a closer examination shows that in the case of these shields they are purely decorative. The real clue to the analysis is to be found not immediately in these qualities, the "whole activity," but by doubling back to the traits, the building-blocks embodied as the separate design motifs. This is because although several may be used on a single shield, the traits or motifs are not all of equal value. In any single shield-design, one or two tend to be dominant, and the other motifs are subsidiary. These dominant motifs are perfectly distinct from each other: they do not, in fact, predict each other, and so the total shield-designs of which they form part also do not predict each other. None really implies that the existence of the others is complementary to it, or that there is a significant degree of functioning interrelationship such as one would expect to find in a unified style. The conclusion is that in these shield-designs, one is dealing not with a single style but with several existing simultaneously in time (since none of the known shields can be older than the turn of the century), and in a limited space —a single village. The problem is to discover how such a situation came about.

To mention simultaneity is not, of course, to fall into the trap of a synchronic point of view—it is merely to refer to an historical accident, the date of European contact, when the shields began to be collected and, owing to political pacification, not long after became obsolete as functioning weapons. An appeal to history would be normal if we were faced with a similar problem in western art styles. The art historian of literate cultures is fortunate in that his sequences of objects can be matched against rich concurrent sequences of texts, which are so inevitably a part of his equipment that their existence is accepted as a norm; only the conclusions drawn from their cooperative selves are open to discussion. With such until recently non-literate societies as New Guinea, neither native written records exist, nor has there been the extensive archaeological research which might establish an alternative framework. The study of stylistic history has, in fact, by a reversal of the procedure appropriate to literate societies, been recommended as a basis for ethnological history (e.g., Bühler, Barrow, and Mountford 1962:189).

However, in the case of Kubkain it is not the sole resource available: another is a body of oral traditions which is the nearest local equivalent to what we consider history. All are discrete, fairly short sequences covering brief spaces of time. Their view of the past—like that of other groups in this area—includes on an equal level of credibility both myths of origin and stories about the deeds of people known to be more or less recent ancestors. Sometimes these are interrelated, sometimes they are distinct. Those traditions referring to ancestral acts are, to an overwhelming extent, circumstantial and mundane; the persons involved can usually, and ideally always, be traced through genealogies to descendants alive today. If these are historical in quality, others containing episodes which, while not pure myth, have a more remote reference to normal behavior, may be better described as parahistorical. Finally the myths of origin are clearly an eclectic body garnered from different sources; and sometimes they bear traces of having been synthesized into new versions. They are thus artifacts of the culture, and as such, valuable objects to be analyzed for the evidence they can yield, among other things, about their own origins; the same is also true, of course, of the more limited stories about ancestors. By taking all these traditions first, then relating them to an examination of the shields themselves, it may be possible to explain some of the historical problems of style not only for Kubkain, but possibly for other Sepik areas as well.[1]

II. The Kubru

A. THE KUBRU DEFINED

Kubkain is a village on the upper Sepik River at about 142°21E 4°19S, within the Wongamusun administrative census division in the East Sepik District. The inhabitants of this area include a small group of villages speaking a common language, designated Wogamusin (Laycock 1965), with about 340 speakers. Linguistically the entire Wogamusin-speaking group belongs to Laycock's Upper Sepik Phylum (Laycock 1968), with shared vocabulary percentages of 12 percent with the Iwam and 14 percent with the more distant Abau around the Green River. Shared vocabulary percentages in the same phylum with the Tama family languages, spoken by both the Yasyin to the east and by people to the north of them, are between 22 and 37 percent.

Native names of the Wogamusin villages differ from those adopted by European official sources (e.g., Port Moresby 1968: 75) and indicated on most maps. They are, from east to west: Munggwal, known to Europeans as "Washkuk"; Kumba, known as "Yambunumbu" at the mouth of the April (Nigsak) River; Komti, at the mouth of the Wogamush (Nuwha) River, known as "Biaga" (actually the name of the nearby bush); and Kubru (sometimes pronounced "Gubru"), known as "Kubkain." Kubru will accordingly be used instead of "Kubkain" in what follows. Kutbog (= Kutebok, Behrmann 1922: map) was at the mouth of the stream leading inland to Munggwal, but has been abandoned. The village called "Wogumasch," with variant spellings, by early writers (Behrmann *op. cit.*; Roesicke 1914) was originally Kumnau. This is said to have been situated a little upstream from the mouth of the Wogamush River, on the south bank of the Sepik. On leaving this place, which became blocked from the river by the build-up of a sandbank, the former inhabitants of Kumnau settled at Komti (the early explorers' "Wogumasch") and Kumba.

The original site of Kubru was a little up-river from that of today. Well before living memory, the bank of the river began to collapse (or the people suffered from an epidemic, as will be detailed later, or both) and everyone came down-river to the present site. The village is now built on a hillock called Karok, which rises steeply out of the Sepik's water, and on land called Kwamtuk, at the east and south foot of Karok, on the shore of a shallow bay. The small inlet, Karok-kwulkwul, to the west of Karok, is still used as the mooring place for the village canoes. Slightly further west still are two hills: to the west Kubka, and Glrshɔ to the east. The village itself is often called "Kubka" (Behrmann 1922: map), as are the people; but a group of people is commonly indicated by the place-name with the suffix *yon* ("children"): hence "Wogamus*in*," and Kubka'*yon,* or "Kubk*ain,*" after the name of the hill.[2]

The Kubru form a large proportion of the Wogamusin-speaking group—there are some 190 of them, of whom 46 are adult males[3]—but consider themselves a separate and independent body from the other speakers, whom they call collectively "Wogumas." They maintain generally friendly relations with the other villages; there were plenty of accusations of sorcery in traditional stories—some will be quoted later—but there seems to have been little or no actual conflict, and certainly some alliances for fighting. The main enemies of Kubru were to the west: Senap ("Chenapian"), a single village with its own language, and the Iwam-speaking villages Auom (the "Minggi"), Tauri, and Iniyok (the "Ari'yon"). Hauna ("Yauen-ian"), an Iwam-speaking village just beyond Senap, was friendly. To the south the enemy groups were the hill-people the Kubru'yon call "Bulu," probably the Pai and Setiyali. The Kubru traded with Nggala ("Swagab") which is inland to the southeast, and with the villages of the lower April River. Like some of the other villages around it, Kubru was to some extent a frontier, with all the extra opportunity for a range of contacts that such a position entails.

B. MATERIAL CULTURE

The material culture inventory of the Kubru-Wogumas was closely similar to that of other up-river and down-river groups. Out of a general list of some 125 traits, the Kubru-Wogumas omit (compared with the middle Sepik list) only about six. These include areca-nut mortars, bamboo lime-containers, and, most significantly, some ritual musical instruments: the water-drums, water-beating bowls, and percussion planks typical of Iatmul-Manambu-Chambri culture. The Kubru represent the furthest extension west of the area in which a cult of mass-beating of slit gongs is found. The Hauna and other Iwam-speakers again have the same basic list, with only the river Iwam using a limited amount of pottery (traded from Kubru) and canoe-shield ornaments; but all Iwam adding to the list the combined bamboo-and-gourd smoking apparatus used up-river. Paintings on sago-spathes appear to play a far more important role in Iwam art than among the Wogumas.

The main items may be listed as follows,[4] with those which were regularly carved, painted, incised, or otherwise decorated with designs, distinguished by italics:

> Houses: Dwelling houses; ceremonial houses with ceremonial mounds in front of them; *canoe prow shield ornaments* used as gable ornaments; and decorative *bark-paintings*.

Costume: For women: short fiber skirts; for men: aprons of bark-cloth and (? flying-fox) skin with attached boar-tusks; woven brassards, belts, armbands with tusks; leg bands, ankle bands; feather and opossum-fur frontlets; feather hair ornaments; rattle anklets; neck, forehead, ear, and nose ornaments of melo, conus shell, and boar tusk; necklaces of net over a large red seed, and insect carapaces; earrings of fishbone and insect carapaces; cassowary quills worn in pierced noses; shell and boar-tusk pectorals in the form of human faces; net bags decorated with hornbill heads, feathers, lizard skins, boar tusks (Newton 1971:104); penis covers (Kelm 1966–1968, 2:132) of basketry (Schultze Jena 1914: fig. 15; Roesicke 1914: abb. 4) woven on wood forms, of *bamboo* (Kelm 1966–1968, 2:160), and of *coconut shell* (Newton 1971: 102–103); *lime-gourds* (Kelm 1966–1968, 2:133, 134); bone *lime spatulas* (Kelm 1966–1968, 2:135); feather whisks; wigs; rain capes.

Furniture: Headrests; wood bowls; coconut-shell *cups;* paint dishes; *benches; stools; suspension hooks* (Kelm 1966–1968, 3:519 is probably an example); food baskets; net bags; sleeping mats; sleeping baskets; smoke racks above clay-bed fireplaces; brooms.

Tools: Mallets; stone adzes; digging sticks; hand-nets; large fish-nets; sago-washing equipment: fire-making equipment (using stone percussion or string friction); bone coconut graters; thorn fish-hooks; flying-fox bone awls; ochre paints; pottery vessels (Kelm 1966–1968, 2:147) traded from Nggala; bark containers for water heated with hot stones.

Canoes: Canoes with carved *prows* (Bühler *et al.* 1962:77; Haberland 1965: 100; Newton 1971:100); canoe-prow *shield ornaments* (Haberland 1964:101); *paddles* (Newton 1971:101) with lenticular or forked blades.

Weapons: *Shields*; daggers of human or cassowary bone (Kelm 1966–1968, 2:142); *spears;* bows; *arrows* (traded from Siyo on the middle April River); *clubs;* basketry wrist guards.

Musical instruments: *Trumpets* (Newton 1971: 106); *hand-drums* (Haberland 1964: 104, 105); *slit gongs* (Newton 1971:91–93) and *gong beaters* (Newton 1971: 94–95); flutes with carved *stoppers* and *wood* or basketry ornaments (Newton 1971:96–99); bullroarers; *seed* or *clay whistles* (Kelm 1966–1968, 2:144); musical bows; jews'-harps; panpipes.

Ceremonial and ritual objects: Composite bone and wood *instruments* and miniature *adzes* for incising the penis; wooden *gags* for novices; *boards* with relief designs worn on chests and backs of men taking part in

Löl initiations; sacred *masks*. *Masks* worn by fathers to frighten children into weaning. Coconut-shell *tops* (Kelm 1966–1968, 3:547) used in a game played at yam harvest time. A small clay *animal head* (Kelm 1966–1968, 3:527) was probably also of ceremonial significance.

III. Kubru History

A. KUBRU CLANS

To understand the history of any upper Sepik River community, or of the area as a whole, it must be understood that all, as they exist at present, are the result of groups of people, under the pressures of fighting, famine, or for other reasons, having moved about freely and regrouped as they could. Consequently no village is a monolithic unit. It is, rather, a more or less stable congeries of clans having closer ties with each other than with those of other places.

This is an historical fact of which the Kubru are highly conscious. They are divided into a number of patrilineal clans linked in exogamous groups, apparently according to places of origin or shared totems. These clans are: Ula and Wiya; Wahano and Nandi, collectively called Kwal'yon; Yino and Wismi; Bəgərrə and Nəmburrə, collectively the Mulmul'yon;[5] Munggwal and Nasidi, collectively the Munggwal'yon. The historical traditions current in the village refer to the origins and travels of these clans. What follows (below) is an arrangement of such traditions paraphrased, and in some cases abridged, in a chronological sequence based on both the statements of the Kubru'yon about what the sequence should be, and on internal evidence.

Diagrammatic summary of population movements described in Kubru and other upper Sepik traditions

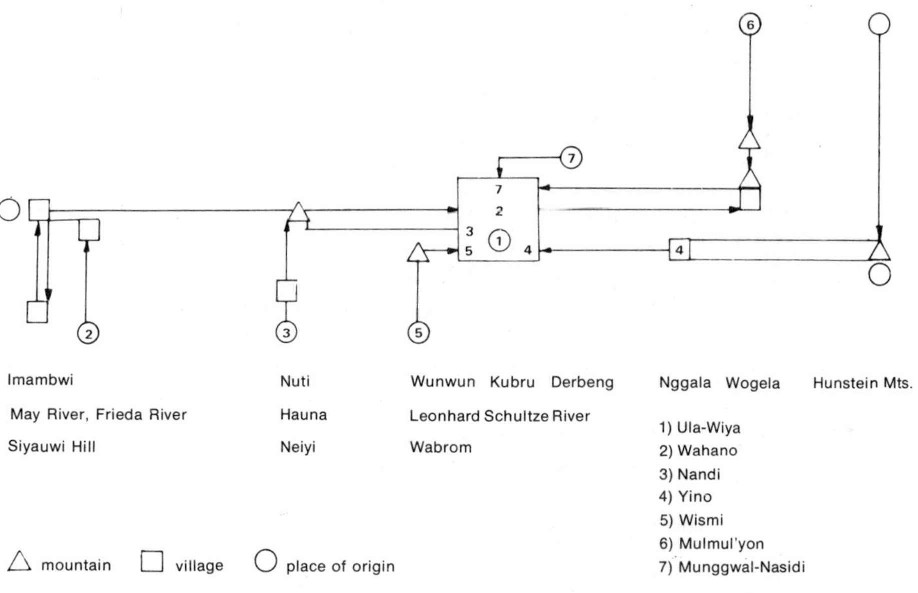

B. ULA-WIYA HISTORY

The earliest tale about ancestors deals with those of Ula and Wiya clans who, it is stated, emerged from a hole in the rocks at Glrshɔ. They lived in the hills before anyone else came to this stretch of the river, Ula at Yuwu, the western peak, and the Wiya at Benip, the eastern.

At that time the people made their canoes by chewing the logs, as they had no proper tools. A man called Wugunut, of Ula clan, was once doing this while Glram, a man of Kumnau, watched from a hiding-place behind a tree. One of Wugunut's teeth cracked, and he leaped out of the canoe exclaiming "Oh! one of my adzes has broken!" He saw Glram and challenged him to show himself. The two sat down to share their food and Wugunut produced some fish, but Glram saw it was only sun-dried, as Wugunut's people had no fire. He therefore made fire and cooked the fish for Wugunut.

Glram set a day for another meeting, and brought to it a fire-stick and four stone blades in a net bag which he gave Wugunut. The other Ula and Wiya were terrified when they saw fire for the first time, and at first the women and children vomited the cooked food. Wugunut went and cut a new canoe with his blades— but he still tore off the bark with his teeth, as before.

The clans then built two ceremonial enclosures, Ula's up-river and Wiya's down-river. The Ula took the initiative in originating the Löl initiation ceremony. First they took nettle and rubbed their penes, then split bamboo slivers, inserted them in their urethras, and broke them off. But the men who did this died, so they abandoned the slivers and instead made instruments for the same purpose from the bones of two men, Gwimbi and Doasklo. They also adopted fuzzy grass stalks to induce the flow of blood, and bamboo knives to incise their penes.

While the clans were at Glrshɔ, a sandbank formed a little below the surface of the river and a white heron came and perched on it. The people asked each other "What, is it standing on the water?" But on the next day the sandbank rose above the level of the water, and the people left the hills to go and live on it.

C. KWAL'YON HISTORY

The original ancestors of Nandi clan were created by two women, Klito and Miyato, at Hauna. One bore a python, while the other bore six boys called Gaulwulshɔ, Gaulwub, Wiyabugruwub, Bishibeiyara, Isabwa, and Yigiku. At first the children merely sang in the voices of birds; eventually their mothers struck their ears with bamboo tongs and at this they began to speak in the languages of Kubru and Hauna. The boys sang spells; the python set out writhing along and creating a furrow which became the bed of the Sepik River as far as Nggala, while his cousins followed him. All of them then returned to the mouth of the Hauna waterway and settled on a hill called Nuti.

This story corresponds to, and probably derives from, the origin legend of the Nauwan clan of Hauna. In this, however, names and geography are quite differently arranged. Here the python, Yausipauwawai, is said to have emerged from Neiyi, a sago swamp near Waruwi, which is a lake south of Hauna. He traveled underground to Yambun, where he emerged in human form, then returned as a python back upstream, pausing at Yasyin, Nggala, Kumnau, and

Kubru in the shape of a man. At Kubru he married two sisters, Kiritu and Meiyatu, then returned with his wives to Neiyi, forming the Hauna waterway by his serpentine track.

To return to the Nandi legend, the Kwal'yon came down-river on a floating mountain called Belesuwi. They encountered the Nandi living at Nuti, who told them to go ahead downstream, and that they would follow. Belesuwi went floating on until it reached the place where the Ula-Wiya lived. Masakwoduwub, one of these people, took a stick and attached a betel pepper to it; using this, he hooked onto a tree on Belesuwi, and tried to make the island fast. The betel pepper was not strong enough to secure the whole island and it broke. The stick and betel fell into the river in front of Karok, and became Kwodusirr and Kwoduwub, a pair of spirits who now live in the river-water at the foot of Karok. Belesuwi itself broke into two parts; the smaller, Karok, stayed where it is now and at least some of the people remained with it. The greater part of Belesuwi drifted on until it finally lodged downstream and became Wɔgela, the Yasyin mountain.

D. YINO HISTORY

Some while later Yinggeiyu, a man from Nggala, went to Glrshɔ in search of land on which to settle. The Ula and Wiya people who lived there told him they had none to give, and sent him to Kubka. He had the pots Nggala women make to trade for Kubru sleeping baskets and net bags. At a market place on a lake called Wansus, he met two Kwal'yon, Yenagai, and Nemnuwa. At this time, the Nggala only ate inferior food: *suk,* a water-weed; *kwos,* a vegetable; and *bok tak,* a large leaf.[6] The Kwal'yon saw this and told Yinggeiyu to throw it away. They took him to Kubru, and gave him fish and sago to eat. Nemnuwa then invited Yinggeiyu to stay, and presented him with sago palms growing south of Kubka. Yinggeiyu became the ancestor of the Yino clan.

E. WISMI HISTORY

The Wismi clan originated at Wabrom, apparently in the hinterland of the Waliyo (Leonhard Schultze) River, and there they created their sacred objects. A man killed a cassowary, took its bones, scraped them, and they made an impressive sound. The Wismi made flutes, but they did not sound well in combination with the bones. They carved a slat of wood into a bullroarer and established it as Gumus, the mother of the bones, which they called Wabsi (below) and Yamsi.[7] Finally they made a flute, called Yulitambeg, as a brother for Gumus.

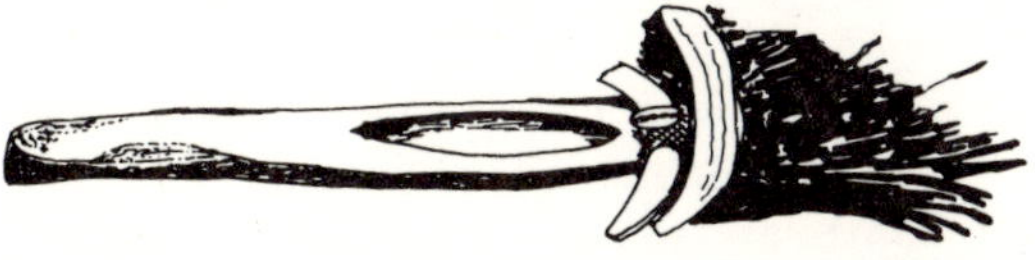

Cult object of Kwal'yon, personal name Wabsi. Cassowary bone with boar tusks (probably referring to Sirrkub), cowrie shell, cassowary feathers, and binding of string and trade cloth; about 12″ long

The Wismi were living near a lake, the mouth of which was blocked by a stone adze-blade called Metauwu. Eventually the people got tired of dragging their canoes over it to get into the lake, so they took the blade away and the lake water rushed out. They fastened the blade on the prow of the canoe Urrmandə, and as it moved forward the blade cut out the bed of the Waliyo River. One of the men also worked at the ground with a stick, helped by a cassowary called Wurrsuwa. But finally the cassowary became hungry and wandered away in search of food. Wherever the bird dropped excrement, as it traveled about, this turned into sago palms.

The man's stick broke, so he threw it away; it fell in Lake Potoma, where it became a water-spirit. The canoe then lodged against a hill called Wunwun; the people called to the cassowary to return and help them again, but it would not. So they took a boar's tusk, called Sirrkub, and went on digging the river-bed until they broke through onto the Sepik River and were able to float downstream to join the other clans at Kubru.

F. MULMUL'YON HISTORY

The people from Wɔgela now living at Kubru are apparently descendants of immigrants. The Nəmburrə and Bəgərrə ancestors are said to have lived in a sago swamp north of the Sepik before Wɔgela came to a halt; and their anthropogenic myth with its hero Wulruwiyanggwet (Newton 1971: 51) corresponds to the Yasyin myth of their culture hero Yinakwut. At any rate, the ancestor of the Nəmburrə at Kubru was Ishimbu. He left Wɔgela because, after killing a cassowary in the bush Numu, he received only a share of the meat, whereas he wanted also a thigh bone to make into a dagger. The other men refused to give it up. As a result of this quarrel he went to Kumnau, where eventually he died.[8] His sons moved to Kubru and were received by the Wismi. Ishimbu was accompanied by two other Nəmburrə men, Mamuk and Kadamun (who has no descendants), and two Bəgərrə men, Wuweiyamb and Wimeg, whose only descendants are two women; the descent line has therefore become virtually extinct in the present generation.

G. MUNGGWAL'YON HISTORY

The Munggwal and Nasidi clans originally lived together at Derbeng on Kumga, a stream which had been cut through the bush called Muwin by the Munggwal man, Nauwurryagyag, using an edible leaf.[9]

The Nasidi left and, in company with a cassowary, went to Wiyamtom. Here sago palms grew up from the scraps of the sago pudding they brought with them. They went by way of Senap to the stream Wubi, which led them out onto the Sepik at Washkuk. Nəgub and Wiyintawi, two important men of Nasidi, decided to go and live at Kubru.

The Munggwal ancestors who had remained behind married many Kumnau women. Angered by this, a Kumnau man, Bisakro, took an arrow and rubbed it with flying-fox and human excrement,[10] which he also rubbed on himself. He shot the arrow in the direction of the Munggwal; through this sorcery the Munggwal all fell ill, and in their weakened state were attacked by all the Iwam and Senap. The Munggwal therefore dispersed; one man, Nambishuwa, went to live at Kumnau. The men there constantly made trouble for him by attempting to seduce his wife; so, one night, he made magic and spat chewed bespelled ginger on his house-posts to put a curse on them, assembled all his goods in a canoe, and went up-river. His two small boys, the infants Wuduru and Nesitsiba, were tired, so he left them to sleep on a sandbank and went on with his wife to Kubru. There Nəgub and Wiyintawi welcomed them; and having collected the boys they settled down. After a year, Nambishuwa asked his wife if she had had any trouble; she said she had not, so they decided to stay at Kubru. In the end Nambishuwa died at the former site of the village.

The wife of Ulau (a man of Ula clan) was constantly beaten by him; she ran away to Munggwal, where she married a man called Salko. But since he also ill-treated her she went back to Ulau taking with her, in her net bag, some of her second husband's shell valuables which she had stolen. Salko followed to reclaim them but Nəgub and Wiyintawi faced him down, sending him away empty-handed. They told him, however, he could take what revenge he liked in the way of sorcery.

Salko got a breadfruit leaf, cut it into shape, and transformed it into an eagle which he sent flying through the air. It went first to Nggala, where the men were sleeping in the ceremonial house; all of them became ill. It flew next to Kumnau, then to Kubru, with the same effect. Nəgub and Wiyintawi helped it in its work, and many people died of sickness. All left the old place, and came—eight canoe-loads only were left—to Karok.

H. SUMMARY AND DATING OF KUBRU HISTORY

The sequence given here is obviously quite loosely constructed, partly on the basis of encounters said to have taken place between ancestors of different clans. As a record it is incomplete. Only the stories of first arrivals at Kubru are given. Further, as is often the case with Sepik area traditions, they deal only with positive presences of clans in the village, or with those remembered because their former presence had a bearing on current conditions. Some clans have certainly become extinct: their names are remembered, but not much else about them.[11] Where such links are missing, any attempt to form a relative sequence runs into immediate difficulties. To overcome these, as a first step one may refer to a group of inter-related genealogies, shown here in abridged form (below). Most of the genealogies

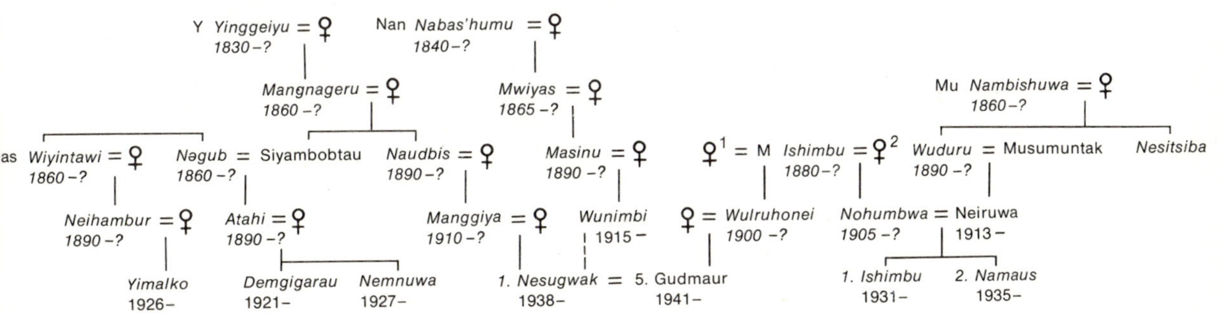

Kubru genealogies

Male names are in *italics*. Numbers before names indicate order of birth.
Dates in italic type are conjectural; those in roman type are derived from Administration census reports.
Clan names are abbreviated as follows:
Mu (Munggwal); Y (Yino); Nas (Nasidi); Nan (Nandi); M (Mulmul'yon).

are very short; this, in itself, would appear to argue in favor of their reliability. The question of the actual time-spans involved is debatable. The generation of twenty-five years, as it is commonly accepted, and used here, can of course only be the most arbitrary of estimates.[12]

The history of Kubru can be divided into two parts, the second beginning with the Nandi and Yino genealogies. In the first period, to recapitulate, some southern hill people moved to a spot close to the south bank of the Sepik River and a little upstream from the present site. These formed the Ula and Wiya clans. Subsequently they were joined by Wahano clansmen from the area of the May River. No dates, however approximate, can be assigned to this period as no genealogy extends back far enough.

The second period begins with the immigrants from Nggala who formed the Yino clan. Yinggeiyu, the earliest ancestor named in the Yino sequence, was possibly born about 1840; the Yino arrival is thus in the mid-nineteenth century. Nabas'humu of the Nandi clan, in the same generation as Yinggeiyu, is reported to have been among the group which moved from the settlement at Nuti hill to Kubru; perhaps therefore also in the middle years of the nineteenth century. The later part of this period is marked by the arrivals of the Munggwal and Nasidi. Nɔgub and Wiyintawi, born about 1870 approximately speaking, arrived at Kubru first; Nambishuwa of Munggwal arrived later, to judge by the presumptive age of Wuduru's birth about 1890. It seems that the Yasyin arrived fairly recently at Wɔgela; the Nɔmburrɔ and Bɔgɔrrɔ presence at Kubru, if we are to accept No-humbwa as their first representative there, must be placed very late: perhaps no earlier than 1920. But if some of the Yasyin who left at the same time as Ishimbu, such as Mamuk, went directly to Kubru, they could have arrived as much as two decades earlier. This earlier date seems more likely. Schmidt (1929:64) describes, and Kelm (1966–1968, 2:136) illustrates, a shield from Kubru with facial designs like those of Nɔmburrɔ clan, collected by the Behrmann expedition. My informants attributed it to Nɔmburrɔ, but also (perhaps more accurately) to Yino. A true Nɔmburrɔ type shield (Kelm 1966–1968, 2:140) was however collected at the same time from "Wogumach."

This last case is a reminder of the fact that the genealogies may be accurate enough as far as they go in terms of the succession of names; but they may be subject to other forms of error. As with Polynesian genealogies, they could be deformed by omissions and—even more misleading—illegitimate inclusions. The sequence of arrival therefore may be generally accurate enough. The dates given, if one presumes that omission rather than incorporation has been practiced, are *termini ante quem* which objectively may err toward being too recent. In any case they have no relationship with the possible earliest dates of origin for the motifs used in the art.

I. OTHER LOCAL HISTORIES RELATING TO KUBRU

The Kubru record substantiates the assertion about the mixed make-up of the village, but it should be repeated that Kubru, far from being unique in this, is not an exception but typical of an upper Sepik community's history. To illustrate this, one may turn to the histories of groups contributing to the Kubru population: the Iwam, Nggala, and Yasyin. Some can be related to certain of the Kubru traditions, and in doing so give a further extension into the past.

The May River Iwam clans are loosely clustered in three large exogamous groups, each named after a totemic tree: Wan (raintree), Yin (ironwood), and Niya:t (sago palm). The Yin are said (somewhat uncertainly) to be immigrants from somewhere on the course of the upper Sepik River itself, more probably from the upper May River. This tradition takes on a further dimension if we return down-river to Hauna—as it will be recalled, an Iwam-speaking community. Its Dunakwan clan describe the creation of the May and Sepik rivers by two brothers, who split open a raintree so that the waters could flow out of the trunk. One of the brothers, Wani, then floated down the Sepik on an ironwood tree with all the items of human food hung on its branches. He disembarked at Luti (= Nuti), the hill near the mouth of the Hauna waterway, and later returned to the May River and summoned his brother to join him at Hauna. More than this, the origin myth of one Nggala group of clans repeats the same theme. The Nggraiyo claim that their ancestor, Yenuwi-bögela, came down the Sepik from a hill called Libamasen, "near the May River," pausing at "Kabaruk" (= Karok) on the way. There is, then, a considerable consensus in the area about the eastward movement of people from the upper Sepik, and the importance of Kubru-Karok in their story, in which the Kubru traditions are only a single element.

Further Nggala traditions detail the immigration of other clans from areas to the east. These include the Hunstein Mountains and the area north of the Kwoma: people from the latter possibly are to be identified with the Nggala clan of the Koriyasi division of the Kwoma.

According to Yasyin traditions, the Wɔgela mountain on which they live at present was originally inhabited by two groups. One, whom they call the Kwanggwarr, lived along the ridge; the other lived at Eiklam. at the foot of the western end of the ridge, and were called "Gumbru."

According to the traditions of the Yambun, the Gumbru people—whom they call "Kobarau"—originally came from far to the east, driven upstream, in fact, by the expansion of the big downstream tribe, the Iatmul. They settled near the Yambun ancestors at Serembu (near the present village of Brugnauwi) and inter-married with them, later abandoning Serembu and moving to Eiklam. After a while, owing to a dispute over rights in a sago swamp, the Yambun raided the Kobarau, who then abandoned their holdings at Eiklam and went upstream to join the Wogumas.

Meanwhile a group of immigrants from the north had moved down the Namblo River to the Sepik, and settled at the eastern end of the Kwoma hills. The Yambun, who have always maintained a strong claim to this land and were probably living at that time in the hills above, raided them. What is said to have happened next varies according to the tribal affiliations of the narrator. The Yambun say that they relented, on the grounds that the immigrants would be useful trade partners and allies, and transported them in canoes across the river to Wɔgela. The Yasyin, on the other hand, claim that after the raids they went on their own initiative, traveling on rafts. They drove off the Kwanggwarr, and the whole mountain was thus open for settlement by the newcomers.

IV. Kubru Shields

A. GENERAL

The conformation of Kubru-Wogumas shields (Wogamusin: *nɔw*) has been de-scribed in detail by Schmidt (1929: 165–166) and Haberland (1963: 113–115). Like those of the Iwam, they are tall oblong slabs averaging 163.5 cm. high, with a width-height ratio averaging 1: 4.2, and parallel sides. The handles are of two types: one consists of two vertical bars projecting from the back, which are bound by two or three horizontal light wood grips; the other of grips attached to vertical bars bound to the slab through perforations in the slab itself, regardless of the decoration on the front. Similar grips are found on the shields of the Iwam and of the Hunstein Mountains groups. As with Iwam shields, the center of the slab is slightly thicker than the edges, producing a slight keel down the middle.

The wood used for shields was from a tree called *wab,* also used for making house-posts. The manufacture was attended by magical procedures: the carver, before starting work, performed the usual incising of his penis which preceded all important ritual undertakings. The pigments used were ochres and charcoal, chewed with ginger root (Schuster 1968–69) and the dried testicles of the cuscus, the mixture of paint and magic ingredients being spat into a half coconut-shell cup. The paints were applied with brushes of the grass used for bleeding the penis. The colors themselves are designated the property of different clans: white belongs to Yino; red and yellow to Yino, Wismi, Ula, Wiya; black to Kwal'yon, Mulmul'-yon, Munggwal'yon. Large areas of a color, in theory, were only to be used by the clan which "owns" it, though any clan was free to use small quantities of the other colors.

All shields are carved on the front face (no decoration ever appears on the back) with very low-relief designs, the raised areas being never more than a few milli-meters high. The raised areas are positive—that is, they carry the significant designs—and are always painted black, irrespective of the prescribed "ownership" of the color. There are two main aspects of the designs on the shields: first, their overall disposition on the field, i.e., the composition; second, the nature of the details, which are the elements forming the composition. Not only individual motifs but the total design assemblies, the Kubru insist, are specialized to indi-vidual clans.[13]

B. COMPOSITION

On the Kubru shields the designs usually cover the entire surface, but in a few examples only the upper half to two-thirds is covered.

The compositions of the Kubru designs fall into three groups:

a. Designs based on bilateral symmetry on a vertical axis. This has two possibil-ities:

　i. the central axis is of secondary importance, and the primary groups of signs are disposed on either side of it;

　ii. the central axis is comprised of a primary bloc of signs, and is bordered by a (frequently) continuous band or bands of secondary signs.

b. Designs based on biaxial symmetry around corner-to-corner diagonals on the field, elements in the four triangles thus formed being primary or secondary in importance, according to size and complexity. The four possible variations can be found by forming a grid of nine rectangles in three registers, each rectangle being divided by a diagonal (fig. 1). If the verticals are designated 1,2,3,4 and the horizontals A,B,C,D, this schema renders the possibilities:

i. AC13 in which the triangles at the ends are primary;

ii. BD24 in which the triangles at the sides are primary;

iii. AC24 in which triangles at the corners are primary, leaving a central diamond negative; and

iv. BD13 in which the corner triangles are negative, leaving the central diamond primary.

c. A design in which only the upper part of the field is occupied by a stylized human face.

The geographical distribution of these compositions on shields in the area dealt with here may be summarized diagrammatically:

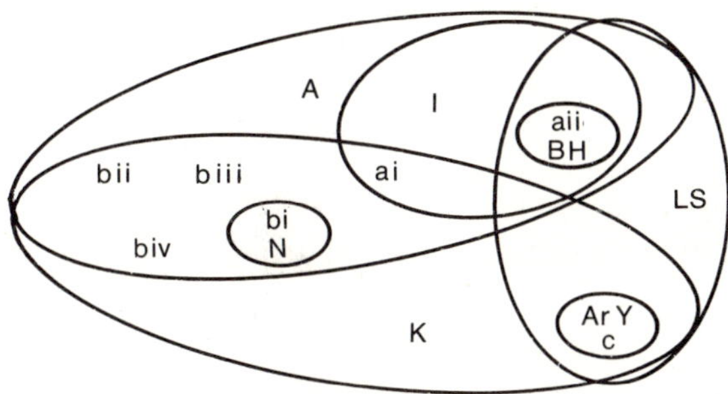

A) Abau   I) Iwam   H) Hauna   LS) Leonhard Schultze River   K) Kubru   Ar) April River
N) Nggala   B) Bahinemo   Y) Yasyin

It will be noted that this includes people to the west, south, and east; the lack of any from the north reflects a demographic reality: a corridor of uninhabited territory some sixty miles long and thirty miles wide runs parallel to the north bank of the Sepik River between the Namblo and Yellow rivers. Taking Kubru as the center point, it is clear that the *a* and *b* types of composition converge on it from the west, and that *c* comes from the south and east.

No examples are quoted directly from one group that is mentioned as contributing to the Kubru population, the Yasyin. No examples of shields from Yasyin itself appear to be available, but a shield (Kelm 1966–1968, 2:45) from "Kamberau" (Kauiyimbei, a Yasyin-Warasei related village) conforms to the type, as do the shields of their neighbors the Kwoma. Other Kwoma and Yasyin works—particularly bark-paintings—use all *a* and *b* types.

C. SIGNS

The designs carved on the shields are based on a number of abstract and irreducible geometric designs—"signs," to use the term proposed by Gardin (1958: 341–345).

These signs are remarkably few: they include only line, crescent, spiral, circle (or oval), angle. The operations, to continue with Gardin's terms, applied to them are similarly few and simple, surprisingly so when Gardin calculates the possibility of six hundred "primary signs" derived from twenty elementary signs subjected to fifteen standard operations. The Kubru repertoire appears to use only linear arrangement, as in rows of angles (triangles); radial arrangement—concentric circles; and symmetrical arrangement—interlocking spirals. One sign results from the combination of crescent and angle into a "tear-drop" shape. The only design on Kubru shields that has a constant representational significance—the human face—is equally made up of the elementary signs. Otherwise, the Kubru repertoire consists of nine primary signs which are operationally irreducible to their elements (fig. 2).

It is at this level, in Kubru eyes, that the primary signs achieve their identity, and each is given the name of a natural object. The natural objects themselves are all, in accordance with the world-view of the Kubru, properties of the various clans. While the number of signs is so limited, they are evidently to some extent considered representational and indeed a few recognizably are so. The limitation of number in itself, however, entails the use of certain signs by more than one clan, with a corresponding number of projective interpretations. These are, formally speaking, secret: although, as will be seen later, a man can use the designs of another clan, he professes ignorance of their meaning. That the designs were involved with jealousy and pride can be illustrated from a Kubru tradition in which a Munggwal man carves his paddle with his designs and jeeringly asks his Yino wife whether her parents can do the same. This is intended, and accepted, as one of a succession of insults which end in the man's murder by the Yino. The designs as a whole, and probably especially the clusters of signs on the shields, were then heraldic, and presumably functioned as statements of clan unity.

Besides this, both the designs and the shields themselves had supernatural connotations. The Kubru believe that all human beings and animals have *sokpas,* an immortal soul that lives on after death. *Sokpas* are to some extent associated with dreams and the bush, where a few men and women have the ability to see them; these visions are always omens of death for the person whose *sokpas* is seen. Other supernatural beings are *mwiyim,* water-spirits, and *diyutim,* tree-spirits. These creatures are able to metamorphize at will; the *diyutim,* that is, hang up in their trees the skins of pig, cassowary, and crocodile which they assume when they wish to move about. *Mwiyim* and *diyutim* are not specifically ancestral beings. However, *sokpas* may be encountered in the form of men in the process of transformation into cassowaries—birds but for human legs: *sokpas* and the tree- and water-spirits are thus analogous if not identical. Slit gongs are embodiments of *mwiyim,* and so are the shields.

The most important sign which appears on the shields is 2; it represents *kɔhan dok:* the d'Albertis creeper, a vine with crescentic scarlet flowers *(Mucuna nova-guineensis)* intensively used in sorcery. This is personified as Dowiya-tau, a female spirit. Another female spirit, Sabɔ-tau, is the personification of one of the types of magic ginger. As part of preparations for fighting, a piece of this was chewed and spat into a lime gourd which was then stoppered with a split areca nut to prevent its *binkip* ("smell," possibly also "soul") from escaping. After further ritual

(Newton 1971: 53), the fighting party smashed the gourds against the *kɔhan dok* carvings, thus creating a fog concealing them from the enemy.

A tabulation of the distribution of the specific signs used by the Kubru in adjacent areas shows that all are used (though this does not exhaust the entire repertoire of locally used signs).

	1	2	5	6	7	8	9	10 (human face)
Abau	x	x						
Iwam	x	x	x					
Hauna	x	x	x	x	x			
Kubru	x	x	x	x	x	x	x	x
Nggala		x	x	x	x	x	x	x
Bahinemo	*x*	*x*	*x*	*x*	*x*			
Yasyin	x		*x*			*x*		*x*

This table is modified by the elimination of signs 3 and 4 as noise, since they occur among all groups. They are the basic signs used on Bahinemo shields, however; and the Bahinemo range is here augmented by the inclusion of signs *x* which, although not found on shields, are within the repertoire of signs engraved on arrow foreshafts (5, 6, 7). The inclusion of signs 1 and 2 takes this adoption for the sake of the table to a further remove: it is based on their coincidence, in three-dimensional form, with the Bahinemo cult-hooks *(garra)*. The connection, though it may be regarded as rather tenuous in strictly formal terms, is perfectly viable in visual terms.

A similar shift in media has been adopted in the case of the Kwoma-Yasyin signs; sign 8 does not occur on Kwoma shields, but is a major design in pottery and bark-paintings; the face is also a major painting design, and occurs in modified form on Kwoma shields. Granted that these signs can be legitimately included in the table, the distribution of the group as a whole shows a west-east gradient similar to that of the distribution of composition principles.

D. COMPARISON OF KUBRU AND OTHER LOCAL SHIELD-DESIGNS

Kubru shield compositions and signs, as separate characteristics, are well integrated into the art traditions of the area; an examination of the assemblies of these on Kubru shields also shows coincidences with such assemblies as they are found in other areas.

It will be noticed that the signs on Kubru shields are usually more susceptible to precise definition than are the compositions, in which there is sometimes a certain ambiguity owing to the richness of the total decoration scheme: K3, for instance, is called here a *biv* composition but could also operate conceivably as a *biii*.

Ula-Wiya and Yino-Wismi (Y)

Kubru: Composition: *bi*

    Signs: sign bordering 8 at each end. Below each sign 8, two signs 7 converge toward the center. Narrow bands frame the 8-signs and converge to the center also.

Y1 (fig. 3): the triangular forms with the bands are bordered with sign 2.

Y2 (fig. 4): in the upper triangle, between and below the signs 7, two signs 6. Below is a band of 0. On either side of the center, sign 8 is repeated with sign 2 above it.
Y3: no framing bands; two signs 8 form the central design, with sign 1 (chevrons on all four sides) between them.

Nggala: Composition: *bi*
   Signs (fig. 5): sign 8 at both ends with sign 6 below on the converging triangular forms bordered with sign 2. Framing lines surround 3-signs at the mid-points of the sides.

Kwal'iyon (K)

Kubru: Composition: *ai*
   Signs: K1 (fig. 6): a vertical row of signs 6, flanked by two vertical rows of signs 5. This design is used by both Wahano and Nandi.

Iwam: Composition: *ai*
   Signs (fig. 7): a vertical double row of signs 4, flanked by two vertical rows of signs 5. Compare also a Hauna shield (fig. 8), and see the comment on it in the following section.

Kubru: Composition: *bii*
   Signs: K2 (fig. 9): four 7-signs divide the field in the form of a St. Andrew's cross, the narrow ends converging at the center; their outer borders are elaborated with sign 2. In the angles of the cross, at top, bottom, and sides, are (apparently slightly anthropomorphized) transforms of sign 8; these refer to the leaf of *wur*.

Iwam: The crossed arrangement of signs 7 occurs on Iwam shields (Haberland 1963: pl. III, 5, from Mauwi village), and on bark-paintings (Schuster 1968–1969: 43; 1969: 6). Another painting design follows the total composition even more closely (fig. 10). A related design appears on shields from the Leonhard Schultze River (Schuster 1968–1969: 41, from Waliyo village), where it represents fish.

Abau: A skeleton version, mainly expressing the composition, appears on a shield (fig. 11).

Kubru: Composition: *biv*
   Signs: K3 (fig. 12): On the vertical center line are two signs 6. On either side is a vertical sign 1, restricted, and terminating at both ends in sign 5: each of these could therefore also be expressed as 2-signs, restricted and doubled (i.e., as multipled versions of *wur,* which the whole design is said to represent). The whole design is specified as belonging to Nandi.

Abau: Composition: *biii*
   Signs (fig. 13): sign 2 at each corner, with a large sign 3 in the center (Kelm 1966–1968, 2: 209).

Iwam: A similar design appears in relief on a hand drum also from May River (fig. 14).

Munggwal'yon shields (Mu)

Kubru: Composition: *ai*
  Signs: Mu 1 (fig. 15): sign 9 is the vertical central feature, with its central length expressed as an elongated sign 6. The signs on either side are ambiguous, but appear to be each a doubled and restricted version of sign 2; they possibly represent *wur*.

Abau; Kwoma: No analogues of the design seem to exist on shields from the area, except on one from Abau (fig. 16); both this and Mu may be referred back to K3. In a version lacking the central feature it is, however, a bark-painting design used by the Kwoma (Wanyi clan, Tongwindjamb village), where it is named for Rumbapwi, a water-spirit.

Mulmul'yon (M)

Kubru: Composition: *c*
  M1:   Signs (fig. 17): sign 10, with two signs 6 above and two below it. The face is that of the hero Wulruwiyanggwət, who is said to have created the design on seeing his face reflected in a pool; while the border of sign 4 around it represents *wur* (Schuster 1968–1969: 11).
  M2:   Two 6-signs on either side below sign 10; said to belong to Nöök clan, now extinct.

Kwoma: The nearest equivalents are Kwoma bark-painting designs (fig. 18), as remarked above.

E. RELATIONSHIPS OF KUBRU WITH OTHER SHIELD-DESIGNS

It is apparent that not only the Kubru use on their shields compositions and signs which are common to the areas around them, but that the total designs also correspond to total designs from the same areas. Most important, the total designs of each clan can be shown to have analogues in the direction from which that clan states that its ancestors originally came. Whether the "fit" is relatively good or bad, the implication in all these cases is that the designs were brought by incoming groups to Kubru, and retain, even though with obvious modifications, the characteristics found in the respective groups' places of origin.

This is actually made explicit in one case: the Yino claim that their Nggala ancestors brought their shield-design to Kubru and sold it to the Ula and Wiya ancestors. The same claim is made about the village's carved canoe prows. The simplest form (for individuals' canoes) is a slightly flattened ovoid pierced with a comma-shaped aperture, attached to the body of the canoe at its broader end; a bar in the form of two or three stylized birds extends from the back of the ovoid to the trough of the canoe; a larger version of this was made for communally owned canoes (e.g., Bühler 1960: pl. 18 center; a Yino-Wismi-Ula-Wiya canoe). In a still larger version two doubled ovoids were carved in silhouette on either side of a very large prow (Shurcliff 1930: pl. opp. p. 260).

These forms duplicate exactly those of Nggala; and the Yino claim to have introduced the basic form to Kubru, selling the right to make it first to the Ula-Wiya, then successively to the other clans which came to the village. The Yino call the ovoid form their totemic bird, *kali;* the other birds on the bar include the hornbill. The canoe prows of other clans are distinguished by minor variations in detail, and paddle handles have carved ends which are miniature versions of the prows. Such variations do not occur on Nggala prows, but at Kubru they account for the fact that the clans call the prow and paddle designs different birds and creatures—the Mulmul'yon design, for instance, represents the butterfly; the band of sign 4 on the tip of the Nasidi prow is its *dok hɔ* cane. The same ovoid occurs as the terminal of slit gongs (Newton 1967: fig. 15) and their beaters; again for some clans (Mulmul'yon and Wismi) it can represent the butterfly. Other designs represent naturalistically human heads, and cassowary and crocodile heads (Haberland and Schuster 1964: 100). The legend of Wulruwiyanggwɔt relates the carvings on slit gongs to the story of his presentation of human heads as trophies, which were thus the latest to be carved on slit gongs.

The canoe prow shields (*ba: l wulru,* "canoe cassowary") of Kubru are markedly smaller than those of Nggala. The masks attached to them are relatively long, narrow, and convex in section (Haberland and Schuster 1964: 101) in contrast to those of Nggala, in which the mask is flat and surmounted by a long, vertical extension up which runs a series of hooks, with a bird's head at the top (Bühler 1960: pl. 9). However, one extant mask from Kubru also shows these hooks and a bird's (? cassowary) head (fig. 19). It seems probable that this form also derives from Nggala prototypes.

These rows of hooks recall the Bahinemo *garra;* and in turn suggest that the origin of the Nggala shield itself may be illuminated by the history of that village's clans. To recapitulate: the Nggraiyo clans describe their origin from the area of the May River; the Wolbi from the Hunstein Mountains; and the Dogoshowa from north of the Kwoma. The Nggala shield-design, analyzed with this in mind, seems to show an amalgam of the iconographic traditions of these three areas. The median rows of hooks may refer to the Bahinemo *garra;* the 8-signs to the identical Kwoma sign, *ab'gimbi* ("flying-fox"); while the outer, border design is clearly related to the K3 shield-design (fig. 12) and its Iwam analogues. The Nggala shield is, in fact, a syncretic assembly of elements selected from various sources; the development from it of the Y variants will be taken up later.

Similarly the origin of the K1 design (fig. 6) may be looked for at an even earlier remove than the passage of the Iwam Wan clans from the May River to Kubru and perhaps beyond. The Yaku subclan of the Wan moved from the south, somewhere on the Niyap (Frieda) River, to the Sepik itself, then westward to the May River. While the ethnographic state of the Frieda–Leonhard Schultze interfluvial area remains obscure, it seems at least possible that the 5-sign and its variants originally formed part of the graphic vocabulary: this is certainly the case east of the Leonhard Schultze River and throughout the Hunstein Mountains.

The example of the relationship between the Nggala and Y group of shields has a number of implications concerning the possibilities of originality, change, and persistence. In the first place, it is suggested that the Nggala design could have been a local invention based on the sources of the Nggala population, and thus not merely deriving from Nggala history but in a sense summarizing it. The Y1 shield, subsequently, derives directly from the Nggala prototype; as K may be said to derive directly from an Iwam shield.

This presumed coincidence presupposes the persistence of at least basic designs over a period which may be considerable. There is no doubt that not merely persistence but identity was deliberately intended, among the Kubru'yon as among other groups—for instance, the Abelam as described by Forge (1967: 83–84). The Kubru'yon themselves affirm that canoe prows, when the body of the canoe deteriorated, were cut off and preserved. This was done precisely in order that the carver, keeping it beside him as he worked, could use an old prow as model for the new prow he was making. That the same procedure was followed in carving shields seems likely, from my own experience. In 1967 there were no old shields at Kubru, and only a couple of recently made examples. I left, at their request, a set of photographs of old shields; by the following year they had produced a considerable number of new ones for sale, and in 1970 it was explained to me that they had been enabled to do this by having the photographs in hand to copy.

In practice minor variations in successive versions would almost inevitably be introduced by individual artists, but these would not involve such major iconographic shifts as can be seen in Y2 and Y3. However, if the shield-designs reflect an articulate process of social change in the village, rather than random invention or acquisition of the designs, the same may well be true of transformations within a single design. Among the Kubru, as among the Iwam, a man can carve the designs of both his father's and his father-in-law's clans. In one case, a Yino man with a Nəmburrə wife carved shield-designs Y2 and M; but each shield was unmodified from the established design. This is not to say that modifications could not be made, or never have been made in the past; some Iwam, although the rules involved (if any) are obscure, attribute the wide extent of their repertoire of shield and bark-painting designs to this dual usage. The period during which the Iwam can do this is said to be limited to the period between marriage and the birth of the first child, during which the husband is formally assimilated into the wife's family. Obviously the restriction does not apply so strictly among the Kubru, at least at present; and it seems likely that other socially based modifications were possible. According to Kubru statements, the original Nandi design was identical with one still current at Hauna (fig. 8), and an example was so carved by Wunimbi, an old Nandi man. But Wunimbi is also the adoptive father of a Yino man; and recently he carved (for prospective sale) a shield of *bii* layout, with the converging elements as *kɔhan dok* and the Yino 8-sign at either end. His use of 8 was legitimized, of course, by his relationship to the young man. When finished the result was transitional between Y and K2 type shields.

These few examples demonstrate rather clearly the versatility of the Kubru socio-artistic system. Built into its logic was the possibility of maintaining a traditional succession of designs, but also the option—not to say the obligation—of variation. It might be going too far to speak of *innovation;* whatever novelty could be introduced must have been within circumscribed limits, owing to the nature and number of the primary designs. (On the other hand there is no reason to suppose that we have inherited anything like the full range of shield-designs: many must have vanished through the attrition of clans and the obsolescence of the shields themselves.) It is, however, this flexibility which has given the art of this village the right to be designated a "Kubru style."

V. Conclusion

This article began with an appeal to an archaeological definition of "style," and a proposal that style in this sense implies certain limitations. By their nature, such limitations allow some definition of the styles' durability and the kind of distribution for which they are available. Combining these considerations with an examination of historical and parahistorical traditions, and including those embodied in myth, results in a more or less satisfactory approximation of an art history for Kubru village. This is an approach which treads a narrow path between true archaeology (which uses a considerably broader spectrum of traits than "designs and patterns") and art historical techniques which have often been based on the isolation of traits and the description of their transformations.

It may seem that the correlation of Kubru narrative material with ethnographic material is simplified to the point of being simplistic: that both are treated as artifacts of an equal order of validity. It is indisputable that the accuracy of the traditions is variable, and in the best of circumstances is only at a closer rather than more distant radius from the original historical facts. They are hearsay evidence which has been deformed by the injection of mythology and probably also by the false claims required by rivalry and pride. The versions quoted here are very possibly incomplete, and I have not attempted to conceal the fact that there are lacunae in the Kubru record which there are no means at present to restore. But to reject this testimony out of hand is more indicative of bias against the chance of its containing usable material than a demonstration of its lack of value. Even in the most clearly mythological phrasing, there can be the trace of historical fact. The floating mountain Belesuwi, or the python Yausipauwawai, are not convincing as geomorphogenic phenomena, but this is not the point; the most significant aspects of the stories about them is, at one level, not the images involved, but the actions they perform. At another level the significance of the stories lies in the extent and range of their distribution.

If, however, it is conceded that the traditions have a broad basis in generalized fact, and if the "non-predictive" principle of the designs is accepted, we are left with a positive hypothesis. This is that the designs were not acquired at Kubru in the random manner we associate with aesthetic choice, or copied at will from sources exterior to the village. They must have been introduced into Kubru by a process of accumulation of population, which took place in historical sequence. This is because various clans had, or acquired, the right to use certain prescribed compositions and signs which they retained in moving from earlier to later locations. The result is not a monothetic "Kubru style" but the interdigitation of a number of styles of diverse origins, which have in some cases been modified or recombined into new formats. (In another sphere of the culture, this is also reflected in the anthropogenic myths of various clans.) While the bias of the present account is in favor of demonstrating that the distribution of the visual material—the designs—

is explained by the information given in the verbal material—the narratives—it can be noticed that the converse could also be true. This, of course, returns us to the position of those who postulate historical events on the strength of material culture. The assemblage of distinct styles at Kubru in itself could be taken as revealing the degree to which separate bands of immigrants have formed strata of the population.

Kubru is taken as an example here because it particularly clearly illustrates a process. It is not to be considered as unique, as the references to the Nggala and Iwam indicate, with their hints that the designs from "earlier locations" are themselves products of an untraced number of still earlier locations and corresponding styles. It would be a mistake to look upon the rest of the area as either remaining artistically static, without a similar series of local transformations, or simply as feeding into Kubru without any reciprocal activity having taken place: although none—for lack of material—has been detailed here, it seems perfectly possible that it has done so, thereby contributing to the complication of the scene. Kubru, in fact, can only be taken as a small and localized detail of a very large picture—the Sepik District, with its enormous wealth of art; which itself is only one part of the even greater scene, New Guinea. Its interest is in the way it shows how other details of that large picture may have been built up, and their relationships to each other.

Much of the actual vocabulary of composition and sign described here can also be found elsewhere: and even extremely close coincidences. A number of paintings from the "lower Sepik," but unmistakably Kambot work, are possibly from Kambaramba (Kelm 1966–1968, 3: 286–292, 296, 299). One group shows a face, in the local convention, at the top of two parallel rows of sign 5; the other is a *bi* composition, with a human face at either end similar in some cases to sign 8; and with 3-signs at either side of the converging chins of the faces. The borders of the faces, and the connecting form between them, are often edged with sign 2 "hooks." Not only in general composition, but in specific details, these paintings coincide almost exactly with the design of the Nggala shield.

Why do they? Coincidence does not mean that designs inevitably (particularly not, over a wide area) form a linked group in either a contemporaneous sense or through an evolutionary development from each other. The existence of a sign in one place might easily inspire random experimentation with it which would lead to combinations already established in the art of another place. The results could be incorporated or not in the art of their new place, according to taste or necessity. This sort of experimentation—and subsequent elaboration of the results—is obviously very easy when, as is usually the case in the areas under discussion, the design elements themselves are extremely simple and there is a marked inclination to a set group of compositions. In other words, the use of minimal signs permits a maximal possibility of permutations, making independent invention not only possible but almost inevitable. To put it another way, when a large area exists in which artists are using a limited number of signs, these may be transformed at one location into a number of allomorphs, of which the transformations at another location, having followed different routes, are isomorphs. On the other hand, the possibility of independent invention having taken place decreases in inverse proportion to the affinity of the quantity of design elements, and the relationships between them, in the art of two areas. With full correspondence, independent invention would be based on such a degree of coincidence in methods and materials of creative thought as to render them so nearly identical in the first place that the most elegant course would be to assume a genuine identity, at least of intention. To determine this, one might refer to historical causes, to the elucidation of which, in recent times at least, oral history can be a valuable tool.

NOTES

[1]   The information given here was collected in 1967, 1970, and 1973 during field work for which The Museum of Primitive Art granted me leaves of absence and financial support. The Wenner-Gren Foundation provided grants for travel and equipment in 1967 and 1973. I am much indebted to the Museum and the Foundation for this assistance, and to Mrs. Gertrud A. Mellon, Mr. Harold P. Schneider, and Mr. G. de Havenon for further help.

I also wish to thank my informants at Kubru; particularly Namawas, Nesugwak, Sonu, and Wunimbi.

My wife, Kathleen Haven Newton, kindly undertook the difficult task of drawing all the most complex shield-designs: figs. 3, 4, 5, 6, 9.

[2]   "Kubka": the name means "the place of entrails"—those of her victims heaped up up a vengeful water-spirit.

[3]   The population figures are based on Administration census information.

[4]   This list is probably incomplete. It is based on notes on the collections of the Museum für Völkerkunde, Basel; Museum für Völkerkunde, Berlin; Field Museum of Natural History, Chicago; Peabody Museums of Archaeology and Ethnology, Cambridge and New Haven; objects collected in 1965, 1967, and 1970, now in the Papua New Guinea Public Museum, Port Moresby, and in the American Museum of Natural History, New York; and a list of Wogamusin material culture terms compiled in 1967.

[5]   "Múlmulion" in Schuster 1968–1969:28. Wogamusin: *yon,* "child" (Laycock 1968: 52).

[6]   Probably pidgin: "tulip" (*Gneton gnemon*), as is definitely so for note 9.

[7]   Wabsi and Yamsi belonged respectively to Kwal'yon and Wismi. Yamsi is now in a private collection in Australia. Kwal'yon is associated with these objects as the Wismi encountered some of the former during their migration.

[8]   This theme of unfair division leading to emigration occurs also several times in Kwoma traditions.

[9]   See note 6.

[10]   Human excrement—female in the case of the Manambu—figures largely as an ingredient in fighting magic; the use of flying-fox excrement (*kaimb ndjodja*) in sorcery is attributed by the Nggala to the Bahinemo.

[11]   These include Ga: girruli, Noək (clans of Mulmul'yon).

[12]   See Reay 1969: 471–472 for objections to such a convention. An examination of Administration census figures for "Kupkain" is fairly revealing, although it is likely that some of the dates of birth recorded, particularly early ones, are based on guesswork. Thirty-seven men with offspring are listed, with dates of birth from 1901–1941, in the censuses from 1960–1970; the father's average age at the birth of the first recorded child is 31 years (3 men had their first child at 16–18 years; 28 between 20–30 years; 6 between 33–38). A number of variables cannot be assessed; among them the effect of infant mortality in the earlier part of the period. Whether recruiting, with resulting long spells of absence from the village on such occupations as plantation work, has had the result of raising the age of marriage it is also impossible to say. It may be observed, however, that the seven men with recorded birth-dates of 1901–1917 (that is, before much European contact) still come out with an average age of 27 1/2 years at the birth of the eldest recorded child. In the circumstances, 25 years seems a reasonably close figure for the length of a generation.

[13]   The attributions of the designs to clans were given me by several men, consulted separately or in groups, to whom I showed photographs of the shields in the Basel, Berlin, Frankfurt, and Stuttgart collections. The level of accord was high. K3 was at first attributed to Yino (on the basis of the discs; taken as "coconuts"), but this was corrected by a Nandi man who recognized one such shield as made by his father.

Bibliographical References

Behrmann, Walter
1922   *Im Stromgebiet des Sepik.* Berlin

Bühler, Alfred
1961   "Kultkrokodile vom Korewori (Sepik-Distrikt, Territorium Neuguinea)," *Zeitschrift für Ethnologie,* 86:183–207

Bühler, Alfred, T. Barrow, and C. Mountford
1962   *The Art of the South Sea Islands.* New York

Craig, Barry
1967   *Houseboards and war shields of the Mountain-Ok, Central New Guinea: analysis of an art style.* 3 vols. Unpublished thesis, University of Sydney

Cranstone, B. A. L.
1968   "War shields of the Telefomin sub-district, New Guinea," *Man,* n.s. 3: 609–624

Forge, A.
1967   "The Abelam artist," *Social Organization,* ed. Maurice Freedman. London

Gardin, Jean-Claude
1958   "Four codes for the description of artifacts: an essay in archaeological technique and theory," *American Anthropologist,* 60: 335–357

Haberland, Eike
1963   "Schilde vom oberen Sepik aus dem Völkerkunde-Museen Frankfurt am Main und Stuttgart," *Tribus,* 12: 105–121

Haberland, Eike, and Meinhard Schuster
1964   *Sepik: Kunst aus Neuguinea.* Ausstellung in Städels'schen Kunstinstitut, Juni–August 1964. Frankfurt-am-Main

Kelm, Heinz
1966–1968   *Kunst vom Sepik.* Berlin. (Veröffentlichungen des Museums für Völkerkunde Berlin, N. F. 10, 15. Abteilung Südsee 5–7. 32)
1969   "Kunstgegenstände aus dem Sepik-Gebiet (Neuguinea)," *Baessler-Archiv,* N. F. 17: 303–364

Laycock, D. C.
1965   "Three upper Sepik phonologies," *Oceanic Linguistics,* 4: 113–118
1968   "Languages of the Lumi subdistrict (West Sepik District), New Guinea," *Oceanic Linguistics,* 7: 36–66

Newton, Douglas
1967   "Oral tradition and art history in the Sepik District, New Guinea," *Essays on the Verbal and Visual Arts. Proceedings of the American Ethnological Society,* 1966: 200–215. Seattle
1971   *Crocodile and cassowary. Religious art of the upper Sepik River, New Guinea.* The Museum of Primitive Art. New York

Port Moresby
1968   *Village directory*. Department of District administration, Territory of Papua New Guinea

Reay, Marie
1969   "Myth and tradition as historical evidence," *The History of Melanesia*. Second Waigani seminar, the University of Papua New Guinea. The Research School of Pacific Studies, Australian National University, Canberra: 463–476

Roesicke, A.
1914   "Mitteilungen über ethnographischen Ergebnisse der Kaiserin-Augusta-Fluss-Expedition," *Zeitschrift für Ethnologie*, 46: 507–522

Schapiro, Meyer
1952   "Style," *Anthropology Today*, ed. A. L. Kroeber. Chicago: 287–312

Schmidt, E. W.
1929   "Die Schildtypen vom Kaiserin-Augusta-Fluss und eine Kritik der Deutung ihrer Gesichtsornamente," *Baessler-Archiv*, 13: 136–177

Schmitz, Carl A.
1972   *Oceanic Art. Myth, Man, and Magic in the South Seas*. New York

Schultze Jena, Leonhard
1914   *Forschungen im Inner der Insel Neuguinea*. Berlin (Ergänzungsheft nr. 11 der *Mitteilungen aus den Deutschen Schutzgebieten*)

Schuster, Meinhard
1968–1969   *Farbe, Motiv, Funktion zur Malerei von Natürvolkern*. Sonderaustellung vom 2. Juli 1968 bis 23. Februar 1969 (its *Führer*). Basel
1969   "Die Maler vom May River," *Palette*, 33

Shurcliff, S. N.
1930   *Jungle Islands*. New York

1. Compositional principles
   of Kubru shields

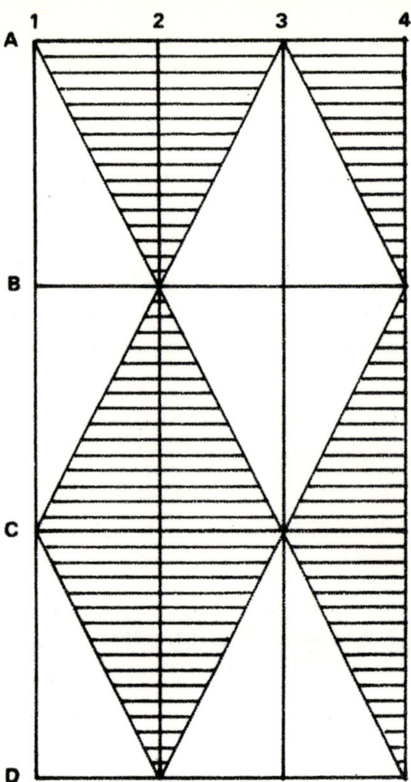

2. Primary signs used on shields.
   Some Kubru interpretations:

1. Yino: antennae of shrimp (?).
The central pointed element is Nasidi:
magrinek, a water insect.
Unidirectional chevrons are the human spine
(see fig. 4)

2. Kwal'yon: *kɔhan dok*, d'Albertis creeper

3. Yino: coconuts

4. Nasidi: *dok hɔ*, wild sugar cane.
Open serial chevrons are Yino: *baisas dok*,
areca; or *mumt*, snake

5. Munggwal: *wur*, vine with thorns;
to a lesser degree this is also Mulmul

6. Yino: *bok wir duan*, coconut weevil;
enclosed version is *suk, bok tak*
(see fig. 4 and p. 199)

7. Crocodile mandible; variant with
internal chevrons, human ribs

8. Yino: coconut husk

9. Birds on floating log;
also variant of *wur*

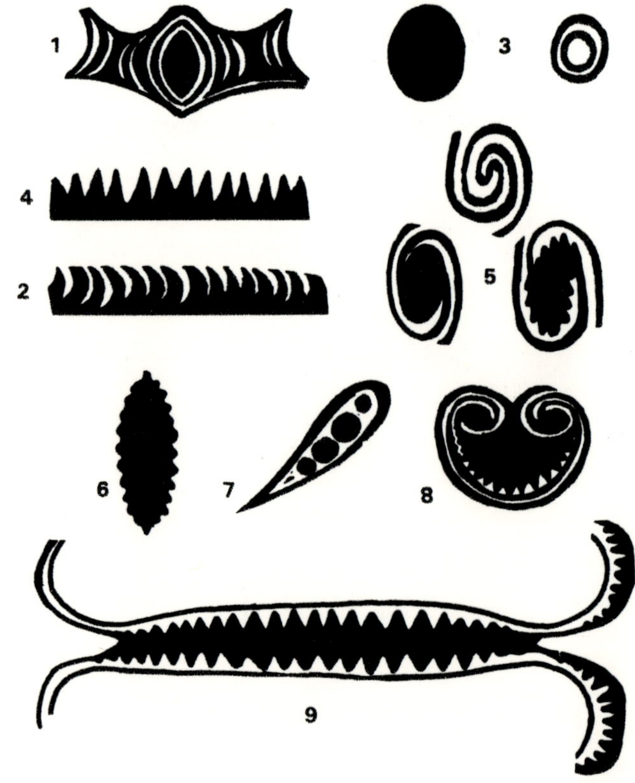

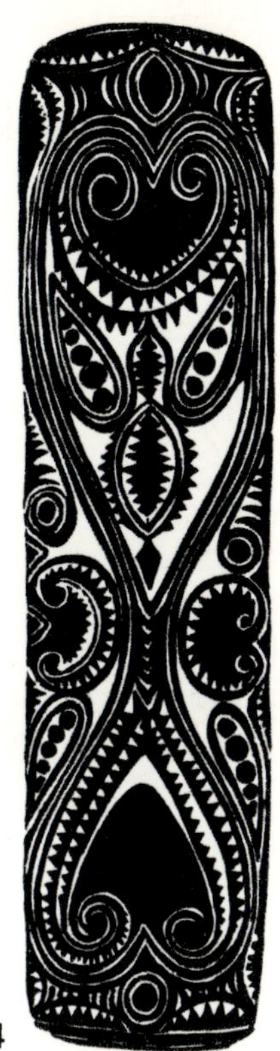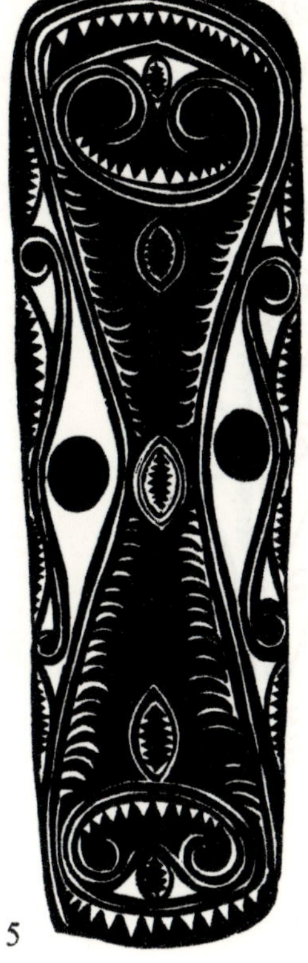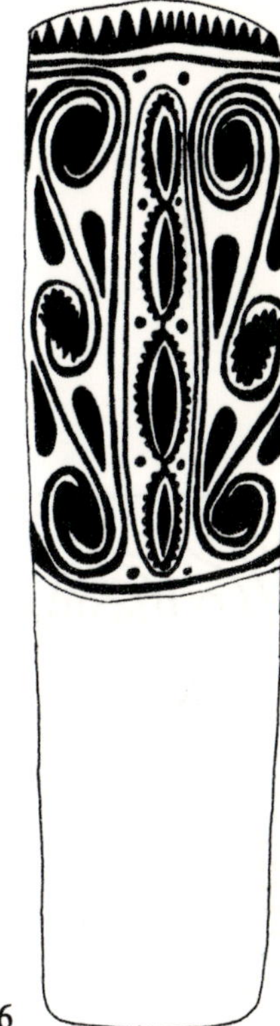

3. Shield. Yino clan (Y1). Kubru
(after Kelm 1969:356). Berlin VI 49 371

4. Shield. Yino clan (Y2). Kubru
(after Schmitz 1972:pl. 113). Basel Vb 15 949

5. Shield. Nggala (after Kelm 1966–1968, 2:167).
Berlin VI 42 058

6. Shield. Kwal'yon clan (Kl)
(after Kelm 1966–1968, 2:157).
Berlin VI 39 383; attributed to "April River."
An almost identical example from Kubru
is Basel Vb 15 954

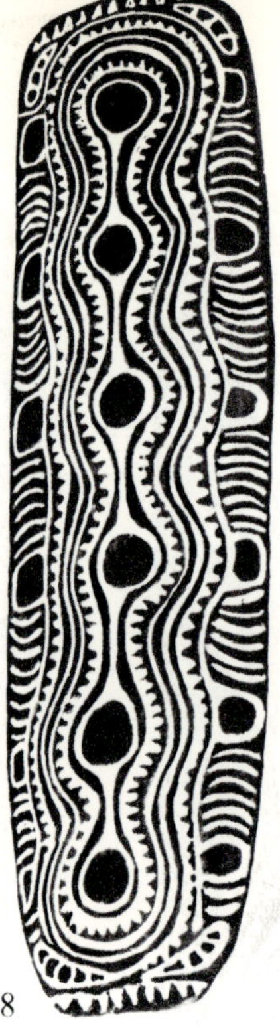

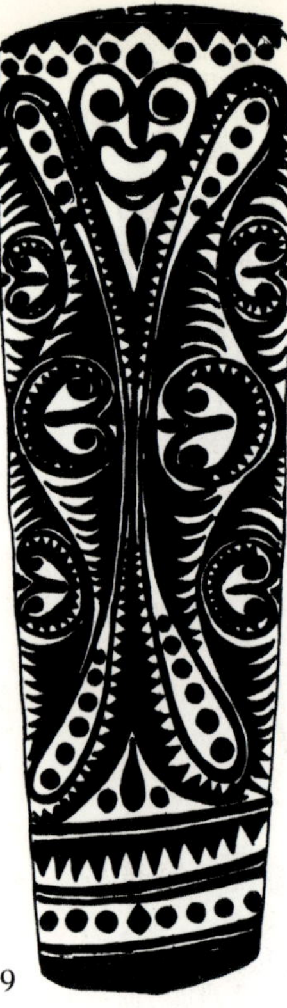

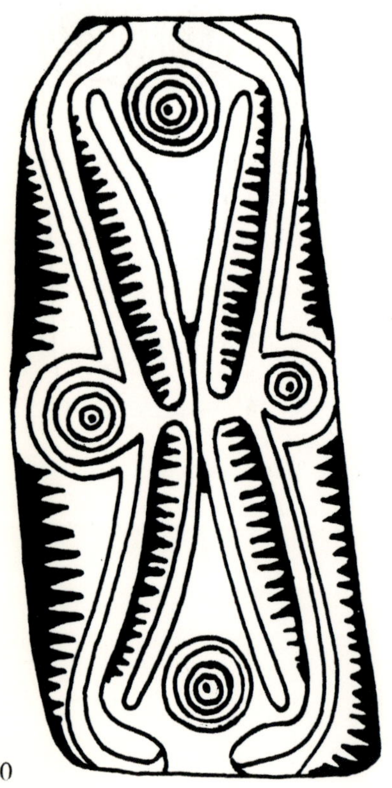

7.   Shield. May River Iwam
(after Bühler 1960:22). Basel Vb 15 965.
Attributed by Iwam informants (1967)
to Wan and Dunak clans

8.   Shield. Hauna: Sepik River Iwam.
Made about 1970.
Papua New Guinea Public Museum, Port Moresby

9.   Shield. Kwal'yon clan (K2). Kubru.
Basel Vb 15 946

10.   Bark-painting. Mowi: Sepik River Iwam. Basel

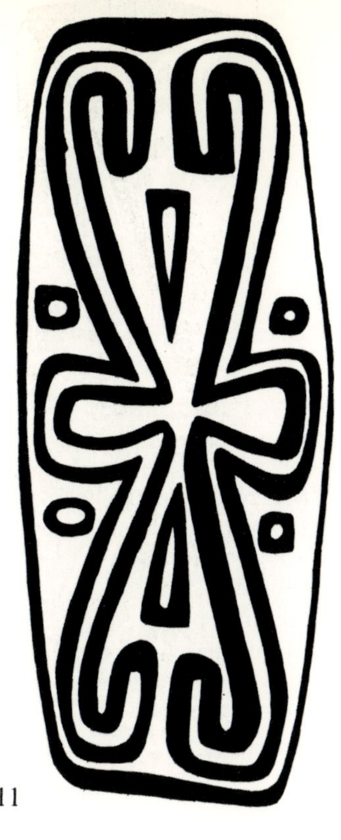

11

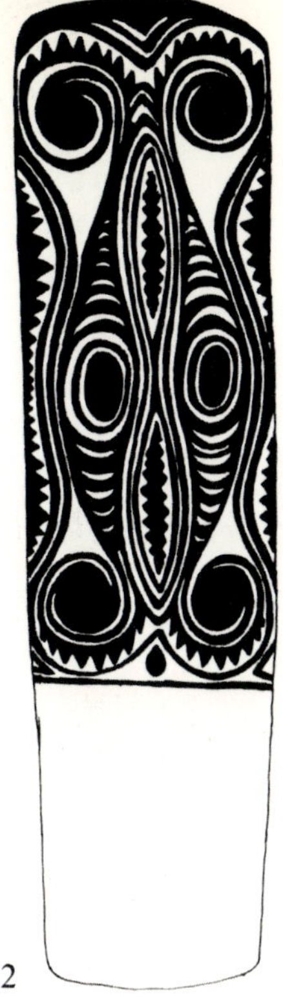

12

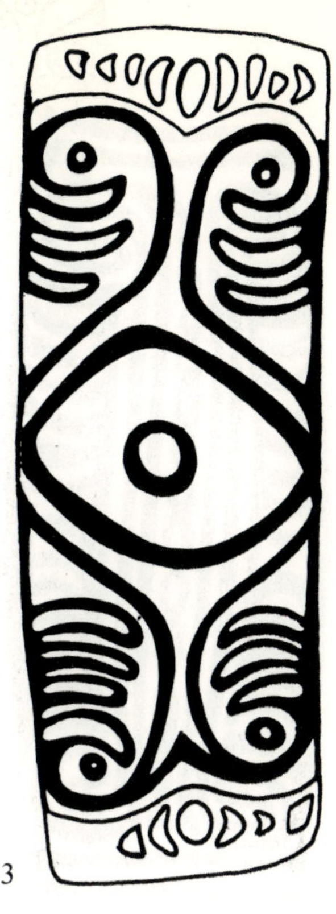

13

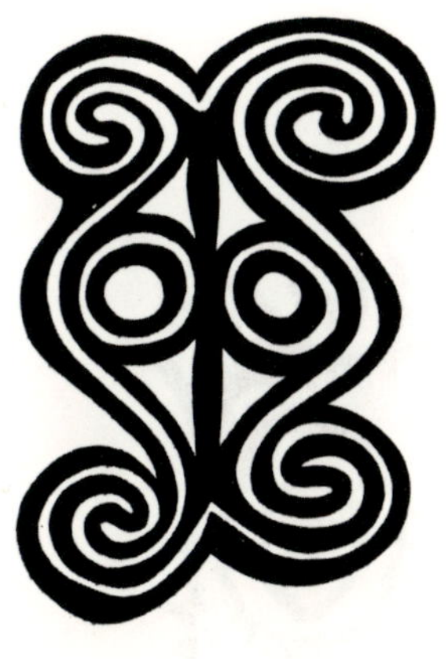

14

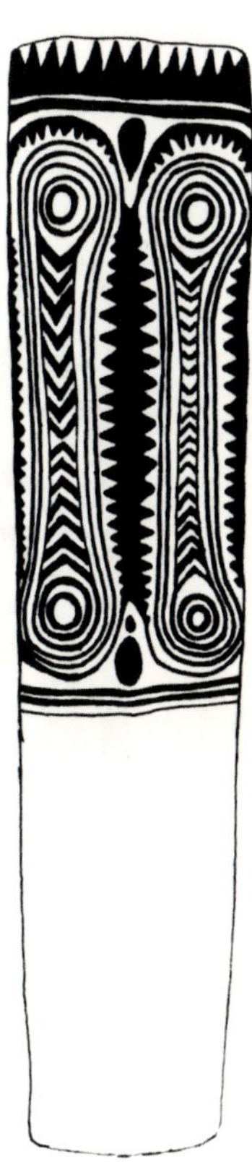

15

11. Shield.
Abau (after Kelm 1966–1968, 2:218;
compare also 232, 236). Berlin VI 41 751;
"Dorf beim Endlager"

12. Shield. Kwal'yon clan (K3).
Kubru. Basel Vb 15 953

13. Shield.
Abau (after Kelm 1966–1968, 2:209).
From "Dorf I/II oberhalb
des Grenzjäger-Biwaks"
(between the Hordern and August rivers)

14. Design on hand-drum.
May River Iwam.
Private collection, New York

15. Shield. Munggwal clan (Mu).
No provenience
(after Haberland 1963:Taf. II, 5;
compare II, 4 from Kubru).
Frankfurt NS 30 870

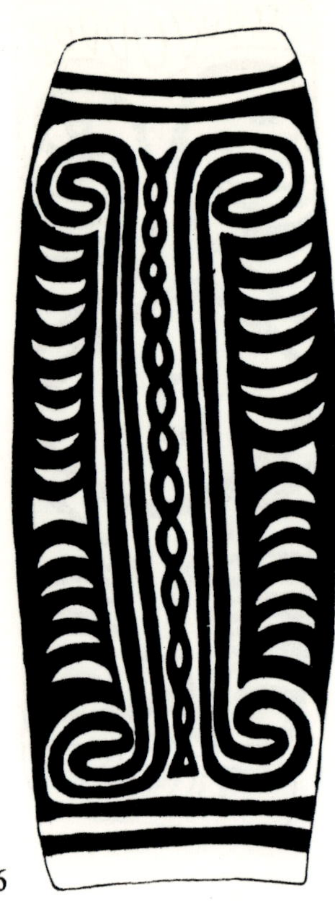

16

16.   Shield. Abau (after Kelm 1966–1968, 2:203).
Berlin VI 41 515; "Dorf oberhalb des Mäander-Berges"

17.   Shield. Mulmul'yon clan (M). No provenience.
The Museum of Primitive Art 69.16

18.   Masək-nggaamba
("Head ghost": a head living in a pool),
a character in the Kwoma version of the legend of
Wulruwiyanggwət. Kwoma, Tongwindjamb village;
detail of painting by Nggeipfuk, 1965.
The Museum of Primitive Art 69.19

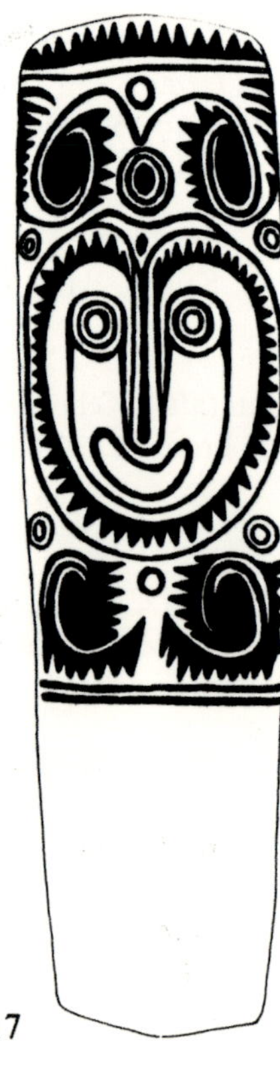

17

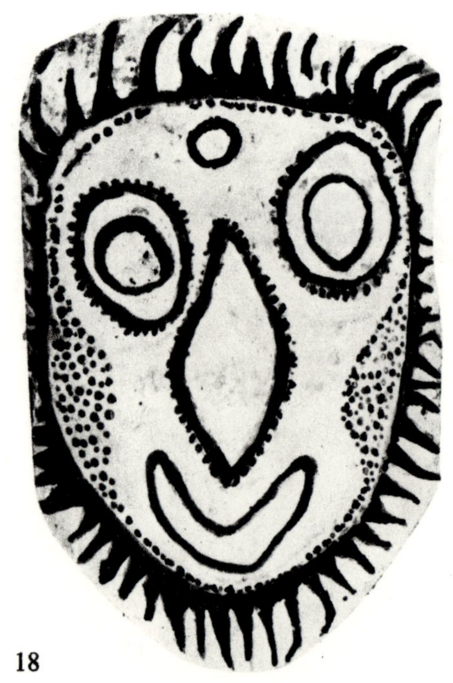

18

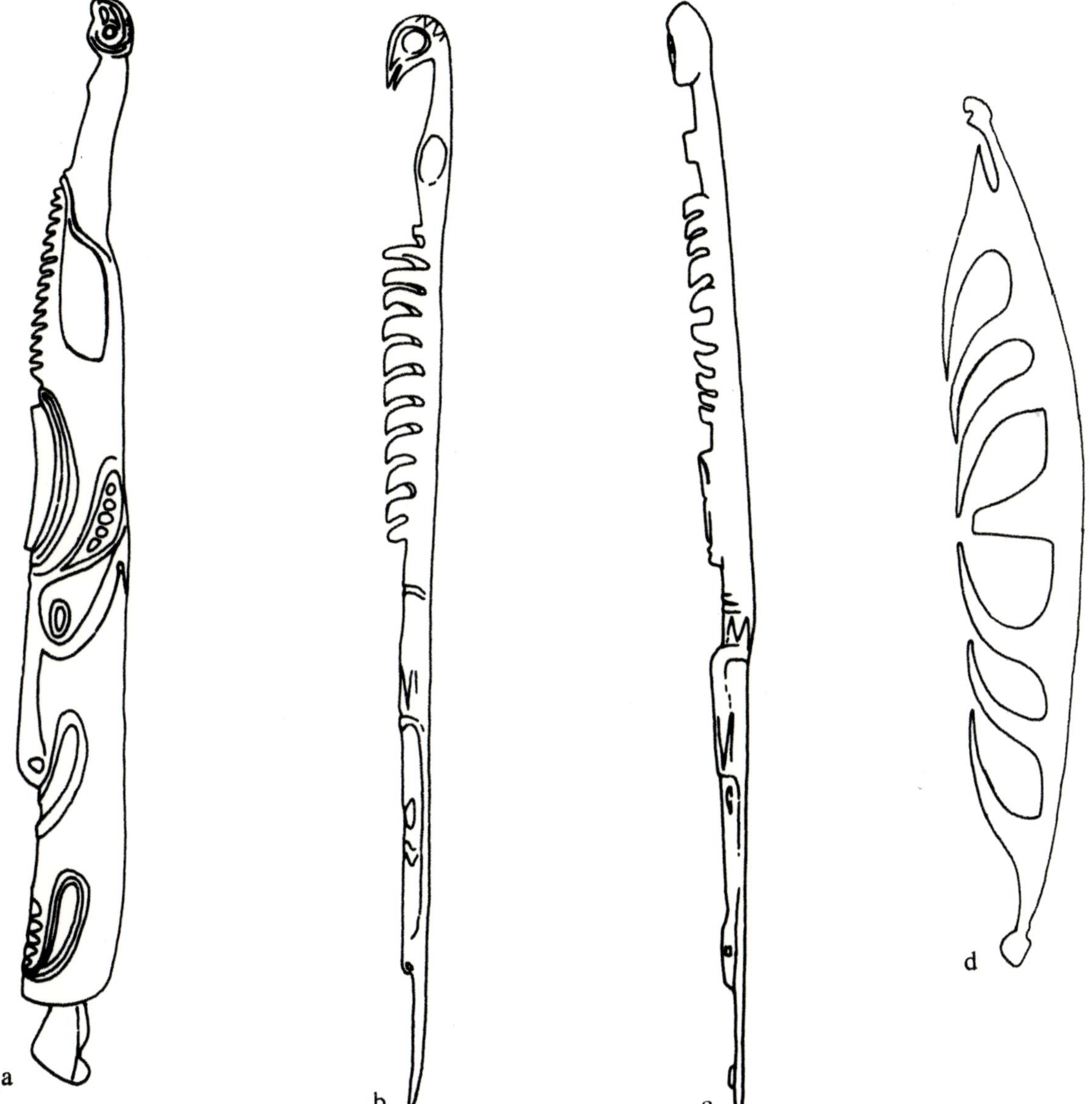

19.   Profiles of masks from canoe prow ornaments:
a) Kubru; Basel b) Nggala; Basel c) Nggala; Basel
d) Sacred object, *garra,* Bahinemo;
Private collection

19

STUART PRESTON

A Puritan in Paradise:
Henry Adams in Oceania

Writing to John Hay on June 23, 1890, Henry James commented: "Henry Adams's journey to the South Seas is one more ray of light on the fact that the world is fast growing too small for its worldlings." To what surprising adventure on the part of the great American thinker and historian does this refer, and what were the reasons why the journey took place? What induced Henry Adams to forsake the amenities of life in Washington and Europe, the adulation of eminent friends, and the echoing chamber of his intellectual remoteness in order to spend a year and a half roaming about Oceania, then beyond the pale of Western civilization? Was he not sufficiently an expatriate at home? What did he find there, and how did he reconcile his discoveries with the accepted American ideas of 1890 and the profundity of his own thought?

In 1890 Henry Adams was fifty-two years of age, a rich retired scholar, a recent widower, and in full possession of his exceptional intellectual powers. If he liked to consider himself a "failure," that conviction rose solely from the fact that he had failed to reach the political eminence of his great-grandfather John Adams, second President of the United States; of his grandfather John Quincy Adams, sixth President of the United States; and of his father Charles Francis Adams, American Minister to England during the Civil War. He believed ruefully that the new post-Civil War America, vulgar, imperialistic, and increasingly heedless of the stern morality of New England's founding fathers, had no further use for a person of his type and breeding. And because he not so secretly held a high opinion of himself he became more and more contemptuous of the contemporary world. Nonetheless, social and intellectual distinction was an inadequate substitute for political power. America had failed him, rather than he it. Not that his career was hitherto undistinguished. He had served his father diligently in London; he had taught history at Harvard and had written books on American history which still hold their own today. He was also the anonymous author of two rather waspish novels about society in Washington, where, in the 1880s, he built a handsome house on Lafayette Square right across from the White House, whose successive occupants he observed with sharp and amused derision. Nothing about Adams is simple. Yet very few human beings have left behind them more abundant, contradictory clues to their actions. The complexity of motives behind his Pacific journey deeply illuminates Adams's ambivalent personality—so longing for a certainty and so sceptical of there being one.

As usual, Henry James got to the heart of the matter, Adams's motives being partly personal and partly springing from the intellectual predicament shared by so many thoughtful persons at the time. A profound malaise weighed down on the last decade of the nineteenth century, pessimism replacing the optimism of earlier years when industrial and scientific discoveries and the spread of democracy seemed to promise the millennium. High hopes began to dissolve as new, unforeseen perils rose the world over—militarism in Germany; nationalism in France; nihilism in Russia; rumblings in the Far East; decadence in art and letters everywhere; and financial and political corruption in the United States, where the gap between the intelligentsia and the inordinately rich and powerful new moneyed class widened menacingly. As the most sensitive barometer of the day, Adams recorded all these storm signals, finding himself deeper and deeper in trouble with the new American dream. Furthermore he had personal reasons for feeling that the world was too much with him late and soon. The shock and horror of his wife's suicide in 1885 had permanently wounded him. "I am glad to be dead to the old existence," he wrote, "which was a torture, and to forget it, in a change as complete as that of another planet." Again, more mildly, "Every now and then, in my bourgeois ease and uniformity, my soul rebels against it all, and I want to be off on my wanderings again."

Yet Adams was no escapist, wishing to abandon an unbearable present for some land of heart's desire. His perpetual disillusionment succeeded in sharpening his sense of reality instead of lulling it in the fogs of nostalgia. A vein of tough-mindedness underlay his cynical pose. He liked testing his physical endurance, and his real curiosity about new experiences as well as a passionate interest in history and sociology were eminently active traits. In any event, ennui and despair cannot fully account for the vigor and enterprise with which he embarked on this pilgrimage, concluded with such rich results.

Adams did not travel alone, finding in the distinguished American artist John La Farge, a man of congenial tastes and similar inquiring mind, an ideal companion well accustomed to Adams's ways, having toured Japan with him in 1886. Like Adams, La Farge detached himself from the vulgarity and commercialism of the age, consequently suffering, as a biographer wrote, "the disadvantage of being a full-grown, sophisticated man in a country and period which was more ready to resent than to recognize one." Born in New York in 1835 to French parents, he had studied in Paris and returned to this country to pursue an active artistic career as a landscape painter, a muralist, and a designer of stained glass. Many important commissions came his way in recognition of his outstanding ability to fuse the decorative arts and architecture: If anything, La Farge was over-cultivated, painting being merely one of the many accomplishments that his rich and versatile nature required. The blight of culture mars most of his work, where beautiful thoughts are devitalized in execution. Not so, however, the sketches he made in the South Seas, which are brilliant and direct (fig. 1). He gave Adams lessons in watercolor, thus sharpening his friend's visual responses which had hitherto been sacrificed to intellectual disciplines. "I go on," wrote Adams, "trying every day to make pictures, and every day learning, as one does in a new language, a word or two more, just to show that the thing is laughable. Still, I have learned enough, from La Farge's instructions, to make me look at painting rather from the inside, and see a good many things about a picture that I only felt before." He even developed a painter's eye, describing the Samoan landscape at midnight as "toned with one general purplish wash with the most exquisitely delicate gradations . . . even the whites have an infinite gradation of violets, when contrasted with the dead white of a ship or a house." The South Seas provided more than one lesson in Adams's education. The friends set each other off well. "Adams, you reason too much," said La Farge one day. On which Adams commented, characteristically, "He should have blamed him [Adams] for being born in Boston."

For most people in 1890 the South Seas was no more than a vague geographical term with even vaguer romantic associations. Few Western travelers had gone out there, the best known, Captain Cook and Bougainville, having done so in the eighteenth century, while more scientific reports were brought back later by Darwin and Lewis Henry Morgan. Still, the legend persisted of "happy shores without a law / where all partake the earth without dispute." This was not exactly true. Aggressive missionaries had harshly attempted to make the natives mend their Arcadian (i.e., to the missionaries, sinful) ways: the French had established a little outpost in Tahiti in the 1840s, and toward the close of the century German and American trading and political interests squabbled over the area of Samoa. Nonetheless, by 1890 no more than three hundred Europeans and Americans had settled in that almost limitless expanse of island territory. Adams could justly boast that he and La Farge were "the first Americans who ever came to these islands as great chiefs travelling for pleasure."

However, far-seeing empire builders were beginning to envision the South Pacific as a crucial area of global politics in the future. Adams ranked among them although he claimed to have gone to Samoa "for the beauty and the art, not the utility." On the one hand he succumbed to "the moon and the Pacific"; the "butterfly blue" of the sea, and the "lilac grey" of the cumulus clouds. On the other his ever-active political sense foresaw, and rightly, a future struggle for the control of the Pacific sea lanes as the direct door to the Far East.

On August 23, 1890, the two travelers steamed away from San Francisco for Honolulu, their first landfall. Hawaii captivated them although civilization had made ominous inroads there, the names Dole, Dillingham, and Spreckels being already in prominence. But away from the town they discovered primeval beauty, "where the land and the ocean meet like lovers, and the natives look almost natural," sights which La Farge excitedly sketched and about which Adams wrote letters home in near-ecstatic terms. "Every ravine was more beautiful than the last, and each was a true Paul and Virginia idyll, wildly lovely in ways that make one forget life." Young women with "sufficient old-gold quality and blood to make them very amusing" hung leis about their necks. All in all he could forget his old complaint that civilization had become "an intolerable bore." New sensations mixed strangely with the past when he would "get gently intoxicated on the soft violets and strong blues, the masses of purple and the broad bands of orange and green in the sunsets, as I used to griser myself on absinthe in the Palais Royal before dining at Véfour's, thirty years ago." Back in Honolulu Adams quickly recovered his cynical, bantering, world-weary self, forgiving local society for having ignored him, having caught "glimpses enough of it to imagine worse than Washington horrors." Feelings of disdain appear to have been mutual, Adams confessing naïvely that he found it "strange that no one ever suggests our doing anything social." But they were granted an audience by King Kalakaua, "a somewhat superior Chester A. Arthur; a type surprisingly common among the natives, though not, like our own magistrate, an example of the Christian virtues. I would not be thought to prefer Kalakaua to Benjamin Harrison, but I own to finding him a more amusing subject."

For all its attractions, Hawaii offered no more than a foretaste of what lay ahead, an agreeable hors d'oeuvre to the banquet of Polynesia, to the still genuinely archaic world, "what Hawaii was a hundred years ago, except for a tinge of missionary, disagreeable but not so bad as elsewhere." They were welcomed with literally open arms, the natives regarding Americans as their saviors and dearest friends. Once on the island of Vaiale in Samoa they were invited to drink kava in the houses of all the chiefs. Other delights followed swiftly. "We have had a great siva dance at the house of Sewmano in defiance of missionary remonstrance and even of the women's opposition," at the end of which Sewmano's daughter "pranced about, approaching and retreating, till at last she came up close to me as I sat cross-legged on the ground, and then bending over, put her arms around my neck and kissed me, amid shouts of applause and laughter from the whole village." Shades of Quincy and of Mt. Vernon Street! But Adams still had a prudish side and was anxious to reassure his correspondents that his virtue lay in no danger and that he played the part of a passive, although entranced, observer. "As far as I know or can learn," he primly wrote, "the women of rank here are in their own way perfectly respectable . . . Of open license I have seen no sign. Neither man nor woman has said a word to me, or even made a sign suggesting indecency or immorality." Nor did Adams lose his social caution. "We have associated only with the first society," he commented complacently, as if from London or Paris, "the families of the powerful chiefs, and I know nothing of the common people except as I see them pass by."

La Farge was equally bowled over by the siva dance and, quivering with emotion, "expressed endless contempt for Carmencita." Confusedly he tried to find equivalents for this physical grace and beauty in classical allusions and in European painting. "The Samoan youngster," he rhapsodized, "who rose shining from the sea to meet us, all brown and red, with a red hibiscus fastened in his hair as beautiful as any carved ornament, was the Bacchus of Tintoretto's picture." And again, in the bookish language of 1890 cultivation: "So those lovers of form, the Greeks, must have looked, anointed and crowned with garlands, and the so-called dance that we saw might not have been misplaced far back in some classical antiquity." He pitied the sailor, the missionary, and the beachcomber, "witnesses of things they did not see because they had not read." However Adams scorned La Farge's timid classical allusions. "Greece was nowhere," he wrote. "I imagine he [La Farge] never approached such an artistic sensation before. For my own part, I gasped with the effect of color, form and motion, and leave description to the fellow that thinks he can do it." Reality surpassed all expectation.

A highlight of their Samoan stay was meeting Robert Louis Stevenson, who had settled there in desperate search of a cure for his incurable consumption. Their encounter was an experience that, initially, raised all Adams's social hackles and brought out disagreeably his considerable snobbishness. Moreover, in the flush of his own delight in setting Western foot in what he thought was nigh-virginal territory for one of his own eminence, he was chagrined to find Stevenson, years his junior, a great local hero and the acknowledged European champion of Polynesia. Adams's amusingly malicious account of the visit reveals more about himself than about the tragically doomed novelist.

Adams and La Farge rode up to Stevenson's house "Vialima" on the mountains above Apia. "There," the former wrote, "Stevenson and his wife were perched —like queer birds—mighty queer ones too. Stevenson has cut some of his hair; if he had not, I think he would have been positively alarming. He seems never to rest, but perches like a parrot on every available projection, jumping from one to another, and talking incessantly. The parrot was very dirty and ill-clothed as we saw him, being perhaps caught unawares, and the female was in rather worse trim than the male. I was not prepared for so much eccentricity in this particular, and could see no obvious excuse for it." Despite the "weird and grimy" impression that Stevenson made on his prickly visitor, his charm won out and his entertaining talk interested Adams immensely, giving him much valuable information on the islands and on local Samoan politics, and verifying the visitor's impressions of the natives being "always respectable, while some of the whites are degraded beyond description." Adams's whole caustic account of the visit was written to John Hay, who, amused by his friend's discomfiture, could not resist sending him Stevenson's account of the visit: "Two Americans called on me yesterday . . . one an artist named La Farge . . . the name of the other I do not recall." "Bear up under this," commented the teasing Hay, "like a man, in the interest of science! It completes the image of the shabby parrot."

Once the wonder and strangeness of Samoa, as a visual spectacle, became familiar, Adams's historical, ethnographical, and sociological curiosity was aroused by the Samoans themselves. No subject was left untouched in the long conversations he held, through a native interpreter, with native chiefs. He particularly inquired "about the old customs, families and religions," and suspected shrewdly "that all matters involving their old superstitions, priesthood and family history, are really secret, and that their Christianity covers a pretty complete paganism." The feudal structure of society gratified him, and the fact that an American frigate nearby was named "Adams" raised him in native esteem. "I am rejoiced to find," he wrote with characteristic irony, "for the first time in my life, that my name is worth something to me, but the natives are solid aristocrats to a man, and they evidently know a swell when they see one." He and La Farge were "school-boys on a lark. We have been as amused as though we were supernumeraries at the opera. Every day brings us some new variety of childhood's fables."

Yet their conclusions were gloomy. "Social changes are steady," Adams wrote, "and another generation will leave behind it the finest part of the old Samoan world. The young chiefs are inferior to the old ones. Gunpowder and missionaries have destroyed the old life of the nobles." La Farge's regrets were more poetically expressed and in more fin-de-siècle language. He wished "to sleep forever in the trade winds under the southern stars, wandering over the dark purple ocean, with its purple sense of solitude and void." But he, too, realized that these haunting dreams of Arcady were dissolving in the light of the immediate future. "There will soon come a day," he mused, "when even for those who care, it will be no more; when nowhere on earth or at sea will there be any living proof that Greek art is not all the invention of the poet—the mere refuge of the artist in his disdain of the ugly in life."

Their time in Samoa was drawing to a close. Goodbye to the fading island paradise. Goodbye to their good friend ex-King Mata-afa ("At last, La Farge, we have met a gentleman"). And goodbye to the Stevensons. "I must say no more in ridicule," Adams wrote, "for he has been extremely obliging . . . but I dare not see him often for fear of his hating me as a Philistine and a disgrace to humanity." For all that, they had many interesting political conversations, La Farge summing up Adams's shrewd arguments in the following terms: "The Pacific is our natural property. Our great coast borders it for a quarter of the world. We must either give up Hawaii, which will then inevitably go over to England, or take it willingly, if we need to keep the passage open to Eastern Asia, the future battleground of commerce."

"Tahiti! does the word mean anything to you?" wrote Adams to his adored friend Mrs. Cameron from Papeete, the capital, on February 6, 1891. "To me it has a perfume of its own, made up of utterly inconsequent associations; essence of the South Seas mixed with imaginations of at least forty years ago; Herman Melville and Captain Cook head and heels with the French opera and Pierre Loti." He felt half angry to find it was "a real place, and not a pantomime." And even angrier that Stevenson's rosy picture of it proved so false. He had assured Adams that the Tahitians were by far finer men than the Samoans, and the scenery more beautiful. Consequently Adams's disillusionment was as great as that of Gauguin who arrived there six months later, although unlike Adams, Gauguin was able to transform sordid reality into a golden dream that never existed outside his fevered imagination. For Tahiti was a French trading post in the worst sense, a hotbed of squalid intrigue, abounding in colonial administrators and traders who swindled the natives; grotesque missionaries who forced them to clothe their glorious bodies and instilled into them the sense of sin and shame; drunken and diseased sailors who completed the havoc; and raw European corruption without the veneer of dignity. "Great Pan was dead, the old beliefs forgotten." Adams cursed Stevenson for giving them "an idea of Tahiti that Paradise could not satisfy."

The travelers lost no time lingering in Papeete, mercifully finding the countryside less corrupted. At Tautira, a pretty place, he sat, looking out as usual "through the eternal cocoanut trees over the eternal surf," concluding that "it has done me a lot of good. I am more like a sane idiot than I have known myself to be, in these six years past." He described Tahiti as "an exquisitely successful cemetery. One would like to be buried here. Everything is dead, more or less . . . the sense of death is not painful here, but just a bit sad and sunny . . . La Farge works, but I only doze even when I pretend to be doing something." Every prospect pleased and yet the natives were not the "gay, big animal creatures of Samoa," and the "atmosphere was tinged by a South Seas melancholy, a little sense of hopelessness and premature decay." Inevitably a reaction set in. "Never have I known what it was to be so bored before, even in the worst wilds of Beacon Street, or at the dreariest dinner-tables of Belgravia."

As often before, intellectual interests came to his rescue. He geologized in an effort to account for the building of the coral reef atolls, "all to the confusion and defeat of Mr. Darwin" whose theory was "nothing but theory." Confounding eminent experts on their own subjects was meat and drink to Adams. Far more congenial, and a task that irresistibly appealed to his sense of the past and his cult of faded glory, was the chronicling of pagan Tahiti: old songs, superstitions, and customs, all of these gathered from members of the Teva family, the deposed rulers who had adopted Adams and La Farge as members of the clan. The task provided more than a moment of amusement to vary the monotony of island life. The great authority on these matters was Queen Marau, divorced wife of King Pamare, "with no functions whatever except to drink." Hour by hour, ever more entranced, Adams listened to Tahitian chronicles going back to the time of Captain Cook. His enthusiasm captured the interest of old Queen Hinari, "who astonished her children by telling me things she would never tell them; and as they had to act as interpreters, they caught the disease one by one, and are hard at work, making out the family genealogy for a thousand years back." Adams's subtlety soon detected the resemblance between the story of the decline and fall of the Teva family, once powerful and still the noblest tribe on the island, and the fate of the Adamses, both having fallen from high estate. Inevitably the chronicle became more personal and reminiscences dovetailed in spirit.

Their leaving from Tahiti was an occasion of genuine sorrow. The venerable Queen kissed him on both cheeks, and "made us a little speech, with such dignity and feeling, that though it was in native, and I did not understand a word of it, I quite broke down. I shall never see her again, but I have learned from her what the archaic woman was." On June 5, 1891, they sailed for Rarotonga in the Cook Islands, eventually arriving at Suva, capital of the Fiji Islands, on June 16. There they stayed with the British governor, Sir John Thurston, whose house was staffed with former cannibals, "of the most gormandising class." Adams was delighted, finding that the cannibal's "impression of human nature is evidently favorable. He regards men as I regard snipe." Then the old regrets broke forth. "Romance is gone but prettiness remains." They left Fiji on July 23, arriving early in August in Australia, "an unavoidable bore, a second-rate United States."

The tour was over and Adams satisfied. "We have done our South Seas at last," he wrote to John Hay, "clean cooked and eaten . . . I am almost sorry—yet rather glad—to have accomplished the queer sensation of realising so old a vision, and one so fixed that the vision and reality still manage to live peaceably in my head—two South Seas, not at all alike, and both in their ways charming." And, more drily, to Henry Cabot Lodge: "The South Seas swarm with laughable satires on everything civilised, and especially on every known standard of morality. They flourished in outrageous defiance of every known moral, economical, social and sanitary law, until morality and economy were taught them, and then they went, promptly and unanimously to the devil . . . I do not attempt to draw a moral from their euthanasia." He was obviously pleased with his experiences, although, as always, clothing his pleasure with epigrammatic irony. Needless to say, La Farge's response was more esthetic and tender. He was captivated by the exquisiteness of "this rustic Greece"; by the cult of physical beauty; and by the intensification of all feeling that the islands offered. "I have lived for a season in the Order of Old," he wrote, comparing it sadly with "the weariness of civilized life." For both men, the profound thinker and the sensitive artist, the trip was, in different ways, a spiritual pilgrimage, and a richly rewarding one. They went at just the right moment, when the past, going out, met the present at the door. And they left precious records of their journey. Adams's wonderful letters and La Farge's delicately revealing watercolors preserve forever their experiences of a vanishing world.

Neither man made further record-breaking journeys. La Farge returned to New York and Newport and to his art which never justified its early high hopes. He died in 1910. His record of the journey with Adams is contained in a posthumously published book, *Reminiscences of the South Seas,* which appeared in 1912. If La Farge's career ended dimly Adams went on from strength to strength. To the latter years of his life belong the two great books by which he will always be remembered, *The Education of Henry Adams* and *Mont-Saint-Michel and Chartres.* He died at the age of eighty in 1918.

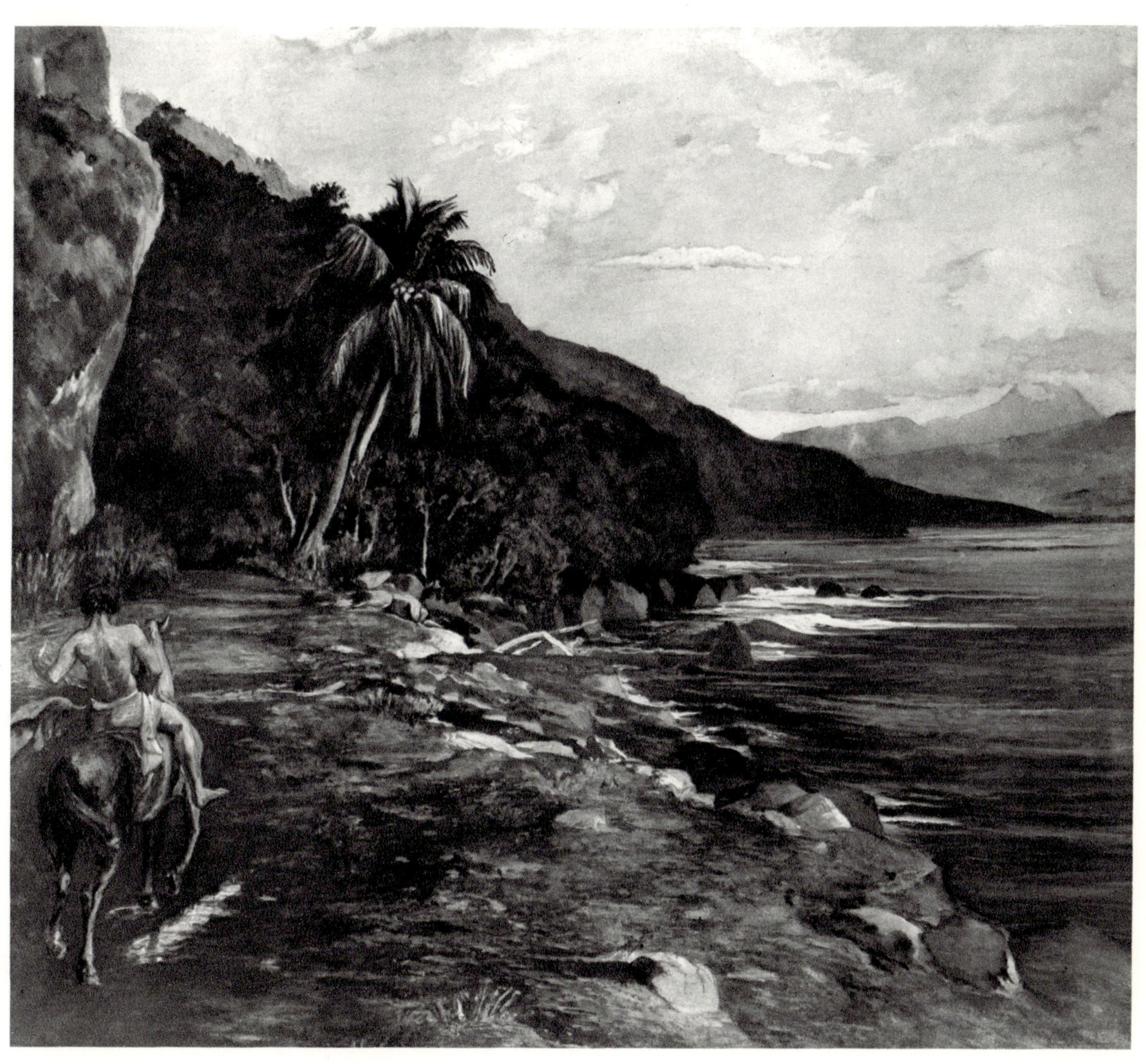

1. JOHN LA FARGE. *Bridle Path, Tahiti.* 1891. Fogg Art Museum,
Cambridge, Massachusetts.
Gift of Edward D. Bettens to the Louise E. Bettens Fund

20

WOLFGANG STECHOW

The Crisis in Rembrandt Research

The crisis which has gripped the state of research on the paintings of Rembrandt shows no signs of abating. The painting with *David before Saul* (fig. 1) in the Mauritshuis and the spectators in the *Prodigal Son* (fig. 2) in Leningrad have already been taken away from the master, together with many less famous pieces, and it is certain that the end has not been reached. At the same time, debates concerning the iconography of some of Rembrandt's major works are in full swing and show signs of increasing frustration and confusion. The great painting in Leningrad, the subject of which was for a long time almost universally identified as the *Downfall of Haman* (fig. 3), has more recently been called *David's Departure from Saul and Abner* and *Joseph Turning away from Judah and Reuben;* the Cologne *Laughing Self-portrait* has been shifted from *Rembrandt-Democritus* to *Rembrandt and Terminus*—and back.

In both areas—style and iconography—definite advances can fortunately be registered. Some attributions of former periods have been dropped to the satisfaction of most; some new identifications of subject matter have convinced and pleased everybody. Yet there is much dissent in each field, some of it violent. Here I want to give a sketch of one inquiry, which I feel would have interested Milton Fox: Is there a connection between these two areas of trouble, and if so, which?

Let us consider first the question why the matter of authenticity of so many paintings can possibly be so complicated in view of the fact that a considerable number of the doubted works are signed with unimpeachable signatures. The leaders of the main group of sceptics have been vague in referring to the method which in their opinion enabled them to state that Rembrandt had the right to sign works executed by his students. In his *apologia* Gerson says only: "It seems . . . that Rembrandt sold his pupils' work," and for this statement he refers to the document of ca. 1635 which does say that Rembrandt sold (*verhandelt*) some works by "Fardynandus" (presumably Ferdinand Bol) and "Leendert" (presumably Leendert van Beyeren). Gerson continues: "Did he overpaint them, *did he sign them* [emphasis added]?" and leaves it at that, except for repeating later, equally tentatively, that "there have been (probably) studio-works signed by Rembrandt himself." The step from Rembrandt as seller of works by two of his pupils to his signing them with his name is a crucial one, and not a single proof of its ever having been taken is available; in fact, the inscription "Rembrandt verandert. En overgeschildert 1636" on the Munich version of the Leningrad *Sacrifice of Abraham* speaks strongly against that assumption, even though its exact meaning is still being debated.

But that assumption is surely the only possible explanation of the astonishing neglect of Rembrandt's signatures. To mention but one example: In Gerson's new edition of Bredius' corpus of Rembrandt's paintings one finds the following entry on *Portrait of a Young Student* in the Cleveland Museum (fig. 4): "Signed (?): Rembrandt 16 . ." There is no record in the Cleveland Museum that anybody has ever inquired about the authenticity or non-authenticity of that signature. Renewed laboratory investigation has confirmed that it is perfectly genuine—and such a confirmation is indeed possible today, in spite of Gerson's perfectly correct statement that "it is difficult to differentiate between a genuine and a faked signature." The rest of Gerson's entry reads: "Bauch (1966, p. 47) attributes the work to Carel Fabritius (possibly); I am reminded of early pictures by Aert de Gelder or Barent Fabritius. An attribution to Rembrandt is probably not right." Thus, we have here the "probable" elimination of the artist who signed the picture in favor of a possible attribution to three totally different artists, one of whom was almost a generation younger than the two others. To be sure, the surface of the picture has suffered from "ironing" and abrasion, as is the case with so many other paintings by Rembrandt, but that certainly has no bearing on its attribution—although lots of confusion has resulted from insufficient consideration of this fact.

If signatures are of no consequence, what do we have—in the absence of other documentation? One will have to answer this question with one word: Opinions. Gerson's opinion is that in the case of *David before Saul*—which, I hasten to add, is (now) unsigned—"the painterly execution is superficial and inconsistent; Saul's turban is shining and variegated, and rather pedantic in treatment, in contrast with the clothing and the hand, which are painted loosely, in one monotonous tone of brownish red. All this points to an execution in Rembrandt's studio, after a design of the master in the manner of Benesch C. 76 (which is itself a copy)." This means that a "shining and variegated" turban cannot be expected to contrast with a "loosely painted" clothing and hand in a genuine painting by Rembrandt (and one may also ask why Rembrandt did not see to it that these discrepancies were eliminated if the picture was executed in his studio). But what if Rembrandt was bent upon making a special display of that turban as a symbol of Saul's worldly power and royalty, which just at this moment, through David's playing, is made to appear so worthless, and therefore did not hesitate even to make that turban "rather pedantic in treatment"? And what if the "loosely painted" hand was deliberately meant to signify lassitude and renunciation of the javelin which lies powerless in Saul's arm—even to the extent of looking "monotonous"? It is even more difficult to explain how Haak could have been offended by the fact that the spectators in the *Prodigal Son* "contribute little to the main theme," without realizing that such silent witnesses are a most characteristic feature of exactly some of the latest and most powerful paintings by Rembrandt.

It seems to me that recent debates about such cases have suffered from a rather wide-spread tendency, particularly among our Dutch colleagues, to carry the (entirely legitimate) fight against the "romanticized" Rembrandt image too far. If Gerson connects the enthusiasm for the *David before Saul* in the Mauritshuis with its appeal "to the Dutch public of the Josef Israëls generation," what shall one say of *Titus as a Capuchin Monk* (fig. 5) in the Rijksmuseum (unless the attribution of this picture, too, be doubted)? Is this the kind of seventeenth-century interpretation which we are so urgently admonished to expect of Rembrandt because he was a seventeenth-century Dutch painter? The pendulum has indeed swung to the other extreme. Perhaps the problematic nature of this situation struck Gerson when he said of this *Titus* picture: "It was quite within Rembrandt's thinking (*and not only a nineteenth-century interpretation* [my italics]) to imbue an 'historic portrait' with the likeness of an actual one." Regardless of whether this is Titus as St. Francis (Bauch) or Titus as a Franciscan (Valentiner), it is Titus in a most extraordinary guise and in an elegiac mood (I don't think this is saying too much). If anybody else painted such a subject in the seventeenth century it certainly did not resemble this one in any significant way, just as there is no parallel to Rembrandt's etched *St. Francis* of 1657. We may see reflections of such things in works by Rembrandt's pupils; but reflections presuppose a light source.

If the cases of *David before Saul* and the *Prodigal Son* show that the relationship between features of style (and technique) and of interpretation of a known subject is not always sufficiently understood, where do we stand when the subject matter is under debate?

Our decisive handicap in this area is the fact that we know next to nothing about commissions entrusted to Rembrandt, particularly for his religious paintings. Who—or what—inspired Rembrandt to paint such a miracle as *Jacob's Blessing* (fig. 6) in Kassel and the vast majority of his other greatest biblical stories? We don't know. In other words, we know nothing about the functional role of such a work within contemporary society (an extremely complex society!) and with that, we lack a decisive aspect of it. Even if we can arrive at an understanding of the synthesis of content and form in such works, its historical locus is still only dimly discernible. That *Jacob's Blessing* was probably commissioned by a Christian, rather than a Jewish, patron can perhaps be concluded from the halo around Ephraim's blond head, but even that is not certain, and in other cases we are left entirely in the dark. And when there are actual uncertainties about the subject we are quite helpless, while even the meagerest document about its commission would solve at least the problem of the story that was expected by the patron.

The latter reservation is indeed important. It has been argued convincingly that on the whole Rembrandt restricted himself to traditional biblical subjects and that it is one of the main tasks of research on Rembrandt iconography to relate carefully the master's works to the pictorial tradition, with additional support from later works in which his own formulations may have been reflected. But this most reasonable method has as yet enabled no one to solve to general satisfaction the problem of the Leningrad painting mentioned at the beginning of this essay (as well as some others). Why is this? Let us assume for a moment that the commission for this picture—which, incidentally, has also sometimes been doubted, though not by Gerson—is known and that it stipulates a "Downfall of Haman." Rembrandt had shown in 1660 (in the wonderful picture in Moscow) how he conceived of the banquet during which Haman was exposed by Queen Esther to the wrath of Ahasver; this was one way of depicting the downfall of Haman. Now let us also assume that a few years later another patron of Rembrandt's—or Rembrandt himself, considering his previous depiction, his last word on that particular scene—desired to see this downfall represented in a significantly different manner—as happened in quite a number of comparable cases. With his deep understanding of the tragic elements which characterize such a downfall, whether it is "deserved" or not, Rembrandt would then naturally have concentrated on the pitiful figure of Haman as he leaves the palace of Ahasver in a dejected mood, completely aware of his fate; the deafening silence around him would be expressed through the other two faces watching his departure in awe but without wrath; any action or specific comment would be as superfluous here as it already had been, to a degree, in the Moscow *Banquet* and as it was to be more fully in the *Prodigal Son*.

But what about the objections that have been raised against this identification? How valid are they? Let me state the two main ones briefly.

Objection no. 1: Rembrandt could not have made an enemy of the Jews the main person of a picture. In the two other examples of this kind, which are cited as only seemingly acceptable parallels, the *Balaam* and the *Belshazzar,* "Rembrandt shows us clearly that their role has already ended." Is this not the case here? I find it hard to think of a more convincing pose and gesture for a man who was powerful only a moment before but now, though still wearing the insignia of power, goes to his doom. True, Haman—an Amalekite—was considered by the Jews to be inherently evil, rather than temporarily insane as was Saul when he raised his javelin against young David. But even Flavius Josephus had elaborated on Haman's downfall in a spirit which evinces the presence of more pity with the Amalekite than the biblical report had shown, when he described how Haman "left [the palace] in consternation and told his wife and his friends with tears what had happened to him." The gap between tears of dejection and tears of contrition, such as the young Rembrandt (1629) had put into the eyes of the repentant Judas—certainly a greater evil-doer than Haman in Rembrandt's eyes—does not seem to me too great to have been bridged by the old master.

Objection no. 2: The Book of Esther does not describe such a scene; "there is no tragic departure in that scene, nor any reason for all three figures to be so deeply concerned." The tragic departure is Rembrandt's interpretation of the fate of great sinners—the kind of interpretation for which an exact parallel in the Bible is no prerequisite and for which there exists not always a fully comparable pictorial representation either. The two other figures witness this departure with sad (not hostile) glances; their concern is that of people who were ordained to be the instruments of such an abysmal downfall.

If these main objections do not invalidate the identification of the subject of the Leningrad picture as the *Downfall of Haman,* how certain can we be that this is really Haman? There is no certainty. But it is nevertheless true that this picture, seen as Haman, most clearly and convincingly corroborates previously broached ideas about that new dimension of the art of the late Rembrandt which can be subsumed under the concept of isolation. It is in such cases in particular that Rembrandt needed no specific biblical text and no specific pictorial tradition. Haman alone, his fate only echoed in the quiet countenances of two witnesses, is like the inseparable group of father and repentant son, "attested" rather than aided or commented on by a few bystanders (Leningrad), like the *Jewish Bride* (Amsterdam), where the pair, Isaac and Rebekah, is now even shown *alone,* deliberately divested of the figure of the spying king Abimelech which was still before Rembrandt's inner eye when he made the preliminary drawing. The two new attempts to explain the subject of the Leningrad picture would necessitate assuming a similar amount of abstraction from the respective biblical scenes—but in their case we would have to think of a much vaster extent of reduction of the number of figures involved in the story and of the basic elements of the setting as they appear in the Bible—too vast in contrast to what we have in the biblical account of the Haman story, for which only two or three figures and "a room" are needed.

If we are sure of so little we shall have to work harder. In doing so we must consider all facets of this incomparable oeuvre with equal care: signature, technique, condition, style, subject matter, personal interpretation of that subject matter, pictorial tradition, workshop conditions, cultural ambiance, related drawings and etchings by Rembrandt; and we must compensate for the crucial lack of documentation with a double effort at a full and unbiased study of all those other aspects—and, before all, of their interrelationship.

BIBLIOGRAPHICAL NOTE

Most references to Gerson are to *Rembrandt: The Complete Edition of the Paintings,* by A. Bredius, revised by H. Gerson, London–New York, 1968; the one to his *apologia* is to "Rembrandt: Oratio pro domo," *Gazette des Beaux-Arts,* 1971, p. 195. The doubts about the spectators in the *Prodigal Son* are voiced by Bob Haak, *Rembrandt, His Life, His Work, His Time,* New York (1969). The most recent identifications of the subject of the Leningrad *Haman* are found in *The Burlington Magazine,* CXIII, 1971, p. 473 (A. Bader), and in *Oud Holland,* LXXXVI, 1971, p. 32 (S. Nijstad); for the last discussion of the Cologne *Self-portrait,* see *Jahrbuch der Hamburger Kunstsammlungen,* XVI, 1971, p. 33 (C. Tümpel). The most recent arguments in favor of identifying the subject of the Leningrad picture with the downfall of Haman were published by C. Tümpel (*Jahrbuch der Hamburger Kunstsammlungen,* XIII, 1968, p. 108) and by M. Kahr (*The Burlington Magazine,* CXIV, 1972, p. 551, with what seems to me an unnecessary display of intolerance and over-confidence).

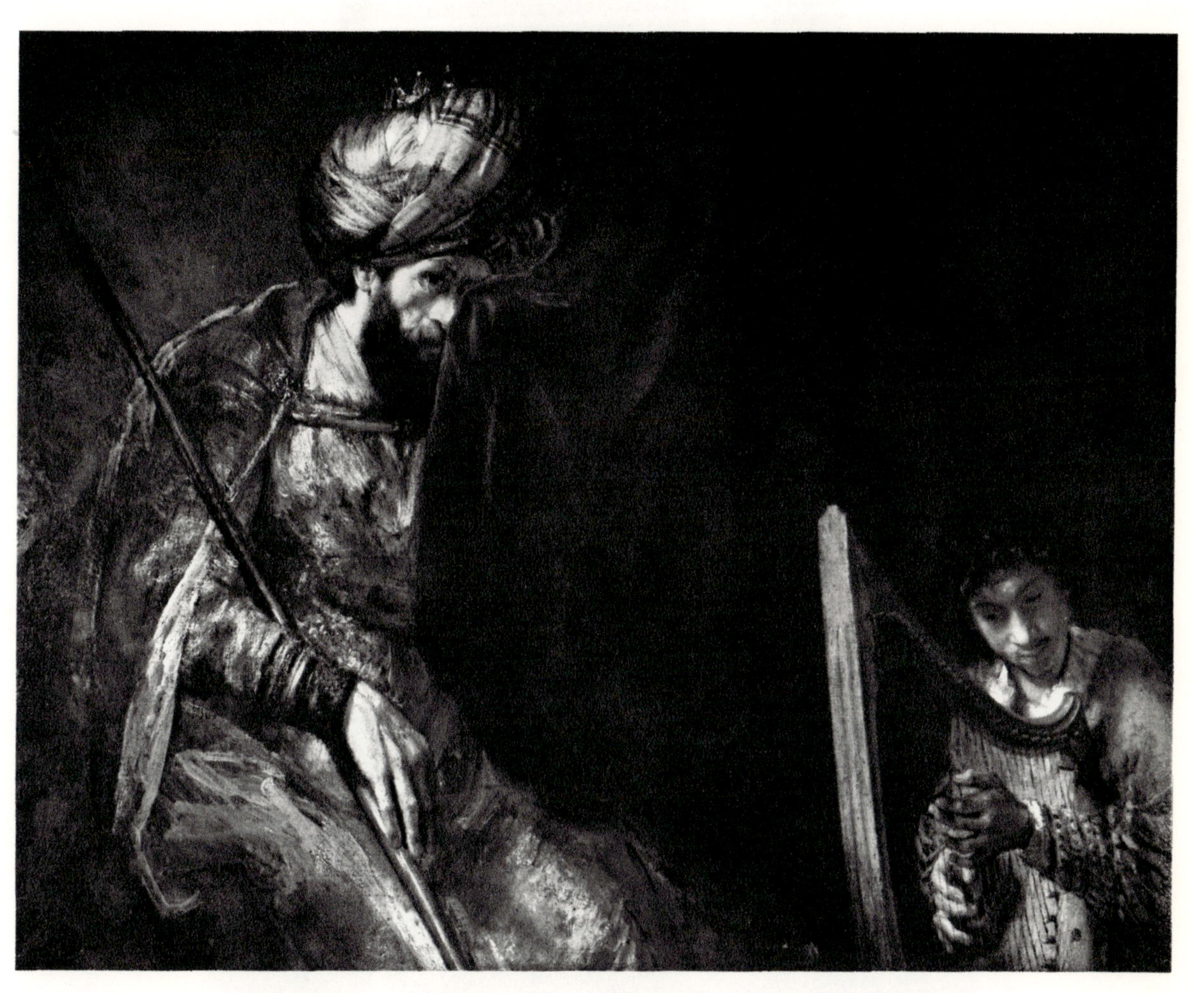

1.   REMBRANDT. *David before Saul.* c. 1657–58. Oil on canvas, $51\frac{3}{8} \times 64\frac{1}{2}''$.
Royal Picture Gallery, Mauritshuis, The Hague

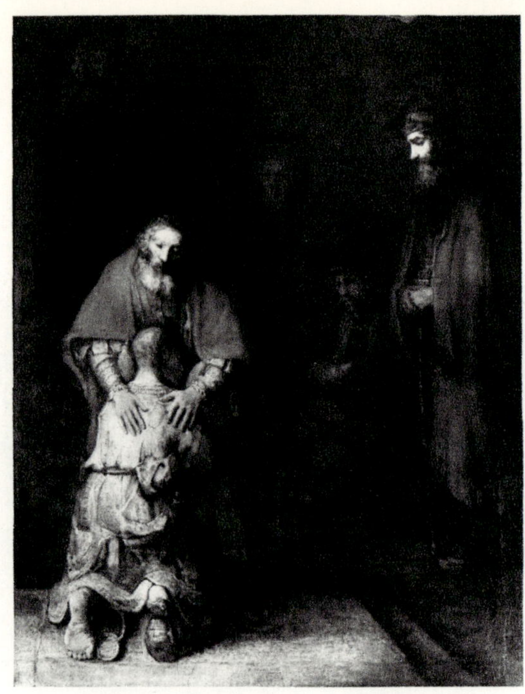

2. REMBRANDT. *Return of the Prodigal Son.* c. 1665.
Oil on canvas, 8'8" × 6'8¾".
The Hermitage, Leningrad

3. REMBRANDT. *Downfall of Haman.* c. 1665. Oil on canvas, 50 × 45⅝".
The Hermitage, Leningrad

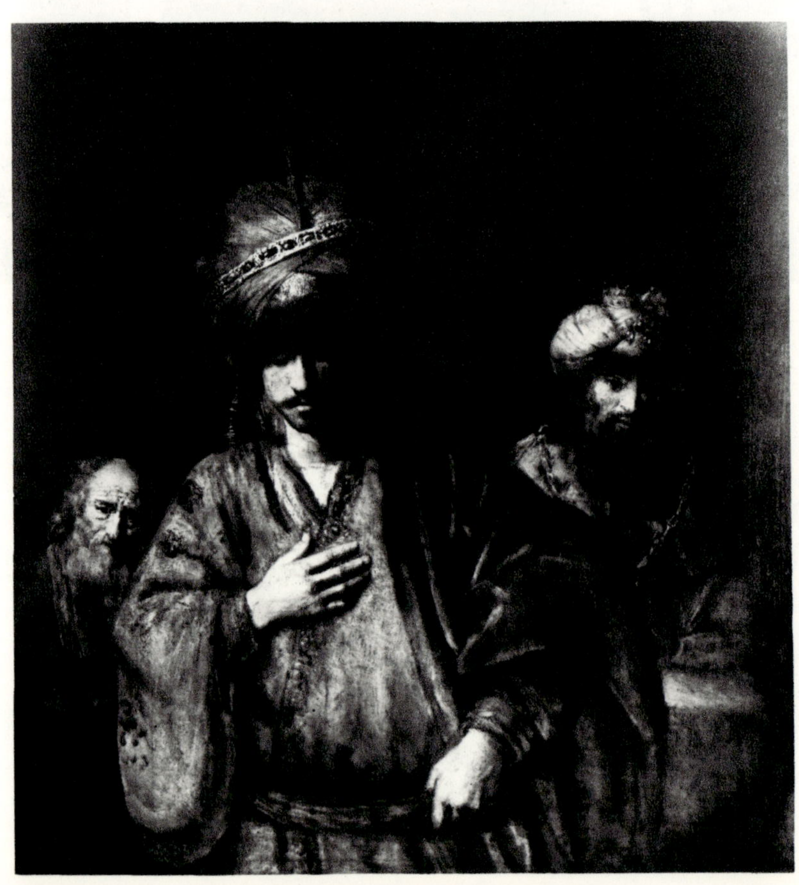

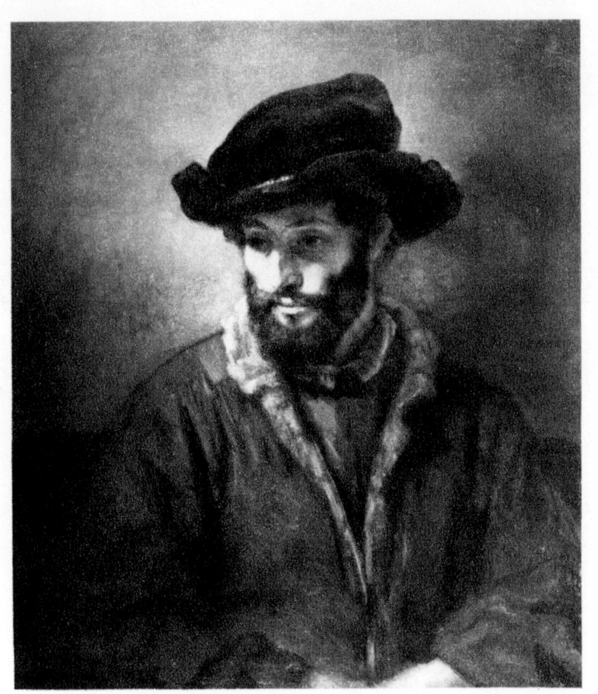
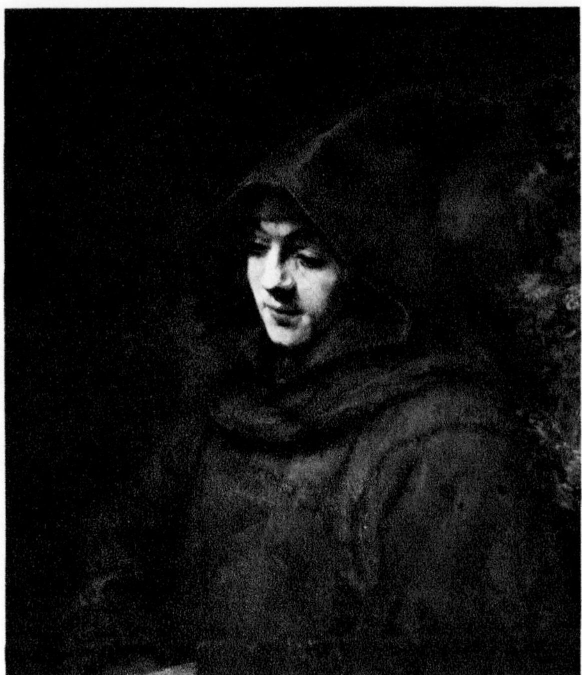

4. REMBRANDT. *Portrait of a Young Student*. Oil on canvas, 33¼ × 27¼".
The Cleveland Museum of Art. Gift of the Hanna Fund

5. REMBRANDT. *Titus as a Capuchin Monk*. 1660. Oil on canvas, 31¼ × 26¾".
Rijksmuseum, Amsterdam

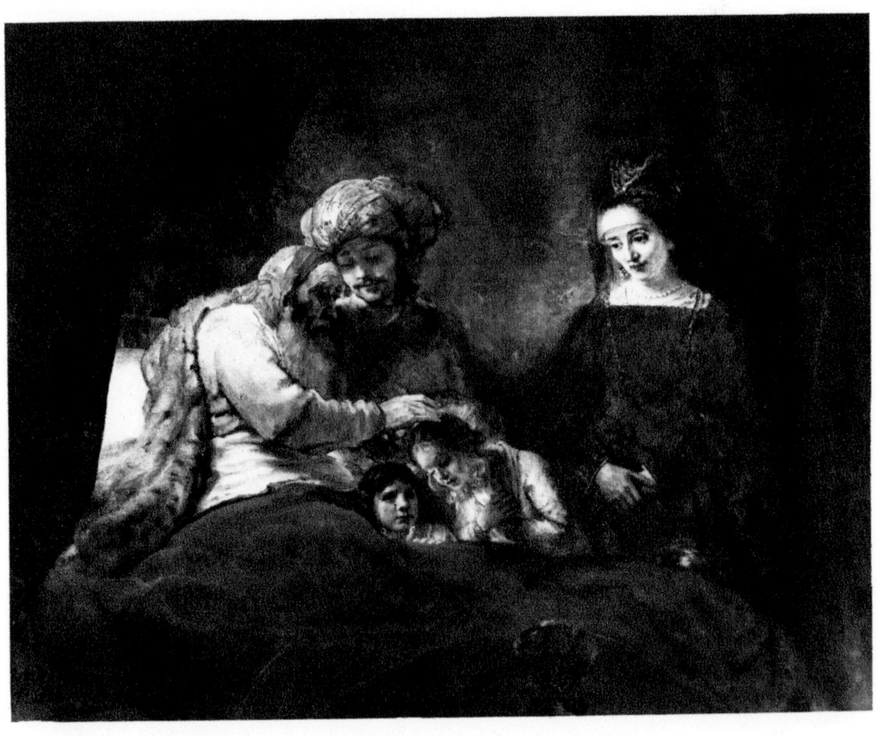

6. REMBRANDT. *Jacob Blessing the Sons of Joseph*. 1656.
Oil on canvas, 68½ × 83½".
Staatliche Kunstsammlungen, Kassel

21

JOHN WALKER

Two Paintings of the Gerbier Family

The National Gallery of Art in Washington recently acquired one of the most important paintings by Rubens to come to America (fig. 1).[1] The picture is well known, having been exhibited in the nineteenth century and, for the last time, in 1927 at the great exhibition of Flemish and Belgian art, held at the Royal Academy in London. Roger Fry in an article in the *Burlington Magazine* of March 1927 wrote: "Rubens has conceived it [*The Gerbier Family*] in a manner all his own. . . . The group is admirably balanced. The poses combine to make an almost sculptural unity. . . . As to colour it is one of the strangest and most unexpected of Rubens's creations."

Even more unusual in Rubens's work is the mood of introspection which pervades the painting. Why does Madame Gerbier appear so withdrawn, as though meditating on some inner problem? Her son gazes at her almost beseechingly, seeming to ask her to reveal her thoughts. The baby alone is oblivious to this mood, which is one of apparent serenity, yet not without overtones of strange foreboding, suggested by stormy bursts of light in the distant sky.

But how easy it is to invent the psychology of others, especially in paintings! There is, however, in this case reason to believe that Lady Gerbier had many problems in her life, which might well have made her pensive, if not melancholy. She was married to a scoundrel, and her expression, as Rubens caught it, may have reflected sorrows she had experienced and premonitions of tragedies to come. Sir

Balthasar Gerbier, secret agent, art dealer, artist, architect, schoolmaster, and cicerone, seems to have had only one loyalty, to Rubens, who was his guest in London, his companion in Brussels, and his fellow intriguer in many diplomatic missions. Toward all others he was consistently treacherous. For example, while British Minister in Brussels, he betrayed a conspiracy to overthrow Spanish rule— a plot he had helped to organize—with the result that the chief conspirators were hanged. At the same time he implicated quite gratuitously Charles I who had befriended and trusted him. When the Civil War was about to begin and the King was under attack from all sides he accused Cottington, the King's close friend, of the betrayal of state secrets, of the disclosure of those very conspiratorial plans which he himself had sold to the Spaniards for 20,000 crowns. After the death of Charles, to curry favor with the Commonwealth he wrote a vicious pamphlet justifying the regicides. And toward the end of his life, having persuaded the Dutch government to send him to Guyana in search of gold, and having dragged along his wife and three of his daughters, he managed through his intrigues and treacheries to stir up such hostility that his followers mutinied and at Cayenne one of his daughters was shot and killed and another wounded. If Lady Gerbier foresaw the anguish of her life—debts, treachery, frauds, even murder—she had every right to be melancholy.

But Gerbier was impervious to his crimes. He wrote innumerable pamphlets justifying himself; and having designed for his last patron, Lord Craven, a tasteless country house, which has mercifully disappeared, he died tranquilly at Hampsted Marshall in 1667. He was the ancestor and one of the most brilliant of all curators; for in his youth he had assembled the collection of the Duke of Buckingham at York House and managed the acquisition for his patron of Rubens's own collection. As the inscription for his grave, however, he chose a single word, "Architect," a profession at which he was judged to have been a total failure.

The reason we can identify Lady Gerbier and her children is that the group they form was copied in a large picture now at Windsor Castle, which includes Sir Balthasar Gerbier and five additional children (fig. 2). The Windsor picture shows the Gerbier coat of arms, and once had an inscription identifying the family. As Gerbier was not knighted until 1638, the vase on the right, bearing his coat of arms, must have been painted after that date, but otherwise we are uncertain of which year in the 1630s the copy was executed.

The Windsor painting presents us with many problems, two of which are paramount: why was Gerbier omitted in the Washington version, which seems to be entirely by Rubens's own hand; and why did he wish this picture repeated by an inferior artist? The answer must remain speculative until further documents are discovered; but though we do not know under what circumstances Rubens decided to paint Gerbier's family, a consideration of the relations of the two artists will, I believe, permit an hypothetical answer to these questions.

Rubens and Gerbier met in Paris in 1625. Rubens was then the agent of the Infanta Isabella, Regent of the Spanish Netherlands, and Gerbier of the Duke of Buckingham. Both wanted Spain and England to end their quarrel, which formed a part of the Thirty Years' War; neither had much authority; and both pretended to more than they had.

The complications of these shifting alliances and belligerencies cannot be unraveled in a short space. Suffice it to say that Rubens was above all loyal to his own country, namely, the Spanish Netherlands, and then by association to Spain. As a diplomat he was trusted by his patroness, the Infanta Isabella; but for a time he was disdainfully looked upon by her nephew and ruler, Philip IV. As the Spanish king wrote his aunt, "It is a cause of great discredit to this monarchy, as may easily be understood, for its reputation is bound to suffer if a man of so little importance [Rubens] has to be approached by ambassadors bearing such weighty proposals."[2] In spite of the disadvantage of his common birth Rubens maneuvered his affairs in such a way that he was finally summoned to the Court in Madrid. There his popularity as an artist, for he painted the King, the Queen, and other members of the royal family, and his modesty as a man, overcame Philip's prejudice. Rubens was selected to go to England to prepare a treaty and an exchange of ambassadors. To increase his importance he was made Secretary of the Privy Council of the Netherlands. Nevertheless, because of the disadvantage of his birth, it was never possible for him to be named Spanish ambassador to the Court of St. James's.

Charles I decided, when Rubens arrived in London, that a fellow painter, his old friend Balthasar Gerbier, should be his host. So Rubens, with his brother-in-law Brant and a retinue of servants, lodged with the Gerbiers for nine months. When their stay was over Gerbier wrote Cottington, then Chancellor of the Exchequer, that "The King has taken from Gerbier a cordon of diamonds and a ring to give to Rubens. God knows when Gerbier will be paid—as also the charges of ten months entertainment for Rubens. It is a poor reward to be put to charges and still to be excluded from confidence."[3] Gerbier soon received at least a partial payment. But in view of the reluctance of the king to pay him at all, it is difficult to agree with Burckardt that the Windsor painting was ordered from Rubens's studio by Charles I, presumably as a gift for Gerbier.[4]

Diplomatic negotiations during his nine months in England had left Rubens little time for painting. Though Gerbier's studio was available he seems to have executed only two important portraits during his English sojourn, both now in America: *The Earl of Arundel* at Fenway Court in Boston and *Dr. Theodore De Mayerne* at Raleigh, North Carolina; and he probably carried out two or three noteworthy compositions: *St. George and the Dragon* now in the Royal Collection, which may have been finished after his return to Flanders; *The Allegory of Peace and War,* a gift to Charles I and presently in the National Gallery, London; and presumably *Mars and Venus* in Dulwich. For an artist as prolific as Rubens this is a surprisingly small production, even granting the omission of a few less significant pictures. Furthermore it is curious that he did not do a state portrait of Charles I when one considers his numerous portraits of Spanish royalty. In London he would seem to have spent less time at his easel than in Madrid. Under the circumstances had he the leisure to paint *The Gerbier Family,* which most, if not all, scholars have attributed to his English period?

To answer with certainty is impossible, but an answer is implied by the ages of the children on the right of *The Allegory of Peace and War* (fig. 3), and the same children in the Washington portrait (fig. 1). The date of *Peace and War* is known, since on his departure from London Rubens gave it to Charles I, as a token of gratitude for the King's hospitality and cooperation in establishing peace between

England and Spain. During the nine-month period of Rubens's stay in London, from May 25, 1629, to February 22, 1630, three of the Gerbier children must have posed for him. There are drawings of them in Rotterdam, Berlin, Weimar, Leningrad, and Vienna. Rubens apparently loved children and these three seem to have particularly fascinated him. He gave them a conspicuous place in *Peace and War,* where their presence has always seemed to me somewhat contrived.

Gerbier's children were available models, and quite possibly their mother, born Deborah Kip, also posed. The nude holding her breast in the center of the same picture, a figure usually identified as the Goddess Pax, and a second nude, the Venus in the Dulwich *Mars and Venus,* bear a strong resemblance to the seated lady in the Washington and Windsor paintings (figs. 1 and 2).

Now compare the children in the Washington picture and in a detail of *Peace and War* (fig. 4). Is it fanciful to think that in the Washington and Windsor paintings they are more mature, look a little older? Their names are not precisely known, but it is generally thought that George served as the model for Hymen, the boy who holds the torch and crowns the maiden, probably his sister Elizabeth. The youngest child staring at the spectator would then be Susan. George also appears a second time with his arm around Elizabeth. Look first at George as we see him in the Washington painting. His face and body are heavier, and he would seem to be in his early teens. Next consider Elizabeth on the extreme right, who coolly appraises the spectator. Isn't she already a young lady? And Susan, doesn't she seem to have outgrown the plump baby face we see in *Peace and War* (fig. 5)? Their mother, too, has definitely aged, if she posed for the goddesses Pax and Venus. If this is true then it follows that the two versions of *The Gerbier Family* must both have been painted in Flanders.[5]

There is a second but less certain reason to suppose that Rubens executed the Washington picture after he had left England. Madame Gerbier and her children are dressed in the Flemish fashion, as Sir Oliver Millar helpfully pointed out to me. Though it is possible that they would have worn these clothes in London, it is more likely that they dressed themselves in this manner when they were in the Netherlands.[6] Thus the ages of the sitters and their clothes seem to me evidence, not conclusive but persuasive, that Madame Gerbier and her children posed again for Rubens after their return to the Netherlands.

We do not know the exact movements of Gerbier himself in the year immediately following Rubens's visit to England, but in the spring of 1631 he was appointed English Resident at Brussels. His wife and children accompanied him on June 16th of that year. Judging by the ages of the children it would seem likely that Rubens painted them in 1631 or 1632. We know that Charles I stood godfather for the youngest son who bore his name.[7] This is probably the baby in Madame Gerbier's lap whose birthdate we do not know. Assuming the christening took place just before the Gerbiers departed from England in June 1631, it is likely that the Washington picture was painted shortly after their arrival in Flanders.

Rubens was indebted to Gerbier not only for his hospitality in England, but also for the sale of his collection to the Duke of Buckingham some years earlier. Rubens's gift of the Washington painting to his friend would therefore have been appropriate, but cannot be proved. It is also possible that Gerbier, who dabbled in art dealing, may have bought it as an investment.

But why was Gerbier himself omitted from the picture? There is no certain answer, nor is any likely to be more than an hypothesis with the knowledge at present available. Gerbier was continuously in the Netherlands in the years following Rubens's visit to England. It would therefore have been easy for the master to do a drawing of his friend, but so far as we know he didn't. Gerbier seems to have been snubbed. Why?

The most obvious reason is that he wasn't on hand when Rubens painted his family. This, however, is unlikely, as he continued to be English Resident at Brussels for nine years. But perhaps there is some subtler explanation. Was the painting in Washington ever intended to be a group portrait? True, certain individuals posed for the painting, but Rubens may have wished to go far beyond their individualities, to transform a mother and her children into an allegory of family unity. Madame Gerbier holds her baby protectively in her lap and her son looks up at her yearningly, while her two daughters gaze coldly at the spectator, as though challenging the intrusion. The whole group seems a symbol of matriarchal solidarity. They are an archetypal family, harmonious, united, devoted, but also, the mood of the painting implies, vulnerable, potential victims of fate, of the unhappiness Rubens himself had known with the death of his little daughter and of Isabella Brant. Perhaps such tragedies in his personal life are reflected in these somber overtones. But in the Windsor picture, with the introduction of Gerbier and the additional children, this mood is destroyed. There is no longer a sense of universality, and instead the scene is reduced to a group of individuals who happen to pose together. That inner unity so conspicuous in the Washington version has vanished.

There is further evidence that Rubens intended the Washington picture to be more than a mere group portrait of the Gerbiers. He not only omitted Gerbier himself, but I believe he purposely left out the additional five children we see in the Windsor painting. The generally accepted explanation is that they were not yet born, but if one looks at their apparent ages this becomes highly improbable. Furthermore, Gerbier in a letter of July 1629 refers to a "large family";[8] and in the Calendar of State Papers there is preserved a document which states that when Gerbier arrived in Dover in June 1631, preparing to cross the Channel, he had with him his wife and "many children."[9] There is also the documented story involving Elizabeth, Mary, and Susan, who enjoyed considerable notoriety, for in 1643 they escaped from their father's custody and entered a Catholic convent in France, where for a time they began their novitiate.

Assuming Susan was six when the Washington picture was painted about 1631, she must have been born in 1625, and Mary, perhaps one of the twins on the steps in the Windsor picture, in 1624. They would then have been seventeen and eighteen in 1643, just the right ages for their escapade; whereas if Mary had been born after the completion of the Washington painting, she would have been too young to enter her novitiate. Moreover, if the ages of the children are what they appear to be in the Windsor painting, then reading from left to right, the baby would be less than one, Susan five to six, George (who by 1638 had gone off to war) thirteen or fourteen, Elizabeth ten to eleven, the twins on the steps seven, the seated girl four to five, the kneeling boy eight, and the girl with the arrow nine. Assuming the Windsor picture to have been painted shortly after the Washington canvas (with the vase and its coat of arms added later, for which the X-ray offers evidence), there is no discrepancy in the ages of the children. Is it not logical to suppose that Madame Gerbier had her babies in rapid succession while she was still young? She was born in 1601 and was thirty when she returned to Brussels. If the five additional children shown in the Windsor painting were born in the Netherlands, one must suppose that a woman in her thirties had five children in about six years. Surely it is more probable that her last child was the baby in her lap, whose birth may have inspired Rubens to paint the picture, using as models for the other children in his ideal family group the three who had posed for *Peace and War*.

It is possible that if the Washington picture was owned by Gerbier, he concealed the identity of the sitters and gave them more exalted and more saleable titles. This would explain how the painting came to be known as the Duchess of Buckingham and her children, the family of Gerbier's first patron. But whether or not Gerbier owned the Washington painting he must have decided that he wanted it copied and woven into a portrait of himself and the rest of his family.

This replica with additions (the Windsor painting) was undoubtedly executed in Rubens's studio, probably shortly after the completion of the Washington picture. It appears to have been painted at two different periods by two different hands. During phase 1 artist A chose a rectangle of canvas to which were added strips at top and bottom. The whole was large enough to include a copy of the Washington picture with Gerbier on the left behind his wife and a small dog at his feet. Perhaps this was Gerbier's first idea. Then he may have decided he wished the rest of his children included. In any event during phase 2 more canvas was added on the right and artist B continued the work. Artist B was less able than artist A and also used a lighter palette. Where a vertical seam indicates the final addition, the picture is in a different color key and the drawing of the figures less adept. Finally some time after 1638 the vase with its coat of arms was added.

There is, however, one perplexing problem in the relationship of the Washington and Windsor paintings. In the Washington picture as we now see it the boy pushes the curtains apart with his right hand; but the X-ray shows that originally he drew aside the curtains with his left hand. This, the left hand, he also uses in the Windsor painting. Since in both pictures the boy once had the same posture, either the Washington canvas in its original form was copied from the Windsor picture, or the painting at Windsor was copied from the Washington version before it was altered. Which is more likely, and why in either case was the Washington picture changed?

On the basis of style there is convincing evidence that the Washington painting is by Rubens's own hand and that the Windsor painting could only be by someone working in his studio. About this there is general agreement among those who have specialized in the study of Rubens's work. The touch throughout the Washington picture has the vibrancy and sparkle of Rubens's brush, whereas in the Windsor canvas the handling by artist A is smooth and monotonous and by artist B flaccid and at times incompetent. Moreover, the central group at Windsor compared to the Washington painting is cramped and fills the space inharmoniously. This is largely because the curving contour of Madame Gerbier's back has been straightened and made more vertical to provide room for Gerbier. The same is true of the outline of the girl on the right, the eldest daughter. Her bodice and skirt in the Washington picture are fuller. In the Windsor painting these clothes have been contracted to make room for the inclusion of her sisters. As a result the figures do not combine, in Fry's words, "to make a sculptural unity," that closely interknit relation of forms which marks all the great achievements of Rubens's maturity. Instead those in the central group, compared to the Washington version, appear stiff and isolated.

But there is also a curious bit of internal evidence that the Windsor picture is a copy. In *Peace and War* and in the Washington *Gerbier Family* the little girl identified as Susan Gerbier has a coil of hair at the back of her head. In her portrait in the collection of the Earl Spencer, as Mr. Jaffé has pointed out to me, she wears the same coil of hair (fig. 6). But in the Windsor painting this coil is missing (fig. 2). If the Washington painting were copied from the Windsor canvas, why would the coil of hair have been added? A copyist scarcely ever improvises in this way. Surely it is more likely that copyist-artist A omitted the coil of hair, which is in shadow, to eliminate an unnecessary complication—a tendency toward simplification that often appears in copies.[10]

Assuming then that the painting at Windsor is demonstrably a copy, how does one explain the puzzling alteration in the boy's arm? To arrive at a tenable solution let me restate my previous hypothesis. Gerbier either did not own the Washington group portrait, or if he did, he intended to sell it; he wished in either case to retain a copy and he wanted this made in Rubens's studio; his orders were to include in the new version his own portrait and those of his other children; the Washington painting was then sent to Rubens's studio to be duplicated. While it was there Rubens looked again at his own painting, checking perhaps the original and the copy on behalf of his friend, and decided to improve the picture now in Washington by altering the arm of the boy. The child's original gesture, which we see in the Windsor painting, implies a *contrapposto,* since he is standing with his right side to the draperies. A much more natural action would be to push the curtains aside with his right arm, the arm nearest to them. The change in his posture is an obvious improvement, and the touch in the altered passage seems to be that of the master. As Rubens had no interest in the copy, he left the arm in the Windsor picture as the copyist had painted it.

The hypothesis that Rubens altered the Washington canvas to improve its effect is supported by another modification. The position of the tassel hanging from the heavy draperies has been changed, and what an extraordinary improvement results! In the Windsor painting it is silhouetted against the sky, and thus becomes a distracting element, for it draws attention away from Madame Gerbier, the focal point of the composition. In the Washington picture, on the other hand, it is properly subordinated and plays, as it should, a minor role in the over-all design.

Having proposed an explanation for the existence of the Windsor and Washington paintings, and for their relationship to each other, we are still not out of the woods. We are at once confronted with a further puzzle. Where were the pictures between the 1630s and the middle of the eighteenth century, when George Vertue records both? All we know is that Gerbier left the Spanish Netherlands for good in 1640. Before departing he wrote affectionately to Rubens, who was desperately ill, "I hope that with the approaching fine weather you will be better, and that we shall be able to embrace one another yet again for the last time, for I count on leaving this place whenever the good King shall command or permit."[11]

Gerbier departed under a cloud. His one-time secretary, Sidney Bere, wrote, "He intends his family shall creep away by degrees and the rest stay here to clear his debts, as he gets in his arrears, which will be slow enough."[12]

One may suppose that the Windsor canvas was left as collateral for some of these debts. The smaller and more valuable Washington picture, however, Gerbier may have managed to take with him to England, assuming that he owned it. We do not know who bought it from Gerbier (if, as I surmise, Rubens gave or sold it to him), but the most likely person is the first Earl of Radnor, an exceptionally wealthy man. We know that it was in the sale of the possessions of the second Earl of Radnor in 1724.

With this sale we are on firmer ground. From then on we can trace both the National Gallery of Art painting and the picture in Windsor Castle. Our guide is George Vertue. In 1749 he was asked to examine a sketch sent from Flanders of a painting offered to the Prince of Wales, purporting to be of Sir Balthasar Arundel and his family. Vertue soon established that no one of that name ever existed. Nevertheless the Prince engaged "General Guise a great Connoisseur & Mr. Goupy" to go to Flanders and look at the picture. By the time they arrived it had been rechristened "Sir Balthazar Buckingham or Sheffield." In spite of Vertue's warning "the great Connoisseur & Mr. Goupy" bought it for the Prince, who hastened "from Clifden to see it, and was there as soon as the picture in the Cart came to the Gate." Vertue was called in again. He examined the purchase and found an inscription half erased: "La Famille de Balthasar Gerbier Chevaliere." He also identified the Gerbier coat of arms. The Prince was shocked and said to Vertue, "How shall I come off of this? I have for this month past told many persons of quality that I have purchased a family piece of the Sheffield ancestor to the late Duke of Buckingham . . . as I was assured it [was] . . . be said the truth that dealers in pictures are like false moneyers." The picture the "false moneyers" sold the Prince is now in the Rubens room at Windsor Castle correctly labeled "The Family of Sir Balthasar Gerbier."

The National Gallery of Art picture, on the other hand, according to Vertue, "was sold at Lord Radnor's in St. James Square, there I saw Lord Burlington bid five hundred pounds for it [this is corroborated by the catalogue of the sale], and Mr. Scowen bought it. . . . many years afterwards Mr. Scowen being obliged to sell it . . . it was bo^t by a Gent of the Law, who lately sold it to Mr. Gideon the Jew." One of his descendants married into the Fremantle family and the National Gallery of Art painting has been owned by them until now.

While owned by Thomas Scowen, Vertue states it was copied. In his words, "Barwick the painter who took an Exact coppy of the picture or family peece of Rubens or Vandyke at Mr. Scowens observes that the cloth of that picture which was Ld Radnor's before—is pierced down one side to make it larger—and also at the bottom. . . . A relation of Mr. Scowen has this picture and would dispose of it for no less than 400 £." Barwick's copy has disappeared, but that the National Gallery picture is the original he copied is proved by the seams in the canvas, which are exactly in the location shown in Vertue's diagram.[13]

On the various occasions when it was exhibited in the nineteenth century the identity of the family was usually confused. In 1860 it was once more put up for sale, as "The Mistress of the Duke of Buckingham and Her Children," bringing the highest price ever paid for a Rubens at auction up to that time. The London *Times* of July 2, 1860, reported: "It was put up at 1,000 guineas and advanced 500 guineas at each bidding, till it reached the enormous amount of 7,500 guineas, at which sum it was knocked down to Mr. Ward. Great applause followed the adjudication." Nevertheless the owners were dissatisfied and the picture was bought in. They were wise, for though the National Gallery of Art has not disclosed the price paid, one can be sure it was many times the final bid made in 1860 by Mr. Ward, when he received great applause following "the adjudication."

NOTES

[1]   In connection with its sale Mr. Clovis Whitfield, the librarian of Thomas Agnew and Sons, has done some astute and interesting research into the history of the painting, which he found mentioned in several unpublished letters in the British Museum written by George Vertue. He has most generously permitted me to use his notes for this article. Mrs. Carolyn Wells, my research assistant, by her invaluable advice and criticism, has kept me from serious mistakes, especially in the confused chronology of the children's births. I am also indebted to Mr. Michael Jaffé, the leading authority on Rubens and one of the first to recognize the importance of the Washington version of the *Gerbier Family*, for his kindness in checking my first draft; I have made additions he has not seen.

2   Roger Avermaete, *Rubens and His Times,* London, 1968, p. 122.

3   Hugh Ross Williamson, *Four Stuart Portraits,* London, 1949, p. 35.

4   Jacob Burckhardt, *Rubens,* Vienna, 1939, p. 172.

5   I am indebted to Sir Oliver Millar for the suggestion that there appears to be a difference in age between the Gerbier children in *Peace and War* and the same children in the Washington and Windsor group portraits.

6   For a very similar costume to that of Madame Gerbier, especially the cap, which is almost identical, see the painting reproduced by L. Puyvelde (*Rubens,* Brussels, 1952, p. 70) as a portrait of Helena Fourment.

7   Williamson, *op. cit.,* p. 36.

8   W. Noel Sainsbury, ed., *Original Unpublished Papers Illustrative of the Life of Sir Peter Paul Rubens,* London, 1859, p. 136.

9   See Williamson, *op. cit.,* p. 36.

10   It is just possible, though unlikely, that artist A used for this one figure Rubens's original drawing of the child, now in Weimar, where her hair is straight. Since the Washington picture was cleaned the coil of hair has become more conspicuous.

11   Gerbier to Rubens, April 3, 1640, in Sainsbury, *op. cit.,* p. 218.

12   Williamson, *op. cit.,* p. 43.

13   There is a canvas in the Brussels Museum called "Flemish School XVII Century" (fig. 7) which repeats the composition of the *Gerbier Family*. It must have been commissioned by the lute player as a group portrait of himself, his wife, and their children giving some kind of concert. One may suppose that it was painted in Rubens's studio when the Windsor picture was being copied from the Washington canvas, since both seem to have had an influence: the boy draws the curtain with his right hand as in the Washington version, whereas the father is placed on the extreme left as in the Windsor painting. The unknown artist of the Brussels picture was of so little ability that it is remarkable the painting was ever attributed to Rubens. Sir Oliver Millar has called my attention to two other copies based on the Washington painting, one at Sheffield and the other sold at Christie's on April 11, 1968, and again May 21 and November 4, 1971.

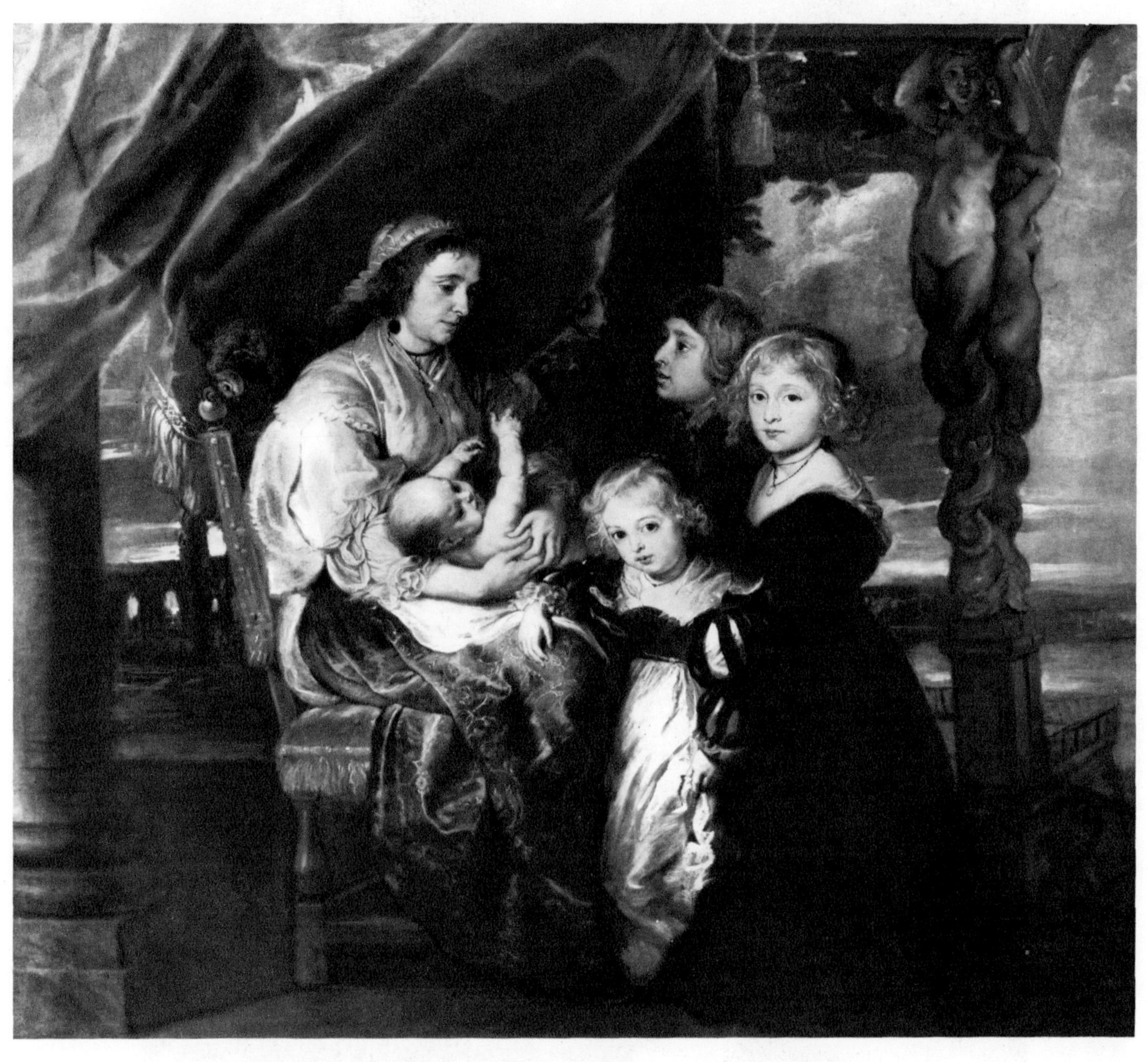

1. PETER PAUL RUBENS. *Deborah Kip, Wife of Sir Balthasar Gerbier, and Her Children.*
Oil on canvas, $65\frac{1}{4} \times 70''$ (165.8 × 177.8 cm.).
National Gallery of Art, Washington, D.C. Andrew W. Mellon Fund, 1971

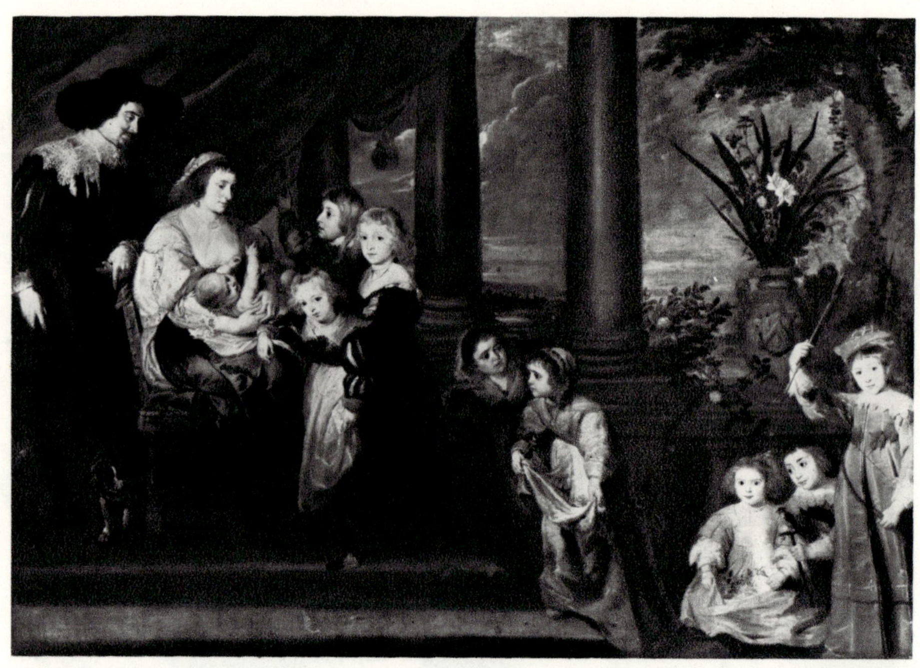

2. RUBENS. *The Family of Sir Balthasar Gerbier* (studio copy?). c. 1635–40.
Oil on canvas, 7′ 1½″ × 10′ 1⅞″.
Windsor Castle. Collection Her Majesty Queen Elizabeth II
(Copyright Reserved)

3. RUBENS. *The Allegory of Peace and War*. 1629–30.
Oil on canvas, 6′ 8¼″ × 9′9¼″.
The National Gallery, London

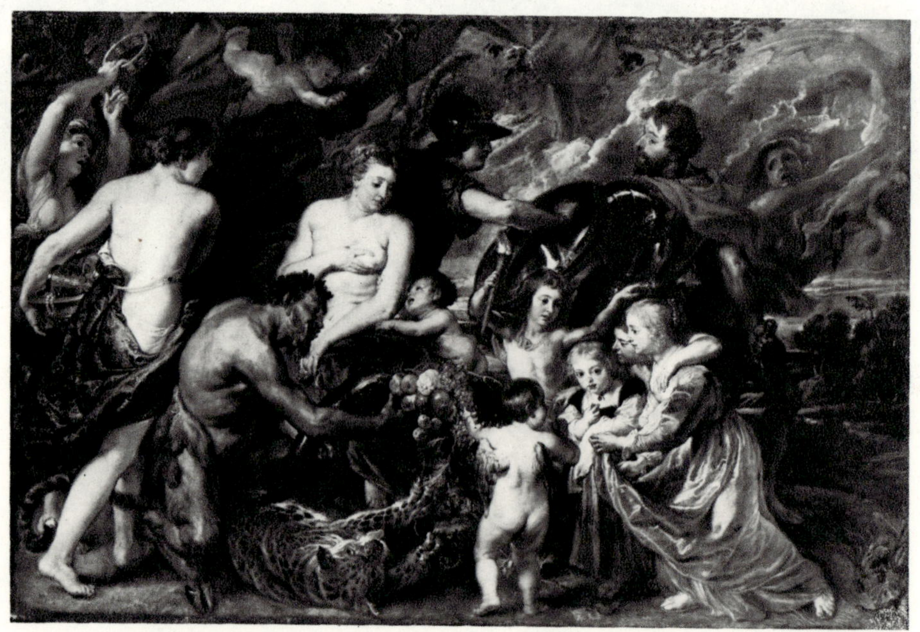

4. RUBENS. *The Allegory of Peace and War*. Detail of children ▶

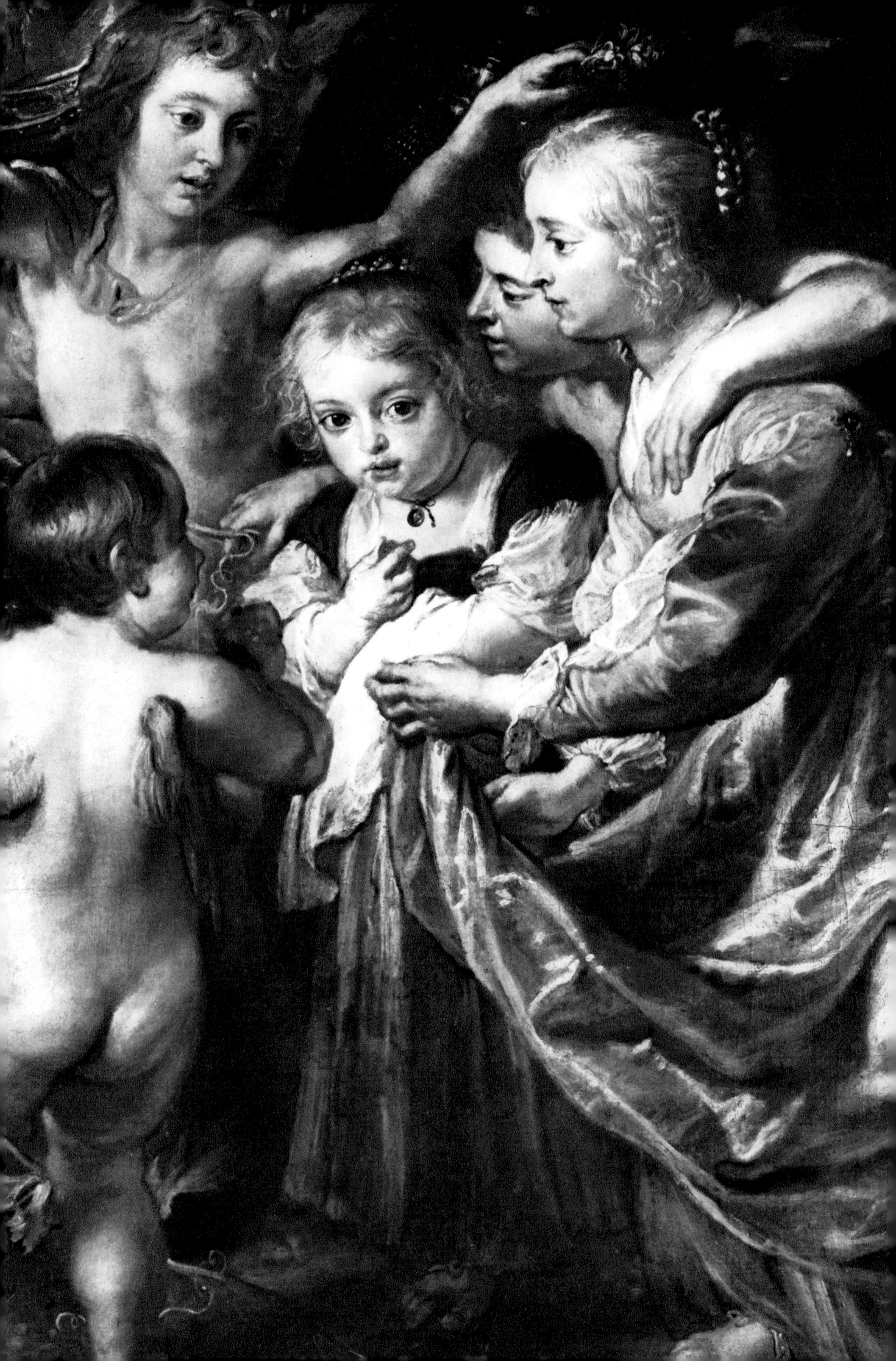

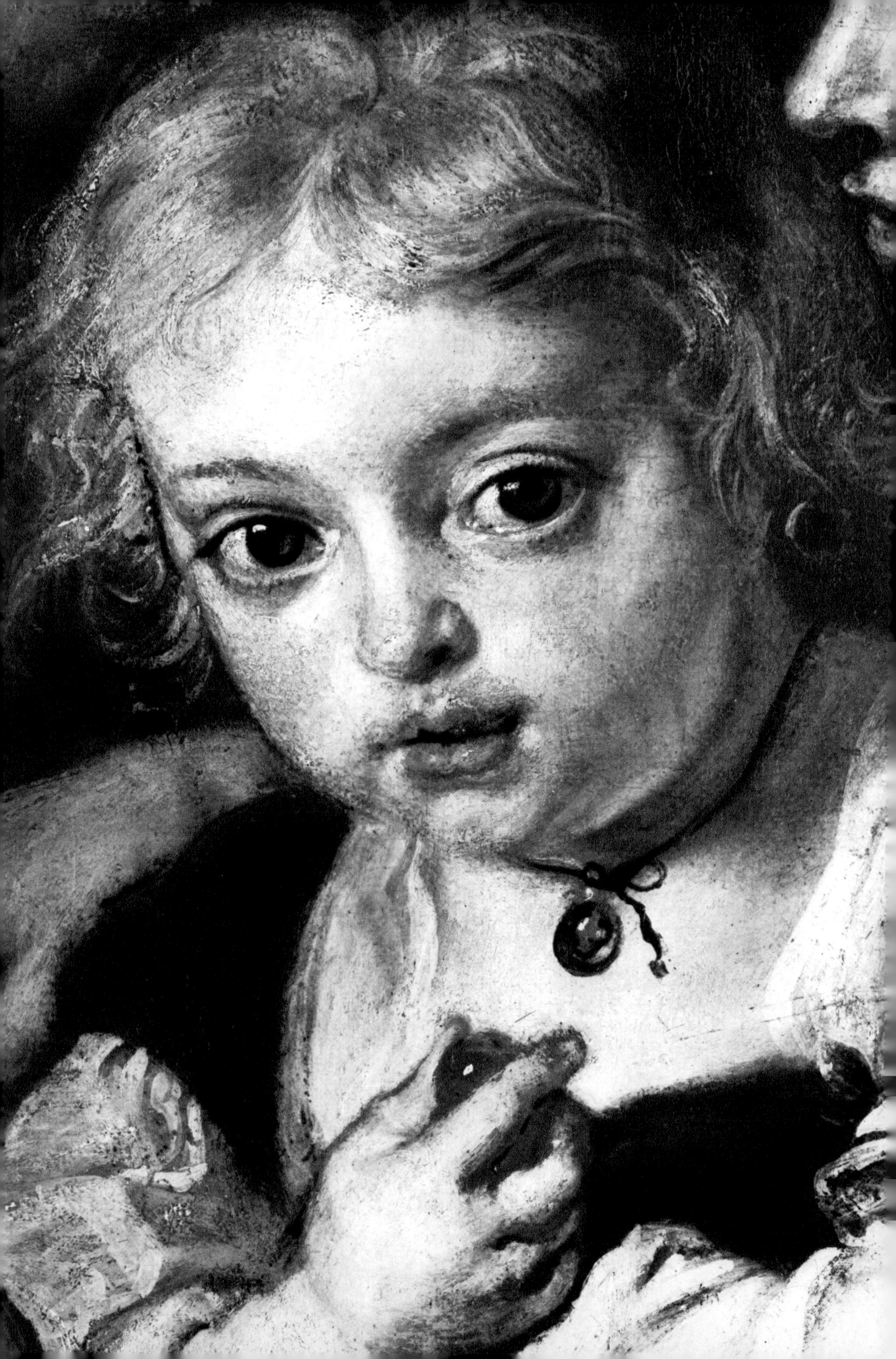

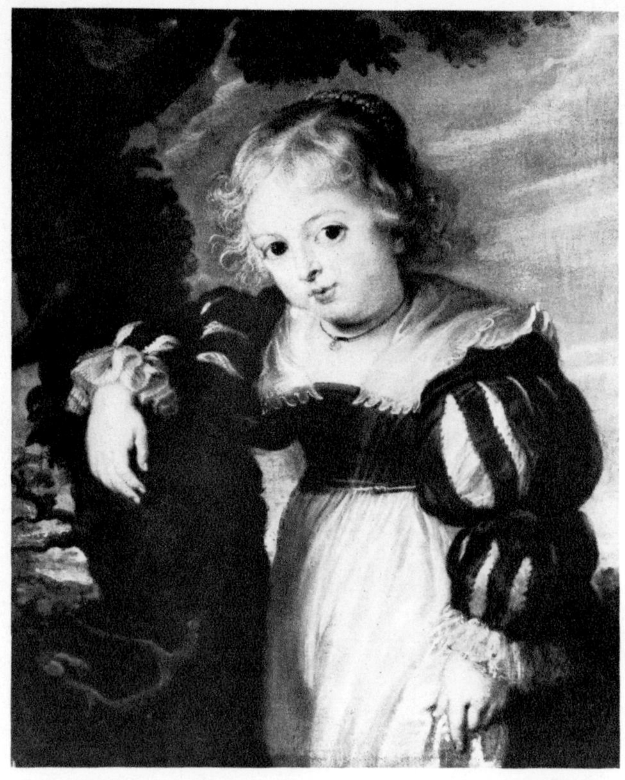

6.   RUBENS. *Susan Gerbier*. Oil on canvas, 26 × 21 ″.
Collection the Earl Spencer, Althorp, Northampton, England

◀5.   RUBENS. *The Allegory of Peace and War*. Detail of Susan's face

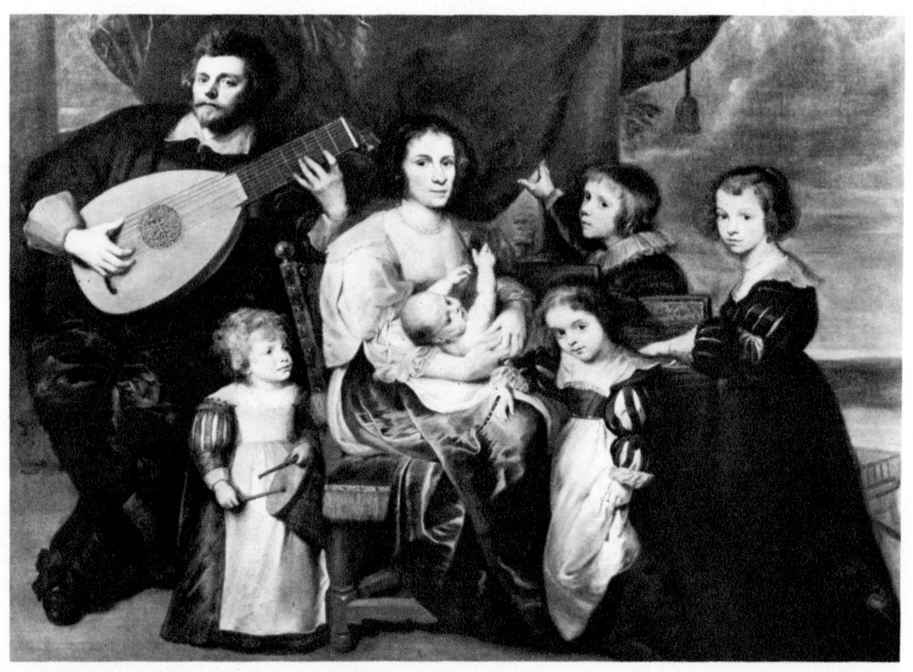

7.   Flemish School, 17th century. *Family Portrait*.
Musées Royaux des Beaux-Arts, Brussels

22

JACK WASSERMAN

The Monster Leonardo Painted
for His Father

Leonardo was charmed by the by-products and curiosities of thought and feeling, by the mysterious and the unknown. He befriended alchemists and consulted fortune tellers, and he invented strange allegories, and exotic tales of make-believe experiences he presumably had had in the East. This eccentric turn of mind was many times applied to devising fanciful toys and other divertissements. He invented an animal that flew when blown up and fell to the ground when the wind abated and he fabricated that famous mechanical lion whose chest suddenly opened after he had walked a few steps to reveal a bouquet of lilies, to the surprise and pleasure of the French monarch.[1] These were playful and charming novelties; but he was capable also of pranks upon the gullible that were sometimes mocking and even cruel. Vasari cites several of them. He writes that Leonardo while in Rome (after 1513) "would often dry and purge the entrails of a mutton and make them so small that they could be held in the palm of one hand. In another room he would set up a pair of bellows and fasten the entrails to them, and then he would blow them up so that they filled the room, which was a large one, and whoever was in the room would have to back into a corner."[2] Another of his bizarre pranks was to fasten onto an especially weird lizard the scales he had plucked from other lizards, as well as eyes, a horn, beard, and wings covered with bright silver that would quiver as the lizard walked. This animal, Vasari concludes, terrified all the friends to whom he showed it.[3] Some of these "follies" *(pazzie)*, as Vasari termed them,[4] for all their jocular character, may in fact have been at least partially conceived by Leonardo in the spirit of scientific and mechanical experiments. Others he raised to the level of art and imbued with the virtue of a creative act: "The painter," he wrote, "is the master of all things that can occur in man's mind . . . ; if he wishes monstrous things that frighten, or that are comic and induce laughter, or that are truly piteous or doleful, he is lord and creator of them all."[5] Leonardo demonstrated this principle in the famous monster he painted for his father in the 1470s.

The painting of the monster disappeared long ago and can be recovered only in a passage by Vasari: "It is said that when ser Piero [Leonardo's father] was at his country seat he was requested by a peasant of his estate to get a round piece of wood painted for him at Florence. Accordingly, Piero asked Leonardo to paint something upon it. Leonardo . . . began to cast about for what he should paint that would terrify all who beheld it, having the same effect that the Medusa had. To a room, to which he alone had access, Leonardo took lizards, newts, snakes, butterflies, locusts, bats and other strange species of similar animals, and out of this multitude, which he variously arranged together, he conceived a monster very horrible and frightening, of poisonous breath, issuing from a dark and broken rock, belching poison from its open throat, fire from its eyes, and smoke from its nostrils."[6]

However detailed Vasari's description may be, it is still vague enough to make us wonder about what Leonardo's monster looked like. The starting point for such a discussion must be the fact that the monster was a collage of insects and animals and therefore basically different from the dragons he drew on a number of occasions, either singly or in combat with a horseman (fig. 1). These dragons were modeled on specimens that are commonly seen in fifteenth-century drawings and paintings, especially in representations of St. George and the Dragon; to paint another of this species, Leonardo would not have had to bring together such an extravagant collection of insects and animals.

There are at least two other possibilities. One is that Leonardo had kept the insects and animals whole and intact when he constructed his monster, arranging them into some sort of fierce, dragon-like configuration. This procedure would be comparable to the manner in which the Milanese painter Giuseppe Arcimboldo (c. 1527–1593) some fifty years later painted his proto-surrealistic human heads (fig. 2). It is pertinent to this hypothesis that Arcimboldo's father, also a painter, may have been on friendly terms with members of the later circle of Leonardo's followers in Milan (e.g., Bernardino Luini)[7] and that Leonardo's most intimate disciple, Francesco Melzi, was, at the time Arcimboldo painted his heads, systematically putting together Leonardo's notes and drawings in his villa at Vaprio near Milan. The impact of Leonardo's art may have made itself felt on Arcimboldo by these links. In fact, Leonardo's famous drawings of men and women with grotesquely exaggerated facial features have often been cited in partial explanation of Arcimboldo's fantasies, but more as a freeing of the imagination, an opening up of taste for the bizarre in art, than as a direct, formal influence.[8] Finally, it may also be relevant to our discussion that Leonardo's monster was purchased by Lodovico Sforza in Milan[9] sometime before 1500 and may still have been visible to Arcimboldo in the 1550s.

It would, perhaps, be more reasonable to assume that the monster had been compounded of the parts of diverse animals and insects, not of whole ones, in a form similar to those strange demons that were conceived by Leonardo's exact contemporary, the Dutch artist Hieronymus Bosch (fig. 3). There is precedent in Leonardo's own activities for this approach. The reader may recall the real lizard he had adorned with wings, eyes, horn, beard, and scales of other lizards.

Grafted images have figured in art since antiquity and are found in abundance as devils in medieval and Renaissance representations of the *Last Judgment*. Figure 4, in fact, which reproduces a monster from Bosch's *Last Judgment,* has a curious likeness to Vasari's description, mainly in its dramatic aspects, in which he speaks of Leonardo's monster as "issuing from a dark and broken rock, belching poison from its open throat, fire from its eyes, and smoke from its nostrils." This might suggest that the two artists were both dependent for their monsters on the visual tradition of the *Last Judgment,* although cross-fertilization between them should not be ruled out. Nevertheless, I believe that a source was available to Leonardo that possibly had a stronger impact on his imagination, namely, the travel accounts of geographic explorers. A good example of what I have in mind is a description by the sixteenth-century explorer, Antonio Pigafetta, of a guanaco he had seen in South America. "This beast has its head and ears of the size of a mule, the neck and head of the fashion of a camel, the legs of a deer and the tail like that of a horse."[10] Pigafetta made a real animal that was unknown to his readers recognizable by referring to parts of animals that were familiar to them. This analogical method of describing animals, including imaginary monsters, and its use in other realms of thought, had been an established and popular literary device already in the Middle Ages and was still a deeply ingrained habit of mind in Leonardo's time, as Pigafetta's text indicates. It governs, for example, Leonardo's conception of the universe: "We might say that nature has a vegetative soul and that its flesh is the earth and its bones the stratifications of the rocks of which the mountains are formed, its cartilage the tufas, its blood the springs of water. The lake around the heart is the ocean, and its breathing and the increase and decrease of the blood in the pulse are like the flow and ebb of the sea. The head of the soul is the fire infused in the earth."[11] It governs also his own instructions on how to paint imaginary animals: "You know that you cannot invent animals without limbs, each of which, in itself, must resemble those of some other animal. Hence if you wish to make an animal, imagined by you, appear natural—let us say a dragon, take for its head that of a mastiff or hound, with the eyes of a cat, the ears of a porcupine, the nose of a greyhound, the brow of a lion, the temples of an old cock, the neck of a water-tortoise."[12] It is only natural, therefore, that Leonardo should have devised his monster as a composite of different creatures, although the character and species of those he used for his painted monster, unlike those in his description, were unpleasantly evocative ones.

Leonardo seems to have succeeded in his effort to terrify his father with his painted monster, as the continuation of Vasari's account reveals: "Accordingly ser Piero went to his [Leonardo's] room one morning for the round panel [on which the monster was painted] and knocked on the door. Leonardo opened it asking him to wait a moment, and returning to the room set the panel in the light on the easel and arranged the window in such a way as to make the light dim and then let his father enter to see the painting. Ser Piero, at first not paying too much attention, suddenly became agitated, not believing that the figure he saw was a painted one, and turned to flee. Leonardo detained him, however, saying: This work has served the purpose for which it was made; take it then, carry it away. This thing appeared utterly miraculous to ser Piero, and he praised enthusiastically Leonardo's whimsical intent."[13] This self-indulgent and prankish turn of Leonardo's mind rivals and is incongruous with the aspects of his character that we would more readily accept as fundamental: his charm, largesse of spirit, generosity, and especially his kindness, which is exemplified by his tender treatment of animals and his love for birds, as witness the story of how he bought birds and then freed them from their imprisoning cages.[14] One suspects, therefore, that the dissonance of temperament that led Leonardo to perpetrate his sometimes repellent practical jokes may have been an acquired one, taken from the old Italian tradition of the *beffa,* a phenomenon of culture admired by Boccaccio and Ariosto, for example, that fostered the cruel joke invoked at the expense of another's weaknesses and credulity.

The question of the readiness of Leonardo's father to be taken in by Leonardo's painting deserves some comment. I contribute no fresh information when I point out that monsters and other imaginary creatures were prominent in Western literature from antiquity to the Renaissance and beyond. Common among them were hybrid centaurs, sirens, and one-eyed giants. There were also the three-headed dog Cerberus and that archetypal monster, the Medusa. The centaur, for example, became a part even of Christian iconography and is found in scenes of the life of St. Anthony. More important, monsters were believed actually to exist, even by men of sophistication and thought, although usually in some remote part of the world. It is common knowledge that fifteenth- and sixteenth-century explorers, in their travels, were in constant expectation that the monsters they had read about in medieval and contemporary travel books (e.g., the fourteenth-century *Travels* by Mandeville) would appear before them momentarily, as alive and real as any animal of the familiar world, and they fostered the belief in their existence by sending back to Europe precise and vivid reports of unicorns, men with heads growing out of their shoulders, two-headed men, dog-headed men, man-headed animals, and men with one leg.[15] Sir Walter Raleigh, who spoke of headless men, is a prominent example. These hypothetical monsters were even introduced into maps of new-found lands, as we can see in an atlas of 1513 by Peri Reis, a Turkish cartographer. The atlas is purported to be a copy of a lost map that Columbus had made in 1498 and contains several such abridged and grafted monsters.

Now, if explorers came so close to monsters as to describe and illustrate them in such careful detail and with such conviction, could not these and other monsters have found their way back to Europe on some explorer's ship, perhaps, or so it might have been thought? It has not been long, after all, since reasonable men and women were reporting sightings of flying saucers driven by strange mutants. And how many of us do not half expect that our astronauts will one day meet these inhabitants of remote planets? I do not, of course, say that Leonardo believed in monsters. Certainly he did not, but stories about them must have stimulated his very receptive and sensitive imagination when he set about to paint the panel for his father and when he devised his other practical joke, that with the live lizard. On the other hand, it seems quite likely that his father was disposed to believe in them, under the influence of the geographical explorations that had brought to

the level of consciousness in Renaissance man the existence of frightening monsters
and a heightened sense of fear of them, just as the explorations had elevated the
expectation of a catastrophic deluge. Leonardo obviously was counting on this to
achieve his desired effect (Chastel has called it "shock aesthetics"), as he had with
his Medusa, whose head he had crowned with a garland of snakes.[16] So all he had
to do was create a suggestive atmosphere by manipulating the light and then let
the painted monster do the rest to provoke ser Piero into his startled reaction.

Notes

[1]   Vasari-Milanesi, IV, pp. 46 and 37.

[2]   *Ibid.*, p. 46.

[3]   *Ibid.*

[4]   *Ibid.*, p. 47.

[5]   See J. P. Richter, *The Literary Works of Leonardo da Vinci,* 3rd ed., London, 1970,
I, p. 54, no. 19, for the Italian text.

[6]   Vasari-Milanesi, IV, pp. 23f.

[7]   B. Geiger, *I dipinti ghiribizzosi di Giuseppe Arcimboldi,* Florence, 1954, p. 18.

[8]   F. C. Le Grand and F. Sluys, *Arcimboldo et les Arcimboldesques,* Paris, 1955, p. 29.

[9]   Vasari-Milanesi, IV, p. 25.

[10]   *The Age of the Renaissance,* ed. Denys Hay, New York, 1968, pp. 338 f.

[11]   See Richter, *op. cit.*, p. 178, no. 1000, for the Italian text.

[12]   *Ibid.*, p. 342, no. 585.

[13]   Vasari-Milanesi, IV, pp. 23 f.

[14]   *Ibid.*, p. 44.

[15]   *The Age of the Renaissance,* pp. 338 and 330 for illustrations. See the study by R.
Wittkower, "Marvels of the East—a Study in the History of Monsters," *Journal of the
Warburg and Courtauld Institutes,* 5, 1942, 59–197.

[16]   Vasari-Milanesi, IV, p. 25.

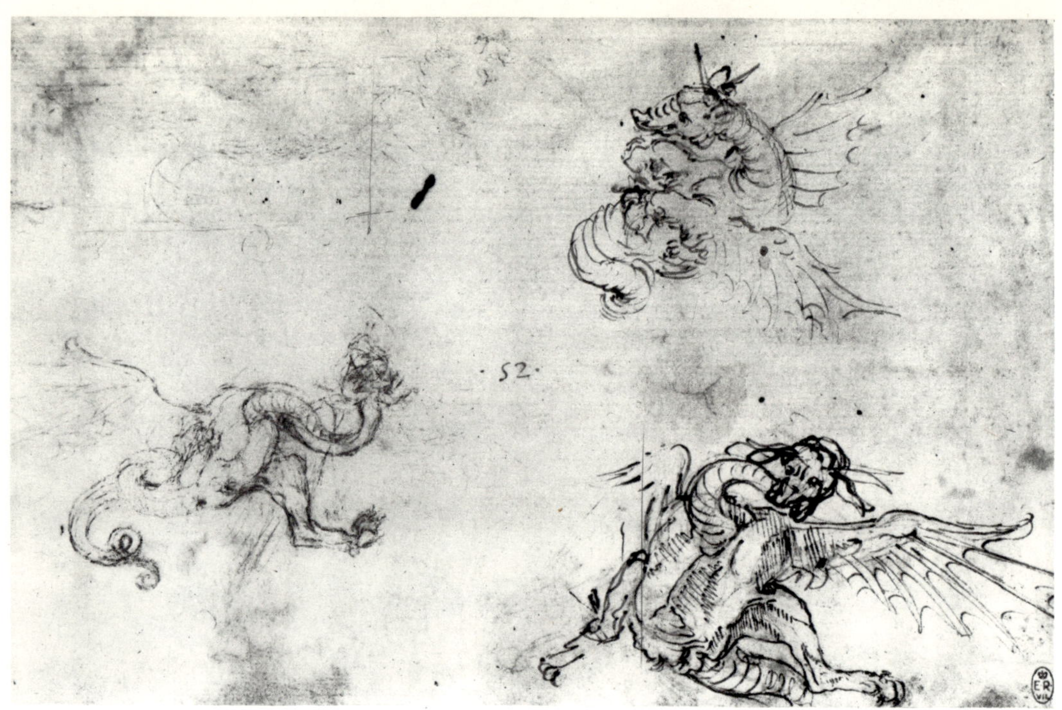

1. LEONARDO. Drawings of dragons. Library, Windsor Castle
(with gracious permission of Her Majesty Queen Elizabeth II)

2. GIUSEPPE ARCIMBOLDO. *Water* (from the series *Four Elements*).
Kunsthistorisches Museum, Vienna

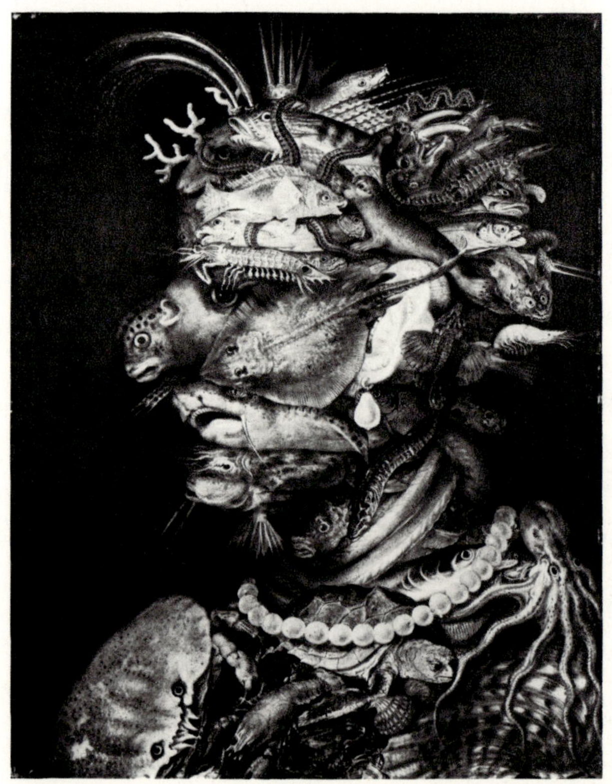

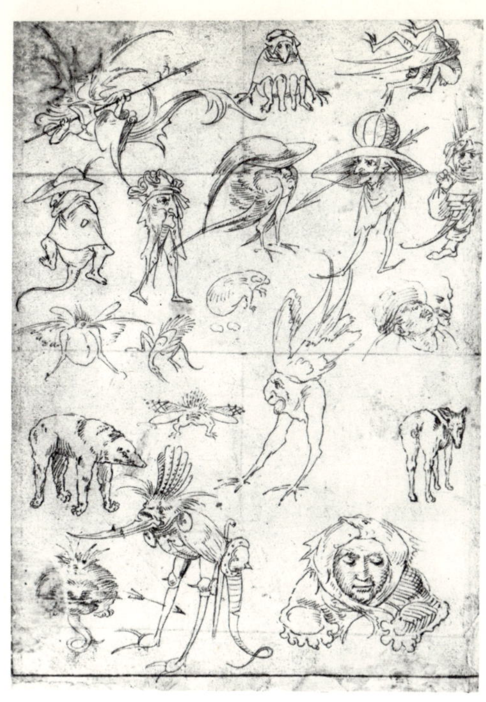

3. HIERONYMUS BOSCH.
Drawings of monsters.
Ashmolean Museum, Oxford

4. HIERONYMUS BOSCH.
Last Judgment. Detail.
Gemäldegalerie der Akademie
der bildenden Künste, Vienna

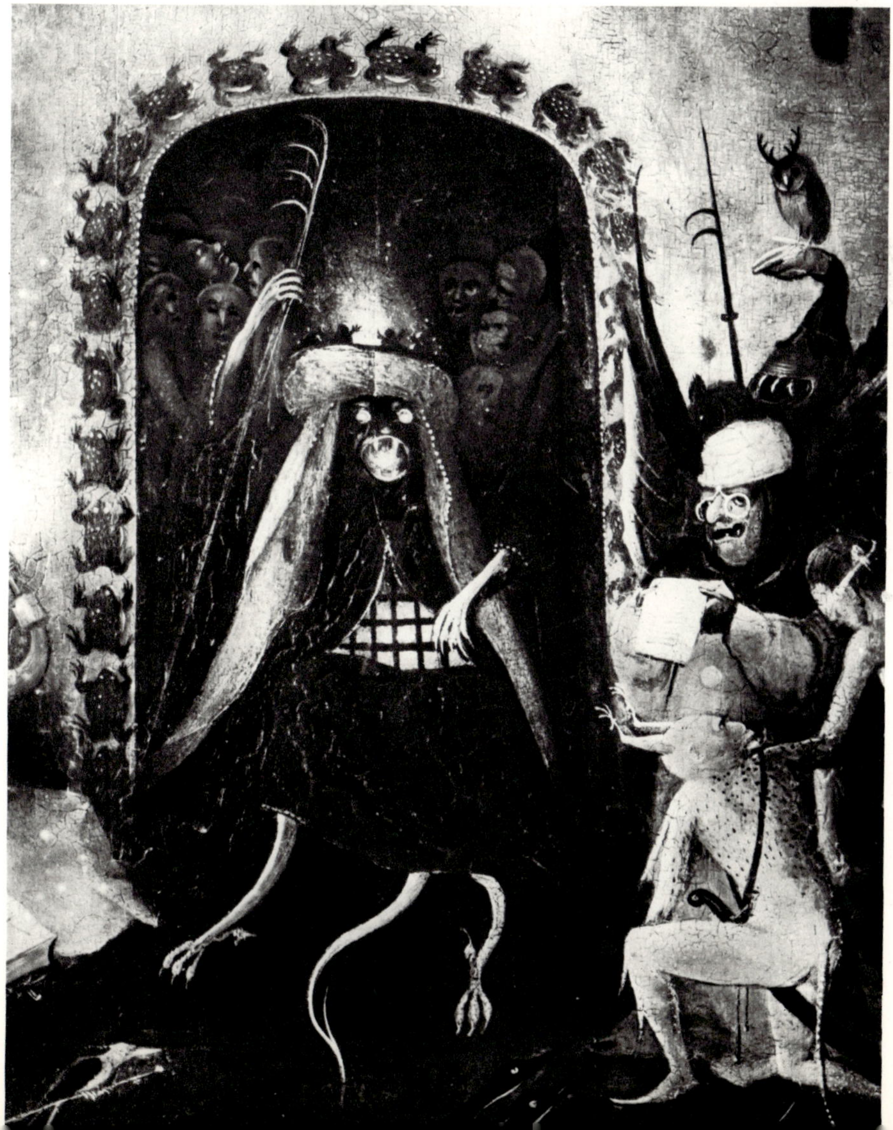

23

JUNE WAYNE

The Male Artist as Stereotypical Female

We artists complain about the same old problems year after year no matter how obscure or famous we may be. We ask each other how to get a show, or a better gallery, or how to move our dealers to promote our works more vigorously. We gossip a lot about the museums too: how a certain trustee collects the art of so-and-so which explains his retrospective at the Modern: or a certain balding young curator is mounting a whole exhibition to prove his pet esthetic gimmick. Every year yet another lawyer/dealer combination is reported to be raiding yet another artist's estate. And obviously every issue of every art magazine proves anew how stupid critics can be.

Sooner or later one of us casually drops the word that Joseph Hirshhorn just blew into town and "bought out the studio" but no mention is made of the prices he paid—nor do we ask. We know the idiosyncrasies of all the collectors and we'd just as soon not be reminded what "making it" can mean. Artists lick their wounds for nourishment, not for healing.

Over the years I have pondered why guilds and royalties, which work fairly well for actors, writers, composers—even for scientists and inventors—were never developed for visual artists too. Perhaps because we are unworldly about the practical matters of sales and careers. Neither art schools nor university art departments provide courses in the business and professional problems of being an artist. A master's degree may qualify the student to replace the teacher but not to bargain with a dealer. Anyhow, who could teach such courses? Art professors cannot hack it in the art market either, so new artists fare no better than preceding generations.

A union or a guild needs an industry *against which* to organize but the art scene has no single nexus of power to bargain with. As for public agencies, they dissolve into lay committees which have neither the concern nor the authority to address the grievances of artists. The art world lives in an ebb and flow of guerrilla warfare. Such citadels of power as there are—museums, foundations, arts councils, the national endowments—are held by *them,* not us, and only rarely can one find that an artist is a member of one of *their* committees. So we learn very early to see ourselves as esthetically unique and morally superior—which is a palatable way of saying isolated and powerless.

But neither the hostile ecology of the art milieu nor the inadequacies of art-department curricula fully explains why artists, who have as much common sense as other people, fail to use even the most elementary protections when it comes to their art. For instance, why do so many artists consign their work to obviously inept or venal or fly-by-night dealers without asking so much as a receipt, let alone a contract or a credit reference? I could list many examples of idiot behavior by otherwise intelligent artists. Why does our cynicism, which is based on painful experience, only express itself in hostile passivity instead of prideful self-protection?

In recent years, the many freedom movements have sharpened my awareness of similarities between the behavior patterns of artists and other minority groupings. There is a direct relationship between the power of any oppressor and the self-esteem and self-evaluation of those who are held in check. In this context feminist literature set me thinking about the relation between women artists and sexual stereotyping. The practical utility of treating the male artist as though he were a woman struck me forcefully, for it would explain much that puzzled me about the interface of artists with the rest of the art world's professionals.

It appears to me that society unconsciously perceives the artist as a female and that artists act out the feminized stereotypical patterns projected onto them. Inasmuch as these patterns are self-destructive and profoundly inhibiting to independent action, the ease with which artists are maintained in a state of disenfranchisement endures for generation after generation. It becomes profitable to many people to view the artist as one unable to cope with the real world of money and trade, although a pedestal is where the artist, like the woman, waits while others are alleged to cope in his behalf.

Although there have always been artists of both sexes, only males have survived into art history. Yet even for male artists one is more apt to believe that Leonardo and Michelangelo were homosexual than that Peter Paul Rubens was a diplomat. For the ancient but still powerful demonic myth prepares us to accept the warped and bizarre personality as an indicator of talent, even as proof of genius. Some of the characteristics given to artists by the demonic myth are, surprisingly, almost identical with characteristics described by Betty Friedan in *The Feminine Mystique.* So profound is the stereotype of the artist as the inchoate, intuitive, emotional romantic that both the public and the artists themselves find it difficult to imagine that we can be anything else.

The demonic myth presents the artist as one possessed of mysterious forces that well up during creative seizures, as it were. The work of art is alleged to be produced without the exercise of the artist's will and may even seem to be unmodified by knowledge itself. The artist "can't help it" or "doesn't know how it happened" or whence came the inspiration. Should the artist try to analyze, control, even to think peripherally about the creative moment, it may be vitiated or even destroyed. The artist is thought to be a sort of medium through whom creative miracles are manifest and unless one is *born* an artist, neither effort nor intelligence (not even surgery) makes one into an artist. So the demonic myth presents the artist as biologically determined—born with Promethean fires, as it were.

The feminine mystique also is based on biological determination. The woman is alleged to be born to procreate and to spend her life in servicing her procreation. No effort of will or intellect is needed in order to reproduce her kind. She is a sort of medium through whom the procreative miracle is manifest. If one isn't born a woman, no effort of will or intelligence (not even surgery) can transform one into a woman. The biology of the woman, like that of the artist, is proposed as her destiny.

Obviously the artist makes art and the woman makes babies, but the word *create* is commonly used to describe both processes. That the will and the brain are said to be unnecessary and even antithetical to the function of women and of artists encourages the elision of the male artist into being perceived as a female by the public. Semantic confusion causes operational distortion in many kinds of human experience: this is why the do-it-yourself hobbyist tells you he loves being "creative" and shows you a bookshelf to prove it. Creativity, procreation, and "making something" are used interchangeably in our society as though synonymous.

Lurking just below the surface of public consciousness is a pervasive assumption that any man whose feelings, intuitions, and purposes are inchoate in source and unusual in product must be a homosexual. Even the most macho of male artists faces this problem and the recent tributes to José Limón particularly emphasized as remarkable that he brought a masculine aspect to the art of the dance. Do *real* men "go for" ballet, poetry, pictures, or do they go for sports? Isn't the culture sector the province of the ladies' committees? Aren't the arts seen as girlish frills in the educational system? What papa is pleased that his son wants to be an artist? Why are art reviews published on the women's page (between the cranberry sauce and the Simplicity patterns) in nearly every newspaper in this country?

Many authorities have insisted that womanhood is incompatible with profundity of thought, intellectual discipline, or worldly accomplishment, but none puts this position more succinctly than does Helene Deutsch, Freud's eminent but submissive disciple. In *The Psychology of Women* she writes that "Woman's intellectuality is to a large extent paid for by the loss of valuable feminine qualities. Her intellectuality feeds on the affective life and results in its impoverishment." Change only two words and Deutsch's formulation will sound as though it had been written about artists. "The *artist's* intellectuality is to a large extent paid for by the loss of valuable *creative* qualities. The *artist's* intellectuality feeds on the *creative* life and results in its impoverishment." A perfect fit.

That critics, art historians, and even artists accept the cliché that the brain is a threat to creativity would explain why, if an exhibition is reviewed as "cerebral" or "intellectual," the words are understood as pejorative, not complimentary. There is a special limbo for Robert Motherwell who often is called the most intellectual of contemporary artists. Who envies Motherwell that niche? Not that he surely is the *most* intellectual of the artists: there are others who may be more so. But Motherwell lets himself be seen as such whereas most artists hide their minds under a bushel. Richard Diebenkorn, during a conversation with me, once called it "maintaining a low profile." Reaction to a brainy artist is like reaction to a female intellectual: neither is quite to be believed.

After I had noted the interchangeability of "artist" and "woman" I played with feminist literature, substituting artist for woman, and found myriad examples where the substitution worked perfectly (I won't take time or space to illustrate this here since you can verify it easily for yourself). Next I rearranged the actors of the art milieu according to sexual roles: artists as women, regardless of actual gender; dealers, collectors, curators, patrons, critics, public functionaries, et al., as men, regardless of actual gender. Now the passivity of artists and the aggressiveness of these other categories became logical and predictable.

How natural that artists are stereotyped as inept, unworldly, insecure, gossipy, cliquish, capricious, flirtatious, indirect, devious, manipulative, over-imaginative, emotional, intuitive, unpredictable, colorful, overly aware of costume and image. Why expect artists to understand money, contracts, business? Why indeed. One must *help* artists, *support* them; they cannot cope. Accordingly we artists look for help not equality, for support not self-determination. We expect "them" to take care of us, get us into the fashionable collections, and make us famous. And we anxiously await results of their efforts while grousing in the studio or rapping at Barney's Beanery or sunning on the beaches at the Hamptons in the summertime. We might as well be Lana Turners awaiting stardom at a Hollywood soda counter.

Nor are our fantasies so inappropriate: what dealer does not claim to know more about nearly everything (including art) than does the artist? What curator is unsure of superior judgment of what the artist is *really* doing? What critic or reporter feels obliged to ask an *artist* what the work is all about? What collector sees the artist as anything but a freak, however lovable?

But if all this is true, why are *women* artists discriminated against? If male artists are acceptable as quasi females in female postures, why not women artists too? Because the male artist is camouflaged by the demonic myth, not by the feminine mystique. He rides motorcycles, not subways; pops drugs, not iron supplements. Groupie girls with pale sheafs of stringy hair trail after him, not his kiddies. A hundred romantic props comprise his demonic image and most are macho to the hilt. But the woman artist is only underscored as a woman by the feminine mystique. She is an instant Mrs. So-and-so living in a tract house with hubby and the babies. She is thought to dabble in oils in the family den which only she refers to seriously as her studio. And her art is assumed to be a matter of tight little landscapes and flower arrangements or decorative, derivative abstractions displayed over the couch in an all too dreary and domestic living room. To be a wife, a mother, and forty is to suffer from a fatal syndrome; no matter what the truth or how large her talent or accomplishment, she is only a woman trying to "pass" as an artist.

A few of us have achieved some recognition but we clearly carry demonic markings that hide our female stigmata. We live in lofts and storefronts and other wildly unconventional spaces just like the male artists do. We dress in unisex or as fantastic eccentrics. Nevelson and O'Keeffe do not shop at Peck and Peck. As successful (women) artists we *must* prefer lovers to husbands and be on guard every moment against conventionalized female gestures. If one is lesbian, so much the better: this demonizes the image and gains one the wife that every artist needs to do the scut work of a career.

For an artist's wife, whether she is an artist herself or not, holds the outside salaried job that pays the studio rent. She also assists within the studio, looks after the framing and shipping, writes the letters and does the phoning. She may even verbalize "his" esthetic, too, while *he* maintains the demonic posture of not knowing what he is doing when he is creating in the studio. She plans the cocktail parties to which collectors and curators and critics are invited and she also will stand patiently aside while a female collector (whom *she* fished in) exercises the male prerogative of seducing her husband. What man would do as much for an artist wife?

But all these efforts, no matter how devotedly performed, are seldom to much avail. The reality is that only a few artists at a time can be promoted in the art market as it presently functions. The art market is a secretive, unregulated, labile arena which the jargon of the Securities and Exchange Commission would describe as untidy. Although it is a young market insofar as contemporary American artists are concerned, already it's incestuous and even sclerotic in some respects.

When women and minority artists clamor to share the recognition and rewards available till now to a few white males, they merely add themselves into an over-crowded talent pool which art marketeers cannot serve in any case. Although no formal studies have been performed on the size and nature of the artist population, some careful estimates suggest that *there are something more than three hundred esthetically valid artists without dealers for every artist of comparable quality with one.* Furthermore, I doubt that more than one artist of the fifty who do have galleries lives from the sales his dealer generates. Every industry needs a labor reservoir from which to draw its talents but a ratio of 12 percent of unemployed for teachers and engineers, for example, is considered extremely high. Unemployment of 25 to 50 percent among black males under the age of 25 is the worst ratio in the nation. So you can see that three hundred artists for every gallery slot is a redundancy of intolerable proportion.

Some would say there are too many artists but I believe that these figures represent the underdevelopment of the market system and that the galleries serve neither the general public around the nation nor the artist population. The art dealers cluster in a few big cities where they cater to each other in alliances of ownership of particular works of art and sell these to an interchangeable clientele of moneyed urbanites. Like the two men with one diamond who sell only to each other at constantly rising prices, much of the traffic in art involves a small circle of international dealers and collectors. Since collectors have limited ability to absorb works of art (some museums have reached their limits too), sooner or later they begin to trade and their collections reenter the market to compete with newer works. So the word "collector" is fast becoming another word for trader—as in stocks.

Unfortunately the tax deductible structure, which was intended to encourage support for cultural institutions, can now be seen to encourage art speculators by providing downside protection against risk. Much more needs to be written about taxes, the museums, the market, and the problems of artists but I only refer to them here as a frame of reference for my comment that it is profitable to some people that artists remain demonized—that is, feminized—that is, lobotomized.

The future of the art world in this country will, I believe, be profoundly influenced by the self-reevaluation of women artists and minority artists who are reversing a previously passive acceptance of outside pressures. Many women artists note that half of nothing is nothing and that to share what the male artist has been getting is to move from our harem to his. By contrast such militancy as male artists are beginning to express these days concerns itself more with the loss of teaching jobs on campuses than with changes in fundamental attitudes toward participation *as equals* in the art milieu.

The shape of the art scene of the future depends on how profoundly, how philosophically, and yes, how *cerebrally* artists come to understand themselves. Will we reject romantic stereotypical behavior that serves to keep us down? Will we use for problem solving those intellectually creative aptitudes that we artists possess, actually in somewhat higher measure than most other people?

Obviously if the battles for the freedom of the press and for the restoration of checks and balances in the Congress are lost, artists will go down the tubes like everybody else, but if the nation makes a new commitment to freedom and life enhancement, then many options open up for artists that we did not have before. Assuming peace and freedom, by 1980 the art marketing apparatus as we know it will have enlarged somewhat but will have been mostly by-passed by self-help activities of artists. The opening of studios to the public that is now in evidence will expand, I believe, into substantial artist-owned cooperative corporations comparable to the cooperative structure used by the Canadian government on behalf of Eskimos, and similar to the consumer co-ops that have a long tradition in this country. I do not mean the simplistic "share-the-rent, share-the-cleaning" cooperation we see among artists just now, but rather the professionally run business cooperatives that have considerable tax and legal muscle within our society. Artists probably will be showing and selling through their own co-ops, and may also share housing, studio facilities, medical care, insurance, and many kinds of professional services as well—I refer to PR, accounting, legal, and even catalogue and mailing services.

Everywhere artists are talking about organizing themselves one way or another. I believe the best approach will be the formation of a guild something like the Screen Writers Guild rather than a "membership" grouping for various social action purposes. A guild with a full-time professional staff could lobby out the terrible tax inequities that burden artists and ruin our families when we die. Such a guild also could lobby out (and win, I have no doubt) the right for artists to pay our income taxes with our art—as is a norm in Mexico. Such a right would then permit the government to start an art bank or library from which every sort of tax-exempt institution could borrow works of art for use at community level in schools, hospitals, and public buildings.

It would take such a guild to implement residual rights for artists, and to police the implementation of such rights and collect our royalties for us. But all this depends on whether we ourselves decide to form a guild: residual rights will not arrive as a fancy gift from the "johns" who feel they have been keeping us, like aging call girls, as an act of charity. Once artists form a power block, our guild will be able to work with other arts institutions to open up the news media to the culture sector, to provide arts news to the people, and to end the blackout of creative people. The arts should have visibility comparable to that afforded sports. Perhaps in the next few years we will see the appearance of a cultural news wire service which, like the AP, UP, and IP and the Farm News Wire Service, will provide teletyped professionally written stories to all media, printed as well as electronic. When will arts reporters be a norm on every TV news team?

I believe that within the next few years museums will be at least partially financed by the federal government and that, as a result, there will be a forced clean-up of many of the conflicts of interest now rife within museum operations. I trust the interlocking boards of trustees will be broken up and that an artists' guild will have its representatives sitting on all museum policy-making boards. But, of course, with federal money will come the increasing danger of political interference in the culture sector. It could happen that the museums, theaters, opera companies, etc., may find themselves cannibalized by politicians as now is happening before our very eyes to educational television.

I believe that artists must intensify discussion as to our own functions beyond the role of makers of objects as a sort of cottage industry. Art is more than product and I can see how self-determination could lead directly to the formation of a national civil service of creative people of every kind to perform those life enhancement services that reevaluation of the quality of life suggests is necessary to the survival of the species.

Freed from the hopelessness that our own banal and stereotyped behavior of the past imposed on us, both the possibilities and the problems of the future take on new and daring dimensions. I wish I had more confidence that we artists will meet the challenge. For the moment I will be content if more of us accept ourselves with the intellects we have. This first step could lead us almost anywhere—and anywhere is up from where we are.

24

ALFRED WERNER

Soutine:
As He Saw Himself and as Others Saw Him

Schopenhauer claimed there were three sources of happiness: in a man's personality ("What a man is"); in his property ("What a man has"); and in his renown ("How a man stands in the estimation of others").[1]

Most artists will agree with the philosopher that the first of these springs is the most important: "What a man has in himself is . . . the chief element in his happiness." The German thinker echoed the sentiments of an ancient Greek sage: "The happiness we receive from ourselves is greater than that which we obtain from our surroundings."

In the light of Schopenhauer's findings, one is inclined to accept at face value the reply that the painter Chaim Soutine (1893–1943) made to a woman intellectual, Andrée Collie, who asked him whether he had had "a great unhappiness" in his life. Soutine proudly retorted: "What makes you think that? I have always been a happy man."[2]

One must realize that for an artist the term "happiness" stands for something different than it does for the average man. The artist is more capable of enduring long years of poverty and concomitant misery than his non-artistic neighbor. He may very well want to have a wife and to raise a family, but he can do without all of this. A creative person, it seems, can never be entirely unhappy. Beethoven, deaf and isolated, wrote in a letter that only the artist or the scholar "carries his happiness with him." Rodin considered true artists "almost the only men who do their work with pleasure."

Andrée Collie's conversation with Soutine took place in Paris, some time in the 1930s. She had not known him when, having run away from the wretchedness of life in Tsarist Russia—in the ghetto of Smilovichi where he was born, and in Minsk and Vilna—he became, more through circumstances than through his own desires, the most bohemian of the bohemian artists on the Left Bank, a *peintre maudit,* a *peintre tragique* beyond comparison in the annals of anti-traditional modern art. She met the celebrity, whose pictures sold well and who had adequate funds at his disposal, not the starving young man who would wait at the counter of a bistro in the hope that some kindly soul would buy him a morsel of food or a drop to drink. One wonders whether his answer would have been the same a few years later, when Soutine, suffering more than ever before from peptic ulcers, was rushed from his hideout to Paris in great secrecy—for he was a Jew, and France was under Nazi occupation—to be operated upon, under an assumed name and without much chance of success: "I have always been a happy man."

For how much can a man endure—even an artist? Soutine had conveniently forgotten that at one point he had been so desperate as to have tried to put an end to his wretched existence. Mlle. Collie's assumption was not as naïve as the artist, protesting too much, made it out to be. Even if she had not heard the stories about the pre-1923 Soutine which circulated in Montparnasse—*la légende de Soutine,* which contained a great deal of truth—even a glance at his pictures, seemingly painted in blood rather than regular pigments, would have revealed to her an abyss, a wound that could never completely heal.

It is not known whether she saw any of the several self-portraits he produced.[3] Two—the self-portrait of about 1918 (fig. 1), in the collection of Mrs. Henry Pearlman, New York, and the other, done about 1922–23 (fig. 2), in the Musée d'Art Moderne de la Ville de Paris—were exhibited in the Soutine show of the Los Angeles County Museum of Art in 1968. A third, about 1920, was reproduced in black-and-white (with the note "whereabouts unknown") in that show's catalogue, authored by Maurice Tuchman. They are remarkable for a variety of reasons, but particularly because of their wide departure from the traditional self-portrait in Western art, in which, as a rule, the artist presents himself as he would like to appear: handsome, strong, a prince of the world. Artists may be too reasonable to tremble at the beauty of their faces, like Narcissus when he saw his reflection in the water. But they are always ready to "overcompensate," to make strenuous efforts to see themselves and to make others see them in the most favorable light. Max J. Friedländer recognized this inherent desire when he wrote: "The painter wants to cut a figure; he takes himself overseriously, portrays himself in a definite situation . . . self-portraits are aggressive and dramatic, and not infrequently theatrical. They convey to us less what the painter looked like than what he wanted to look like. One may speak of the rhetoric of the self-portrait."[4]

For reasons unknown to us, Soutine belonged to the small minority of artists—among them Rembrandt, Goya, Van Gogh—who did not use their skill in portraiture to deceive the world, and perhaps themselves as well, about their looks. But Soutine went further than these three. Possibly a persevering and sympathetic psychoanalyst could have found out, after many sessions, why Soutine went so far as to caricature himself more ruthlessly than anybody else did (with the exception of Toulouse-Lautrec, whose distaste for his misshapen body caused him invariably to make fun of himself). What made Soutine—who, while not the tinsel type of Hollywood beauty, had no repulsive features, to judge by the surviving photographs—portray himself (notably in the picture owned by the Musée d'Art Moderne de la Ville de Paris; fig. 2) as a revolting monster, somewhat like the anti-Semitic cartoons adorning Julius Streicher's *Der Stuermer*? To be sure, had this picture reached the hands of the Nazis, they would have given it a special place of "honor" in their "Degenerate Art" exhibition of 1937!

Soutine's procedure was the very opposite of that of Albrecht Dürer who, when he painted his self-portraits, stressed his extreme male beauty. These pictures are clearly acts of over-compensation, unconvincing protests despite all their aesthetic magnitude. For the heads that Dürer drew in his youth are devoid of self-flattery; they foreshadow a man who was to be tortured by fits of melancholy and afflicted with severe physical ailments (suffering and death are frequent themes in his work). In a late drawing of himself in the nude, where his finger points to a sore spot, Dürer is haggard and clearly ill; he had no need to stoop to deception, as the sketch was made for the doctor he was about to consult. By contrast, in the painted self-portrait that hangs in the Munich Pinakothek he presented himself as a superman, healthy, proud, full of self-confidence; he is dressed in expensive clothes and his coiffure is impeccable. Time and again viewers of this picture have resented what they considered arrogance bordering on blasphemy, since apparently Dürer wanted to show himself as a Christ-like figure (there is a pronounced and probably intentional resemblance to the traditional ecclesiastic portrait of Christ). Had the artist succeeded in obtaining from himself a happiness greater than that which he got from his surroundings? Compared to the outcast from Smilovichi, the Nuremberg master lived and died like a prince. Yet he, too, had financial difficulties, and, as far as the "estimation of others" was concerned, one recalls his bitter statement that in his very hometown he was treated like a *Schmarotzer,* a parasite.

There is a stark discrepancy, on the other hand, between Leonardo da Vinci's written portrait of the typical painter, based, no doubt, on his own experience, and his drawn self-portrait believed to be authentic. For in his *Notebooks* Leonardo gives a vivid description of the pleasant life of the painter who "sits in front of his work at perfect ease. He is well-dressed and handles a light brush dipped in delightful color. He is arrayed in the garments he fancies, and his home is clean and filled with delightful pictures, and he often enjoys the accompaniment of music or the company of men of letters, who read to him from various beautiful works to which he can listen with great pleasure. . . ."[5] Yet in his drawing, in the Biblioteca ex-Reale, Turin, there remains no echo of the glamour described. Leonardo is an old man, with deep lines in his face and with a mouth that expresses bitterness and disappointment.

Neither Dürer nor Leonardo showed himself with any of the tools of his trade. As for Soutine, he did portray himself with a canvas, but without palette and brush. The most famous of the pictures in which an artist appears with all the necessary instruments, and also in his studio, is probably Velásquez's self-portrait in the left-hand section of *The Maids of Honor* (Prado). He is standing before the easel in the chamber of the royal palace which he was allowed to use as a workshop. The brush is poised in one hand, the palette in the other. The center of the canvas is, of course, occupied by the royal princess, the Infanta Margarita.

Unlike Soutine, Velásquez is carefully and expensively dressed. He may have "improved" on his looks, for though he is in his late fifties, his face is without the slightest wrinkle and there is not a trace of gray in his hair which flows down to his shoulders in dark chestnut richness. On the other hand, his face shows little emotion. He stands modestly in the shadow, as he knows his place. Though a court painter to the king of Spain, he is, in the last analysis, as much a servant as any jester or lackey. By contrast, the uncouth Soutine shares the space with nobody else. He is a free agent, free to paint what he pleases and as he pleases, free to act in accordance with the dictate of his soul, but also free to starve in a hole (as he often did).

Soutine was born toward the end of the century which at its opening had given rise to the doctrine that the artist was free. The artist's freedom (or "alienation") actually started right after the French Revolution, when Crown and Church ceased to be the principal and, for all practical purposes, most reliable patrons: "The artists become to themselves a separate, superior class amid their inferiors, the philistines or bourgeois. The artist is driven in on himself, lives in an ivory tower of his own fashioning, breathes the thin, high air of his own fancy, and loses robustness, sympathy, and understanding of his fellow-men. The typical artist of the century is a rebel or a pure dreamer, through no fault of his own . . .When the artist becomes an alien, he becomes as naturally a social dissenter. He must live from his own moral resources, or at best from the support of a small group. He has little like-mindedness with his nation or with society at large."[6]

The modern self-portrait faithfully mirrors this development, anticipated by Rembrandt in his late self-portraits, the painter seen in work clothes and with expressions neither haughty (like Dürer) nor self-effacing (like Velásquez). These works forecast the self-portraits done by the angry men who came to the fore in the final years of the nineteenth century—such as Gauguin, Van Gogh, Ensor, Munch —or, about the time of the outbreak of World War I, the members of the *Brücke* and Kokoschka, Schiele, and Beckmann. They all took themselves very seriously, they all were highly introspective, they all yearned to achieve the "happiness" that can neither be bought with money nor furnished by the public's applause: "It is the quest of our age that drives us along the eternal and never-ending journey we must all explore," Beckmann once observed; "What am I? This is the question that constantly persecutes and torments us."[7]

Soutine was less analytical, less philosophical, than most of these men. More uprooted, more anti-bourgeois than any of them, he was always at variance with the world around him. Without a wife, without a fixed nationality, without any religious affiliation, he was not even in close contact with those who, like himself, inhabited the tiny cells in La Ruche ("The Beehive") or patronized the cafés of Montparnasse. Compared to him even his only friend Modigliani was a bourgeois, for the Italian remained in touch with his family and even raised one of his own. Modigliani managed to look elegant even in straitened circumstances, and, as a painter, he never entirely departed from the Renaissance tradition he had imbibed in his youth. In Modigliani's only painted self-portrait (in a private collection in Brazil) the artist, gaunt, thin, and on the verge of death after years of sickness and privation, still retains the aristocratic bearing and spiritual refinement noted by all who ever met him.

By contrast, Soutine's three major self-portraits evoke the idea of a wild man, uncouth both as a person and as a painter. The one done about 1920 I first saw in a black-and-white reproduction in the *Parnassus* of April 1937; it was shown that year in the gallery of Mrs. Cornelius J. Sullivan, New York, with other works by the artist, but I have never seen the original or a color reproduction.[8] The artist is posed before a curtain; his arms hang against his body; his face has a hauntingly angry look.

The Pearlman self-portrait (fig. 1), however, painted about 1918, has been included in every major Soutine show and reproduced repeatedly, both in color and in black-and-white. The artist is clad in a coarse blue jacket and wears tie and shirt. The background is a yellowish green. The head is done in more or less naturalistic colors, yet the thick lips of the pouting mouth are painted in deep cadmium red. The ears are large and protruding. There are no hands, and there is neither easel nor brush. Yet nobody could possibly believe this to be a portrait.of, say, a patron standing next to a picture. What one actually sees of it is part of a canvas; the picture is probably held by the artist, since no support is visible. The figure on the back of the canvas is puzzling: is it supposed to be another self-portrait? The idea that it was meant as an ironic reference to the artist's poverty[9]— he is forced to use both sides of a canvas—must be rejected, for there was no room for anything subtle or sly to be found in this rather naïve, direct, and straightforward man.

Truculent and even savage, Soutine deliberately accentuates the crudeness of his features. "Take me as I am," the picture shouts, "or, better still, don't bother me!" He tries to frighten us away—yet he himself is frightened by the onlookers. In this "Portrait of the Artist as a Free Man" the hypnotizer is hypnotized himself. In the ungainly face there is tension, but also the strength and vigor of a young man who knows what he is, who does not care what he owns, and who is disdainful of "the estimation of others."

The self-portrait in the Pearlman collection was probably painted in Cagnes; the second—mentioned above, whose whereabouts are unknown—and the third (in the Paris museum; fig. 2), which was done about 1922, were executed during a prolonged sojourn at Céret, in the Pyrenees; all three are products of a period which resulted in some of the wildest, most ferocious, most Expressionist works Soutine was ever to paint (to describe his own state of drunkenness, Modigliani once quipped that everything was dancing around him as in a landscape by Soutine—one done in Cagnes or Céret, that is).

To call the third picture a self-portrait is not quite correct; it is more like an outpouring of unmitigated self-hatred, like an ideological suicide.[10] The artist is seen seated in front of an indistinct greenish and brownish background. Again the hands are cut off (hands of whose delicacy Soutine was known to have been proud). Unpleasant reds, yellows, and greens prevail. The nose is enormous and deformed. The protruding lower lip, painted in strong red, is as slack as in pictures portraying idiots. The eyes—sharp and determined in the Pearlman picture—are here small and piggish. The ears stand out from the head like wings. The shoulders are hunched; the arm is unusually long (like that in Cézanne's *Boy in a Red Vest*— but there the head is free from deformities).

If the Dürer self-portrait in Munich presents the artist as a God-like figure, here the artist Soutine has deteriorated to the status of a cretin. It is actually not a caricature, for it does not make us laugh; it produces no mirth in us; it does not arouse our pity, as do the self-portraits Rembrandt painted in his last years, or those Van Gogh produced before ridding himself of his own life. It is revolting, it is repulsive.

But its existence is easier to understand if we view it not in isolation, but within the context of modern art and, especially, Soutine's art. Rodin strongly insisted that only that which possessed no character was ugly, and he asserted that the emaciated *St. John the Baptist* by Donatello (he must have meant the one in Siena), the deformed dwarf painted by Velásquez, and the old, worn-out peasant depicted by Millet were a thousand times more beautiful than the vacant "beauty" manufactured by Beaux-Arts professors. He himself angered the public with *The Man with the Broken Nose* and *The Old Courtesan*. Nearer in time to Soutine were Suzanne Valadon and her son, Maurice Utrillo: showing one of his canvases to his mother, young Maurice asked, "Is this ugly?" only to receive his teacher's answer, "It can't be ugly enough." The two were discussing a landscape, but the response would have been the same for any genre of painting.

Soutine "caricatured" all his sitters. One wonders how his close friend Modigliani, who was as handsome as men come, would have looked if he had ever been "treated" with Soutine's loaded brush! Why, then, should Soutine have spared himself, if in all his "portraits" he stressed the commonplace, the misshapen, and the clumsy, and inserted these qualities even where they were not actually to be found. He made no exception in the cases of his colleagues, the painter Moïse Kisling, the sculptor Oscar Miestchaninoff, his benefactress Mme. Madeleine Castaing, or the actress Maria Lani, known for her beauty. As a matter of fact, to anything he painted he gave his own unhappy mental features, as it were. As Manuel Gasser put it, "Even the inanimate objects that he painted have something of the self-portrait in them, for how else could he have painted a plucked hen so that it chills our spines as we look at it and makes us feel that we are faced not by a still-life but by the picture of a tragic fate?"[11]

The third and last self-portrait seems to have been painted, or at least started, before Soutine was discovered early in 1923 by the American collector Dr. Albert C. Barnes, the event which catapulted him to fame and fortune. No self-portrait done between that year and Soutine's death two decades later has come down to us. Luckily, the historian is not limited to the three pictures. Soutine was painted by at least three colleagues, and there are also several photographic snapshots. There is a vast gap between, say, the third picture—aptly described by Maurice Tuchman as "a pitiless, ruthless work, ridden with self-contempt"[12]—and Modigliani's likenesses of his friend. Modigliani has left us several drawings and, more importantly, four oil portraits of his *copain,* then a young man of twenty-four. They present the sitter in a peaceful and, twice, even a meditative mood, either because the older man exerted a pacifying, soothing influence on the excitable Russian immigrant or, more likely, because Modigliani endowed all he saw with his own grace, elegance, and sweetness. "Modigliani saw only that which was beautiful and pure," Madame Lunia Czechovska commented.[13] Unlike Soutine, Modigliani nearly always stopped well this side of caricature, and never allowed malice to enter a portrait.

All four of Modigliani's portraits are from the year 1917, that is, roughly a year

before the Pearlman self-portrait was painted. The least developed is the one painted on wood—on the door that separated Soutine's Paris atelier from that of
Modigliani at No. 3, Rue Joseph Bara.[14] Soutine is seen standing. He wears a
broad-brimmed hat and has a young, almost girlish face, slit pupil-less eyes, and a
spatulate nose, and his head is tilted to the right. The work is in the nature of a
sketch, based on irregular splotches of color, and is faintly reminiscent of the
Neo-Impressionist technique which Modigliani adapted to his purposes while
painting his portrait of the collector Frank Burty Haviland.

Two of the pictures, however, are as complete as any Modigliani can be. In the
one in a private collection in Paris, Soutine is sitting with his hands, palms down,
resting on his knees. He wears a coarse brownish workman's jacket, buttoned up
to the collar. The long hair comes down to his ears; he appears to have masculine
strength, and his face has a certain ruggedness. More famous is the other, similar
picture, once owned by Chester Dale (whose wife was among the first to write
about Modigliani) and now in the Chester Dale Collection of the National Gallery
of Art, Washington, D.C. (fig. 3). Soutine wears a dark suit, a black pullover, and a
white shirt with the collar half open. The tie is carelessly knotted. He sits with his
hands folded in his lap. For a change, accessories—a table and a glass half filled
with liquor—have been introduced, as much for compositional needs as for a
suggestion of ambience. There is a certain formality about this picture as though
the model were posing, a bit stiffly, for a photographer. All of Modigliani's stylistic
mannerisms are present: the thinned-out body, with long neck and lengthy, narrow
head, is posed against a nondescript green background. Indeed, there is a lot of
green and red in this picture—these were his friend's favorite colors.

The Staatsgalerie in Stuttgart owns a fourth portrait (fig. 4). Unlike the others,
it shows only head and neck, both vastly elongated in the mature Modigliani style.
Here, Soutine's usually solemn, pouting mouth is shown in a half smile.

In reality, Soutine was a bit short and stocky, and had a rounded face. The later
portrait of him done by another Russian-born member of the École de Paris, the
somewhat younger Constantin (Kostia) Terechkovitch, is probably closer to the
exact physical data. The sitter, now forty (the picture is dated 1933; its present
whereabouts unknown), has a flat, oval face, thick lips, and small, protruding
eyes. He is wearing a fashionable dark blue suit, with a colorful scarf tucked inside, revealing a conservative white dress-shirt and a good tie. He is clearly pros-
perous. Yet fame and money were unable to heal the wounds inflicted upon him
by society and by his own unfortunate disposition. He is seen dreaming, but
without even the faintest indication of a smile.

Another Russian who painted Soutine was Arbit Blatas. Soutine was something
of an idol to the much younger man, who encountered his now famous compatriot
in Paris in the mid-1930s. One of several portraits of him that Blatas painted is
now in a small museum in Maryland.[15] In this half-length portrait the sitter's face
is not much different from that in Terechkovitch's painting. The artist wears a grey
felt slouch hat pulled down over his right eye, a heavy overcoat, and a dark shirt.
The mouth is sullen and the eyes look wary. The entire effect is that of a wanted
criminal.

Another portrait by Blatas shows Soutine standing. He appears furtive, his
hands are in his pockets, his shoulders are hunched, he is leaning against a wall for

support. Except for the clothing, which is of good quality and not ragged, one might take him for a *clochard* who does not like to be looked at. Blatas gives this psychologically admirable description of his late friend: "His dark face and burning eyes created a tormented expression; his body huddled into his coat, he seemed a frightened, suspicious man imprisoned within himself, wanting only to be left alone, distrustful of everyone now that sudden recognition had come to him, after years of inner struggle. But I soon realized that he still desperately needed association with people, that he wanted friends, that he was curious about and interested in even those whom he had pushed away from him in his search for solitude."[16]

Of the surviving photographs—they are not numerous—at least two show Soutine smiling. In both he wears coarse workman's clothes, the kind of attire Picasso had made "fashionable" on Montmartre in the not-so-good old days of the Bateau-Lavoir. In one photograph (fig. 5) Soutine is standing beside a dead rooster that is hanging from a wall hook (the rooster theme frequently appears in his work). In another, he and an unidentified young woman are standing at the corner of a brick building, each holding a forepaw of a small dog that is raised up on its hind legs as if it were a child standing between them. A third photograph is surprising. Soutine is now, for a change—and for a short while only, one suspects—assuming the role of an ex-bohemian. He is well barbered and elegantly clad in an immaculate suit with sharp-peaked lapels. A handkerchief is tucked into his breast pocket. He wears a fine textured tie over a starched white shirt, and seems absorbed in the act of drinking from a long-stemmed glass, held daintily in his hand with the little finger crooked.

But there is no lack of verbal portraits! Though Soutine was certainly not gregarious, even after his importance had been trumpeted about by Albert C. Barnes, Georges Charensol, Elie Faure, Waldemar George, and other astute connoisseurs, the number of people who knew him, or claimed to have known him, is amazingly large. Unquestionably, the sculptor Jacques Lipchitz knew him well, and for more years than Blatas. Lipchitz repeatedly talked about Soutine to his own biographers. Irene Patai observes: "For Lipchitz Soutine was always an enigma, a mixture of such idiosyncratic impulses that he found himself constantly asking the question, Is Soutine good or bad or just neurotic? Not quite sure whether to like him or to pity him, continually perplexed by the protean faculty of the painter."[17]

Madame Castaing, whose hospitality the painter enjoyed during several summers at her country home near Chartres, summed him up as "a character out of Dostoevski." Gerda Groth lived with him for some years, even though she was aware of her friend's "idiosyncratic impulses." Long after Soutine's death she told a Parisian critic: "Soutine was extremely sensitive and also extremely diabolic. In reality, he attached no importance to anything outside his work. I had the luck, if that is the way to put it, of finding him when he was ill and when he needed me. If that had not been the case, I doubt very much whether he would have been capable of attaching himself to a woman."[18]

The writer Maurice Sachs watched Soutine walking in the garden of the Castaing estate: "With his bent back, his drooping shoulders, his rumpled hair, his work trousers," Sachs tells us, Soutine had "the appearance of some mournful Jew who, concealing his fine pale hands, was fleeing to the security of the Ghetto."[19]

Sachs' observation was incorrect in one respect, though. Soutine wished to flee from the ghetto, not back to it. There can be no doubt that the miserable youth he spent at Smilovichi—with its prohibitions, restrictions, outmoded rituals, poverty, and medieval backwardness—had a profound impact upon the painter. He was still "in the ghetto" when Monroe Wheeler met him in Paris. Wheeler, who later organized the first comprehensive Soutine memorial show in the United States, first saw him in the late 1920s: "He was pale and slender, hypochondriacal, and under doctor's orders as to his food and drink. . . . The expressions of his face varied a great deal, sullen or suspicious, timorous or arrogant, but upon occasion as friendly as a child's. A man of slight stature, he moved in an uneasy or evasive way, a little onesidedly. His small and delicate hands suggested a more meticulous way of painting than he ever practiced. Occasionally he took pains to be well dressed, but his clothes soon became shabby and dirty. At the end of his life his cheeks grew hollow, his full lips drooped with a suggestion of boredom or bitterness, but when he spoke his black eyes still glittered with romanticism about himself and his art."[20]

Despite these and other attempts by his friends and acquaintances to shed light on his character, Soutine remained inscrutable to the very end (fig. 6). His paintings are the only real clues to his puzzling personality.

NOTES

1   "Aphorismen zur Lebensweisheit," *Parerga und Paralipomena,* Berlin, 1851.

2   "Souvenirs sur Soutine," *Spectateur des Arts,* Dec. 14–18, Paris, 1944.

3   The self-portrait which, according to Tuchman, was done ca. 1920 is twice reproduced, also in black-and-white only, in Pierre Courthion's *Soutine: Peintre du Déchirant,* Lausanne, 1972. Courthion, however, dates it 1915. In the text—but not in the *catalogue raisonné*—its present owner is identified as a Mme. J., in Paris. Tuchman conceded—in notes written for a Soutine catalogue of 1963, published in connection with the Arts Council of Great Britain show—that, in addition to the three self-portraits known to him, "three others are rumored to exist in a Paris private collection." They may be identical with the self-portraits reproduced in Courthion's *catalogue raisonné.* One, of 1916–17, shows the artist's head, done in a somewhat Modiglianesque manner (he wears his hair long, anticipating the present fashion). He has a thin circular beard in the two later self-portraits (1919–20 and 1926–27, respectively). In none of the three cases is the present owner mentioned.

4   *On Art and Connoisseurship,* London, 1942.

5   *Artists on Art,* compiled and edited by Robert Goldwater and Marco Treves, New York, 1945.

6   Frank Jewett Mather, Jr., *Modern Painting,* Garden City, N.Y., 1927.

7   In his lecture "On My Painting," delivered at the New Burlington Galleries, London, on July 21, 1938.

8   Courthion, who saw the original in the collection of Mme. J., thus comments on the picture: "This self-portrait of Soutine shows a striking analogy in craftsmanship to Cézanne's painting. There are the same strokes that flow together but are still separate. The influence is evident even in the manner of allowing the white of the canvas to appear here and there (at the base of the ear, in the eye, in the hair). The luminous color (*lumière-couleur* in the French original) is striking. The palette, with its green-browns on a light gray background, is also Cézanne-like. The cherry-shaped mouth, the lively eyes, a slightly hounded expression, the longitudinal placement of the body with a red scarf around the neck, the hair divided in the middle into two locks—this is the Soutine of the Cité Falguière in his wrinkled clothes, with torn pockets like those of a poor laborer. This portrait is extraordinary in its three-dimensionality, presence, truthfulness and clarity."

9   *Portrait of the Artist,* catalogue, Metropolitan Museum of Art, Jan. 18–Mar. 7, New York, 1972.

10   Courthion, who gives the picture the title *Grotesque (Autoportrait de l'Artiste),* makes this comment: "Soutine had a formidable sense of irony. If he was harsh to the painters of his own generation, he was equally so toward himself. Less ugly than people have said he was, he may have contributed to the diffusion of the legend of his ugliness by a self-portrait like this one. Like Goya, Soutine knew that a portrait is valid only if the painter emphasizes its characteristics, exaggerates the features, and accentuates the

expression. Here he adds to the thickness of his lips, flattens his forehead, turns his eyes into holes and twists himself frightfully. . . . Soutine shows himself stuffed into a coat which looks like the same one he used to wear at La Ruche. He exaggerates his facial characteristics. The mouth becomes an immense double crescent of flabby flesh, the nose is twisted to one side, the eyes disappear beneath the swollen roundness of the cheeks. The posture is that of a man twisted into a cork-screw."

There is also a note on the self-portrait of 1926–27, the second of the two in which the artist is seen wearing a short circular beard: ". . . he is isolated against a background which features an image that could be a cross or a dagger. In this face there is a dramatic complexity. The painter is there, wretched, bare-throated, facing life, which he has not yet learned to dominate."

[11]   *Self-Portraits,* New York, 1958.

[12]   *Soutine,* catalogue, Los Angeles County Museum of Art, Los Angeles, 1968.

[13]   Ambrogio Ceroni, *Amedeo Modigliani, Peintre,* Milan, 1958.

[14]   Reproduced in Ambrogio Ceroni and Leone Piccioni, *I dipinti di Modigliani,* Milan, 1970, but with no mention of the present owner.

[15]   Washington County Museum of Fine Arts, Hagerstown, Md.

[16]   *Soutine and His Circle in Paris,* catalogue, Hirschl & Adler Galleries, New York, 1958.

[17]   *Encounters: The Life of Jacques Lipchitz,* New York, 1961.

[18]   Gerda Groth ("Mlle. Garde"), "My Years with Soutine," *The Selective Eye,* New York, 1956/1957.

[19]   "Soutine," *Creative Art,* New York, Dec. 1932.

[20]   *Soutine,* catalogue, Museum of Modern Art, New York, 1950.

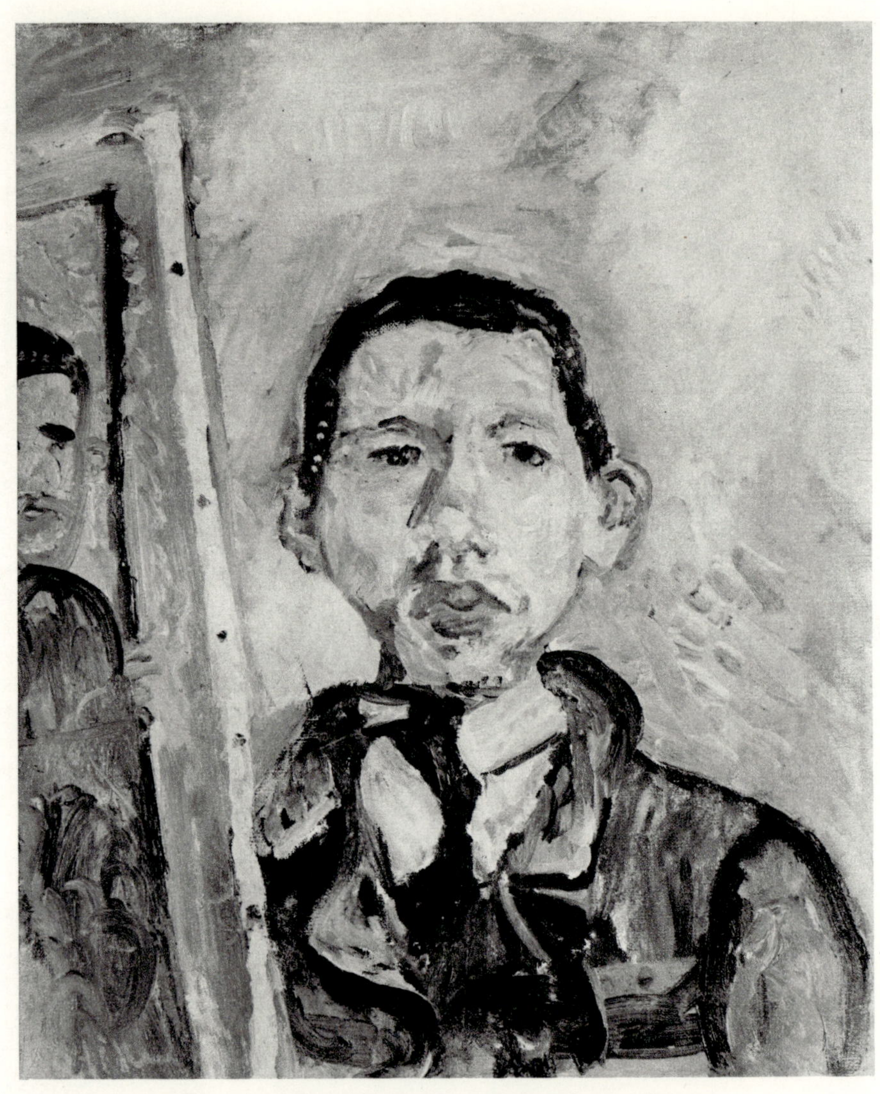

1. CHAIM SOUTINE. *Self-Portrait*. c. 1918.
Collection Mrs. Henry Pearlman, New York

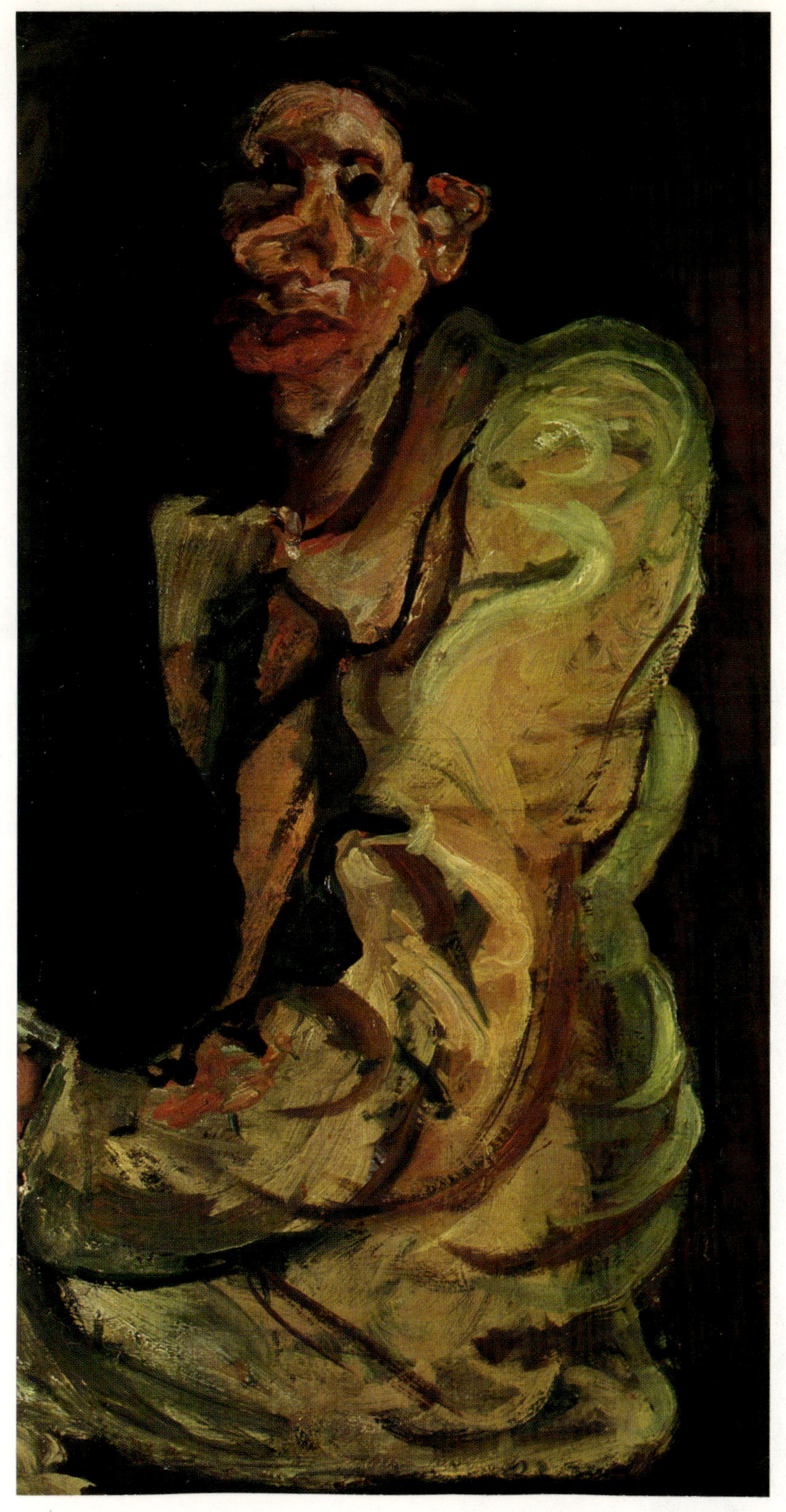

2.   CHAIM SOUTINE. *Self-Portrait*. 1922–23.
Musée d'Art Moderne de la Ville de Paris

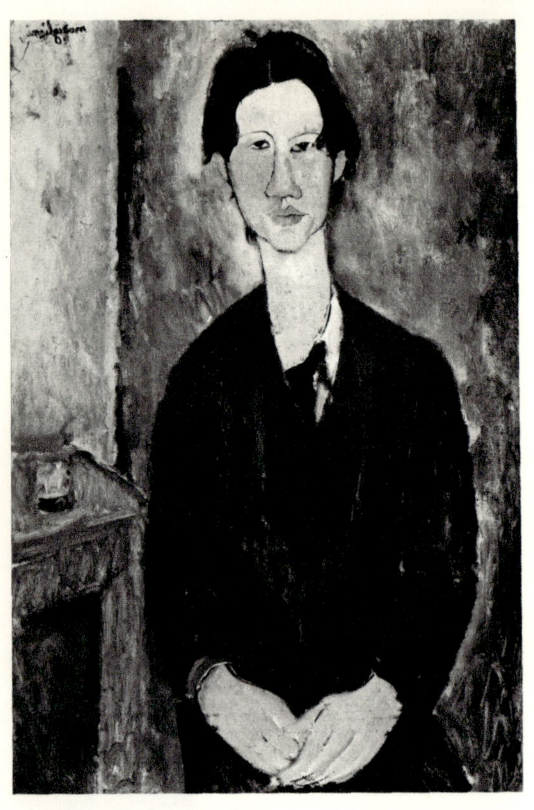

3. AMADEO MODIGLIANI. Portrait of Soutine.
National Gallery of Art, Washington, D.C.
Chester Dale Collection

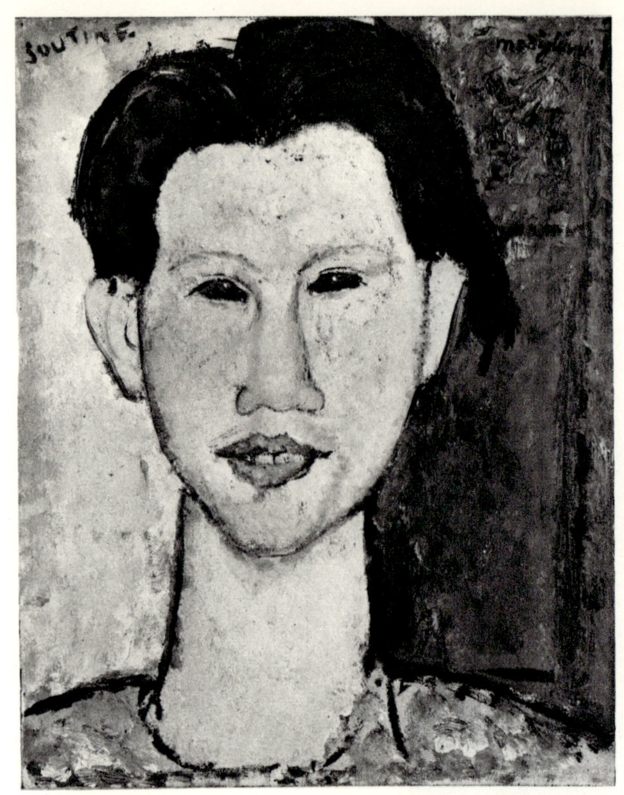

4. AMADEO MODIGLIANI. *Portrait of Soutine.*
Staatsgalerie, Stuttgart

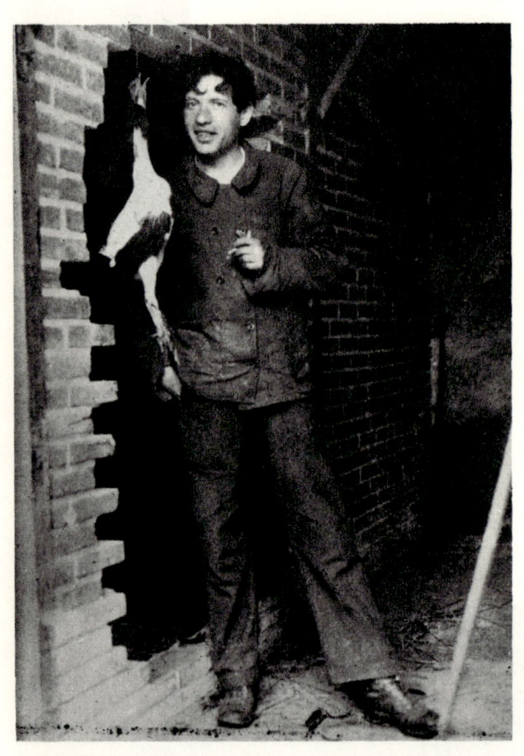

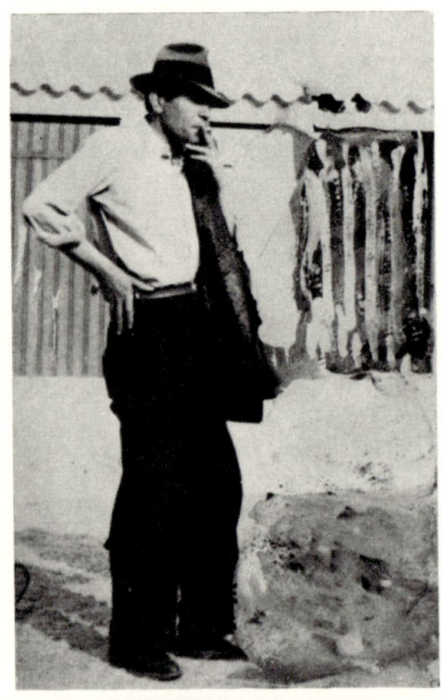

5. Photograph of Soutine with dead chicken.
Late 1920s

6. Photograph of Soutine. August, 1938

25

JOHN WILMERDING

Peale, Quidor, and Eakins: Self-Portraiture as Genre Painting

Ordinarily, one thinks of portraiture as a rather straightforward category of painting. The emphasis is clearly on the sitter or sitters, alone or in groups, surrounded by artifacts, accessories, or identifiable settings which are included primarily to enhance or accent the figural subject. Often more interesting is the subcategory of self-portraiture, wherein artists consciously or unconsciously reveal themselves, in whole or in part, their surface physiognomies or their inner psychological traits. Because of the processes involved, self-examination and confrontation, we are usually given a distinctive intimacy, a special perception, by the artist. Perhaps he will reflect this in a more informal pose, casual composition, unusual lighting effects, or unexpected auxiliary details.

The history and examination of self-portraiture, like autobiography, is surely an intriguing, if monumental, subject in its own right. Even the topic of self-portraits by American artists is too large and diverse to undertake here, although it is a subject that invites comprehensive study. One fascinating modification or amplification of American self-portraiture is its occasional mergence with the area of genre painting. Three painters attract particular attention in this regard for their unusual inventiveness and insight in the ways they paint themselves in the context of broader anecdotal, narrative, or historical subject matter.

Charles Willson Peale (1741–1827) at the very beginning of the nineteenth century was a notable portraitist of both himself and others, as well as the father of subsequent genre painting in America. But almost all of his pictures, and especially his well-known "genre portraits" (as one might call them), like *The Artist in His Museum, The Staircase Group,* and *Exhuming the First American Mastodon,* are in fact autobiographical history paintings.

At mid-century John Quidor (1801–1881), the elusive and imaginative interpreter of tales by Cooper and Irving, appears to have projected himself into the literary characters he painted. Although Rip Van Winkle may not bear the painter's features, the fictional figure is the real artist's surrogate. This may be imaginary self-portraiture, but paradoxically, it is real enough!

Then, toward the end of the century, Thomas Eakins (1844–1916) turned increasingly toward portraiture in the latter part of his career. Not only was his concentration on portrait painting a reflection of his profound concern with humanity, but it was also an act of continual self-definition. His portraits of others tell us as much about himself as about the sitter. Not surprisingly, a series of "genre portraits" of *William Rush Carving His Allegorical Figure of the Schuylkill River* punctuate and bracket his career. Once more, they are not strict portraits of Eakins himself in a photographic sense, yet they are surely images of the artist as he saw himself in time, place, and circumstance.

There are few antecedents to which one can point. These include the eighteenth-century English "conversation piece," such as the family groupings at sport or leisure by Arthur Devis, or the informal portraits by Gainsborough (the most familiar being *Mr. and Mrs. Robert Andrews* of 1755, in the National Gallery, London). There are parallel eighteenth-century French works by Chardin and Watteau: in the latter's *Italian Comedians* and *Gilles* we see the artist projecting himself metaphorically and actually into his subject, and achieving thereby a poignant perception of himself. Earlier, in the seventeenth century, the informal and often narrative portraits of the artist by Rubens, Vermeer, and Rembrandt come to mind. Likewise, there are interesting parallels in nineteenth-century French painting: for example, the artist *at work* as painted by Courbet or Daumier. Yet the American artists seemed to carry these motifs into a special realm, creatively blending history, genre, and portrait painting in new ways, or juxtaposing the real with the imaginary in surprising balances. Together, Peale, Quidor, and Eakins provide a sense of the American artist's ingenuity in adapting traditional types of painting to their own personal or social needs. They illustrate both the continuity and variety of American painting over more than a century.

Peale was the first of a whole family of painters, who numbered more than twenty over three generations and worked in a wide variety of subjects and media. Peale himself was a multi-talented individual, pursuing careers at various times as inventor, painter, saddler, scientist, museum founder and proprietor, soldier, writer, and naturalist.[1] In his youth he was stimulated to take up portrait painting by the belief that he could produce better results than the itinerant artists whose work he occasionally saw. During the 1760s he received some training, successively from John Hesselius in Maryland, John Smibert and John Singleton Copley in Boston, and Benjamin West in London. Although Peale's early portraits reveal the partial influence of these painters respectively, it was West's originality and stature that probably affected Peale most. More than anyone, West was the father of the first national school of American painting. While his own mature career was passed in England, to his studio were attracted a substantial succession of younger Americans who then returned home to pursue their own careers. West was a good teacher and a generous friend; he also set an important example in paintings like *The Death of General Wolfe,* 1770 (National Gallery of Canada, Ottawa), with its new emphasis on contemporary costume and setting for history painting. Two years later he continued this stress on modernity with his depiction of *Penn's Treaty with the Indians* (Independence Hall, Philadelphia), into which he introduced portraits of his father and brother also. Is it possible that Peale was acknowledging this precedent in his own series of modern history paintings, with himself or his family playing the prominent roles?

In the mid-1770s Peale settled in Philadelphia. He served in the Continental Army during the Revolutionary War while managing to execute numerous miniature and fullsize portraits of notable contemporaries. Dating from 1773 is his first major family portrait (fig. 1). Ostensibly, this seems to be a relatively perfunctory group portrait, whose composition Peale may have derived from John Smibert's *Dean George Berkeley and His Party* (Yale University Art Gallery, New Haven) and Robert Feke's *Isaac Royall and His Family* (Harvard Law School, Cambridge). But *The Peale Family* is also more: it is a scene of domestic tranquility and coherence, with three generations represented in a nearly symmetrical balance around the table. Besides the variations in age, Peale also plays off the different oval forms of the faces, not only of the men, women, babies, and dog, but also of the drawn, painted, and sculpted heads in the background and on the table. Most of all, the painting is a portrait of the artist: on the left side is Charles Willson Peale, the only one who holds a palette, and seated before him are his two brothers, James and St. George, the latter making a portrait drawing of their mother from across the table. Thus, art is everywhere—in the busts and painted canvas behind, in St. George's life drawing, by implication in the artificial construct of a still life, and in the setting itself. A little over a decade later Peale was to turn this room into one of America's first museums, displaying his collection of artifacts and portraits. The painting itself also underwent a later reworking around 1808, as Peale added Argus the dog to the foreground.[2]

Peale's art takes on the layers of personal history. The portrait of himself and his family merges into a type of figural still life as well as genre painting in a mode that was totally new for American painting at that time. It was only logical that his painting should be a natural extension and reflection of his life, so much devoted to a wide variety of artistic and scientific activities. In 1795 he was instrumental in founding the Columbianum Academy in Philadelphia, which was to be the antecedent of the venerable Pennsylvania Academy of the Fine Arts. The same year he painted for the inaugural exhibition at the Columbianum his extraordinary *trompe l'oeil* portrait *The Staircase Group* (Philadelphia Museum of Art). On the lower steps of a stairwell stood Raphaelle and Titian, two of his several sons named after artists. Again it was a composition of gentle formal and iconographical balances, and, as always, as much a tribute to the profession of art (Raphaelle holds a palette in his hand) as a portrait. Here, as well as anecdote, are perceptual questions about visual reality, interior landscape, family history, and figural still life.

Perhaps Peale's best realized and most ambitious self-portrait was *Exhuming the*

First American Mastodon (see Essay 5, fig. 1), whose very size, some four by five feet, seems intended to suggest the grandness of his vision and achievements. Here was the fullest blending of his patriotic, artistic, and scientific inclinations. Indeed, the children by his first wife were named for artists, and those by his second for scientists. Now at last are assembled his family, friends, and colleagues in a celebration of American determination and ingenuity. This was the triumph of contemporary history and history painting, with Peale the artist-scientist as the modest hero.

Sometime during 1800 a farmer in upstate New York had unearthed what was believed to be the skeleton of a prehistoric mammoth. Alert to the possibility of gaining unusual scientific information as well as artifacts for his museum, Peale made haste in the summer of 1801 to visit the landowner John Masten in the hope of acquiring the bones. Upon his arrival in Newburgh he first made drawings of the fragments, and subsequently purchased them for two hundred dollars, offering another one hundred to dig the remainder from the ground. The first set was packed and shipped to Philadelphia, and Peale began preparations for the further excavations. President Jefferson provided equipment from the army and navy, writing to the scientific impresario:

> I have to . . . congratulate you on the prospect . . . of obtaining a complete skeleton of the great incognitum, and the world on there being a person at the critical moment of discovery who has zeal enough to devote himself to the recovery of these great animal monuments.[3]

With the help of a wheelwright Peale designed the frame and chain of buckets to be constructed over the swampy hole. It was a cumbersome but characteristically practical machine, and the ensuing excavation naturally attracted the public in wondering crowds. After digging in several spots, the equivalent of an entire second skeleton was unearthed and returned to Philadelphia for display. The less good of the two assemblages was made ready to go on tour abroad, with the implicit assumption that both the art and archeology of the New World were equal to Europe's.

Peale determined to paint a record of the event, the picture to be displayed in the Mammoth Room of his Museum along with the bones. Although some of his earlier works had suggestions of narrative content, this was his first full-fledged attempt at descriptive history painting. It is of course both a self-portrait and family portrait, as well as a remarkably inventive combination of landscape, genre, and contemporary history. At the right the artist himself stands prominently between the symbols of his two primary enterprises in science and art, the excavation machinery and a large drawing of the bones. The large frame of the poles gives the composition a central focus and keeps the wealth of myriad details from dispersing our attention. As if to dramatize the personal, even national, significance of the occasion, a thunderstorm impends in the near background. Thus the aura of the sublime helps to monumentalize everyone's labors.

Evidently, Peale's son Rembrandt was the only other member of the family actually to witness the undertakings, but the artist has taken the liberty of including more family members and several scientific colleagues. He worked on the picture for nearly two years, continuing to add figures; in 1808, the final count numbered some seventy-five of whom at least twenty were identifiable. The owner of the land, John Masten, climbs the ladder in the foreground. A friend and ornithologist, Alexander Wilson, stands before the tent at the left with his arms folded. On either side of the wheel and next to Peale are various of his brothers, in-laws, and children. Appropriately, two of the artist's sons, Rembrandt and Raphaelle, assist in holding the large drawing of the prehistoric leg bone. Like his contemporaries Jefferson and Bulfinch, Peale was a Renaissance man in young America, and this painting fittingly captures the several levels and concentricities of the artist's interests. After all, his life and person had become merged with national aspirations. His autobiographical paintings could only reflect the larger picture of Federal America, of which he was certainly one of the focal images.

The artist at the center of his activities again provided the basis for one of Peale's final masterpieces, *The Artist in His Museum,* 1822 (fig. 2). He stands midway between the symbols of his career, to the left the stuffed birds and to the right his palette and the mastodon's bones. As the curtain was metaphorically descending on his own long and illustrious career, so now he literally raises another to invite the spectator, and by implication the future, into the achievements of his gallery. The setting had its own distinguished history. Shown is a glimpse into the Long Room on the second floor of Independence Hall in Philadelphia, to which the artist had moved his enlarged collection from Philosophical Hall in the early 1800s. A careful perspective rendering of the interior,[4] later finished by his son Titian II, is among the preparatory drawings. It is clear that Peale intended to effect a subtle balance between his own self-portrait in the foreground and the room extending behind him, containing his life's work.

There are, in addition, a number of smaller, related self-studies in oil. In 1821 he painted a pair of bust-length self-portraits with palette in hand for his daughter Sophy,[5] and in 1822 he made a similar study of himself with part of the Long Room visible in the background.[6] A final last portrait on the same scale, completed in 1824, showed him holding one of the giant bones (New-York Historical Society). In these studies he was particularly conscious of the warm light effects, which appear to glow outward from the space behind the figure. Of this he wrote to Jefferson:

> The light I have chosen for my portrait is novel, and before I made a beginning of the large picture, I made a trial on a small canvas to know if I could make a likeness sufficiently striking. My back is towards the light, so that there is no direct light except on my bald pate, the whole face being in a reflected light. You may readily conceive that it required a considerable knowledge of middle tints to make a striking likeness—and whether it is novelty of this mode of portrait painting that captivates the connoisseurs of the art, but so it is, that I have great encomiums on the work, from artists as well as others.[7]

Peale literally and metaphorically stands at the juncture between us, his future public, and his present visitors, seen behind him admiring the Museum's varied collections. His towering form is a finely realized self-portrait in its own right, but the image also reveals the artist's larger world of instruction, both real and ideal. Finally, the blending of formality and gentleness here was related to another marvelous late portrait, the so-called *Lamplight Portrait* of his brother James, 1822 (The Detroit Institute of Arts). Also suffused with the subtle glow of warm illumination, this was a tribute to his brother's career as a painter and by extension to the other artists in the family. For James is shown seated at a table, examining a miniature painted in turn by his daughter Rosalba. The ever-present miniaturist's palette and brush are on the table, images of objects that linked the family almost more closely than blood. These celebrations of character and achievement, whether of his immediate family or of himself, make Charles Willson Peale's portraits among the most inventive and enlivening in the American tradition.

The fact that Peale's portraits take on aspects of genre painting makes them important forebears of the major genre school in American art that developed soon after his death. An increasing consciousness of the national landscape and character paralleled Jacksonian democracy. American painters sought to record with new fervor the purity of the landscape and the vitality of the common man's daily affairs. Native literature asserted the distinctiveness of American scholarship, and landscape painting depicted the undefiled beauty of a new civilization. Fictional characters were conceived—Leatherstocking, Natty Bumpo, and Rip Van Winkle—as the Adams in American Edens. Thus, Peale's *Exhuming the First American Mastodon* was a forecast of the exultation in the history and traditions of the young republic. Along with William Sidney Mount and George Caleb Bingham, John Quidor then brought to fulfillment this indulgence in national life and heroes. In fact, Peale's picture appears in retrospect to anticipate Quidor's *Money Diggers,* of 1832 (The Brooklyn Museum), with its group of figures arranged around another pit of excavation.

Quidor was born in Tappan, New York, not far from the familiar landscape of Washington Irving, who was to inspire several of his paintings. During his childhood Quidor's family moved to New York City, where he passed most of his life. He was briefly apprenticed as a youth, along with Henry Inman, to the portraitist John Wesley Jarvis, but neither of these painters appears to have influenced his work greatly. Rather he found most of his sources for paintings in romantic literature by writers like Cervantes, James Fenimore Cooper, and especially Irving. Living in New York, Quidor also could have derived some of his ideas and style from seventeenth-century Dutch and eighteenth-century English genre painters (for example, Hogarth and Rowlandson), who were known in this period through copies in both oil and prints.

Quidor's generation was a more romantic one than Peale's. Landscape and genre painting emerged simultaneously during the first quarter of the nineteenth century in response to the new harmony Americans envisioned in the relationship of man and nature. Quidor's painting of *The Young Artist* (fig. 3) brings together these two central concerns for landscape and genre. While no specific Quidor self-portraits are known, this work obviously objectifies his image of himself. Here the painter is literally immersed in nature: his foot touches the water, his chair is a mossy bank, and the roots of the tree serve as his easel. The artist is at one with his subject. As the individual and the natural worlds become fused, man finds himself reflected in the universal. Quidor in this respect is very much Emerson's contemporary. Once more we see self-portraiture metamorphosed into something larger.

That same year Quidor began the first of his many pictures after Irving's stories, possibly because in them he found characters who so typified his own life and feelings. His highly imaginative style and imagery were not always appreciated by his contemporaries, who rather preferred literal or symbolic realism. He was a largely neglected figure in his lifetime, and even now many of the facts about his life and art are mysteriously elusive.[8] For one period in the middle of his career, almost nothing is known about his whereabouts at all. John Baur and Celia Ruder have perceptively pointed out that a figure like Rip Van Winkle may readily have come to embody for Quidor his own sense of personal and social alienation.[9]

In a number of Quidor's paintings a strangely detached figure stands off in the background (*Antony Van Corlear Brought into the Presence of Peter Stuyvesant,* 1839, Munson-Williams-Proctor Institute, New York) or runs wildly from the action (*Leatherstocking Meets the Law,* 1832, New York State Historical Association, Cooperstown; and *The Flight of Tom Walker,* 1856, private collection). In a pair of scenes about Rip Van Winkle, painted a decade apart, Quidor places such a figure slouching against a tree at the side of his composition. At first glance *The Return of Rip Van Winkle* (fig. 4) appears full of mirth and not too serious consternation. But beneath this hilarity, wild gesturing, and bright coloring lies a poignant seriousness that Quidor no doubt intended. For Rip's return also brings surprise and dislocation. His loss and recovery of identity are profoundly disquieting, as the intense glances and gestures suggest. The youth against the tree is the metaphorical presence of the earlier Rip. Rip's reappearance may be unexpected to the townspeople, but the search for his own identity in time and place is even more unsettling for himself. The paradox is evident in the crucial paragraph from Irving:

> In the midst of his bewilderment, the man in the cocked hat demanded who he was, and what was his name? "God knows," exclaimed he, at his wit's end; "I'm not myself—I'm somebody else—that's me yonder—no—that's somebody else got into my shoes—I was myself last night, but I fell asleep on the mountain, and they've changed my gun, and everything's changed, and I'm changed, and I can't tell what's my name or who I am!"[10]

Stylistically, the figures themselves are powerfully realized, and again suggest Dutch or English inspiration. But there is another source Quidor perhaps knew through reproductions, the art of Michelangelo. Could the Renaissance master's conception of God the Father from the Sistine Ceiling have inspired the hoary face and pointing hand of Rip? could the sculpted forms of the *Bound Slaves* lie behind the slouching youth? Whatever the derivation of Quidor's imagery, his own life must have been more closely depicted in Rip's story than we have thought. A self-portrait? not in the strict or usual terms, yet the fictional narrative here is truly his own.

The later painting, *Rip Van Winkle at Nicholas Vedder's Tavern* (fig. 5), would seem to confirm this interpretation. Now Rip is very decidedly the young man standing alone by the tree at the edge of the group. He is in marked contrast to the others, who are all seated, active, and indulging in physical pleasures. That their backs are turned to him only adds to his lonely contemplativeness. Yet, Irving tells us, he came to the tavern when driven from home, "to console himself"![11] Alas, passing the time for him is not the same as it is for "the sages, philosophers, and other idle personages of the village."[12] Here was the real romantic, and the presence of Quidor's temperament is as evident as if he had included a literal self-portrait. At mid-century, genre painting permitted Quidor to reveal himself through the act of imagination.

Alienation also shrouded the life of Thomas Eakins. His art, like that of his contemporary, Winslow Homer, was firmly rooted in the American genre tradition. But in contrast to painters such as Mount, Bingham, and even Quidor, he reaches a new and deeper level of seriousness. He was born and spent much of his life in Philadelphia. His youthful training at the Pennsylvania Academy of the Fine Arts and at the Jefferson Medical College together provided him with a solid grounding in the accurate rendering of the human figure from life. At the close of the Civil War he went to Paris for study at the École des Beaux-Arts, where he studied under Gérôme, and also was for a time the pupil of Bonnat. This experience imbued in him a meticulous style based on precise realistic draftsmanship, which was tempered somewhat by a brief visit in 1870 to the Prado in Madrid. Here he discovered Ribera and Velásquez, to whom he responded with particular enthusiasm:

> O what a satisfaction it gave me to see the good Spanish work so good so strong so reasonable so free from every affectation. It stands out like nature itself.[13]

Returning to the United States shortly after, Eakins began a series of interior paintings of his sisters and his fiancée at the piano or seated in chairs. From the beginning his art would show a dual central attention to light and to the human figure. The first was an ambience of affection which surrounded and defined the fragile truths of human character. Strongly present, of course, in these sympathetic records were the artist's own personality and perceptions. Others often provided Eakins with a mirror of himself, in the sense that the human condition was ultimately a profound understanding of self. Like Peale, Eakins began and ended his career painting his family and close friends, for in them he could most resolutely face mortal truths and record them on canvas.

Eakins's earliest self-portraits appropriately appear in the backgrounds of his genre paintings of friends. These were the splendid rowing scenes of the early 1870s, *Max Schmitt in a Single Scull* (The Metropolitan Museum of Art) and *The Biglen Brothers Turning the Stake* (The Cleveland Museum of Art). His presence in a second single scull, looking back at us from the distance, provides a signature that is both metaphoric and literal. The careful drawing and placement of figures in space combined with the radiance of sunlight are the fused legacy of his Parisian and Spanish experiences. Eakins not only paints himself bodily into such pictures, he does so spiritually as well, for these are testaments to youthful endurance and human survival. He equates the discipline of rowing with strength of character. He, Schmitt, and the Biglens are in the prime of life, which is both the triumph and poignancy of mortality. Ultimately, Eakins makes us aware of time that is both stopped for the moment and suspended forever. Time implies age: in the passage of summer to autumn, noon to afternoon, youth to old age, the nineteenth to the twentieth century.

These are the understated themes of his marsh scenes, too. *The Artist and His Father Hunting Reed-Birds on the Cohansey Marshes* (fig. 6) is an outdoor portrait, wonderfully fresh and intimate yet in no way sentimental. The two men contrast in their age and posture—the one physically straining, caught off balance; the other thoughtfully concentrating, poised—yet both united by bonds of love and activity. Finally, the peaceful expanse of landscape and warm sunlight complete the harmonious order of the whole. Just as Peale and Quidor had discovered before him, Eakins required more than an isolated self-portrait to convey the largeness of his perceptions about self. Genre painting paradoxically allowed his introspective vision to render the outer world with unique comprehension.

The balance of thought and action, of intelligence and emotion, of age and survival, was at the heart of his greatest painting, *The Gross Clinic* of 1875 (The Jefferson Medical College of Philadelphia). Intended for the Philadelphia Centennial the next year, it was inadequately shown and poorly received, bringing great disappointment to the artist. Its vivid details and harsh realism, dramatically isolated by the Rembrandtesque lighting, offended genteel Victorian society and marked the beginning of the mutual disaffection between artist and public during the next decade. For in spite of *The Gross Clinic*'s rejection, Eakins the same year began his prominent teaching and directorial career at the Pennsylvania Academy, only to be dismissed from this position in 1886 because of conflicts in social, moral, and artistic attitudes with his patrons.

This crucial central period in Eakins's life must have been one of building personal tensions. We find some of them in *William Rush Carving His Allegorical Figure of the Schuylkill River* (fig. 7), painted in 1877. Rush was a familiar and respected Philadelphia sculptor of the early nineteenth century, and Eakins sought to show that the earlier artist's depiction of a model from life was a prudent and discreet precedent for his own life classes. Two observers are present to insure the dignity of the proceedings: Rush's sculptured figure of George Washington (who was also a friend of Rush), and the model's chaperone seated and preoccupied with her knitting. That Eakins had very much in mind the constraints and paradoxical suppressions of contemporary society is clear from the primary juxtaposition he makes of the strongly tactile nude figure and her elaborate pile of clothing in the center of the composition. Both are more precisely drawn and intensely lit than anything else in the painting. No doubt the features of the carver in the background loosely resemble those of Rush, but not surprisingly they also suggest the general demeanor of Eakins. More importantly, Eakins found in the subject of Rush and his carving of the nude another vehicle for the realization of his own condition. As such, the genre portrait of Rush became his own, in the same way Quidor intuitively found in Rip Van Winkle the image of himself. Eakins must have had such a transposition in mind, for he returned to the Rush theme in other versions (The Brooklyn Museum; The Honolulu Academy of Arts) at the end of his unhappy career.

One other painting of nude figures included Eakins's self-portrait, *The Swimming Hole,* 1883 (fig. 8). The artist and his dog Harry are swimming in from the lower right toward the group. This celebration of man in nature recalls his friend Walt Whitman's poem "Twenty-Eight Young Men Bathe by the Shore" from *Leaves of Grass;* a few years later, after his dismissal by the authorities of the Pennsylvania Academy, Eakins painted the poet's portrait with the vitality and sympathy of a shared spirit. Meanwhile, *The Swimming Hole* was the culmination of a type he had begun with his early rowing scenes. The diving figure caught in mid-air reminds one even more of the photographic vision, as Eakins again holds in equilibrium our awareness of time and timelessness. A related picture from the same year was titled *Arcadia* (The Metropolitan Museum). For a last suspended moment the beleaguered painter envisioned an American Arcadia, full of Whitmanesque optimism and power.

After this, Eakins's view darkened and turned inward. From here on he painted interior scenes, often shadowy and dimly lit. Increasingly, he painted the single figure, frequently one of his friends, family, or a sympathetic spirit such as another artist, teacher, or student. He was also at his best in painting musicians, doctors, and priests, who similarly possessed creative or spiritual will. Mirrored in their faces were his own anxieties, and together they reveal his ultimate achievement of self-understanding. In 1902 he completed a standard self-portrait (National Academy of Design). It conveys the accumulated weight of age, which the artist nonetheless bears with full self-acceptance. Through all of his late paintings we are made conscious of the artist's sense of humanity, his own and that of others. *The Swimming Hole* was one of his most evocative summaries of personal autobiography. As it had been for Peale and Quidor, in different period styles and attitudes, genre painting became for Eakins the unlikely, yet notably effective vehicle for expressing and describing himself.

NOTES

[1]   The definitive biographies of Peale are Charles Coleman Sellers, *Charles Willson Peale,* 2 vols., Philadelphia, 1947; and the same author's updated *Charles Willson Peale,* New York, 1969. For summary information see Jules David Prown, *American Painting from Its Beginnings to the Armory Show,* New York, 1970, pp. 50–53; Charles H. Elam, ed., *The Peale Family,* Detroit, 1967, pp. 39–40; and John Wilmerding, *Audubon, Homer, and Whistler and 19th-Century America,* New York, 1972, pp. 4–5, 87.

[2]   See Elam, *op. cit.,* p. 35; and Sellers (this and all references hereafter are to the 1969 biography), pp. 79–81.

[3]   Quoted in John Howat and John Wilmerding, *19th-Century America: Painting and Sculpture,* New York, 1970, No. 11. See also Sellers, *op. cit.,* pp. 293–303.

[4]   Collection of the Detroit Institute of Arts. Illustrated in Sellers, *op. cit.,* p. 340. See also the ground plan of the museum in *ibid.,* p. 334.

[5]   One is in the collection of Lester Hoadley Sellers, and is illustrated in Sellers, *op. cit.,* Pl. XII; the other was formerly owned by descendants of the family. See "American Masters, 18th and 19th Centuries," exhibition catalogue, Kennedy Galleries, New York, 1972, p. 12.

[6]   Sold at auction 1971; private collection, Philadelphia. Illustrated in Sellers, *op. cit.,* Pl. XII, and in "American Paintings, Drawings & Sculpture of the 18th, 19th and Early 20th Century," exhibition catalogue, Parke-Bernet Galleries, Inc., New York, 1971, pp. 48–49.

[7]   Quoted in Sellers, *op. cit.,* p. 403.

[8]   John Baur, *John Quidor,* New York, 1965, is the principal source of information.

[9]   *Ibid.,* p. 14.

[10]   *Ibid.,* p. 24.

[11]   *Ibid.,* p. 36.

[12]   *Ibid.*

[13]   Quoted in Sylvan Schendler, *Eakins,* Boston, 1967, p. 18.

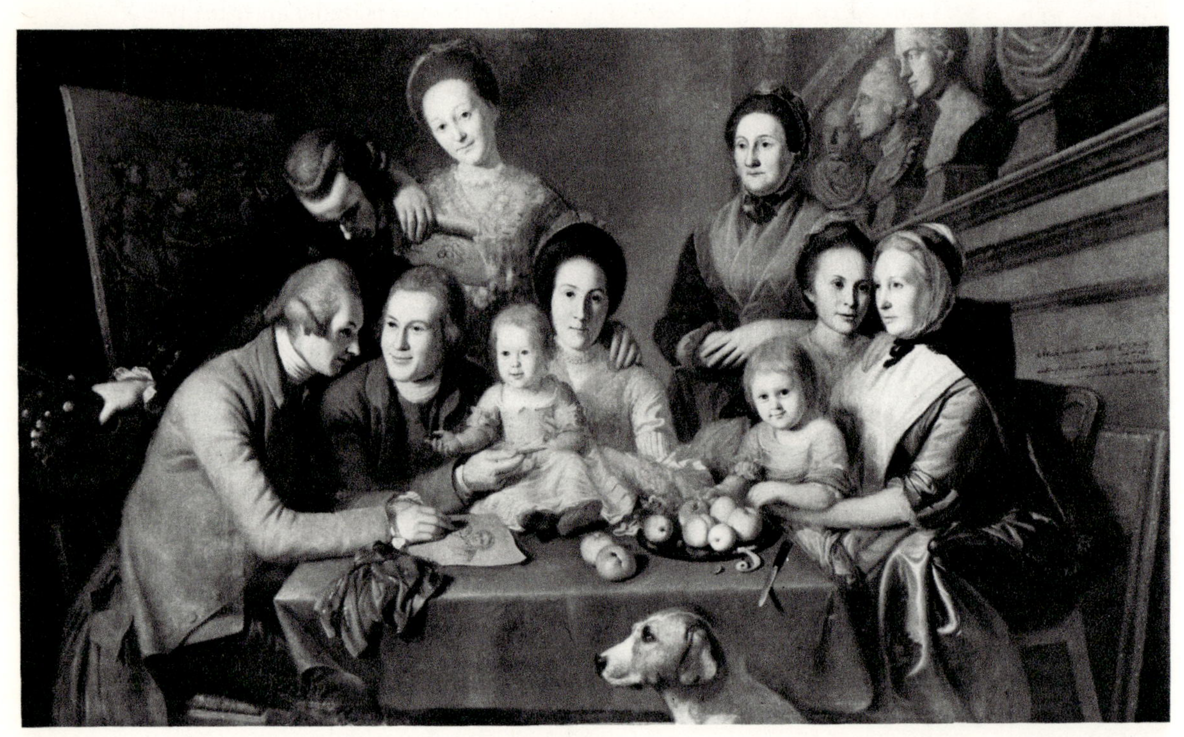

1.   CHARLES WILLSON PEALE. *The Peale Family*. 1773. Oil on canvas, $56\frac{1}{2} \times 89\frac{1}{2}''$.
The New-York Historical Society

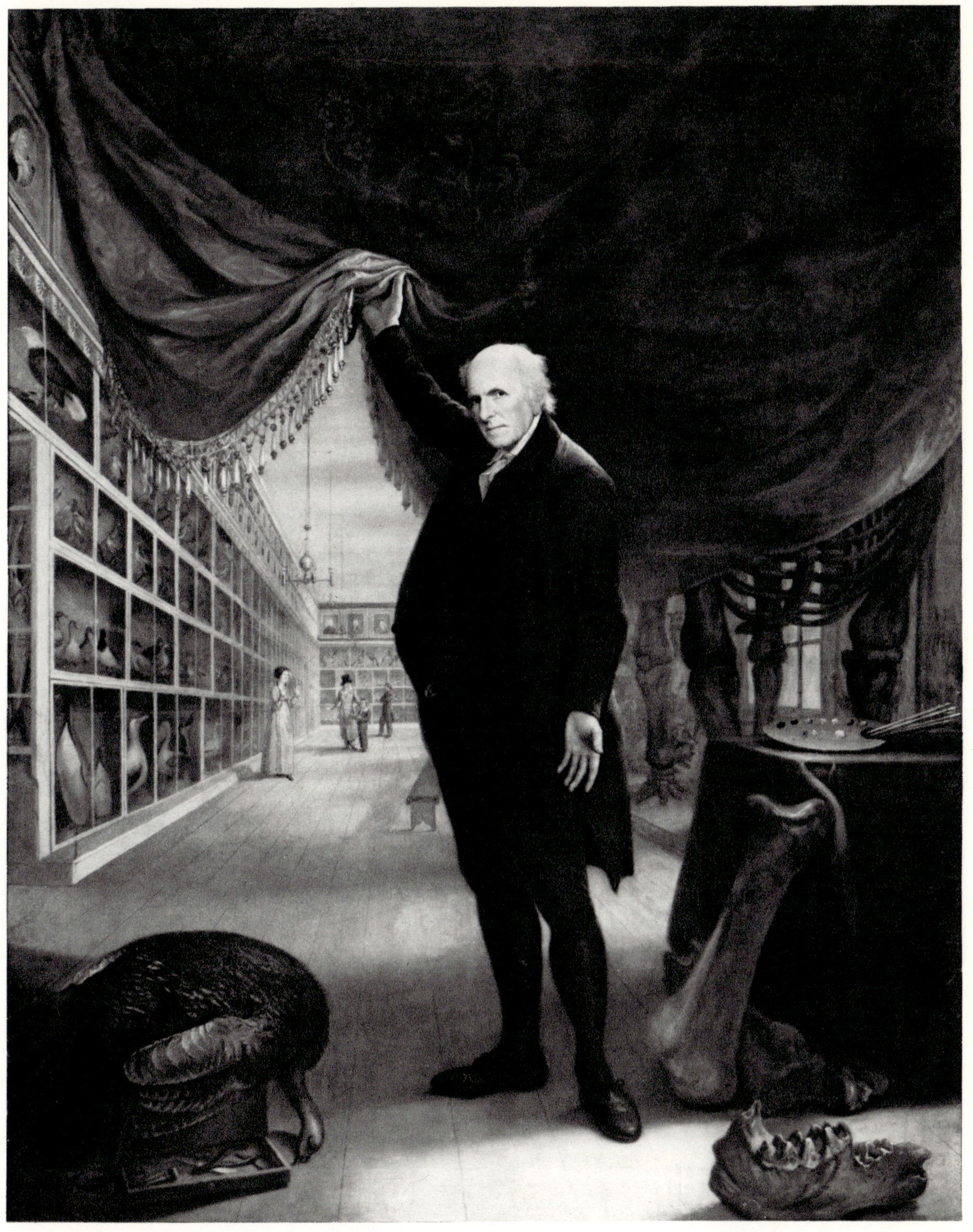

2. CHARLES WILLSON PEALE. *The Artist in His Museum.* 1822.
Oil on canvas, $103\frac{1}{2} \times 80''$.
The Pennsylvania Academy of the Fine Arts, Philadelphia.
Joseph and Sarah Harrison Collection

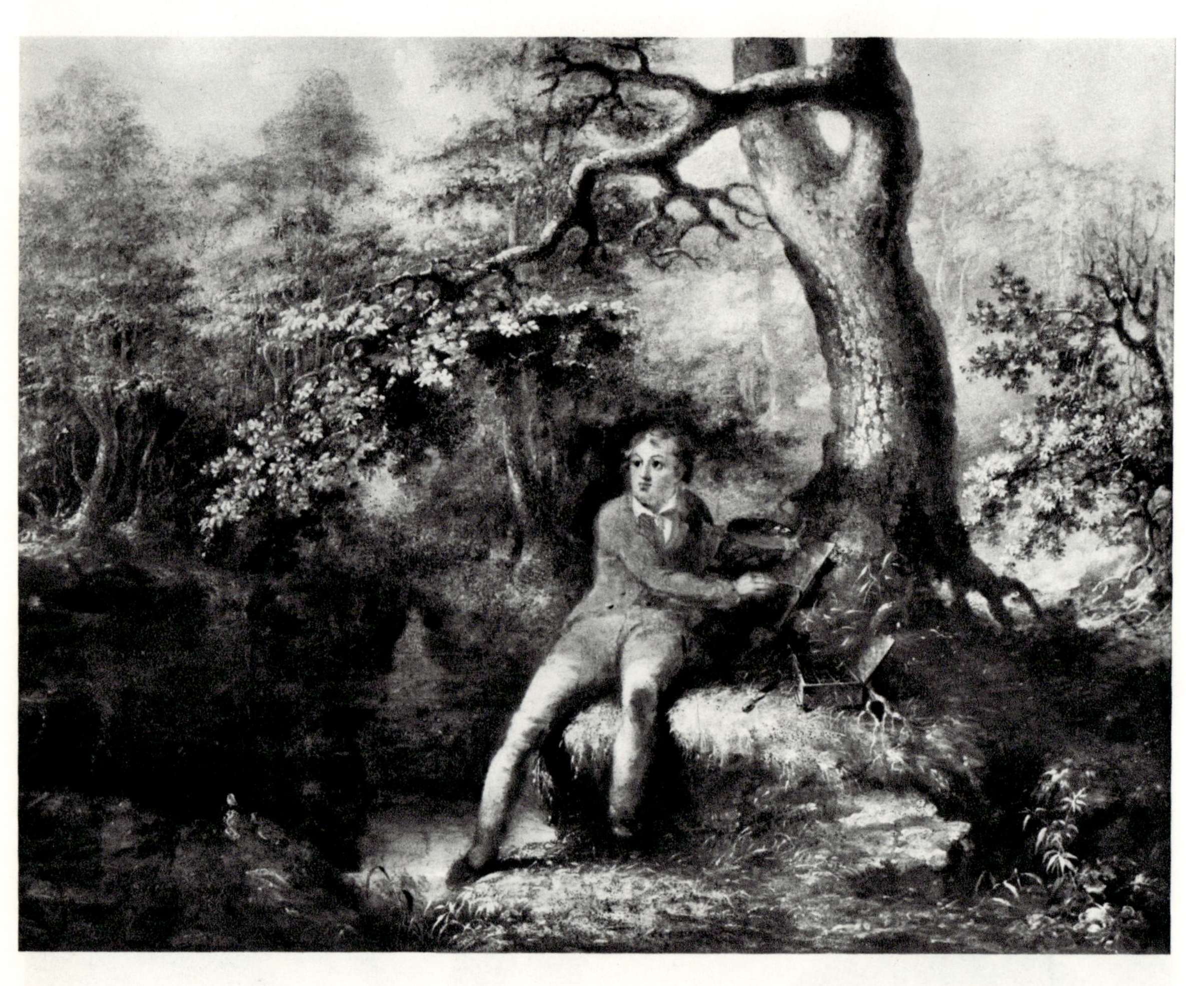

3. JOHN QUIDOR. *The Young Artist*. 1828.
Oil on panel, $20\frac{1}{4} \times 25\frac{1}{4}''$. The Newark Museum

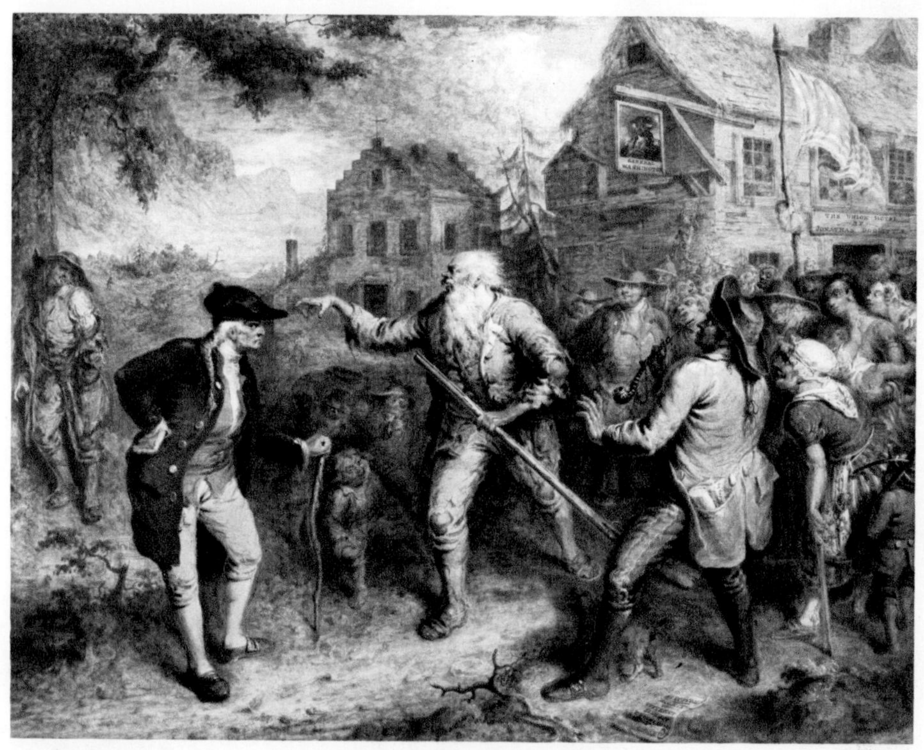

4.   JOHN QUIDOR. *The Return of Rip Van Winkle.* 1829. Oil on canvas, $39\frac{3}{4} \times 49\frac{3}{4}''$.
National Gallery of Art, Washington, D.C. Andrew W. Mellon Collection

5.   JOHN QUIDOR. *Rip Van Winkle at Nicholas Vedder's Tavern.* 1839.
Oil on canvas, $27 \times 34''$. Museum of Fine Arts, Boston.
M. and M. Karolik Collection

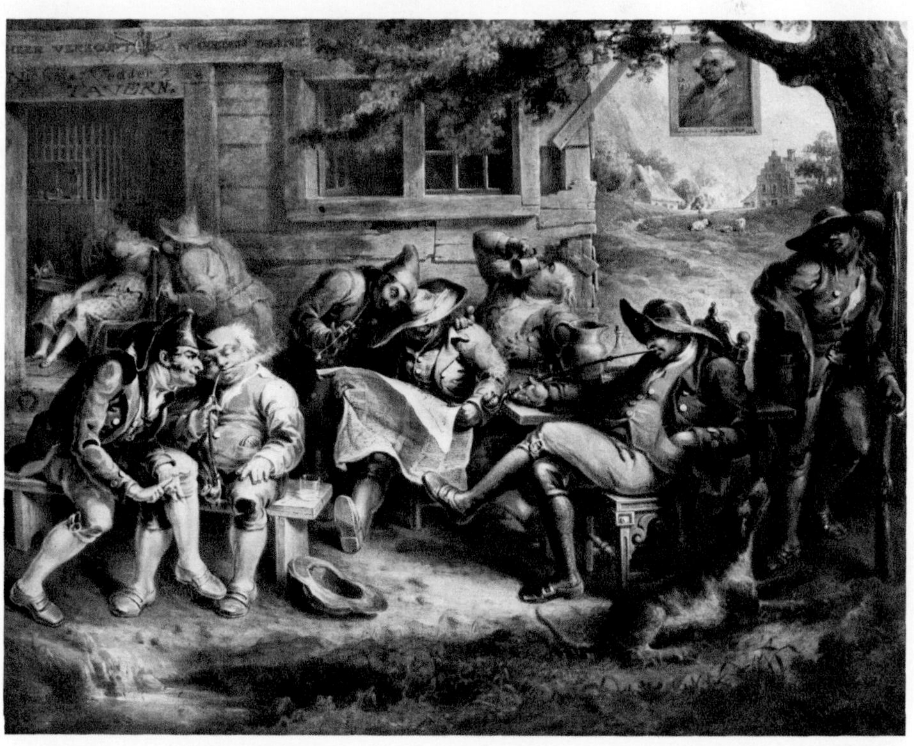

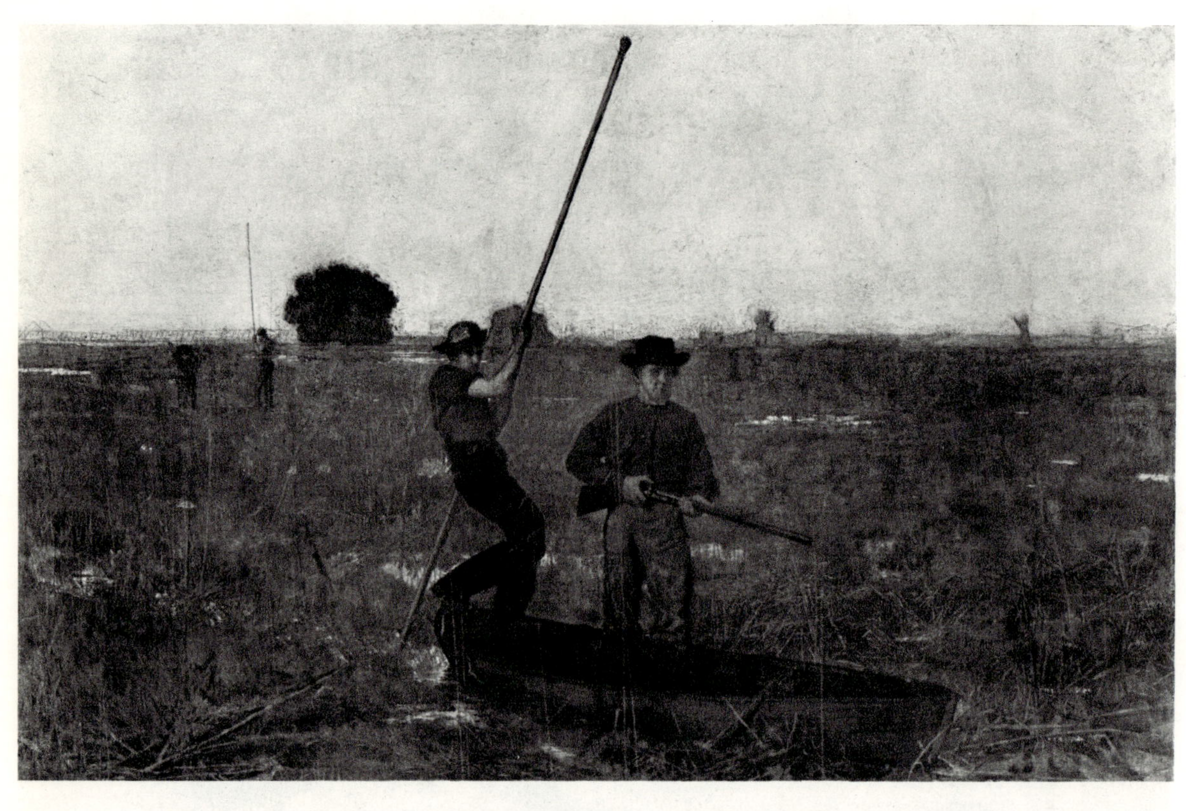

6.   THOMAS EAKINS.
The Artist and His Father Hunting Reed-Birds on the Cohansey Marshes.
c. 1874. Oil on canvas mounted on panel, $17\frac{1}{8} \times 26\frac{1}{2}''$.
Collection Mr. and Mrs. Paul Mellon, Upperville, Virginia

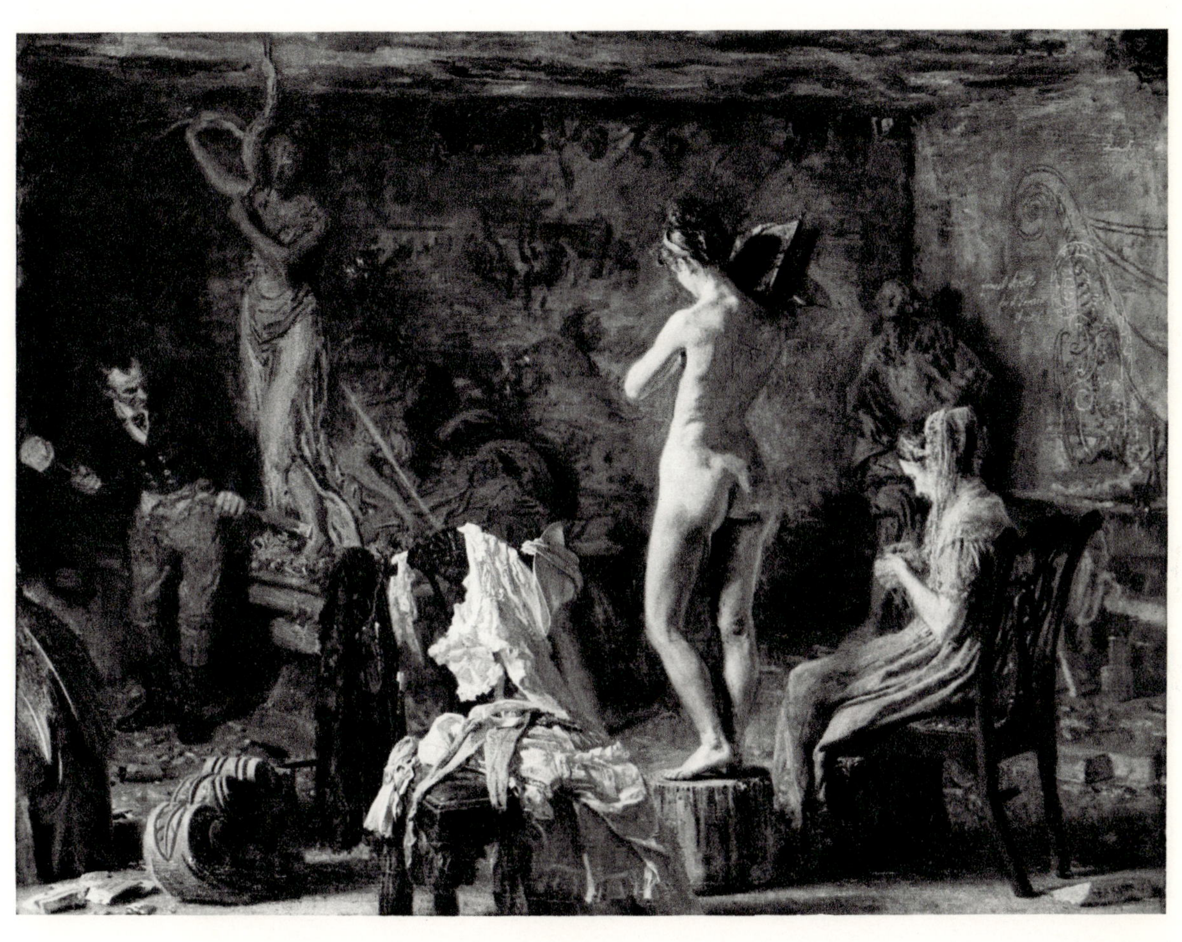

7.   THOMAS EAKINS.
William Rush Carving His Allegorical Figure of the Schuylkill River. 1877.
Oil on canvas, $20\frac{1}{8} \times 26\frac{1}{2}$″. Philadelphia Museum of Art

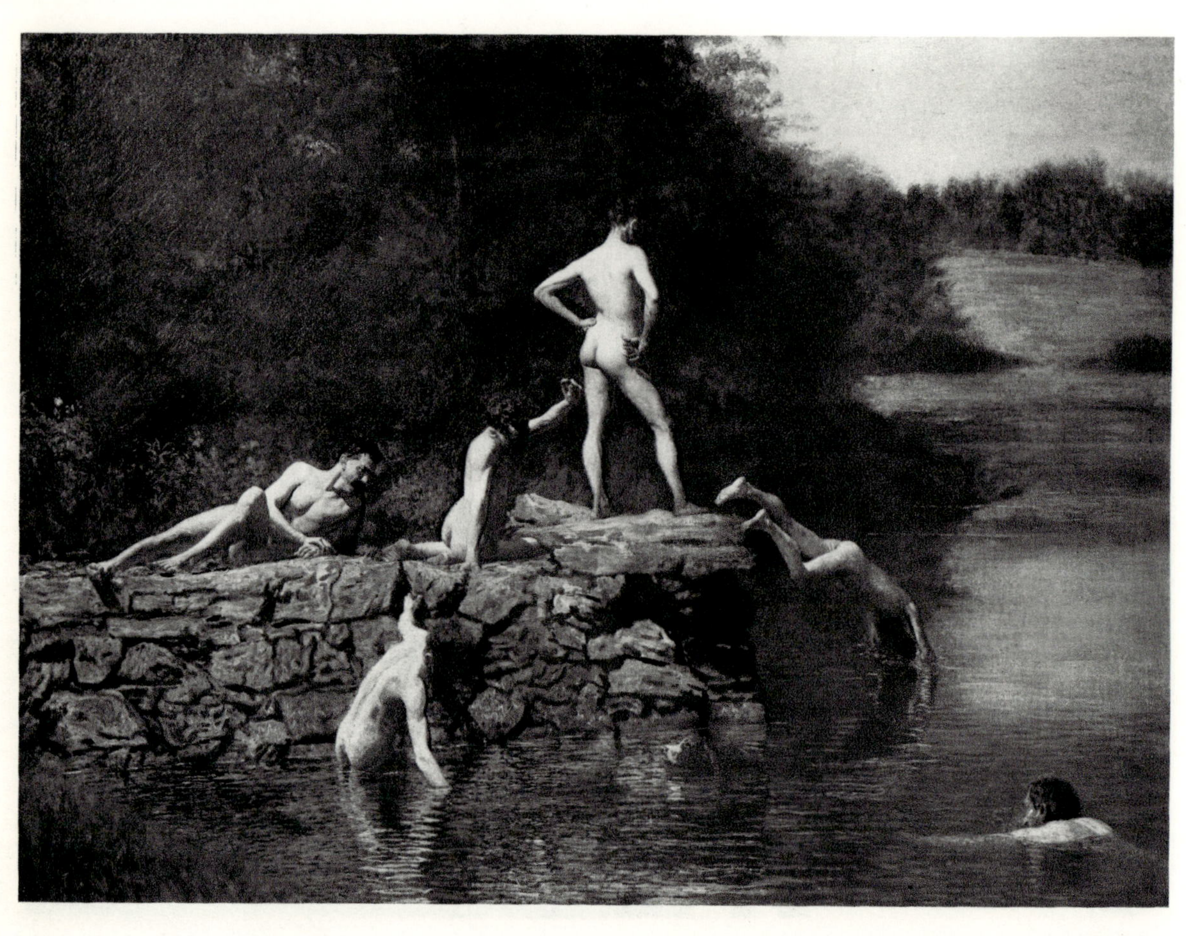

8.   THOMAS EAKINS. *The Swimming Hole.* 1883. Oil on canvas, 27 × 36".
The Fort Worth Art Museum

List of Photographic Credits

The authors and publisher wish to thank the libraries, museums, and private collectors for permitting the reproduction of paintings, prints, sculpture, and drawings in their collections. Photographs have been supplied by the owners or custodians of these works except for the following, whose courtesy is gratefully acknowledged. Numerals in parentheses refer to the essay in which the work is illustrated.

A. C. L., Brussels: (21) 7; Agraci, Paris: (13) 2; Alinari, Anderson, Brogi: (7) 5–7; (8) 1–3, 6, 7, 14, 16, 23–26, 28, 29; Archives Photographiques, Paris: (7) 3; (8) 9; Eugenio Cassin, Florence: (8) 10; Editions Cercle d'Art, Paris: (20) 2, 3; Geoffrey Clements, New York: (3) 7; (13) 3; Deutsche Fotothek, Dresden: (13) 1; A. Dingjan (The Foundation Johan Maurits van Nassau, Mauritshuis), The Hague: (20) 1; Fototeca Unione, Rome: (8) 5; Gabinetto Fotografico della Soprintendenza alle Gallerie, Florence: (8) 12, 13, 15, 17–19, 21, 22, 27; Alexander Georges, New City, N.Y.: (3) 3; Greenberg-May Prod. Inc. (Albright-Knox Art Gallery), Buffalo: (12) 1; Hedrich-Blessing, Chicago: (3) 1, 2; Laboratoire du Musée du Louvre, Paris: (11) 1, 2, 4, 5, 8, 9; Laboratoire de Recherche des Musées de France: (11) 3, 6, 7, 10; Foto Marburg: (7) 1, 4; Eric Pollitzer, Garden City Park, N. Y.: (3) 9; Roger-Viollet, Paris: (24) 5; Service de Documentation Photographique, Réunion des Musées Nationaux, Paris: (4) 5; (8) 20; Joseph Simon Studio (Pennsylvania Academy of the Fine Arts), Philadelphia: (21) 2; John Weber Gallery, New York: (6) 2; A. J. Wyatt (Philadelphia Museum of Art): (25) 7